A Crown of Thorns

By the same author
PRIEST AND PENITENT
CARDINAL HINSLEY
OUR FAITH
MY LORD AND MY GOD
COUNCIL AND CLERGY
NOT THE WHOLE TRUTH

A Crown of Thorns

An Autobiography 1951–1963

John C. Heenan

HODDER AND STOUGHTON
LONDON SYDNEY AUCKLAND TORONTO

ACKNOWLEDGEMENTS TO ILLUSTRATIONS

1 *The Yorkshire Post*; 2 *Liverpool Daily Post and Echo*; 3 ATV Network Ltd.; 4 Fox Photos Ltd., London EC1; 5 The Press Association Ltd., London EC4; 6 Keystone Press Agency Ltd., London EC4; 7 The Associated Press Ltd., London EC4; 8 The Central Press Photos Ltd., London EC4.

ILLUSTRATIONS

facing page

St. Anne's Cathedral, Leeds   32
Bishop Martin, Archbishops Ramsey and Coggan
   and their wives with Bishop Murphy   32
High Mass at St. Anne's Cathedral   33
First Communicants' Party   33
A centenarian Sister of Notre Dame   64
Hospital visitation   64
Parish visitation: blessing of the children   64
Korea   65
Malaya   65
Japan   65
Hiroshima: Peace Memorial Hall   128
Hiroshima: where the bomb fell   128
Whitby Abbey: Centenary Mass[1]   129
Lourdes[2]   160
Television discussion with Barbara Ward[3]   160
St. Nicholas Pro-Cathedral: enthronement   161
A happy occasion in Liverpool[2]   224
During a parish visitation   225
Liverpool University[2]   225
Sir Frederick Gibberd displays Cathedral model   256
Inspecting the work of the Cathedral builders[4]   256
View of the Metropolitan Cathedral, Liverpool[5]   257
Opening of the Cathedral, May 1967[5]   320
Last look at the Cathedral building   321
Last ceremony as Archbishop of Liverpool[6]   321
Leaving Liverpool[2]   352
Arriving for enthronement at Westminster Cathedral[7]   352
Westminster Cathedral: after enthronement[8]   353
With Pope Paul   353

STILL NOT THE WHOLE TRUTH

Some readers were shocked at my declared intention of not telling the whole truth in the first volume. My motive, of course, was to reassure former parishioners and other friends who might have feared betrayal of their confidences.

For the same reason I have been selective also in the present volume. I undertook to write an autobiography, it may be remembered, to avoid long interviews with a potential biographer. I preferred to tell my own story. In recent years I have therefore spent my holidays recording experiences and impressions gathered in many parts of the world while I was Bishop of Leeds or Archbishop of Liverpool. This book is the result.

I returned as archbishop to my native diocese of Westminster in September 1963. Events since that time are too recent for me to treat them objectively. That is why I do not propose at present to add a third volume of autobiography.

There are only two books I still want to write. I would like to give a public starved of devotional reading two short books. One would be on the Blessed Sacrament and the other on Our Lady.

If God grants me time to do this writing I shall then gratefully lay down my pen, reach for my breviary and recite the *Nunc Dimittis*.

† JOHN CARDINAL HEENAN
Christmas Day 1973.

PART I—LEEDS

CHAPTER
ONE

THE YEAR 1951 DID NOT BEGIN AUSPICIOUSLY. MY BROTHER DIED IN January, my sister lay dying of leukaemia and I was nominated Bishop of Leeds. The full burden of becoming a bishop cannot be known except by experience. The first shock is the sudden loss of privacy through becoming a minor public figure. Casual remarks of a new bishop over a cup of tea become a talking point wherever clergy meet. Jocular remarks at a school prize-giving are reported solemnly in the local paper ("Bishop confesses he was always bottom of the class") and may even feature in the national press. Old friends and colleagues begin to address you with cautious respect. Those nearest to you multiply your worries by failing to disclose important information to spare you worry. In order not to appear to have favourites you cultivate no intimate friendships among your priests or people. The laity of whom you are now shepherd are so numerous that it is not possible to know them all personally. You will become acquainted only with heads of organisations, mayors, members of parliament, doctors, matrons and directors of education. But you will no longer know the Christian names of the school children. That, perhaps, is the most constant reminder that you have left behind you the joy of being a parish priest.

The great compensation is that with the co-operation of zealous priests and laity you will have wider opportunities of doing good—but usually at one remove. These opportunities are surprisingly limited. The inexperienced imagine that a bishop has only to write an *ad clerum* (notice to priests) or a pastoral letter (read out in every church in the

[9]

diocese) to achieve any plan he may have in mind. The written word addressed to a body of people is, in fact, rarely effectual. People soon forget what has been read out to them once. Only if a priest also happens to be enthusiastic about a bishop's message are the faithful likely to be stirred to action. The bishop is a more or less remote figure seen possibly once in two or three years. The priest in the parish is the man who can inspire the people to take action. It is now customary to describe the laity as ever eager to take the initiative in pastoral and even theological enterprises. The picture is unreal. Catholic people await a lead from their priests. That is why the bishop is effective only when his priests support him. The most popular pastoral letter I ever wrote was on the Christian duty of giving. This inspired the clergy to order copies for distribution to their parishioners. In unprecedented fashion priests from other dioceses also read my pastoral from their pulpits. The appeal of my more spiritual flights has been markedly less widespread.

The idea most people have of a bishop is largely illusory. However hard a bishop may try to be close to his flock he is bound to remain in some measure isolated. Sooner or later every bishop realises that the major spiritual power of the Catholic Church is wielded not by bishops—not even the Bishop of Rome—but by zealous priests. It is to them rather than bishops that Catholic people look. The priest without zeal exercises little influence on his people. They are dependent on him for spiritual ministrations but will not follow him. The power for good of a devoted priest, on the other hand, is immense. In the homes of parishioners, by the bedside of the sick, in the confessional, from the pulpit and at the altar he is a man sent by God. The Vatican Council did not exaggerate in describing the priest as another Christ. The greatest sacrifice a bishop has to make is to give up most of the direct and intimate cure of souls. This is the chief joy of a priest but the bishop is by definition only an overseer.

One day just before the war I was summoned to Westminster. When I arrived I found Cardinal Hinsley in his room trying on a new mitre. In playful mood he put it on my head. It fitted perfectly. The Cardinal's face became serious. "One day," he said, "you will wear a mitre of your own and you will find it a crown of thorns." Aphorisms are never more than partially true and the Cardinal's is no exception. It will be seen in the chapters which follow that a bishop's life is not all suffering. He continues to enjoy an abundance of the pleasures he knew as a priest. There are even advantages in being a bishop, but on balance the burden of responsibility outweighs the gratification of being in a position to take decisions. President Truman is alleged to have put over his desk the notice: 'The buck stops here.' The same could well find its place over the desk of a bishop. The final decision rests with him. Discussion may be prolonged and consultations multiplied, but eventually it is the bishop who has to accept responsibility. The member of a committee gives his vote knowing that his is not the final and irrevocable judgment. It is said—probably wrongly—that a firing squad is furnished with rifles of which one has a blank cartridge. Thus no member of the squad can be certain that his was the fatal shot. Pope Paul found that the pontifical commission on population and the family created by Pope John still left him with the duty of making up his own mind before God whether or not he ought to jettison the teaching of his immediate predecessors John XXIII, Pius XII and Pius XI on contraception.

I have already described the telephone conversation in which the Apostolic Delegate informed me that the Pope wished me to become Bishop of Leeds. From the time of the appointment there is usually a delay of about ten days before a public announcement is made in Rome. These are difficult days for any bishop-elect but they were especially difficult for me. As superior of the Catholic Missionary Society I continued to receive letters daily from priests requiring the services of the C.M.S. in the coming months when I would no longer be responsible for our programme. I had to deal also with parish priests anxious to discuss details of missions I had undertaken to give but for which I would no longer be available. I needed leisure to prepare myself for a new apostolate and to leave everything in order for my successor at the Mission House but I had no choice but to act as if no change was impending. I was in the Good Shepherd parish in Nottingham when the news was published. I finished the mission there and hurried back to the Mission House. It was the middle of February and the date of the consecration had been fixed for 12th March, the feast of St. Gregory the Great. The interval was short because Easter was early in 1951 and Leeds was anxious not to have a second Holy Week without a bishop.

My ever faithful friends, the Ursuline nuns, set to work on my old black cassock and added the requisite purple trimmings. Dr. Poskitt, my predecessor at Leeds, had been of more or less my own height and build. I was therefore fortunate in not having to buy any episcopal regalia. This was gratifying because I had no money left after three years as a missioner. I was spared the need of asking the diocese to provide money for my robes before I had even set foot in Yorkshire. I had more than enough to worry about without thinking of clothes. A bishop-elect usually spends eight days in retreat before his consecration. This was to be impossible for me because I had undertaken a public debate due to take place only a few days before I was to be consecrated in Leeds Cathedral. If it had been a normal engagement I would have passed it with all my other commitments to one of the other C.M.S. priests. But this was a very special assignment which would have to be cancelled if I could not appear in person. The debate had been arranged in a most unusual way.

Towards the end of 1950 I was preaching a mission in Bolton, Lancashire. Father Chronnell, the parish priest, was very old and little preparation had been made for the mission. The parishioners and the general public had been given no warning that I was coming. The old priest had even forgotten to have the customary mission bills and posters printed. On the first night of the mission I spoke in a half-empty church. The second night of the mission was little better but after the mission service two men came into the sacristy and introduced themselves as the Morris brothers. Both were lawyers, one a solicitor and the other a barrister (subsequently a judge). These keen laymen were distressed at the poor attendance and complained that the mission had not been advertised. They made a bold suggestion. I was to preach next evening on a subject of social as well as spiritual interest. They would see that newspaper reporters were present and in this way the mission would receive free advertisement in Bolton and the surrounding districts. It was decided that I would preach on justice with special reference to political systems offensive to man's nature and dignity. This would give the journalists something to write about.

The experiment was uncomfortably successful. The *Bolton Evening News*—as in many provincial towns there was no local morning paper—gave headlines to my 'indictment of Soviet Communism'. Its quotations from my sermon led the secretary of the Manchester communist party to write a letter to the editor challenging me to a public debate. The letter appeared in the afternoon edition and the Morris brothers came round at once to the presbytery. They offered to be my agents for the planning of the debate and my seconds for the actual fight. Within a few hours they had booked the Albert Hall, Bolton, for the first available night—5th March, 1951—and arranged for the editor of the *Bolton Evening News* to take the chair at the debate. I was amazed that the

Communist Party had invited public discussion because at that time this was not part of their usual technique. Issuing his challenge the secretary of the party had complained that the pulpit is a coward's castle. He was confident, he wrote, that I would lack the courage to take part in a public discussion on Soviet communism. He must have been very naïve because it was the communists who needed courage to defend the Soviet Union in 1951. The party bosses in King Street knew that it was not so much courageous as foolhardy to attempt to defend Stalin's record. At that time (as the whole world now knows through the revelations of Khrushchev) terror was still the rule of law in the U.S.S.R. Communist headquarters in London therefore took the debate out of the hands of the local party and put up Mr. Andrew Rothstein, a founder member of the Communist Party of Great Britain, to defend the Soviets. The debate had already been given nationwide publicity by the time I was appointed Bishop of Leeds. If I had called off the debate to go into retreat the communists would undoubtedly have given the word 'retreat' a literal interpretation.

Tickets were equally divided between communists and Catholics. Since the former were unable to find sufficient supporters to fill their half of the spacious hall we gladly bought their share for the many Catholics from other parts of the country who wanted to hear the debate. Now that television brings discussions into our homes every day, people might not be so inclined to fight for seats for a debate. In March 1951 some were prepared to pay the price of ringside seats at a prize fight in order to be present at Bolton. The British public were apprehensive of Stalin's Russia—much as they had been a decade earlier of Hitler's Germany. Stalin was no less sinister than Hitler and the Soviet Union in the 1950s was as unfriendly as Nazi Germany had been in the 1930s. A little more than a year later the Korean war reminded the western powers that a third world war was not a completely remote possibility. Although nothing so dramatic as the confrontation between Kennedy and Khrushchev over Cuba occurred in his time, Stalin held a dreadful fascination for the war-weary British.

The title of the debate was 'That liberty of the citizen is possible only in a Soviet Socialist State'. I did not really care what title was chosen provided I had the last word. I instructed the Morris brothers who conducted all negotiations to agree to any formula which required the communist to begin the debate. This was not a dishonest device to enable me to produce an argument at the last moment to which my opponent would have no chance of replying. The reason for my insistence was simply that I did not want to give my opponent an opportunity of adopting this well-known strategy. To my surprise the communists were most co-operative. I think that they had already begun to regret the whole enterprise but could not withdraw their challenge without unthinkable loss of face in Lancashire. In appointing Rothstein they had an intelligent and urbane defender of their faith. Nobody could have been less alarming either in appearance or manner. He gave a rather defensive opening speech in which he pleaded for the heroic Soviet Union, our gallant ally in war, which now received nothing but insults from our capitalist society. He gave a picture of social security in the Soviet Union which made our welfare State seem pinchbeck by comparison. The sick and aged in Russia were so well looked after that nobody needed to save for a rainy day. Poverty and illiteracy had been abolished. Because the people were economically free true liberty existed in the Soviet Union while in Britain the poor, enslaved by capitalism, enjoyed only the illusion of freedom from want.

One or two of the speeches made since 1951 have special significance and will be included here. This particular speech, delivered only a few days before my consecration as bishop, marked the end of any sustained attack on communism on my part. In years to come I would still occasionally remind audiences of this evil system which continued to exist after it had outgrown Stalinism. But once I became a bishop the cares of a diocese with its manifold social and religious problems left me little leisure to continue my role as Torquemada. At the Mission House we had an all-purpose title to cover any speech on communism. It was 'Vatican and Kremlin'. Covering any line of thought on social justice it could be used for publicity before we had actually written the speech. We all grew fond of this comprehensive title at the Mission House. When we acquired a puppy and a kitten it seemed natural to call one Vat and the other Krem. The Bolton speech can be regarded as the swan song of the Vat and Krem brigade. It was the last of my speeches directly on communism. The debate was unreal because there was simply no case to be made for Stalin's Russia.

One of the engagements I had to cancel at short notice in March 1951 was a series of lectures in the Oval Hall, Sheffield. The city of steel is one of the largest in England and its Catholics had greater initiative than I had seen elsewhere. Each year the Sheffield Council for Catholic Action organised a week of lectures. It needed great courage to book the biggest halls in the city for a whole week for nothing more exciting than a monologue. I had given the talks the previous year in a well-filled hall. I wondered about this year because television had grown rapidly in twelve months yet was still enough of a novelty to anchor people to their armchairs. I have no idea if I would have been able to attract the crowds in the changed circumstances of 1951. I had been unwilling to go a second time on the general principle that the Catholic Missionary Society did not foster personality cults. The organisers, however, insisted that lectures unlike missions are not spiritual exercises. Until the other members of the C.M.S. became known my name was a useful bait. In the event the organisers were proved wrong. Father Holland went in my place and proved a greater attraction. This might not be evident to the reader of the short article in the *Catholic Gazette* which reported the Sheffield talks and the final meeting at which I spoke. It is therefore important to know that the anonymous writer was Father Holland who was so little known that he was not recognised by the people sent to meet his train.

Father Holland was the man. *The Catholic Church and You* was his subject. February 25th, 26th, 27th, 28th, March 2nd and 4th were the dates.

The series was to have been Act II (six scenes) of Dr. J. C. Heenan's piece which he began in 1950. And this year it was to have been a musical. The best concert organ in the world was on tap (or pipe). The night when David Garrick (or was it Burbage?) fell sick and they literally played *Hamlet* without the Prince of Denmark was long remembered at the Globe Theatre (or was it the Mermaid?).

In some such way it is agreed among all good cutlers that this week of talks will be remembered at Sheffield. The Council of Catholic Action who organise the talks have to be steel-hardened cadres in a place like Sheffield. Yet they were shaken, so far shaken, that Dr. J.C.H.'s substitute passed through their ranks coming from the train without registering on the steely retina of any one of them.

However people came: about 850 the first night, upwards of 520 the second (in the smaller hall), less than 520 the third, upwards of 1,000 the fourth (large hall), well over 520 the fifth (small hall) and 3,000 the sixth (large hall including balconies not previously booked).

The sixth night (Sunday) was very memorable. The Bishop-elect entered the hall at the end of the main address. He would have to be more than steel-hardened if his heart did not beat very quickly as they welcomed him. He said: "The last time I stood before you I was a wandering missioner who came only to say good-bye. This time I come and—you are my people." All the poor substitute could think (as he saw the slim, vibrant figure in the cloak of flame, *cantantibus organis*, leap to the heart of his people) was: "It's magnificent, but it's not the C.M.S.!"

There is, of course, good Christian people and cutlers all, no defence for such parish pump self-pity. Yet you are people who gently regard a father's sorrow when he gives away the light of his home to another. You do allow him one tear. We crave no more. And in return, if ever another Act of the Sheffield Saga comes our way, we shall ransack our green-room in the interests of Catholicised Steel.

I hurried back to London from Sheffield to make final preparations for my departure from the Mission House. I had little opportunity during the days immediately preceding my consecration to give much thought to the task awaiting me as Bishop of Leeds. Apart from the vast amount of correspondence involved in leaving the affairs of the Mission House in order I had to acknowledge the hundreds of greetings from well-wishers who had written or sent telegrams after my appointment had been announced. I remember especially a note from Ronnie Knox (Monsignor R. A. Knox) who having expressed his satisfaction went on, "I don't suppose you will enjoy being a bishop but at least you can enjoy giving pleasure to your friends by becoming a bishop. Please do not acknowledge this note—not even with one of those horrible little cards which say that the Bishop-elect of Titipu thanks you etc." I did not, in fact, have any horrible little cards printed. I managed to send a personal line to all who had troubled to write. The result was that I left for Leeds without having given thought even to the speeches I would have to make when introducing myself to my new flock. These I prepared during the two days I spent at the Bishop's House before taking possession of the See of Leeds.

There was another reason why it was not easy to concentrate on coming events. My sister, Mary Reynolds, was in a critical condition. She had been treated for leukaemia in the London Hospital where her eldest son, Brian, was a house surgeon. Despite the skill of the physicians, her condition deteriorated gravely towards the close of the year

1950. She was so clearly beyond the help of doctors that her family decided after Christmas to remove her from the London Hospital to St. Andrew's Hospital which was in the care of the Blue Nuns. We all felt that since there was no hope of recovery she ought to be given spiritual consolation by the nuns during her last few days on earth. The consultant in charge of the case was assured that the proposed move implied no criticism of the treatment given her by the London Hospital. The simple issue was that since she could not be cured it was kinder to let the Sisters prepare her for death. The doctor agreed to the transfer but warned us that she might not survive the journey across London.

My sister was a woman of such extraordinary determination that to describe her as strong-willed would be an understatement. She had gone to St. Andrew's to prepare for death but was very much in control of whatever short span of life might remain to her. She astonished the Sisters at St. Andrew's by announcing her intention of being present in Leeds cathedral for my consecration as bishop. On being told by the doctors that a four-hour train journey would kill her she persuaded her husband to hire a private plane. The pilot was instructed to fly the Reynolds family to Leeds on the morning of 11th March. My sister announced that she would go to bed at once on arrival in Leeds and would thus be strong enough to face the long ceremony in the cathedral on the following morning. Her plan was not in fact put into effect because 11th March was so misty that the pilot could not take off. Doctors and nurses sighed with satisfaction that the suicidal journey to Leeds was off. They sighed too soon. Despite the forebodings of her doctors she decided to go by train. Her reasoning was simple. If the journey were to kill her she would cease to be a nuisance to family and friends. So, accompanied by a nurse and doctor, she went to Leeds. Nobody could have guessed that this foolhardy journey was the first stage on the road to recovery.

My sister arrived in Leeds exhausted but in no way repentant of her decision. The following day her spirits remained high but her body reacted to the strain of the journey. She had to be carried up the few steps at the entrance to the cathedral by her husband. Ample cushions had been placed in her pew and she survived the long ceremony without disaster. The next day she received a blessing from the Apostolic Delegate who had been the chief celebrant at my consecration. He had been a student in Rome during the pontificate of Pope Pius X of whose sanctity he was convinced. He brought to Leeds a relic of Pope Pius

[17]

with which he proposed to bless my sister. From that day she began to improve. To the intense joy of her family she eventually made such a remarkable recovery that in subsequent years she was present at the ordination to the priesthood of her younger son Michael, was able to travel to the U.S.A. for the marriage of Brian, her elder son, a surgeon in New York, and, best of all, was in St. Peter's, Rome, for the canonisation of Saint Pius X. Remissions are not uncommon in leukaemia but a dramatic remission in a patient on the point of death is rare—so rare that the case of Mrs. Reynolds was quoted by a haematologist in a lecture to nurses. The lecturer did not know that Angela, Mrs. Reynolds' youngest daughter, was in his audience. Miracle or not, my sister's recovery began after her journey to Leeds.

CHAPTER

TWO

12TH MARCH, 1951, THE FEAST OF ST. GREGORY THE GREAT, APOSTLE
of England, does not remain so vividly in my mind as 6th July, 1930,
my ordination day. Becoming a bishop is, of course, much less
important than becoming a priest. Of the Mass of Consecration only
two incidents remain clearly in my memory. The first was a hitch at
the start which led to a long and baffling delay while the congregation
became increasingly restive. I was dressed in purple for the first time.
I felt young, thin and frail. I had a headache of such severity that I
could scarcely read the print in the missal. I was led by my assistants,
Bishop McCormack and Bishop Petit, to a side altar to vest while the
chief consecrator, the Apostolic Delegate, was vesting at the high altar.
Unfortunately the side altar was out of sight of the high altar. For
nearly a quarter of an hour the master of ceremonies waited for my
procession to emerge from the side chapel while we were waiting for a
sign to proceed. My second recollection is that the opening words of
the sermon of Dr. Downey, Archbishop of Liverpool, were: "This is a
red letter day. The joy bells ring out in the belfry of our hearts." This
was his formula for every big occasion from the opening of a new
church to the jubilee of an old nun. The archbishop had used the
same exordium for twenty years and saw no reason to alter it.

After Mass there was a banquet in the Queen's Hotel. The Lord
Mayor of Leeds that year was a Catholic, a splendid man named
O'Donnell who was to prove a powerful friend in later years. Banquets
of any kind have always bored me and this one was no exception.
There were speeches of welcome from the clergy, laity and, of course,

from the Lord Mayor on behalf of the City. I was not sorry to have to miss some of the speech-making—the most deadly part of any banquet—because I had to leave the hotel to record a speech on B.B.C. radio. Tape-recorders were not yet in use so I had to abandon my guests to go to the Leeds broadcasting station. My message to the people of Leeds was to be broadcast that evening after the Northern news. Introducing myself to the diocese I apologised for not being a native of Yorkshire (the boundaries of the Leeds diocese coincide with those of the West Riding). In Yorkshire they hold that the most important achievement of which a man is capable is to be born in Yorkshire. This is particularly important for boys because aliens are not allowed to play cricket for the county club. Here is the text of my short speech:

I have been Bishop of Leeds for only a few hours. So you won't expect me to give you my views on Leeds or the North. What I imagine you would like me to tell you is how I feel about coming among you as your bishop. I can't pretend to be pleased about the burden of responsibility which will be mine. But since it is God's will that I should carry this burden I thank Him for letting me carry it among the warm-hearted people of the north.

One of the greatest friends I ever had was Cardinal Hinsley. I loved and admired him. That is why I wrote his biography. Cardinal Hinsley was a Yorkshire man—and very proud of it he was! I can't claim to be a Yorkshire man except by adoption—if you will have me. From him I learnt to appreciate the sturdy character of the Yorkshire folk. I remember that the Cardinal began one of his great broadcasts with the words: "To beg I am not ashamed". I am not ashamed either. I want to start begging right away.

May I beg the help of your prayers? Whether you are Catholics or Protestants, Christians or Jews, I regard myself as your servant. I intend to devote all my energies to the souls committed to my care in the West Riding of Yorkshire. I want to be a real pastor and father. Left to myself I would be bound to fail. That is where you come in. You who are listening to me, men, women and children—yes, especially the children—pray that God will guide me and make me generous in his service. You will all have my prayers. Perhaps some of you who are listening to me are sick and feeble. You may feel that you are no longer of much use. Believe me, you can be of great use to me. Pray for your new bishop. God bless you all.

Long after I had left Yorkshire for Liverpool dividends were still coming in. Many unknown friends of various religions gave me a place in their prayers from the day of that broadcast.

After being enthroned as Bishop of Leeds I spent a few days entertaining relatives who had come great distances to be present. Among them were two cousins from the U.S.A., Dominican nuns, and two cousins from Ireland, who were also nuns. For nuns to be allowed to stay in Bishop's House was a great concession in those days. We visited some of the churches and institutions of the diocese and had excursions to York Minster and the Liverpool Cathedral (Anglican). The honeymoon lasted nearly a week. The nuns then returned to their convents and I settled down to learn how to be a bishop. It is inevitable that the Church can provide no training for episcopacy. Men do not decide to become bishops and apply to do a course. What happens is that a priest who probably often complained of the incompetence of bishops suddenly finds that he has been made one of the incompetents. It is hard to see how this lacuna in ecclesiastical training can be filled. A staff college for future bishops is hardly practical. The officer cadet is commissioned as a matter of course. He ascends in rank at regular intervals unless he is unfit to be a soldier. When and if he reaches the appropriate seniority he will be sent to a staff college. Unlike the young subaltern, the young priest has already reached his goal as soon as he is commissioned in the service of the Church on the day of his ordination. The word 'preferment' is not part of the vocabulary of Catholic clergy. The priesthood is their career.

The lack of preparation for the office of bishop can have serious consequences. Apart from the bishop's chaplain (called his secretary, though, in fact, a modern bishop employs lay secretaries) nobody knows the problems and stresses of a bishop's life. The newly appointed bishop is likely to be ignorant of what he has to do and how he ought to do it. I was no exception. I had helped Cardinal Hinsley to prepare speeches and pronouncements but I had never been involved in the work of his diocese. As a priest in Essex I had been immersed in parish work and visited Bishop's House only when summoned. I was therefore completely without curial experience.

After the death or translation of the bishop a diocese is in the care of a Vicar Capitular. Monsignor Hawkeswell had been Vicar Capitular for over a year. A few days after my consecration he came to report on the state of the diocese. The old man handed me a long list of names of priests who had either requested a move or needed to be moved for their own good or the good of their flocks.

Canon law decrees *sede vacante nil innovetur* (nothing may be changed while the see is vacant). Monsignor Hawkeswell had interpreted the rule only too literally. The former bishop had been a sick man for a considerable time before his death. It was not surprising that the list of pastoral problems was long. As a young man Henry John Poskitt had been vicar of a small Anglican parish in Leeds. On becoming a Catholic he had studied in Rome at the Beda College, founded after the Oxford Movement for the training of convert clergymen. He had also studied canon law at the Accademia, the college of graduates destined for the papal diplomatic service, where one of his fellow students was Giovanni Battista Montini, the future Pope Paul VI. Henry Poskitt elected to join the diocese of Middlesbrough doubtless thinking that it might have been embarrassing to be a priest in the city where he had been vicar. When he returned to Leeds as bishop he was therefore not well acquainted with the local clergy. He was, however, well known to Yorkshire farmers and nature lovers. He had a great interest in goats and bees and was the president of the Yorkshire society of goat-keepers. I found the garden of the bishop's house dotted with bee-hives and goat houses and the library stocked with goat books. I have no idea what happened to the bees and goats *sede vacante* but there was neither sign nor scent of them when I arrived. It was just as well because sheep and lambs in Leeds had been impatiently awaiting their new shepherd and would leave me little time for goats. Only a few weeks before my appointment a girl from Leeds Notre Dame High School during a papal audience had boldly asked Pius XII when he was going to give Leeds a bishop. That must have been one of the earliest examples of dialogue. Yorkshire Catholics were resentful at being kept waiting so long. Bishop Poskitt died on 19th February, 1950. My consecration took place on 12th March, 1951.

A year is a long time to keep a diocese without a bishop. I suspect that the Holy See failed after a prolonged search to find a local candidate who would enjoy the confidence of a majority. It is usual on such occasions to look for an outsider. That, I imagine, is how I came to be chosen.

It is unprofitable to speculate whether Leeds would have prospered more under a local priest than an outsider. I am obviously in no position to offer an opinion in this case but from subsequent experience I have no doubt that there are circumstances in which it is wise to choose a bishop from outside a diocese. This is the chief but by no means the only objection to the popular election of bishops. Divisions among priests sometimes create the need for the choice of someone from outside. The laity know little about diocesan clergy and still less of priests from elsewhere who keep out of the public eye. Not even his fellow clergy know a priest really well unless they have lived in the same house. With priests as with other professional people a man's public *persona* may be quite different from his private character. The old, the sick, the poor and children know a man's priestly qualities but theirs would not be a very influential voice in the election of bishops. The present system of gathering confidential opinions from clergy and laity is probably the best way of finding the most suitable candidates. As the exercise of authority becomes increasingly burdensome bishops need more than ever to be chosen for their spiritual qualities. Saints cannot be chosen by ballot. A Francis de Sales or a John Fisher does not appear in every century. The Church has to make do with lesser men. A popular vote is much less likely to produce men of God than the present method. A system based on wide and confidential enquiry is not to be lightly discarded. To this question we shall return as I recount how I was moved from diocese to diocese.

When Monsignor Hawkeswell showed me the list of matters urgently awaiting decision I made up my mind to invite him to be my Vicar General. I would need a great deal of guidance from a Yorkshire man. He was old but for that reason all the more suitable. John Dinn, the previous Vicar General and my contemporary at the English College in Rome, might have been over-anxious not to appear patronising by telling me what to do. I asked Monsignor Hawkeswell to give me the history of the diocese as a prelude to advising me on policy. The great disadvantage of coming as a stranger to a diocese is not to know the clergy. A priest may have gained the reputation of being a rebel for having stood up like a man to a bullying superior. Similarly a parish priest may be condemned as a curate-killer whereas he is intolerant only of lazy curates who will not visit the homes of their people. To deal justly with the many priests whose names had been put before me I would need to know what kind of formation priests of the Leeds diocese had received. I listened patiently while the old Monsignor told me the story of the last fifty years in Yorkshire.

The Vicar General was nearly blind but his mind and memory were clear. He began my historical education with Bishop Gordon who became Bishop of Leeds in 1890 and died just before the first world war. William Gordon, he said, had been known to hit children with his crozier if they did not answer his questions at Confirmation. I remembered from my researches for the memoir of Cardinal Hinsley that Bishop Gordon was an irascible man. Although Hinsley was the founder and first headmaster of St. Bede's grammar school, Bradford, he became so aggrieved by Bishop Gordon's treatment that he left not only the school but the diocese. He was accepted by the Bishop of Southwark and made parish priest of Sydenham. For the last six years of his life Bishop Gordon had been unable to administer the diocese and was given a Coadjutor. Joseph Cowgill was consecrated bishop in 1905 (the year I was born) and lived until 1936. When he died at the age of seventy-six he had been in charge of the diocese for over thirty years.

Bishop Cowgill was known as the children's bishop. Before going on his daily walk he used to fill his pockets with sweets to distribute to his little friends. Naturally they adored him. He was even more beloved by those children to whom he had given not sweets but a home. In the early years of this century poverty was regarded as culpable. When sickness, unemployment or death struck a family there was no dole and few allowances except the humiliating help of the poor-law guardians. The Cowgill Home for orphans was the fruit of his solicitude. It was natural for the children's bishop to be a father of the poor. The bishop himself, the Monsignor said, was something of a child and he found it difficult to issue an order and quite impossible to give a reprimand. When a priest was guilty of a misdemeanour the bishop would send for Monsignor Hawkeswell. The delinquent would then be admonished by the Vicar General in the presence of the silent bishop. St. Paul told the Corinthians that "if the trumpet give an uncertain sound none will prepare himself to the battle". In Leeds the senior clergy hearing not even an uncertain sound had taken to blowing the trumpets themselves. They took over the authority the bishop was reluctant to exercise. They went so far as to appoint or dismiss junior clergy without reference to the bishop. Towards the end of Bishop Cowgill's life there was a breakdown of ecclesiastical authority which would have been disastrous but for the highly dependable character of the clergy who were either dogged Yorkshiremen or tough Irishmen. Between them they held the diocese together.

Before the first world war the diocese had been startled by a curates' strike. By the time I arrived in Leeds the episode was remembered only as a prank but at the time it must have seemed like incipient anarchy. According to the Monsignor, a small number of young priests met to discuss their financial misery. Their annual stipend of forty pounds was inadequate even when supplemented by the meagre offerings of the faithful on such occasions as weddings. Poverty was widespread in the centres of heavy industry where most Catholics sought a livelihood. The young priests decided that on a certain Sunday they would refuse to make the outdoor collection (the chief source of revenue for maintaining Catholic schools). The token strike was crushed with speed and severity. Each young priest was banished for several years to another diocese or even to another country. At a subsequent diocesan synod legislation was introduced forbidding any meeting of curates to take place without leave. There is nobody alive today who was involved in the famous strike. By the year 1951 when I came to Leeds the delinquents had all become venerable canons highly critical of undisciplined young curates.

Monsignor Hawkeswell like everyone who had known him recalled Bishop Cowgill with genuine affection. Through his priestly example and palpable love of his flock he achieved a success which might have eluded a mere administrator or disciplinarian. His successor, Bishop Poskitt, coming from the diocese of Middlesbrough, found Leeds in a healthy spiritual state. He had been summoned to Leeds from Bedale, a small country parish where he could devote much of his time to his garden, his goats and his bees. A shy man, he probably never reconciled himself to the loss of the tiny country parish where he had expected to end his days. As a bishop he was little known and avoided social occasions. Even when visiting parishes to administer Confirmation he rarely tarried in the presbytery much longer than it took to drink a cup of tea. Although a reserved man he was much loved and respected. He was an excellent administrator and a shrewd judge of men. I found the affairs of the diocese in superb order. The delicate task awaiting me was to deal with the personnel problems on Monsignor Hawkeswell's long list.

Having spent several days reading his reports and correspondence I asked Monsignor Hawkeswell many questions. Not wishing to make my debut in the guise of an avenging angel I decided not to limit new appointments to those priests who had been in conflict with authority. If they alone were included in the first batch of moves they might become marked men. I thought it kinder to make a wider sweep so that being given a new appointment would not connote an unsatisfactory record. Studying unadorned diocesan statistics I found that some assistant priests had been in the same parish since ordination ten or fifteen years earlier. It was clear without seeking any confidential information that such curates would become better parish priests if they had been given experience of more than one parish. To the twenty or so who for one reason or other were on the Monsignor's list for fresh appointments I added a similar number of priests who had been left too long without a change. In this way I hoped to remove suspicion from all included in the first batch of moves.

I succeeded only too well. Suspicion was transferred from the delinquents to me. When the new appointments were announced it was asked how I could possibly have learned enough about the clergy to make extensive changes so soon. I could not speak about Monsignor Hawkeswell's list without sacrificing the whole purpose of my strategy. I therefore offered no explanation. Worse was to come. Several parish priests who had taken for granted that they would stay in their parishes until death now thought to rejuvenate themselves and renew their zeal by seeking new appointments. I received requests from parish priests of long standing to be considered for a new post but for the most part they asked me not to let it be known that they had asked for a change for fear of hurting their people. In the event their people naturally blamed me. If the priest were unpopular his people praised me. In fact I deserved neither praise nor blame.

A few months later I found myself with a dozen newly ordained priests and a number of requests for a change from both parish priests and curates. I therefore had a formidable number of appointments to make. It resembled a large movement of troops and became known as the autumn manoeuvres. To many priests (and parishioners) the moves were a breath of life—especially to parish priests still young enough to be uprooted who had grown stale through being too long in the same parish. I heard from their fellow priests that many of them were delighted and rejuvenated by their new appointment. Few told me. Encomia do not fall lightly from Yorkshire lips. The first effect of the changes was to awaken parishes which had fallen asleep. Most of the displaced clergy took up their new appointments with zest but some felt resentful. Since William Gordon the bishops had always been gentle and had interfered as little as possible with their clergy. The former bishops had, of course, been Yorkshire men. This new bishop from London was much too quick off the mark. With an eye on a currently

[26]

popular novel a wag named Leeds 'the cruel see'. Priests were alleged to greet each other not with "How are you?" but with "Where are you?" These things were said with great humour. Priests would gleefully tell me the latest cracks about the Bishop of Leeds. I was on cordial terms with the clergy during all my years in Leeds.

Looking back after twenty years I have no doubt that I acted imprudently. It was right to make the changes but most unwise to make them so soon after arriving in a new diocese. At the time I thought it imperative not to delay in sending weary pastors to new pastures. The period of *sede vacante* had been too prolonged and during his last months the late bishop had been able to do little. That is why I allowed myself to attribute undue urgency to Monsignor Hawkeswell's list. Later experience taught me that little is lost by delay in dealing with human problems. The exercise of judgment requires reflection. During the first world war Sir Douglas Haig declared that news is never so good or so bad as it sounds at first. However urgently action is demanded time must be taken for careful thought. Intuition is a dangerous guide. It is easy for me now to formulate these principles because I have been a bishop in three dioceses. When I went to Leeds I was in my middle forties and lacked the knowledge that comes only from experience and failure. I did not then realise that it was unfair to expect instant co-operation from priests who had experienced a gentler wielding of authority.

Belloc never tired of telling people not to read history backwards. It is nevertheless difficult for me to avoid judging my early activities in Leeds by post-conciliar standards. The Council has altered the manner of exercising authority in the Church. In 1951 the concept of authority was much simpler. A priest recognised himself as above all things the servant of the Church. A bishop had even greater reason for regarding himself as the Church's servant. I had received orders from the Pope to rule the diocese of Leeds. I left my native diocese for Leeds as an act of obedience. To speak of ruling a diocese may now sound slightly pretentious. It did not then. Before the Council we talked of a bishop's enthronement and of his reign. Although we used the language of secular rulers we did not regard bishops primarily as wielding power. Then as now a bishop thought of himself as the servant of his priests and people. The proud title of the Sovereign Pontiff, *Servus Servorum Dei*—the servant of the servants of God—is in due measure also appropriate to the bishop. I was to do my duty by giving orders and the priests theirs by carrying them out. If they disliked my decisions

I was ready to listen to their objections but priests rarely refused to obey. To accept decisions without question makes life easier for the priest and bishop but is not necessarily better for the Church. The present method of greater consultation smacks less of autocracy and is more in tune with the times.

I did not think of myself as an autocrat in Leeds but today I would be so regarded if I were to act in the same way. The gap created by rank is disappearing but the essential features of the hierarchical system remain. The bishop is the head of the body of priests (presbyterium) and his chair (cathedra) in his church (cathedral) is the sign of his teaching authority. By stripping him of much of the outward show of episcopal dignity the Church has brought the bishop nearer to his priests and people. The establishment of elected senates of priests and diocesan pastoral councils has made it easier for clergy and laity to make their views known. They now more obviously share the bishop's pastoral responsibility. Authority has not been downgraded but humanised by its current interpretation. During my six years in Leeds this democratic process had not begun. The bishop was still expected to be a ruler and a father. Paternalism had not yet been invented.

Increased educational opportunity has made people less inarticulate but ecclesiastical titles can still have an inhibiting effect. Being called My Lord (or, for that matter, Your Grace or Your Eminence) tends to set prelates at a distance. Some day all clergy irrespective of position will be addressed as 'Father'. This title of the Pope (papa means father) does not lessen respect for his sacred office. I spent my first year in Leeds visiting the priests and people. The sick were told to call me 'Father' but most of them preferred to use the grander title. Children similarly revel in the use of titles. Thus when I entered their class-room the infants loved to salute me with, "Good morning, my Lord. God bless you, my Lord".

In order to establish close relations with the flock I set aside each Friday to receive visitors without appointment. Open Day, as it came to be called, was a successful experiment. Until the novelty wore off—after three or four years—Friday was the busiest day of my week. Most callers brought matrimonial worries or problems over their children's schooling. Priests and people were equally welcome but priests usually preferred to make an appointment to see me on another day. I realised that an Open Day might attract cranks but I guessed—rightly as it turned out—that cranks would soon lose interest if the bishop were easy to see. Apart from showing that I was accessible there was little practical

[28]

value in these interviews because people's problems usually had to be referred to the priests of the parish or the educational authorities. Without knowing their home conditions I could be of little help to those who brought me problems which ought to have been taken to their own priest. I was sometimes told that they did not want to bother their own priest because he was a very busy man! The most delightful visit I had during my six years in Leeds was from an elderly widow. "When I woke up this morning," she said by way of introduction, "I said to myself 'Today's your birthday, luv, give yourself a treat and go to see the bishop'."

A bishop's most obvious duty is to be leader of the Catholic community in his diocese. In addition to preaching sermons during parish visitations this involves making speeches and writing pastoral letters to be read from every pulpit. Apart from meetings called to discuss specific problems e.g. Catholic schools, a bishop usually reaches the general public through societies in search of a speaker. Invitations to speak multiply as a man becomes well known but a bishop from the outset is assumed to have something worth saying. University unions, luncheon clubs and institutes of every sort fall back on bishops in the absence of politicians, sportsmen, and television stars. Such invitations provide an opportunity of talking to people unlikely to be encountered in church. Preaching to the converted is not so attractive as giving a Christian point of view to a religiously indifferent audience. The chief obstacle to accepting speaking engagements is lack of time. Apart from after-dinner speeches (an unproductive and exhausting expense of effort) most talks require long preparation. My custom is to write out and learn by heart the substance of what I propose to say publicly. Though laborious, this practice is a minor safeguard against indiscretion. Unfortunately even a well-prepared speech can go wrong. A sentence quoted out of context (as all quotations must be) may give the press a field day and the speaker a few more grey hairs.

One of the first lessons I learned as a bishop was the peril of making a speech without supplying the press with an advance copy of the text. This is not necessary on routine occasions such as a prize-giving or the opening of a new church or school. The most perilous occasions are those unimportant functions at which a reporter or, worse still, a penny-a-liner is unexpectedly present. Even when the press has been furnished with a copy of a speech it is impossible to foretell how it will be reported. All that is certain is that any closely reasoned passage will be omitted. If questions are allowed at the end of a speech an impulsive answer is more likely to reach next morning's papers than any of the striking passages in the body of the speech which were chiselled with patient care during the long hours of preparation. Social invitations which involve speech-making present a problem to a bishop which only experience or perhaps old age will teach him to solve. I was fortunate in being given a sharp lesson during my first months in Leeds. Harrogate in the West Riding of Yorkshire is one of the most popular conference centres in the country. In the early summer of 1951 the Catenians, a society of Catholic business and professional men, held their annual meeting in Harrogate and invited me to be the guest-of-honour at the dinner on Saturday night. The speeches were so numerous and prolix that it was midnight before I was called upon to speak. I had to go home to Leeds in the early hours of Saturday morning and return to Harrogate to sing pontifical High Mass for the Catenians a few hours later. This was in the days of the rigorous eucharistic fast when not even a cup of water was permitted. It was clear that social occasions of this kind would soon sap my strength and destroy my pastoral work. Thanks to this Harrogate experience I resolved not to accept invitations to public dinners unless the speech-making were severely restricted or at least that I should be free to leave at a reasonably early hour.

The dilemma of whether to accept or refuse social engagements is immensely difficult to resolve. It is not possible to apply any universal rule. A bishop must be selective unless he is prepared to accept all invitations and attend luncheons and dinners two or three times a week. It is true that mayors dine out almost every night during their term of office but they hold office for only one year. When they take off their chain of office they can rest from social functions for as long as they need to repair the physical ravages caused by too much entertainment and too little sleep. A bishop's chain of office—on which significantly a cross is hung—is laid aside only at death or on retirement. I have often reflected before beginning an after dinner speech (and even more poignantly while waiting for others to end theirs) that nobody in the room would have to be up next morning as early as I. You can train the body to manage on a meagre allowance of sleep but the mind cannot remain alert if that regular ration is withheld. Emerging from the heat and excitement of a public dinner one finds it impossible to go to sleep at once. I have to read or listen to music until the recollection of speeches and conversations has evaporated. Only then can I compose myself to sleep—but sleep is coy when it has to be wooed. To hard-working men and women past the prime of life late hours are a hazard to health and efficiency.

Everyone who carries great responsibility needs rest but it matters little when that rest is taken. It is said of Winston Churchill, who could write best in the quiet night watches, that he often went to bed when most working men were beginning their day. He, of course, was able to arrange his programme to begin at midday but bishops have to be on duty early in the morning. Their lost sleep is never regained. Like his priests the bishop will start the day with prayer but he must pray much more if he is to be a wise and good shepherd. I learned this simple pastoral lesson soon after I went to Leeds. Since ordination I had made half-an-hour's preparation for Mass (it would be grandiloquent to call it meditation) but soon after becoming a bishop I realised that I needed to give more time to prayer now that my responsibilities were so much greater. It was not difficult to adjust my time-table. Here the training of Monsignor Hinsley, the rector of the English College in Rome, proved its worth. In Rome for seven years I had to rise each morning at half-past five. Sluggish rising was heinous according to the Hinsley code. I was grateful for my disciplined youth now I saw that a bishop's *horarium* also needed to be spartan.

In the problems sometimes arising between priests and their people wide discussion is often difficult without breach of confidence. A bishop will consult others but his action will depend ultimately on his own conception of charity and justice. Few realise that the most perplexing problem is to decide how to be charitable to one person without being unjust to others. Some of the most publicised priestly defections of recent years show that the result of a bishop's forbearance may be to allow priests to remain shepherds while inflicting spiritual injury on their flock. Such forbearance is motivated not by cowardice but by misplaced charity. This illustrates the need for prayer in the life of a bishop. While not expecting private revelations he must constantly seek guidance from the Holy Spirit. The paradox is only apparent. As well as the state of grace there is also the grace of state.

The grace of state does not confer personal infallibility on the holder of office. I have made many mistakes both in word and action. The effects of inaccurate or unguarded remarks can be extremely painful. Newspapers print what presumably they consider to be the most significant parts of a speech. 'Significant' may mean not what is important but what is dramatic or shocking. After press reports of my speeches have appeared I have been plagued with letters of criticism, abuse or—what can be more embarrassing—congratulations from those who agree with what I am alleged to have said. Every public figure faces the same hazard. Until he sees the next morning's papers no speaker can guess what the public will be told that he has said. Providing a text in advance is some sort of safeguard but it is not proof against sub-editorial selectivity. In my experience papers rarely mis-report. Reporters do not put into a speaker's mouth words he has not uttered. The difficulty is that by deletion of qualifying phrases the press can distort a speaker's views beyond recognition. This is not deliberate misrepresentation. Newspapers print what they think the public wants to read. If in a thirty-minute lecture on the modern novel I were to devote half a paragraph to pornography it is fairly certain that nothing else would be published. The headlines would run: "Bishop Hits Out at Filth".

During my first year in Leeds I made no speeches which attracted much attention. I spent almost every day visiting parishes and meeting priests. Since thousands of children had been awaiting Confirmation for nearly two years my evenings were mostly spent in parish churches. There was only one speech which had a disagreeable aftermath. It was given in the Town Hall, Leeds, at the end of September 1951. A meeting had been arranged as a routine rally of the Catholic Parents and Electors Association but after the date had been fixed a general election was announced. This made the occasion much more significant and the hall was packed to suffocation point. Catholic electors were expecting guidance and I chose my words with care. Despite persecution of religion and widespread suppression of liberty in Yugoslavia its dictator, Marshal Tito, was highly popular with Aneurin Bevan and his Marxist friends. The Archbishop of Zagreb, Monsignor Stepinac, and hundreds of clergy were in prison. Nuns had been expelled from their hospitals and schools. I had this in mind when I spoke to my audience about the election:

> I am aware of the danger of being misquoted, or of being quoted out of context. Because of the gravity of the times I must, however, offer this advice to Catholics who belong to the Labour Party. There is a section of this party, sometimes described as the left wing, sometimes as rebels, who must not be allowed to control that party's destinies. The men and women I have in mind are com-munist in all but name. If they are critical of the Soviet regime it is not because in their hearts they detest Stalin's policy. They are

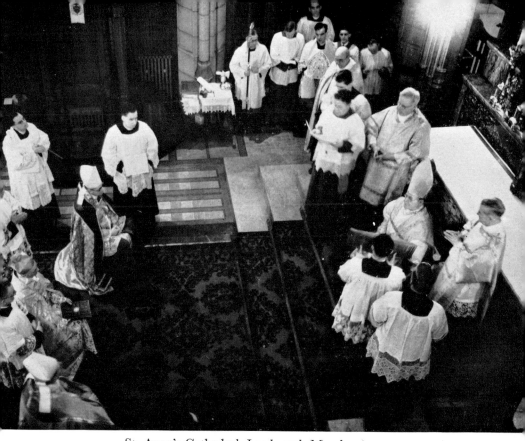

St. Anne's Cathedral, Leeds 12th March 1951.
Back: Bishop Murphy, Archbishops Ramsey and Coggan, Bishop Martin.
Front: Mrs. Martin, Mrs. Ramsey, Mrs. Coggan.

St. Anne's Cathedral, Leeds: the first televised High Mass.
Cathedral parish, Leeds: First Communicants' Party.

Marxists. What they detest is the clumsiness with which the Soviet dictator puts into practice the principles of which they heartily approve.

No one can foretell the outcome of the October elections. As we know from the recent presidential election in America not even a Gallup Poll is a safe guide. As bishop of this diocese I am not prepared to say whether I would prefer a Labour or a Conservative Government to be returned. But if we return a Labour Government to power it would be a national disaster if the Marxists were to gain control. I consider it the duty of Catholics with authority in the Labour movement to urge their leaders to clarify the issues within their own party ... We must concentrate upon choosing a government which can be trusted both at home and abroad. Among the politicians who are making a bid for supreme power in the Labour Party are some who have no respect for our own people and no love of our country. They are guided not by national interest, still less by Christian principles, but entirely by what we have come to call ideology. These are the people who criticise the Stalin regime and therefore claim not to be pro-Soviet but at the same time they praise Marshal Tito's Yugoslavia where liberty and Christianity are bleeding to death. It is the duty of Catholic electors—because as Catholics they should have a universal view of world affairs—to warn their friends of the enemies within our gates.

The sequel to this Sunday afternoon's meeting was utterly unexpected. The morning papers reported the speech without comment. Since only a few months earlier I had addressed a vast rally in the Royal Albert Hall in aid of Archbishop Stepinac it was not thought strange that I should now warn an audience against Tito's friends. On Thursday morning I received an agitated letter from a young man whose name at the time was unknown to me. He was the Labour candidate for Huyton, Harold Wilson. He wrote to say that the Conservatives had hurriedly produced leaflets proclaiming that the Bishop of Leeds advised Catholics not to vote for any friend of Aneurin Bevan. Mr. Wilson said that his campaign workers being mostly Catholics had become troubled in conscience by my words. He asked only that I should tell him in a private letter that I did not have him in mind when I spoke of Bevan's Marxist friends. He undertook to keep my reply confidential from everyone except his conscience-stricken supporters. I replied at once that I had not had him in mind when I spoke in Leeds. I added that my reply was not in any way confidential. I could not see how the Conservative allegation could be countered unless he were free to use my letter. On the eve of the poll leaflets containing the text of my note were distributed. Labour won by only a handful of votes. I did not realise that I had helped to save the day for a future prime minister.

By the end of 1951 I had met all the priests and most of the laity in the diocese. Living among them I soon found that first impressions were justified. Yorkshire people while not being so demonstrative as people in the south or on the other side of the Pennines give staunch affection to the strangers they accept. They are nevertheless in no undue haste to accept the stranger. The clergy and religious, despite the mistakes my inexperience led me to make, gave me their loyal co-operation. They assumed that the policies I was pursuing were dictated by what I took to be the good of souls. Looking back on those early months in Leeds I am more impressed than ever by the zeal and discipline of the clergy. Whatever criticisms they expressed among themselves—in those days priests rarely contradicted a bishop to his face—they did not withhold their support. The many priests who found themselves in new parishes usually worked with renewed vigour. However crude and mistaken my pastoral methods may have been they were blessed through the goodwill with which priests went about their work for souls. There were many saintly men among the clergy and they were by no means confined to the ranks of the ancients.

Nobody can judge a priest's holiness by his demeanour or even by the success of his apostolate. St. Paul has warned us that we can never be sure even of our personal motives and merits. What St. Paul said of himself every priest—and, for that matter, every layman—can echo: "Neither do I judge my own self. For I am not conscious to myself of anything but I am not thereby acquitted: but he that judgeth me is the Lord" (1 Cor. IV: 3, 4). We can nevertheless sometimes be fairly certain of the sanctity of those we meet. Such a man was Father Bernard Harrison who died during the autumn of my first year in Leeds. He had been ordained only five years when he contracted an incurable disease. He had been to see me one Friday morning during the summer to discuss a Mass book for children which he was writing. He was full of schemes for his pastoral work. I knew what a shock it must have been to be told that he would never again say Mass or administer the sacraments to his people. I therefore made my way to the hospital in Halifax in dejected mood expecting to find a very disconsolate young priest. I had prepared an informal homily on not only accepting but positively welcoming the will of God even though it meant accepting a heavy cross. As I entered the hospital I forced myself to smile so that I might give hope and courage to the stricken young priest.

To my astonishment Father Harrison's face was radiant. He welcomed me warmly and gave me what he called his good news. He thought it a wonderful grace, he said, after working such a short time in the Lord's vineyard to be called to his reward. There was no trace of the self-pity I had feared. He expressed no disappointment at being called away from work he had only just begun with such enthusiasm. I know exactly what he said because as soon as I left the hospital I wrote down his words. "I didn't know that dying was like this," he said. "It's wonderful. I feel as if I were someone else looking on. I would not pray to get better. I am completely happy." He was happy and supremely in control of himself. He asked me if it would embarrass me to discuss his funeral. He knew that I liked to speak briefly at the Requiem Mass of a priest. In some places it is the custom to preach a formal panegyric at a priest's funeral. There is no problem in finding words of praise for most priests because they are almost always beloved by their parishioners. It is less easy to speak with sincerity and truth of a priest whose virtues were hidden while his faults were well known to his parishioners and fellow clergy. A formal panegyric tends to turn a requiem into a canonisation to the great disadvantage of the deceased who is thus robbed of the suffrages of his friends. Nobody will pray for the repose of the soul of a saint. "Would you think it awful cheek," Father Harrison said, "if I told you what I would like you to say at my requiem? It is important what is said on an occasion like this. You might just stand up in church after Mass and say what a wonderful priest I was to make my friends happy. That would rob me of prayers and I need all the prayers I can get. They tell me in this hospital that I prescribe my own treatment so I may as well preach my own panegyric."

He was as good as his word. At his Requiem Mass a few days later this is what I said:

I am going to read out what Father Harrison asked me to say. I have written it down lest I should be tempted to interpolate anything of my own. So far as my memory serves me—and mine is not a bad memory—I reproduce exactly what he said:

"There will be, so to speak, three sections in the congregation at the Requiem. There will be the clergy, the parishioners of St. Malachy's and my own family. I would like you to say something special to each of them. I would like you to give them a message.

"First of all the clergy. Of course I am only meaning the young clergy—the people about my own age. It would be impertinent for me to send a message to older priests. I would like you to tell the clergy that what they told us about daily meditation in the seminary is absolutely right. I did not realise it at first. I don't think anybody realises it in the first few years. But if you don't make your meditation every morning the Mass does not mean all it should. We are always telling the people that it is the Mass that matters. But without meditation it becomes sort of mechanical. There is one thing I regret. Of course there are lots of things—small things—that I am sorry about but there is one thing especially that I regret. It is the time I have spent on social things—bazaars and things like that which could have been just as well done by lay people. I suppose it is because my time was so short that I see it so clearly now. But I would like to tell all my priest friends not to waste time on things that are not really pastoral.

"There will be a lot of people from St. Malachy's. I want to thank them for the way they have been praying while I am ill. I have been told that the church is full night after night, and that is the reason why I have had so many graces. If any one had told me a month ago that I was going to die I would have been rebellious. But now I feel absolutely happy; and it is all these prayers. I have had letters from priests who were at All Hallows with me from all over the place, and they have been saying Masses for me. It makes you realise what a big thing the grace of God is.

"Tell the people from St. Malachy's that I know I was not much of a preacher. I never seemed to say just what I wanted to. There was only one thing I tried to say in my round-about way. It is like St. John going round saying 'Little children love one another' and when they asked him why he did not say anything else he said that the whole of Christ's teaching was in 'Little children love one another'. Well what I tried to put over all the time was the second question in the catechism: 'Why did God make you?' Nothing else matters except living the way God wants you to, so you can be happy with Him for ever in the next life.

Of course I always meant what I said. But now I know more than ever that the only success in life is dying properly.

"I hope my mother and brothers won't mind if I give you a message for them. It may be embarrassing for them but I would like it said publicly. I did not have a day off in the week like most priests because my home was so far away. So I used to save up my days off and have a few days together at home. I want to say that my visits home did me more good than making a retreat. My brothers are only working lads, but they taught me more than they can ever know. Going home made me see what Catholic home life should be like, and it made me want to go back to the parish and make other families like it."

Father Harrison was given exceptional graces to support the cross he was made to bear. It would be untrue to say that he was typical but there was nothing unusual about this young priest's outlook. A crisis of identity would have been meaningless to a young priest in 1951 not only because the jargon was not yet in use but because no priest was in any doubt about what he had been ordained to do. The laity had, if possible, even less doubt. In Yorkshire where people pride themselves on their blunt speaking, parishioners were not slow to tell the priest if he was not doing his duty. The priest would soon be called to order by his people if he neglected to visit their homes. In Yorkshire, as elsewhere in England, Catholics expect their priests not only to recognise them at church but to be part of the family circle. The Church in Yorkshire was spiritually healthy and able to withstand the shock of having a non-Yorkshire bishop. Although not a native of Yorkshire I was however no stranger. As a priest of the Catholic Missionary Society I had given missions in Yorkshire parishes and, more important, I had spent two years at Ushaw where the majority of Leeds priests are trained. I had known the majority of the middle-aged priests during their student days.

During my first eighteen months in Leeds I followed a fairly regular routine. Except for the Friday 'open day' I spent most of my time in the parishes. The visitation of a big parish could take two days. In some towns where there were several large institutions I sometimes needed to come back a third day to complete the visits to hospitals. To stop at each bedside and have a word with six or seven hundred patients requires several hours and in some of the great city hospitals a round could take most of the day with a break for lunch with the hospital staff. Although exhausting, these visits were worthwhile. Much joy can be given to long-term patients, especially the old or friendless, by a show of personal interest and the promise of a prayer. A hospital is remarkably isolated from normal social intercourse. It is a world ruled by a medical and nursing hierarchy. There is misery, gaiety and heroism among both patients and staff. That a bishop thinks their world worth a leisured visit gives heart not only to the patients but also to an over-worked staff. Among them there is usually a high proportion of Catholics of whom many come from Ireland or the Commonwealth. In my experience the non-Catholic nurses were just as welcoming as the Catholics. There is an added justification for including public hospitals in a parish visitation. Sometimes misunderstandings have arisen between the hospital and the chaplain. These may have been inherited from matrons or priests no longer in the district but feuds, like reputations, often outlive their cause. An official visitation can lead to a new relationship between hospital officials and the local clergy.

The standard of education in the West Riding was high. The county education authority was under the gifted direction of Mr.—later Sir Alec—Clegg. The county offices are in Wakefield where Monsignor Henry Thompson, secretary of the Leeds Diocesan Schools' Commission, was parish priest of St. Austin's. He had an uncannily detailed knowledge of every Catholic school in the diocese. Urbane and efficient he co-operated closely with all the education authorities in the diocese —Leeds, Bradford, Huddersfield, Sheffield, Halifax, Doncaster, Barnsley and Rotherham as well as the West Riding itself. I soon came to know most of the inspectors, directors of education and chairmen of education committees. During six years in the diocese I grew in admiration of the generous spirit in which the Education Act was interpreted to enable the Catholic community to keep pace with the rapid growth of county school building. My most frequent encounters were with Mr. George Taylor, director of education for Leeds, a man of wide general culture and a considerable musician. I had many dealings with him because as soon as I had taken stock of the diocesan property I realised that both the former Leeds seminary and Bishop's House (in which I was then living) were big enough to be turned into schools. Under Mr. Taylor's guidance I was able to stretch regulations just short of breaking point to achieve these desirable ends.

The old seminary was not far from St. Anne's Cathedral which is in the centre of the city. The seminary was closed before the second world war when it had been agreed that Ushaw could make far better provision for students than the seminary. Ushaw had the pick of the priests of the six northern dioceses for its teaching staff. At the outbreak of war the empty seminary was commandeered by the government to become the general headquarters of the Army Pay Corps. The war had been over for five years when I went to Leeds but it took a further two years to persuade the authorities that our property should be relinquished (de-requisitioned in civil service patois). This I was anxious to do because the cathedral senior schools were severely over-crowded. With the active co-operation of Mr. Taylor the old seminary, after extensive refurbishing, became the senior boys' school. The former Bishop's House in the grounds of the seminary became the diocesan curial offices to which I went each day. This was an immense convenience to priests and people who until that time had to go to Weetwood Lane on the outskirts of Leeds to see me.

I had always regarded the house at Weetwood Lane as unsuitable. The long drive to the front door emphasised the manorial character of the property. This mansion had been acquired for less than the price of a modest villa at a time when large houses were cluttering the property market. They were no longer regarded as desirable residences because of the difficulty of finding domestic staff. This property had been owned in turn by a prosperous bookmaker and the vice-chancellor of Leeds university. Many of the rooms had been closed by the former bishop whose housekeeper could not possibly have looked after so large an establishment. Some of the Franciscan Sisters who had worked in the Mission House in London volunteered to accompany me to Leeds and I was therefore able to make use of the whole house. I used to invite young priests in parties of four to live in Bishop's House for periods of two weeks. During that time my secretary would introduce them to the work of the chancery. For my part I tried to teach them how to prepare and deliver sermons. The young priests did not relish the prospect of staying in Bishop's House but it proved useful for them and for me because we came to know each other well. Today when students and priests feel the need of being close to their bishops the scheme would probably seem more attractive. It is possible, on the other hand, that bishop and priests best preserve friendship by keeping their distance.

I began the experiment because I had read in the life of Cardinal Vaughan that when he was Bishop of Salford he appointed all priests to the Cathedral for their first year after ordination. To this end he built what he called a seminary in which the newly ordained priests from Ushaw, Rome, Paris, Valladolid or Lisbon would be brought together to make each other's acquaintance and be given practical instruction in pastoral theology. The priests lived in a community governed by more or less monastic rules. We do not know how the young priests of the 1870s reacted to this extended tutelage but since it was abandoned long before the bishop was translated to Westminster we may assume that the practice did not match the theory. This was certainly true of the Leeds experiment. The failure probably had the same cause in both cases. Without a staff of competent professors the priests were left to themselves for most of each day and soon became bored. When Bishop's House was turned into a school I lived for some time at the clergy house attached to the cathedral. It would then have become impossible to find room for the young priests but, in fact, the scheme had been abandoned long before that time. This was one of many examples of failure due to lack of experience. During my first years in Leeds I learned much from my mistakes. I assume that while I learned others suffered.

CHAPTER

THREE

IN 1952 THE INTERNATIONAL EUCHARISTIC CONGRESS WAS IN BARCELONA. This event takes place at irregular intervals in the great cities of the world. In the 'thirties Dublin, Chicago and, just before the war, Budapest were the host cities. Usually a city with a large proportion of Catholics is chosen but the 1964 Congress took place in Bombay with its largely Hindu population. Pope Paul attended and was welcomed with as much enthusiasm as the Papal Legate received in Catholic cities in former years. I was at Bombay airport when the Pope's white plane touched down. The reverent greetings of half-a-million Indians, few of whom were Christians, was a unique lesson in courtesy and piety. The Indians although not addicted to dogma are a sincerely religious people. They are aware of the presence of God and respect his law and his whole creation. To the Hindus the Pope was a man of God and as such was to be welcomed. Unlike the Moslems who worship Allah the one true God, the Hindu religion is poly-theistic—but these minor deities may not be far removed from the Christian communion of saints. The risk of holding a congress in honour of the Blessed Sacrament in a city which was not only non-Catholic but non-Christian was justified by events. The same cannot be said of the only occasion on which the Eucharistic Congress was held in England.

It was a brave decision to hold the Congress in the England of the days before the first world war. When the Papal Legate, Cardinal Vannutelli, landed at Dover on Tuesday 8th September, 1908 he was the first legate to set foot on English soil since the arrival of Cardinal

Pole three hundred and fifty years previously. The Congress was successful in giving English Catholics the opportunity of hearing such distinguished speakers as Cardinal Mercier of Malines, Cardinal Gibbons of Baltimore, Cardinal Logue of Armagh and Cardinal Mathieu of the Académie Française. As a public spectacle, however, the Congress was a failure. The Protestant Alliance protested so loudly that Mr. Asquith, a timid prime minister, forbade the procession of the Blessed Sacrament which by custom is the climax of a Eucharistic Congress. The Archbishop of Westminster at the time was Archbishop Francis Bourne, a diplomatic prelate. The enthusiastic Catholics who had gathered from all over the British Isles might well have caused a breach of the peace but for the restraining influence of the young archbishop. Bourne faced the government fearlessly but did nothing to incite his angry flock.

Feeling was high among Catholics but self-respecting Protestants were also outraged by the attitude of the civic authorities. Everybody knew that the prime minister had capitulated to the bigots against the advice of the commissioner of police who foresaw no danger to public order from the procession. The mood of the public is shown by the following extract from *The Daily Telegraph* of 14th September, 1908:

> It is clear from the official correspondence which we publish this morning that Archbishop Bourne and his coadjutors were given to understand by the Commissioner of Police that, so far as he was concerned, there was not the slightest objection to the procession taking place. No fear on the head of public danger was entertained at Scotland Yard. The police had not the faintest doubt of their power to preserve perfect order; nor did they expect any contingency to arise in the shape of organised opposition.

I was three years old at the time of the London Eucharistic Congress. If, as is likely, I was carried to receive a blessing outside Westminster Cathedral from the Papal Legate I do not recall it. The chief reason why I decided to be present at the Barcelona Congress in 1952 was that only one other bishop was going from this country. This was not from any lack of affection for the Spaniards but simply because the English do not find congresses attractive. In 1952 Spain was still thought of as the land from which the Armada had sailed. During the Spanish civil war which ended in 1939 the British press and radio had been almost unanimously anti-Franco. His forces were always referred to by the B.B.C. as the rebels. This was technically true but as the war went on it became evident that the international brigade directed by Soviet intelligence could not fairly be described as government forces. This cruel war might have collapsed in the first few weeks but for the intervention of foreigners—fascists, nazis and communists. I was no better informed than the rest of the public about the rights and wrongs of this tragedy. I did not know who were the villains and the heroes but I did know that during the war the Catholic Church in Spain had been martyred. My journey to the Eucharistic Congress of Barcelona was a pilgrimage to the tombs of the thousands of priests, monks, nuns and laymen butchered in the name of democracy.

Having made up my mind to go to the Congress I wrote to my friend Rafael Masso in Barcelona. Rafael had become known to me through Rosie Rolwing, one of many friends I first met when they introduced themselves on my travels because they saw I was a priest. My first trip to U.S.A. was in 1931 before I took up my first post as curate in Barking. I travelled in tourist class on an obsolescent ship of the U.S. Lines. Rosie, on her way home from a finishing school in Paris, was in first class. The ship's officers did not mind where we went on this small boat provided we ate in the appropriate dining-room. Rosie used to come to my Mass in the tourist library. Though gay and attractive this girl was subject to moods of depression. While she had been away at school in Paris her parents had been divorced. The family home was broken up, her brothers and sisters were married and she did not really know where to make her home. In her distress she regarded my clerical collar as a beacon of hope. She confided in me and I gave her the benefit of such slender pastoral knowledge as I had gained from my text books. I have remained a friend of Rosie—now a grand-mother—and from time to time she has given my address to her friends, who in turn have become my friends. Of this numerous body of friends none is a more original character than Rafael Masso.

Rosie sent him to me on his first visit to London in the early 'thirties. An accomplished linguist he entertained me with stories of his adventures in many lands. Before telling of my stay in Barcelona where he was my host and cicerone I must add a word about this fascinating Spaniard. His business was textiles but horticulture was a hobby which had become a passion. Eventually his hobby developed into an international enterprise. The proceeds of the textile business were used to fulfil his ambition to beautify Spain with flowers. The business developed so rapidly after the civil war that he was soon supplying seeds, plants and bulbs to gardens throughout the country. Before long this amateur gardener had over a hundred husbandmen and floral artists in his employ. Letters from flower lovers throughout the world became so numerous that he had to train secretaries in horticulture in order to maintain correspondence with his clients. He regarded the city clerk with a window-box as no less important than the hidalgos in their castles. Appreciating that lonely people become attached to their correspondents, Rafael gave each of his secretaries a *nom-de-fleur*. Thus when Lily, Rose or Iris left his employ to be married (nothing but marriage would entice them away) her successor inherited her name. In this way the clients never knew that they had lost their friend. In Rafael's garden was a chapel in honour of St. Fiacre, patron saint of gardeners, whose versatility was not exhausted by the four-wheeler to which he gave his name.

All new clients were dealt with in the first instance by Rafael himself. Portuguese, French, Italian, German and English came equally easily to him. Since most enquiries follow a pattern he was able to provide stereotyped letters with which his secretaries could meet most situations. It gave him particular satisfaction to supply the personal needs of strangers. During the second world war, for example, he studied shortages in the various belligerent countries and taking advantage of Spanish neutrality despatched food parcels to friends in every part of Europe. He even sent Winston Churchill a box of cigars when the Madrid press reported—wrongly—that the British prime minister had nothing to smoke. Rosie, who meanwhile had married an Italian, was now living in Rome. When she was in serious difficulties after America entered the war Rafael flew to Rome to organise regular food supplies for her family.

Rafael was malicious in a Robin Hood sort of way. Before the war he did extensive business with German textile firms and had a regular account with the biggest Jewish store in Berlin. No sooner had he heard that the Nazis had confiscated all Jewish shops than Rafael flew to Berlin. He went to his Jewish store in Unter den Linden and ordered bales of cloth in huge quantities. Since his name was well known to the firm no demur was made as he emptied shelf after shelf. Surveying the mountainous piles of merchandise Rafael at last called a halt and asked to see his old friend Saul Cohen, the managing director. The new manager smiled and explained to Herr Masso that the Fuehrer had taken over all Jewish premises. "That's a great pity," said Rafael. "I do business only with Jews. You can put all this stuff back."

Apart from textiles and horticulture, Rafael's chief interest is in friends and even mere acquaintances. In his office he keeps a file of all the people he knows. Each indexed card is designed to give him all essential information of a social nature. Not satisfied with knowing the birthdays of his friends, Rafael makes a note of what they are likely to lack in their own countries. The last entry on the card is *mania* which is the Spanish word for hobby. On one occasion a visitor from Latin America was allowed to leave Barcelona without giving the data for the friendship file. Since the man was staying a few days in Madrid Rafael was able to send a blank card to his Madrid agent with instructions to fill in the required details. It came back with an abundance of information. In the space for *mania* the agent had written *senoritas*. Rafael loved to entertain and, not surprisingly, preferred to give his guests meals in the garden where he has fauna as well as flora. On my first visit I thought I was in a private zoo. It is impossible to have an uninterrupted meal with Rafael because he has a mania (in the English sense) for speaking on the telephone. His friends all know this with the result that the telephone bell rings continuously. No matter in what part of his extensive garden he is walking, Rafael is never far from a phone. All the bigger trees are equipped with telephone extensions so that he can answer without having to return to the house.

It would have been difficult to find a more congenial host than Rafael. Like other Catholics with spare rooms, Rafael had volunteered to accommodate visitors from abroad. Because of his knowledge of languages he had been able to offer hospitality to a pilgrim of almost any nationality and was gratified when his guest proved to be an old friend. I was even more gratified because I would be able to play truant from most of the Congress events without shocking my host. With hundreds of prelates in attendance it was not likely that the absence of one junior bishop would be noticed. This was my first visit to Spain and I did not propose to waste it attending the discussions which proliferate on such ecclesiastical occasions. I intended to be present at the solemn opening, the Legate's Mass and the midnight rally of men. For the rest I intended to see something of Spanish institutions and study the outlook of the post-civil war Spaniard. I visited such widely different establishments as the monastery of Montserrat (famous for its library and the Black Madonna) and Barcelona prison. I saw the spacious up-to-date hospital of the Brothers of St. John of God and a home for lepers looked after by Sisters. Having seen totalitarianism at close quarters in Italy, Germany and Russia I wanted to study the Franco variety.

My impressions were not unlike those of a young couple whom I met on the French frontier when I was making my way to Lourdes to join the Leeds pilgrimage after the Congress. As I was crossing the plaza outside the parish church of the little town of Puigerda, I saw a young man and his wife loading luggage into their car. After greeting them I asked if Spain had come up to their expectations. They told me that it was entirely different from what they had expected to find. Having chosen Spain because the favourable sterling balance would enable them to have a cheap holiday, they had arrived with certain misgivings. Spain, after all, is a dictatorship and the brutality of the civil war was still a fairly recent memory. They had anticipated a military regime coupled with police repression. What had surprised them was the friendly attitude and happy demeanour of the people. Their impressions matched my own. English people who have never visited Spain are unlikely to throw off their inherited suspicions of the country and its people. Every child learns about the persecution of Protestants by Queen Mary, wife of an intriguing Spanish prince. An ill-fated armada once threatened this realm and since Tudor times the Spanish ambassador has been a sinister figure in our literature. We are predisposed from schooldays to believe the worst about Spain. It was inevitable that the myth of aristocratic army officers leading blood-thirsty blackamoors against Spanish workers should gain credence in England during the civil war.

Most freedom-loving British citizens accepted the civil war as a struggle between rich and poor—military adventurers and clergy being on one side with peasants and toilers on the other. Even honest Clem Attlee, a future prime minister of Britain, was proud to be photo-graphed with the International Brigade. There were few who did not feel outraged when troops from Fascist Italy and Nazi Germany were called in to aid an allegedly Christian crusade. It is still too soon to learn the whole truth about the Spanish struggle. Both sides were responsible for pillage, murder, rape and arson. Civil wars are rarely fought between saints and sinners. What surprised a visitor to post-war Spain was the absence of most of the trappings of a totalitarian State. Here was dictatorship unlike any I had seen before. Political freedom as we understand the term did not exist. No opposition party was tolerated and the papers were full of speeches from the Caudillo and his ministers. The press was tuned to the praise of the regime. Thus far Spain was like any other dictatorship.

There were striking differences between Franco's Spain and the other dictatorships I had known. In Hitler's Germany, Mussolini's Italy and Stalin's Russia it would have been literally more than a man's life was worth to criticise the dictator. It was otherwise in Spain. Though easy to control the press it is impossible to muzzle the proud Spanish people. I heard at least as much criticism of Franco and his ministers as one hears of a political leader in England. There is, of course, far less talk of politics in England than in any other European country. We flatter our politicians by talking about them only when they are forced on our attention by a new budget, a domestic crisis or an international disaster. I gathered that even Franco's opponents were mostly glad that Spain had been saved from anarchy or Soviet communism. His critics regarded him as autocratic and insufficiently sensitive to the scandal of poverty cheek-by-jowl with luxury. This social pattern is not unusual in the Iberian peninsula. I was surprised and fascinated by the freedom with which citizens could so openly attack Franco. Franco's Spain is a dictatorship with a difference. Elsewhere citizens in a dictatorship had used a pseudonym—Mr. Johnson (the Duce), Uncle Joe (Stalin)—rather than risk mention of the precious name.

The impressions I gathered during the Eucharistic Congress were of limited value because Barcelona is the chief city of the Catalonians who are little more disposed than the Basques to regard themselves as subjects of the Madrid Government. In Barcelona not even the educated speak to each other in the Spanish (Castilian) language, while the uneducated usually know only Catalan. Far from being the language of illiterates Catalan has a rich literature and ranks its chief poets with Dante, Goethe and Shakespeare. After making allowance for the dislike Catalonians have for Castilians it was possible to form some idea of the civic outlook of Spaniards. Travellers' tales are usually suspect but in Barcelona I met pilgrims from Madrid, Burgos and San Sebastian who were likely to be more reliable witnesses than Spanish exiles living abroad. The picture I brought away was clear enough in outline however vague in detail. Spaniards are genuinely fond of the English. They are unlikely to have heard much about the Spanish Armada since it was a defeat in arms—nations cherish recollections only of their victories. Waterloo has a more prominent place in school text books in England than in France. Only the English perversely recall defeats but contrive to make them sound like victories (the Norman Conquest, the Miracle of Dunkirk).

Spaniards have no idea of the traditional mistrust in which the English hold them. They do know that Franco's victory was regarded here as the death of democracy. They are bewildered when told that most people in this country artlessly believed that Franco's regime had displaced a democratically elected liberal government. The British people knew as little of the burning of churches, rape of nuns and murder of priests in Spain before the civil war as they did of what was happening to Jews in Nazi concentration camps before the second world war. The liberal government in pre-war Spain had originally been popular. By supporting it many thought they were fighting the forces of reaction. With the passage of time and the increase of atrocities they came to realise their mistake. Many who before the civil war had been anti-clerical turned to the Church when they saw how democracy was being degraded by the liberals. All round me in Barcelona I saw relics of the horrors of the civil war. I visited the great hospital of St. Pablo which is staffed by the Brothers and Sisters of St. John of God. This hospital looks after most of the sick poor of Barcelona. The doctors who had been on duty when the communist forces invaded the hospital told me that they had not been molested but every nursing Brother without exception was assassinated. The Sisters were assaulted and expelled. The altars in each ward were despoiled. This kind of experience turned even irreligious Spaniards against the Red government. The communists were Franco's best public relations officers.

Since my days in the Catholic Missionary Society I had taken a special interest in the welfare of prisoners. I imagined Spanish prisons to be among the worst in the world. Before leaving London I asked the Spanish Ambassador for a letter of introduction requesting facilities for visiting the famous (or, as I had gathered from the press, infamous) Barcelona prison. Soon after my arrival in Barcelona I sought permission to inspect the prison. Any penal institution can be made to present a favourable impression if a visitor is piloted away from black spots and the more resentful inmates. From a fairly wide experience of prisons I knew what to look for and I was determined not to be given a guided tour. Before leaving the office of the Director of the prison I told him what I wanted to see. Somewhat to his surprise I asked to be taken to the punishment cells. I had brought Rafael Masso with me as interpreter because in my experience an official interpreter does not always phrase questions as pointedly as the questioner. A detailed account of the hours I spent in the prison might prove dull but I describe here certain features which are of particular interest.

Barcelona prison was the opposite of what I had been led to expect. It reminded me more of Sing-Sing, the New York State penitentiary, than of Pentonville or Wormwood Scrubs. With the exception of some of our modern open prisons there was not at that time a single prison in this country with running water and a w.c. in every cell—as in Sing-Sing and Barcelona. The general conduct of the prison was much the same as in our own but the discipline seemed to be less rigorous. There was no enforced silence and prisoners spent little time locked up in cells (the rules in our own prisons have been revised since the time of my visit to Barcelona).

The main difference, apart from better sanitation, was the civilised atmosphere of the institution. The prison chapel is on the ground floor, in view of the galleries where the men live. When they are not at work prisoners are allowed to attend Mass and visit the chapel for private prayer. This is acceptable because almost all prisoners and officials are at least nominal Catholics. At the time of my visit there were only two non-Catholics among the prison population. Both were foreigners serving short sentences. The religious approach to the treatment of prisoners is emphasised by the presence of a priest of the Trinitarian Congregation founded to care for prisoners. Within the prison there is a convent of nuns whose members have likewise devoted their lives to this work of mercy. These monks and nuns have as their motto: "I was in prison and you came to me" (Matt. XXV: 36). The nuns supervise the cooking and nurse the sick. By Spanish law every prisoner at the age of sixty is removed from the prison proper to the infirmary. He is treated as a sick person and lives in much the same way as he would in a hospital for chronic invalids. Unless they are bedridden the patients spend most of their time in recreation rooms or walking in the grounds. The seriously ill—in all prison hospitals I have visited there are patients suffering from chronic bronchitis or tuberculosis—are accommodated in side wards containing four beds. Since the hospital is under the exclusive care of Sisters the atmosphere is happy and peaceful.

The presence of the priests and nuns naturally has a marked effect on the morale of the hospital. In Spanish prisons—as in our own—the Governor holds court each morning to hear complaints or judge mis-demeanours. Sitting with the Governor in Barcelona prison are the prison chaplain and the mother superior of the convent. This is a better guarantee than any written regulations that prisoners will receive humanitarian treatment. I talked at some length to both the priests and nuns. Much could have been hidden from me as a visitor but they, living in the prison, must have known all the facts. They were able to establish to my complete satisfaction that the rehabilitation of the prisoners is the genuine motive behind the whole prison administration. A priest told me that in all the years he had never had a single example of a dying prisoner refusing the Last Sacraments. This is a way of saying that prisoners do not become embittered. Every experienced priest knows that embittered men will not accept spiritual ministrations even at the point of death.

Because of these favourable comments on Barcelona prison it must not be thought that the Spanish judicial system itself is superior to our own. The contrary is true. Habeas Corpus makes our penal code the envy of the civilised world. In Spain, as in many Latin countries, the alleged criminal—in particular the suspected political offender—is denied the protection a British citizen enjoys. He may be left months or even years awaiting trial. Political freedom is not accorded to the Spaniard. It is not credible, as I was asked to believe, that there were no political prisoners in Spain.

Many people in Barcelona complained at what they regarded as an affront offered by Franco to Cardinal Tedeschino, the Papal Legate. Several times I heard Spaniards deplore the fact that he was not present to greet the Legate on his arrival in Spain. I was not sufficiently expert in matters of protocol to judge, but better informed Spaniards said it was a calculated insult for Franco to make a solemn entry into Barcelona after the Congress had started instead of being at the city gates to welcome the representative of the Pope. Relations between Church and State in Spain were not so cordial as foreigners supposed. Franco, I was told, wanted the Church to accord him all the privileges held in the days of the monarchy by His Most Catholic Majesty, the King of Spain. To the Church, which thinks in centuries, the General is a passing figure. His government, in the ascendant today, may be over-thrown tomorrow. Spanish Catholics held that relations between Church and State in Franco's Spain will always remain tentative and uneasy.

Spain is a poor country. It depends for its economic security on favourable climatic conditions to a degree more usual in Asia than Europe. Even when rain is abundant (in recent years Spain has suffered severe droughts) the country remains poor. Its resources are limited and by our standards the industries are old-fashioned and inefficient. It is not therefore surprising that many Spaniards are poor. What vexes the enquirer is not the number of poor but the contrast between them and the rich. I saw little to throw light on this paradox in a Christian country because in Catalonia, the most prosperous part of Spain, such contrasts are encountered less often than elsewhere. I visited the homes of both rich and poor but Barcelona is not typical of Spain as a whole. Except for those living in the *barracas*, to whom I shall later refer, the poor were not in desperate straits. In other words they were not desperately poor.

The middle class was living in a style unfamiliar in England for generations. Their households had an abundance of servants whose scale of wages would be considered derisory in this country. It does not follow from the fact that there were plenty of servants (Spanish servants and workers were to emigrate soon afterwards in large numbers) that they were content with their conditions. Lack of alternative employment kept them at domestic work. In England any servant could find well-paid work in a factory. For many Spaniards the alternative to domestic employment was a precarious livelihood in an impoverished village. Relations between a family and its servants appeared to be not only easy but cordial. Servants possess the traditional Spanish self-esteem. They do not regard themselves as belonging to their masters and for this reason may be less preoccupied by money than servants elsewhere. This may also explain the happy demeanour of men and women who by our standards were seriously underpaid.

I visited the destitute whose number in the Barcelona area was relatively small. If I had travelled further south I would have seen much larger numbers living in appalling conditions. To what extent the Church was guilty of tolerating social injustice I lacked the information on which to judge. The Church is often credited with power (and therefore responsibility) in Latin countries where anti-clerical politicians are deaf to the voice of the Church. I went with Rafael to the *barracas*. These hovels which disfigured the outskirts of Barcelona were inhabited by squatters. I had never seen anything to compare with this squalor. Many years later I was to see even more degrading conditions in the Middle East, India, Hong Kong and Latin America. Barcelona shocked me because it was my first experience of sub-human living conditions. About eight thousand people lived here in improvised homes made of pieces of wood, tin and cardboard. None of these shacks had windows or chimneys. About a thousand of these people were gypsies who, like most of their neighbours, had come to Barcelona from southern Spain in search of work.

The government did little for the squatters beyond tolerate their existence. They were treated like our own squatters after the war and for the same reason. Little help was given for fear of encouraging them to remain, thus making permanent this disgusting and unsalubrious encampment. I would have left the *barracas* in a mood of unrelieved depression had it not been my good fortune to meet a priest as I was making my rounds. He did not know who I was (I was not dressed as a bishop) nor had he been warned of my coming. With the priest as my guide I retraced my steps and began to revisit this strange territory.

I now saw that the Church was attempting what the government was unwilling or unable to do. Two priests, one the resident chaplain of a neighbouring hospital and the other a Franciscan friar, had made this their parish and were conducting a noble apostolate. They had improvised two chapels which were extended versions of the surrounding shacks. The larger one, a semi-permanent structure, served as church, school and social centre. With the help of unpaid voluntary teachers, the priests conducted a day school for the children and an evening school for adolescents. Nearly all the grown-up boys and girls in these nomad families were illiterate. The priests and their helpers could attempt no more than to teach the four Rs. (In Spain, of course, there are not only three Rs but four Rs of which the first R stands for religion.) I was moved by the obvious affection of the people for their priests. I had assumed that regarding themselves as outcasts they would be anti-social. I was forgetting—or rather I did not know—that most of them were finding a better way of living in Barcelona than in southern Spain. Their conditions seemed more appalling to me than to them. They are feckless, the priest told me, in their whole attitude to life but far from being anti-clerical they see in the priest the one person who has made their interests his own. It was heartening to learn that the Archbishop of Barcelona had ordered all collections made during the Eucharistic Congress to be devoted to providing homes for these destitute families. The Congress by order of the archbishop would mark the end of the *barracas*.

It was strange to be in a country which had not been involved in the second world war. When Spaniards referred to the war they meant their war—the civil war—which dated everything. It was obviously impossible to be in Spain without wondering constantly about the effects of that bitter conflict. It would be facile to picture it as a war between the rich and the poor or between Christians and Marxists. It was, of course, a war between the rich and poor in the sense that economic distress provided sufficient incitement for a crusade by anarchists, communists and liberals against entrenched capitalism. As in any revolution there were many awaiting the chance to attack those against whom they harboured a grievance. I realised that it would be absurd to describe the war as a revolt of the poor or to allege that the Church had previously shown no care for the poor. Some of the most fervent Catholics—the Basques—fought on the Red side hoping for independence from Madrid when victory was won. To the victim I suppose it mattered little who killed him but it was said that no flock, however poor, turned against its own pastor. In Barcelona within hours of the outbreak of the revolution every church except the cathedral was sacked. The archbishop and most of his clergy were murdered. This was hard to credit in 1952 when the whole population of Barcelona was fired with religious fervour. The poorest quarters of the city were as gaily decorated as the palaces and offices on the main processional route. On more than one occasion I asked my Spanish friends how these people could have brought themselves to butcher their priests and nuns or burn their churches. Their invariable answer was that murder and pillage had always been the work of strangers. I suppose this is no greater puzzle than Ireland in her own civil war. It is true that in Ireland neither side turned against the Church or slaughtered the clergy but many a man's hand was turned against his own family and friends. Political strife was no longer evident in Spain though doubtless there was hidden opposition. The main disturbers of the peace had gone into exile. Few accepted the assurance of General Franco that they might return without fear unless they had been personally responsible for crimes. Even if this offer of amnesty was genuine it would have needed remarkable courage to accept it. The main reason for the lack of political unrest was that few in Spain wanted a return to bloodshed. They had been given their fill of the glory of war.

There was a delayed sequel to my visit to Barcelona. During the Eucharistic Congress I met Rafael's family and became particularly friendly with his brother-in-law, Xavier Ribo, an anglophil of deep sincerity. He and Rafael were determined to find an excuse for me to return to Barcelona to see the many friends I had accumulated by the end of the Congress. The excuse came by way of the prison. I was invited to return to take part in a week of festivities which began on the feast of Our Lady of Ransom (the Spanish name for the Barcelona Madonna is Mercedes). This title is connected with the Trinitarian Order founded for the ransom of slaves. A Trinitarian monk would take the place of a slave on the galleys thus giving himself as a ransom for the slave's liberty and, presumably, eternal salvation. The Feast and the following seven days are celebrated as an octave of rejoicing in the prison. Preparations for the octave began several months in advance. It was a splendid exercise in psychology to take the mind of the prisoner off his unhappy state. The prison orchestra rehearsed ambitious pieces for a series of performances. Writers among the prisoners entered literary competitions. Footballers, boxers and tennis enthusiasts went into training for matches to be held during the festival. I was invited to sing a Requiem Mass for the deceased prisoners during the octave (on the Feast itself it was the privilege of the Archbishop of Barcelona to be the celebrant). Each day during the festivities a fresh menu was printed. For the cooks—nuns and prisoners—it was a matter of pride to produce meals to rival those served in the smartest hotels. British penologists tend to look for inspiration to Scandinavia which is progressive and clinical. They may have something to learn also from their Spanish colleagues.

One of my last visits before leaving Barcelona was to a lepers' home. Preventive medicine has almost eliminated the scourge of leprosy from Europe but those who do contract the disease rarely seek medical aid in time to effect a cure. For this reason the atmosphere of a leper hospital tends to be despairing. Those who have lost limbs or are disfigured are more liable than most invalids to traumatic depression. In this home the comfort of the sacraments and the dedication of the nuns combined to produce a peace and happiness not of this world. Of all the places I visited none was so full of joy as this sanctuary of suffering. This visit was to have a special significance for me. In a sense it was the beginning of a journey round the world. As I was leaving the home Cardinal Gilroy, Archbishop of Sydney, arrived. All visiting bishops had been given a list of hospitals, orphanages and charitable institutions of every kind in the diocese of Barcelona. Cardinal Gilroy and I quite independently guessed that this little leper colony might be neglected during the Congress because of its isolation. We both had kindly hosts who put cars at our disposal so it was easy for us to visit the lepers. The Cardinal was delighted to see me because he had been looking for me throughout the week. He told me that in the following year (1953) there was to be a national Eucharistic Congress in Sydney. He had come to Barcelona to pick up ideas for his own congress. He had been looking for me to invite me to preach and lecture in Sydney. I said it would be impossible because as yet I had made visitations of only half the parishes in Leeds diocese. He dismissed the excuse at once. His congress was still a whole year away and by that time I would have completed the round of the diocese. Having always had great admiration for Cardinal Gilroy I easily allowed myself to be persuaded to become his guest.

CHAPTER
FOUR

DURING MY YEARS WITH THE CATHOLIC MISSIONARY SOCIETY I DID LITTLE broadcasting. The only occasion I can recall was a service of prayers and hymns from the chapel of the Ursuline Sisters in Forest Gate. This undistinguished occasion remains in my memory for two reasons. It was my first engagement with the B.B.C. since my frequent war-time broadcasts. It was still more memorable because it was the day of my mother's funeral. I clearly recall the beauty of the children's voices as they sang Newman's 'Firmly I believe and truly' from the *Dream of Gerontius*. It is always difficult to listen unmoved to the purity of children's voices but the hymn meant more to me in my emotional state that day than at any time before or since. I remember receiving a letter some days after the broadcast from an angry colonel who accused me of insulting Winston Churchill. The not very original theme of my sermon had been that we usually turn to God when we want something. I added that even those with little belief in God tend to call on Him when they are frightened. I reminded listeners that the most successful Day of Prayer during the war had taken place on what we all thought was the eve of the Nazi invasion. I remarked—and this is what roused the colonel's anger—that during the war we knew when the news was bad because Churchill then brought God into his broadcasts. I gave as an instance his rallying cry on the Sunday evening after France had fallen and the allied cause seemed hopeless. Mr. Churchill's opening words had been: "Today is Trinity Sunday, my friends."

I had various adventures with the B.B.C. during my six years in Leeds which, although belonging to different periods, may conveniently be related together. Some of these encounters were pleasant while others were painful or at least controversial. A public corporation with a near monopoly in communications is in a vulnerable position. Without claiming infallibility it is liable to act as if it were always right. The B.B.C. is full of men and women of integrity who, having strong personal views, are tenacious of their opinions on matters of policy. Like most regular broadcasters I have had disagreements with B.B.C. officials but I have never doubted their good faith. A producer, especially in television, has dictatorial powers and seems to be subject to no sort of control. I doubt if this is in the public interest but I do not know how or by whom control can be exercised. Rule by committees tends to be asphyxiating. Perhaps there could be an amalgamation of interests with two or three producers having joint responsibility.

Producers and directors—there is a technical difference—must be allowed discretion if they are to provide first class programmes. Rigid censorship would paralyse script-writers, performers and producers. It is nevertheless plain that certain ethical standards must be maintained in programmes destined for people's homes. It is no defence of objectionable programmes to say that viewers are always free to switch off. There is no true parallel between theatre performances and broadcasts. Those who attend a performance by pornographers' dummies in theatres go to some trouble and expense to gratify their desire for titillation. The law cannot be expected to protect voyeurs from themselves but it has a duty to prevent violation of the sanctity of the home. Those seeking dirt should have to forage for it. The solution may be not in stricter censorship but in a greater sense of responsibility in making appointments in the world of broadcasting. In modern Britain this obviously could not be done in the name of religion but it may be more than a coincidence that the decline of religious belief has been accompanied by a lowering of ethical standards.

I have never been in conflict with the B.B.C. over ethical problems but only on matters of taste. Thus I disagreed with the B.B.C. at the time of the death of King George VI. The dispute arose not from one of my broadcasts but from a sermon I preached during a memorial service for the late King. I had been exasperated by the B.B.C.'s treatment of the King's death. On the day he died all programmes were cancelled apart from abbreviated news bulletins which were heralded by recordings of a ticking clock or possibly a death-watch beetle. During the prolonged period intervening between his death and the King's funeral all programmes of entertainment were replaced by uplifting talks or solemn music. The atmosphere generated by the Corporation was one of unrelieved misery. Before my sermon no public criticism of this strategy had been voiced. No doubt many who deplored this unchristian display of mourning hesitated to complain for fear of being thought disloyal to the memory of a much loved monarch. After much thought I decided to risk misunderstanding by making a protest. I had in mind the avoidance of a repetition of this macabre performance on future occasions of national bereavement. I also thought it opportune to challenge the assumption that the expression of religious sentiment needs to be sombre. Here is the text of my short sermon in St. Anne's Cathedral, Leeds.

TRIBUTE BY THE BISHOP OF LEEDS

TOMORROW the body of our King, deservedly revered and loved, will be laid to rest. Tomorrow the sorrow of a nation will reach its climax. Tomorrow the thoughts of all will be centred on the abbey in Westminster and the grave in Windsor. We all knew that high office did not disturb the simple piety of his Christian life. No tributes will be more loyal or more affectionate than those of the Catholics in this island.

We loved him as everyone loved him because he was a sincere and simple man. We admired him as all believers in God admired him because according to his conscience he unfailingly paid his duty of worship to Almighty God. At his Coronation he promised to uphold the Protestant Religion as by law established but he did not conceive it to be part of his duty to persecute the religion of his Catholic subjects. He reigned over them and gave them his service as to all his other subjects. We Catholics in peace and war proved our loyalty to King and Country.

The Catholics of the West Riding feel themselves bereaved. Our sense of loss is deep. If we must say which among the many qualities of the King most compelled our respectful loyalty it was undoubtedly the noble example he gave of Christian family life. We saw him as father in his own domestic circle and in the larger family of the British Commonwealth of Nations. All who have a sense of Christian values are grateful for the steady example given by the royal family during the critical years of the King's reign.

The whole nation has expressed its sorrow. I hope I shall not be misunderstood if I say that this sorrow has not seemed to be a particularly Christian sorrow. For it has been almost unrelieved

[58]

by any sign of hope. Why must we pretend that the death of the King is a great tragedy? It is nothing of the sort. Like the death of any loved one it has brought sadness, especially to the members of his own family. But we have heard little or nothing of gratitude to God for the graces granted to the King in recent months.

Death did not come to him unexpected. Fortified by the prayers of all believers in his kingdom he overcame the great crisis of his last illness. For many weeks he walked with death. His late Majesty, like all men, had to appear before the judgment seat of God. His was the great blessing of being given time to prepare. In the end he was spared the suffering and temptation of a long illness. He had lived a full life. He had seen his children's children. He had lived justly and with honour. It is hard to think it a tragedy that a great and good man has been called by God to his eternal reward.

But how little we heard of gratitude to God for these great blessings. Well might the nation hearken to the words of St. Paul: "We will not have you ignorant brethren concerning them that are asleep that you be not sorrowful even as others who have no hope. For if we believe that Jesus died and rose again; even so them who have slept through Jesus will God bring with Him." (1 Thess: IV: 13, 14).

I do not like to strike a critical note but one thing I must say now because later there will be no opportunity. The British Broadcasting Corporation does not seem to have used its monopoly judiciously during this time of national trial. It wrapped the nation in organised gloom for more than a week. The death of a constitutional monarch need not paralyse the legitimate relaxation of the whole nation for so long. I am not concerned with those in health who can find recreation in countless ways. I am thinking of thousands of people in this country—it would be no exaggeration to talk of millions—who through sickness or old age have come to depend mainly upon the wireless for relief from pain or monotony. I cannot think that the memory of our gracious King was well served either by the melodrama of prolonged silences on the day of his death or by the sombre and mirthless programmes which the afflicted among our fellow-countrymen were offered without alternatives for more than a week.

Catholics hold that sympathy does not spell misery. Our love for the King is best shown by praying for the repose of his soul.

On the day of the King's death I sent the Queen the following telegram: "The Catholics of the West Riding of Yorkshire offer their deepest sympathy and promise prayers for the King's repose and the comfort of the Royal family." Priests and people have prayed and will pray that God may grant eternal rest to our beloved Sovereign. We shall also pray that the guidance of the Holy Spirit be granted to our young Queen. May she imitate her parents. May she give an example as wife and mother that her subjects will be compelled to yield her their admiration as they have already offered her their loyalty and love.

There was little hostile comment on my sermon but an official of the B.B.C. in Manchester in an excess of indignation gave a press interview in which he described my remarks as misguided in themselves and out of place coming from a 'foreign' prelate. If criticism had to be made of the B.B.C., he said, it could come properly only from a bishop of the Established Church. His masters at Broadcasting House in London promptly reprimanded him. He was told that the Bishop of Leeds was a British subject and that a very considerable volume of complaints of the B.B.C.'s handling of the King's death had been received. More powerful voices than mine subsequently expressed similar views with the result that the whole policy of what the B.B.C. calls 'programme content' on occasions of national mourning was reviewed. As a result the death of Queen Mary was treated without hysteria and when Winston Churchill died the B.B.C. combined mourning with reminiscence and pride with gratitude in an altogether satisfactory fashion.

Two years later a much more serious disagreement with the B.B.C. was given world-wide publicity. The original incident was so trivial that it now seems incredible that it could have led to such a storm. On Monday 21st March, 1954 I gave the first of a week of early morning broadcasts in a programme called 'Lift up your hearts'. In it I described the arrest, trial and imprisonment of St. Paul. The title of my talks was 'It could happen today'. I used a technique which has now become common of giving the words of scripture in modern idiom. Some clergy and teachers thought I was reading from a newly published version of the bible and asked for the name and address of the publisher. Here are two samples of the narrative. The staccato style effective in broadcast speech is unattractive in prose but these extracts give an idea of the free style I adopted. Here is a sample from Tuesday morning's broadcast:

"I am a Jew myself," Paul told the crowd, "born at Tarsus—trained by Gamaliel in the Ancient Law and just as jealous for the honour of the law as you are. I tell you that God sent me to preach the Gospel to the Gentiles."

That was enough. You should have seen the way the crowd rose. This is how the bible describes it: "Up to this point they listened to his speech. Then they cried out: 'Liquidate this fellow.' He should not be allowed to live any longer." The captain, who was standing by, when he saw the riot starting all over again and the Jews throwing their clothes on the floor, hustled Paul back into the barracks.

It is interesting to see what he did next. These Romans were all the same. To them the Jews were a bunch of quarrelling natives. The only thing to do with them was hit them. Pilate—remember? —when he didn't know what to do with Jesus Christ, scourged Him. That's just what this captain decided to do with Paul. They stripped him, put him face downwards on the rack; his wrists and ankles were bound with leather thongs. Paul was protesting all the time, but the Roman soldiers didn't know what he was talking about. They only spoke their own language. But when a sergeant came up to make sure all was ready for the scourging, Paul could talk to him in Greek. He said quite calmly: "Is it lawful to scourge a Roman citizen who hasn't been tried?" The sergeant rushed off to the captain. "Sir," he said, breathlessly, "do you realise what we are doing? This man is a Roman citizen."

The captain came running. "What's all this?" he asked Paul. "Are you honestly a Roman citizen? It cost me a packet to become a citizen myself."

"Sure, I'm a citizen," Paul replied "but it didn't cost me a cent. I am a Roman citizen by birth."

The other extract is from Thursday's talk:

Lysias, the Roman captain, was feeling very nervous. Twice he had saved his prisoner from the Jews. He couldn't be sure if his luck would hold a third time. Actually he knew that the Jews had hatched a plot to ambush Paul. He'd got it from Paul's young nephew. This is what the youth told him, according to chapter 23 of the Acts of the Apostles:

"The Jews," the lad said, "will ask you to bring Paul down

[61]

before the Council tomorrow. Don't take any notice. Some of them will be lying in ambush—in fact more than forty of them. They have vowed not to eat or drink until they have killed him."

That settled it. The captain swore the youth to secrecy and sent his prisoner to Caesarea with a guard nearly three hundred strong. "This is too big for me," he thought, "Felix the governor can look after it." So he scribbled this note to the governor—I'm reading from verse 27—

"Your Excellency,

Here's a man the Jews were trying to kill and I rescued hearing he is a Roman citizen. Trying to find out what they had against him, I took him before their Council. I couldn't make head or tail of their accusations. It seemed a private quarrel about their own religion—nothing in the way of a criminal offence. Now I've got definite information that they are out to kill him. That's why I'm sending him and his accusers to you."

The governor acted quickly. In less than a week he summoned Paul. The proceedings were opened by a barrister named Tertullus, representing the high priest, Ananias. He spoke briefly: "This man" he said, "is ringleader of the Nazarene sect. He is out to violate the temple and cause trouble. We arrested him and would have tried him according to our own law if the Roman captain, Lysias, hadn't interfered." Felix turned to Paul. "What do you say to that?" he asked. Paul was cool and clever. "Who started the trouble?" he asked. "Was it me? It all began when I was on my own in the temple. It was some Jews from Asia who started the riot. They, not I, should be before you today. The truth is, Excellency, I'm accused not of rioting but of believing in the resurrection of the dead."

The purpose of my broadcasts was to show the contemporary significance of what happened in apostolic times. I was suggesting that a modern Christian might easily have to undergo the same kind of trial as St. Paul. Today's enemies are not Jewish anti-Christians but militant atheists who persecute all who believe in God. The climactic talk was Saturday's and it was entitled: 'It could happen here'. In those days producers still retained the war-time custom of requiring performers to submit scripts in advance. This mild form of censorship was no doubt regarded as some protection against legal action for broadcasting libel or slander. There was never in my experience any attempt to alter the

[62]

theological content of a script. On the Friday before the final talk Francis House, head of Religious Broadcasts, telephoned to suggest an alteration in Saturday's script. He seemed to be worried about my remarks on the communist persecution of religion. I thought—wrongly as it turned out—that the B.B.C. was afraid of reactions from the Communist Party of Great Britain. Knowing the extent of communist persecution of believers I was not prepared to delete the reference to what was happening in Eastern Europe. But after giving the list of persecuted countries I was willing to omit the following two sentences:

> Anyone who tells you that there is still religious freedom in these countries is either a knave or a fool. Either he does not know the facts or he is a liar.

There was no principle involved and I was not particularly proud of the blunt expression. Late on Friday night I was still brooding over this last minute request for alteration. It was extraordinary because the B.B.C. had been given copies of all six talks some weeks in advance. Dozens of copies had been circulated to officials within the B.B.C. including the editor of *The Listener*. I tried to convince myself that there must be good reasons for the sudden request for a change in the script. At last I thought I could see a glimmer of light. It was true, I reflected, that communists are not the only people to suppress freedom. Perhaps the B.B.C. was right, after all, to object to my isolated attack on militant atheists. I therefore pencilled the following lines at the bottom of the script:

> We are so used to tolerance for minorities in Great Britain we take it for granted. They don't everywhere—in Spain, for example, and Northern Ireland. But their intolerance is nothing compared with the savage treatment of believers where active communists are in control.

In its emended form the relevant part of the text actually broadcast was the following:

> If you have listened all the week you will have realised how thrilling some bits of scripture are. Funny, isn't it, how things that happened hundreds of years ago are so like current events? And people haven't changed much either. What they did to St. Paul

[63]

they are doing today to thousands of Christians. The only really big difference is that a modern martyr is rarely allowed to speak in his own defence. Nowadays, the enemies of God condition prisoners before dragging them before the public. If St. Paul had been tried in Moscow or Warsaw or Peking they would have alleged that he had confessed to sabotage of the government and of being a spy in the pay of foreign imperialists determined to overthrow the Roman Empire. Trials like St. Paul's are always happening and we, safe in England, ought to remember the victims of persecution and pray for them.

You may think I've spoiled a nice week of scripture reading by ugly disconcerting thoughts on this last day of the week. But really I haven't spoilt anything. Obviously, I had a reason for choosing to tell you about the trial of St. Paul the Apostle. You see, there are millions of Christians now suffering persecution who would have laughed at you if you had warned them a few years ago that night would fall. Bulgaria, Poland, Rumania, Czechoslovakia, Hungary, the Ukraine, the Baltic States—they all had their Christian schools and full freedom of worship the other day. But not now. We are so used to tolerance for minorities in Britain that we take it for granted. They don't everywhere—in Spain, for example, and Northern Ireland . . .

There was no reaction from Spain but in Northern Ireland the anger was immediate and intense. Telephone lines to the B.B.C. were choked with calls. An official complaint was lodged without delay. The Northern Ireland government sent a telegram of protest not only to the Director General of the B.B.C. but also to the British Prime Minister. After the broadcast I had left Leeds for Bradford where I was due to give some lectures. I was therefore unaware of the tornado I had created until I returned to Leeds in the evening to find a crowd of reporters awaiting me. They told me that after the one o'clock news the announcer had apologised for my misdemeanour. Without mentioning my name he expressed regret that a speaker in a programme of encouragement and worship had seen fit to accuse the government of Northern Ireland of intolerance. A spokesman for the B.B.C. in Belfast told the press that the Roman Catholic Bishop of Leeds, having submitted a talk which had been approved, waited until the producer's back was turned and altered the script in order to launch an attack on the Northern Ireland government.

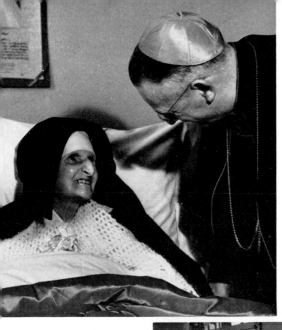

A centenarian Sister of
Notre Dame.

Hospital visitation.

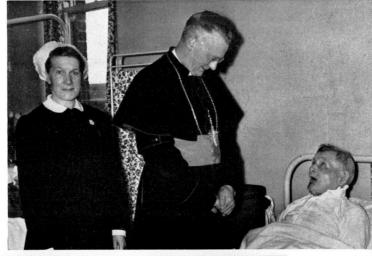

Parish visitation:
blessing of children.

Korea

Malaya

Japan

It now seems incredible that such a furore was aroused by a short sentence which today would be regarded as a serious understatement: "they do not take tolerance for granted in Northern Ireland". What is even more incredible is that the Northern Ireland government, not content with the apology of the B.B.C., inflated the incident to such proportions that on 30th March there was an adjournment debate in Stormont. The debate was widely but briefly reported in the British press. In Ireland each paper gave full reports of the speeches made by members of the party it supported. The official report occupies no less than forty-one of the fifty-seven columns of Hansard recording that day's proceedings in parliament. In view of all that has happened in Northern Ireland since March 1954 these extracts from Hansard repay reading. They show that members of parliament in Stormont did not all take tolerance for granted. Even those not interested in politics will relish the hibernian repartee which enlivened the debate.

MR. MINFORD: I should like to refer to a telegram sent by our Prime Minister on Saturday. I think I can discuss that, because the Prime Minister did it on the Estimates regarding a particular point. The Prime Minister sent a very strong protest regarding a very misleading statement, a vicious statement, against Northern Ireland. I have it here.

MR. STEWART: Anybody can send a telegram.

MR. CONNELLAN: Send a telegram yourself.

MR. MINFORD: I say that the honour of Northern Ireland is at stake, and I am going to stand up here and defend it. I feel that I am in order. The television and radio are black-balling Northern Ireland. This telegram was sent on Saturday morning pointing out the views of our Government, and I advocate that stronger representations be made to other quarters regarding these points, because, as far as I can see, if we do not do something we are not going to get anywhere.

MR. GORMLEY: Listen in to Radio Eireann.

MR. MINFORD: Ah, shut your mouth. I would cremate the old Bishop if I could get my hands on him. (Interruption.) Millions of people are hearing these statements about Northern Ireland. There is no truth at all in them, and I think the time has come when in this House we should have the right and liberty at any time to speak about these matters. That is what I intend to do today. I say that the statement made on Saturday by Bishop Heenan is

[65]

completely incorrect and should never have been made, and his apology in the press afterwards is a perfect disgrace.

MR. STEWART: He did not apologise.

MR. MIDGLEY: Give the man a chance.

MR. MINFORD: After the telegram was sent on Saturday morning we had a statement in the press from our Chief Whip stating that the reply of the B.B.C. was utterly inadequate. I say that the reply to this telegram was altogether hopeless. I am asking this House and this Government to take the firmest action in this matter, and to say that they are not satisfied with the steps taken by the B.B.C. and by the Imperial Parliament . . .

MR. PORTER: I think the Roman Catholic prelate should have some regard to his remarks. If he wants evidence of our position in Northern Ireland I will refer very briefly to one or two examples of our toleration here. First of all, we have a number of Roman Catholics who occupy positions as nurses in our hospitals. A bus is provided on a Sunday so that these Roman Catholic nurses may be able to attend Mass, but no bus is provided for Protestant nurses.

MR. CONNELLAN: They do not attend Mass.

MR. PORTER: The very fact that the Bishop of Leeds should have made this attack on Northern Ireland would make one wonder if the slogan of our forefathers—No peace with Rome; No Popery— was not justified.

MR. SPEAKER: The hon. Member must refrain from introducing religious topics in this House, and he has just made a statement which I think he should withdraw.

MR. HEALY: In the few minutes I shall take I hope I shall deal with the matter in a reasonable way. The utterance by Dr. Heenan to which objection is taken is as follows:

"We are so used to tolerance for minorities in England that we take it for granted. They don't elsewhere—in Spain, for example, and Northern Ireland . . ."

MR. MIDGLEY: Why link us with Spain?

MR. HEALY: I will tell you in a minute.

". . . but this intolerance is nothing compared with the savage treatment of believers where active Communists are in control."

That is a very moderate statement of fact. I do want to correct something which has been said in the local newspapers in the last few days, namely, that after the official of the B.B.C. had passed the script Bishop Heenan altered it to read as I have just indicated. As a matter of fact, the script was not altered from those words, and the officials had an opportunity of seeing it if they had so desired.

MR. MIDGLEY: Who told you that?

MR. HEALY: I have the Bishop's word for it. Surely the Bishop's word is as good as that of some of the gentlemen opposite, gentlemen about whom I will have something to say in a few minutes. The whole issue here is one of tolerance. I will tell you a few facts about the amount of tolerance we receive in this area. I will start with Derry City. There is a majority of Nationalists there. They are peaceful and well-behaved people, yet they are not allowed to walk within the walls of their own city on St. Patrick's Day. Other political parties, even a group of Communists, would be allowed to march carrying whatever colours they liked.

DR. NIXON: No, they would not.

MR. HEALY: The Bishop has made no apology for the words he used, and he has no right to do so. I say that because in my opinion he did not go far enough.

HON. MEMBERS: Oh.

MR. HEALY: The fault of the Bishop was that he did not make it clear that here is a country dominated by a secret society.

HON. MEMBERS: No, no.

MR. LYONS: I will contradict you—you are wrong.

MR. HEALY: The hon. Member is not capable of telling the truth.

MR. TOPPING: On a point of order. The hon. Member for South Fermanagh has said that the hon. Member for North Tyrone is not capable of speaking the truth. He should be asked to withdraw that statement.

MR. DIAMOND: On a further point of order. If the Chief Whip requests a withdrawal of that sort, I would also ask you to ask for the withdrawal of a statement made earlier by the hon. Member for Antrim. I took a note of it at the time. He said he would cremate old Bishop Heenan, of Leeds. No further comment is necessary on intolerance in Northern Ireland.

MR. SPEAKER: I think the hon. Member is going a little bit too far. I certainly did not hear the hon. Member say that. I am sure that if the hon. Member for South Fermanagh stated that the hon.

Member for North Tyrone was not capable of telling the truth he certainly did not mean that.

MR. HEALY: If I said anything unparliamentary I withdraw it, but the hon. Member said previously—and this was a retort to him—that I was not telling the truth.

MR. LYONS: My remark was quite correct; he was not telling the truth.

MR. HEALY: Then I say the hon. Member is a liar.

MR. J. W. MORGAN: Lift up your hearts.

MR. DIAMOND: You want to watch yourself.

MR. MIDGLEY: I will be able to watch myself and keep you in control as well.

MR. DIXON: The people of Ulster will read this Debate and they will accept the orgy of intemperate talking here today as a measure of their trust in their representatives. That intolerance exists in Ulster I believe, and I believe it exists proportionately to the population, Nationalists and Unionists. Intolerance exists in every country where religion exists. It is wrong for hon. Members on this side of the House to abuse hon. Members on the other side of the House, and it ill-behoves hon. Members on the other side to abuse us.

Frankly, I am sick of this religious bigotry. I am fed up with it. I have said before in this House that I am heartily ashamed to have visitors in this House and for them to see us behaving like this. It could well be that the Roman Catholic Bishop of Leeds made what he considered to be an honest statement, but that he is qualified to make that statement I deny. The manner in which he made the statement is one to be deplored. Whether he interpolated another statement in the prepared script after it had been scrutinised is one matter. I believe he said he did not, and I am prepared to believe him, but it is another matter if he pencilled it in. The statement went out to millions to do us harm religiously, commercially, and in every conceivable manner to try to destroy us.

While the controversy continued with customary ferocity in Northern Ireland I tried to preserve a sense of proportion. It was, of course, impossible to let the matter rest. The B.B.C. by apologising for what I had said, created the impression that I had behaved in an underhand way. The accusation made by the B.B.C. spokesman in Belfast that when left alone in the studio I had made a surreptitious interpolation had been widely reported. The issue now was not whether tolerance is taken for granted in Northern Ireland but whether I was lacking in integrity. Even if I had been willing to pursue it no further the question had now gone beyond the personal level. The Catholic community and, irrespective of their religious beliefs, the Yorkshire people were angry with the B.B.C. Letters appeared in the national press and in great numbers in Yorkshire papers. It was felt that the B.B.C. had slandered me to appease Lord Brookeborough, the prime minister of Northern Ireland. The B.B.C. was challenged to withdraw its apology. (The enterprising editor of *Punch* published an article by Christopher Hollis on 'The B.B.C. Department of Apologies for Apologising'.) Before correspondence began in the press I had a private exchange of letters (eventually made public) with Francis House, head of the religious division of the B.B.C. He was a man of peace and a personal friend. He deplored the fact that a religious programme had been the cause of so much bitterness. He also realised that had he not asked me to alter my script at the last moment there would have been no crisis.

Cathedral House,
Leeds 2.
29th March, 1954.

The Rev. F. H. House,
Broadcasting House,
London W.1.

My dear Francis,

Needless to say, I am very sorry about the upset over Saturday's Talk. The press reporters tell me that the B.B.C. intends to hold an enquiry. I imagine that this is unlikely but I thought you might want to know the facts.

Before giving them, however, I must express surprise that the B.B.C. made the regrettable apology after the one o'clock news. The apology, as reported, does me less than justice. But apart from that, the B.B.C. should not so quickly lay blame publicly on those who are serving them. Such a thing would not happen, for example, in the civil service. I must add that I do not imagine the Religious Division to be responsible for the apology. I am quite sure that you, personally, had nothing to do with it.

[69]

Here are the facts:

On Friday I was asked by the B.B.C. to reconsider the following passage: "Anyone who tells you that there is still religious freedom in those countries is either a knave or a fool. That is either he does not know the facts or he is a liar. The Church is enslaved wherever Communism is in control."

For the record it is important to say explicitly what objections were raised.

(i) The B.B.C. felt that I should insert the word 'full' before 'religious' so that it would read: "Anyone who tells you that there is full religious freedom . . ."

(ii) Knave, fool and liar were all felt by the B.B.C. to be rather too strong.

(iii) The B.B.C. objected to the sentence—"The Church is enslaved wherever Communism is in control"—on the ground that it was against B.B.C. policy to condemn Communism. It was explained that it is part of the general understanding between the B.B.C. and political parties that no attack on a Party will be allowed unless in a specifically Party broadcast.

(i) I rejected, without hesitation, the suggestion to insert 'full' before the word 'religious'. I said that the only qualifying word I would use was 'real'.

(ii) I agreed to think about the offending epithets—knave, fool and liar.

(iii) It was the B.B.C.'s anxiety to be fair to the Communists that caused the most trouble. I said on the phone that I would be willing to insert 'atheistic' before 'communism' since the political Party does not call itself by that name. I said that I would think the whole thing over during the day.

Now comes the question of my personal integrity. The public has been told one story by the B.B.C. and another by me. The B.B.C. says that I made a last-minute interpolation. Belfast goes further and says that as soon as the producer left me alone I took out my pencil and stealthily changed the script. Let me assure you that mine was no last-minute interpolation. The B.B.C.'s anxiety to be fair to the Communist Party set up a train of thought in my mind. I do not, for a moment, accept that a broadcaster should tone down references to religious persecution for fear of wounding Communists in England. But, at least, it is a point of view. So I began to question whether it was fair to talk of religious persecution in Communist-controlled countries while making no reference to other kinds of intolerance elsewhere. Spain immediately came to mind. I know that there is no religious persecution there but there is intolerance of minorities. So I decided to mention Spain—a State associated in the public mind with Catholics. But if Spain—why not Northern Ireland where also there is intolerance? So, having had all day to think about it, on Friday night I deleted the paragraph to which objection had been taken and inserted the following:

"We are so used to tolerance for minorities in England that we take it for granted. They don't elsewhere—in Spain, for example, and Northern Ireland. But their intolerance is nothing compared with the savage treatment of believers where atheistic Communists are in control."

These are the facts. I expected that Falangists in Spain and Orangemen in Northern Ireland would resent reference to intolerance. But I must ask you to believe that when I broadcast on Saturday I did not think that there was any dispute about the *fact* of intolerance either in Spain or Northern Ireland. The only controversy, I imagined, concerned the causes and extent of intolerance.

I must say once more how sorry I am that you, personally, and Father Agnellus have been involved in this unpleasantness. As I have said, it never occurred to me that my remark would cause offence to any but fanatics. Perhaps it didn't. However, this puts you in a difficult position regarding my own services to the B.B.C. I am due to record a programme on Thursday in the Leeds Studio. I shall quite understand if you would prefer this to be cancelled. I shall also be ready to resign from C.R.A.C. (Central Religious Advisory Council), if you think that I would no longer command respect in that assembly. Please believe that I am ready to do whatever is best for the cause we both have at heart.

I am,
Yours sincerely,
† JOHN C. HEENAN
Bishop of Leeds.

Broadcasting House,
London W.1.
30th March, 1954.

The Rt. Rev. J. C. Heenan D.D.,
Cathedral House,
Leeds 2.

My dear Bishop,

I was very grateful for your letter of the 29th which at last makes clear the nature of the misunderstanding which has had such regrettable consequences. It was most unfortunate that circumstances beyond our control necessitated discussion of the script indirectly and by telephone. The basic fact is that my suggestions for merely verbal changes were misinterpreted as requiring much more fundamental revision of your script. In particular my suggestion that in the sentence—"The Church is enslaved wherever Communism is in control" the word 'Communism' should be replaced by 'Communist governments' or 'regimes' apparently reached you in a form which led you to suppose that some serious question of broadcast policy was at stake. This was not my intention at all. There is no Corporation policy in relation to Communism of the kind you were apparently led to suppose. Actually, when it was reported to me that you were prepared to insert the word 'atheistic' before 'Communism', I said this did not meet my point, but did not follow the question up because I attached so little importance to it. This explains how we were at cross-purposes; unknown to me you were worrying about a supposed request to make a change of a kind which I had never intended to suggest.

Secondly, I can assure you that the reference in the broadcast apology to a 'last-minute interpolation' was not intended to reflect on your personal integrity or to imply that anything underhand had been done. On Saturday morning the information reached London that the alteration had been made at the last minute. This information was based on the fact that you had said nothing to anyone earlier about a change, and that you had written something into the script at the last moment. It was naturally assumed that this was the sentence in question. When we got in touch with you on Saturday morning, the question when the addition was made

[72]

was not directly asked, and we were consequently still left under the impression that the alteration had been made in the studio. The apology was therefore drawn up on the supposition that there was agreement on this point. It was not until we were at last able to get in touch with you again at 8.00 p.m. that we knew that you had made the major alteration on Friday, and that only the kind of minor changes, which are customarily made in the studio by experienced broadcasters, had been made at the last minute.

Thirdly, in view of certain comments that have reached me, I must explain that in the apology the phrase "in a programme of encouragement and worship" was added merely to distinguish talks in "Lift up your hearts" in which a right of reply to a controversial statement could not be provided for, from other talks and discussions in which controversial issues could be handled.

Fourthly, as it has been suggested that the handling of the question of the apology was discourteous, I must explain that we made every effort to get in touch with you as soon as the question arose; that we did let you know confidentially that an apology might have to be broadcast; and that there was not time to consult you again between the time at which the decision to broadcast the apology was taken and the actual broadcast. Repeated efforts to get in touch with you again all through the afternoon were unsuccessful. No discourtesy was intended.

Fifthly, as it has been stated that we could have seen the script in its altered form had we wished to do so, I must add that after telephone exchanges on Friday, I thought that nothing but minor verbal changes were in question, and you had been told that I was available if further consultation was required. In fact your alteration introduced a new idea involving delicate and controversial material. The B.B.C. has responsibilities in view of which I am sure you will now agree that we had the right to have been informed of your intention.

I very much hope that what I have written clears up all causes of misunderstanding. The B.B.C. does not, I understand, at present intend to make any further statement to the press on this matter, but please feel yourself at liberty to make any use you wish of the information I have given in this letter. I would only ask that if you do decide that it is necessary to say something more in public, you would be kind enough to let me have a copy of what you decide to say.

I need hardly add that there is no change in the plans for your recording on Thursday and no question arises of ending your membership of C.R.A.C.

I can only end by saying again how very much I regret the misunderstandings which have caused so much unnecessary trouble and distress.

Yours sincerely,

FRANCIS H. HOUSE

Head of Religious Broadcasting.

The storm rumbled on for eight or nine days. The average duration of public interest in scandal is three or four days unless sex and well-known names are involved. In that case interest can be kept alive by clever journalists for as much as two weeks. The *Yorkshire Post*, a Leeds paper, naturally gave wide coverage to the controversy in both news and correspondence columns. Sir Linton Andrews, the editor, gave a summing up of the situation in a feature article on 6th April. At this time I had only a distant acquaintance with Sir Linton. Knowing that he was Protestant by religion and conservative in politics I was surprised at the virtuosity with which he defended a Catholic bishop. He wrote as usual under the initials W.L.A. (William Linton Andrews) and his article carried a double headline:

WHAT WOULD A JURY SAY?
FAIR PLAY FOR THE BISHOP

We now have the detailed evidence before us in the case of Bishop Heenan, the B.B.C. and the Government of Northern Ireland. What would a fairminded jury say about it? Let us put aside our religious preferences and try to be impartial. The main questions are these:

(1) Did the Bishop say anything unfair?

(2) Did he surreptitiously put in the broadcast something the B.B.C. might have cut out?

(3) Was the statement by Lord Brookeborough, Northern Ireland Prime Minister in the Northern Ireland House of Commons, fair and reasonable comment based on established facts?

(4) Have the B.B.C. been fair to the Bishop?

I suspect that most of those who have sent me angry letters do not know the general nature of the series given by Dr. Heenan in a programme of encouragement and worship. He spoke of the Acts of the Apostles and compared the treatment of St. Paul in the Courts with modern Anti-Christian trials in Communist countries. The series made a deep impression on those who heard it, whatever their religious faith—'beautiful' and 'inspiring' were among the words applied to it by a Leeds Nonconformist. But controversy, or most of it, has fastened on a single sentence:

> "We are so used to tolerance for minorities in England that we take it for granted. They don't elsewhere—in Spain, for example, and Northern Ireland—but their intolerance is nothing compared with the savage treatment of believers where active Communists are in control."

1. FAIR COMMENT

The Bishop did not accuse the Government of Northern Ireland of religious persecution. He merely expressed his belief that some intolerance existed in both Spain and Northern Ireland. He did not say this with provocative emphasis, but used the point to show how much worse, infinitely worse, was the extreme of intolerance reached in Communist-controlled countries. Cases are reported in which persons in Northern Ireland have suffered for their religion, perhaps by being refused employment because they are Roman Catholics. I have often seen the intolerant phrase, 'To Hell with the Pope', posted up in Belfast, and in the countryside. These expressions of un-Christian feeling, though deplorable, are not to be compared with the ghastly sufferings of, say, Roman Catholic missionaries and nuns in Communist China.

The Bishop's argument seemed to me clear and fair. It may be said that he should not have introduced the subject in a devotional series, but how can Christians meditate on the sufferings of St. Paul without thinking of the hardships to which some of the Christians of today are subject?

My verdict would be that the Bishop said nothing that deserves rebuke. Legally, and I think morally, what he said was fair comment.

2. ALLEGED TRICK

At the end of the one o'clock news on Saturday, March 27th, the B.B.C. said: "This morning in 'Lift Up Your Hearts' the speaker made a last-minute interpolation alleging religious intolerance in Northern Ireland." That reference to a last-minute interpolation was based on a misapprehension. So was the suggestion, published in Belfast but presumably originating in this country, that when the B.B.C. representative left the Bishop alone in the Leeds studio to give his talk—the producer, announcer or representative often goes to listen with the technicians on the other side of the glass wall—the Bishop took out his pencil and stealthily changed the script. What a monstrous fiction! We now have the plain facts. The B.B.C. on getting the script in advance decided that the Bishop's reference to the Communists was against their rules since they were held to attack a political party in a non-party broadcast, and he was asked to alter certain wordings. Clearly the Bishop did his best to obey the B.B.C.'s request. He altered the script on the day before delivery. So where was the trick? It may be said that he introduced a fresh subject, but the phrase about Spain and Northern Ireland was used, quite fairly, to strengthen the condemnation of atrocious Communist methods.

3. LORD BROOKEBOROUGH

In view of this explanation, what are we to make of Lord Brookeborough's complaint of cunning conduct by the Bishop? Lord Brookeborough, in his statement in the Northern Ireland House of Commons, said: "It is an uncontested fact that the Bishop's reference to Northern Ireland was not in the script approved by the B.B.C." From my contacts with Lord Brookeborough I believe him to be a man of integrity, but this statement in his speech is most unfair to the Bishop, since it suggests that *after the script had been approved by the B.B.C.* the Bishop made a cunning, uninvited, secret interpolation. But the script in its original form, the script of which Lord Brookeborough was speaking, was not fully and finally approved by the B.B.C., since, as we have seen, the Bishop was asked to modify part of it. He did this in what he thought was a reasonable way and must have been startled at the later outcry.

One of the oddest incidents is that the B.B.C., after suggesting alterations in the script, do not seem to have followed up the point and checked the alterations. Why not? Presumably whoever read the script in London attached so little importance to the proposed amendments that no arrangement was made to check them in the

Leeds studio. The B.B.C. representative there evidently believed that the script, as left in the Bishop's care, was authorised. It probably never occurred to him to ask: "Have you made any changes since London saw the script?"

Lord Brookeborough therefore is utterly mistaken in saying that the Bishop "chose to slander Northern Ireland by innuendo and did it behind the backs of the B.B.C."

4. THE APOLOGY

The B.B.C. apology was a curious one. The Corporation expressed "regret for broadcasting a statement of this nature in a programme of encouragement and worship." They did not take sides in the issue between the Bishop and the Northern Ireland Government, and presumably what they really regretted was that such trouble arose. But the reference to a last-minute interpolation was baseless and created an impression most unfair to Bishop Heenan. The B.B.C. told me yesterday afternoon that nothing more would be said about the broadcast.

It seems to me very odd of the B.B.C. to ask a broadcaster to amend a script, not bother to see the amendments and then denounce them as an interpolation. This conduct is not usual on the part of the B.B.C., of whose fairness and consideration to broadcasters and care in supervising the script at all stages I can speak with long experience.

I thanked the editor for becoming my champion and received the following charming acknowledgment:

The Yorkshire Post

Albion Street,
Leeds 1.

8/4/54

My dear Bishop,

Thank you for your kind note. I am sorry you have had all this trouble. But at least you can say with Voltaire: "My prayer to God is a very short one: O Lord, make my enemies very ridiculous." God has granted it. But the story put out by the B.B.C. official at Belfast was not merely ridiculous. It was a gross slander.

Yes, the yelping pack is at my heels. How can I, a professed Anglican, defend a Roman Catholic? And so forth.

But the incident will be forgotten in the next excitement.

Yours very sincerely,
W. L. ANDREWS.

To close this account of the troubles which resulted from the broadcast it is amusing to read what a prominent performer on B.B.C. television of those days had to say. Gilbert Harding was an enigmatic character. He had a lively, encyclopaedic mind and an unequalled gift for civilised vituperation. He was such an artist that it was impossible to know if his virulent outbursts were the outcome of real or simulated anger. At that time I had not met him. Later we became friends and I learned to feel compassion for this highly successful and deeply insecure man. His mother lived in Bradford and as a young man he had tested his vocation as a monk in the Anglican monastery in Mirfield. When he became a Catholic he was enthusiastic about the faith and aggressively loyal to the Church.

18 Cadogan Place,
London S.W.1.
31st March, 1954.

Dear Lord Bishop,

I write for three reasons: one to express my deep sympathy with you in all the kefuffle and brouhaha about the B.B.C. talk. I suppose it's useful as an indication of the enormous amount of latent hostility to which the Church is still exposed.

Secondly, to say how much I enjoyed the television broadcast from the Cathedral: thirdly, to say that in a hazy and somewhat harassed way I remember being asked, and refusing, to come to Leeds for some garden party or fete, and to say that I intend to visit Leeds and Bradford within the next three months and could be at your disposal for some sort of money-raising project if necessary. Wednesdays, Thursdays and Sundays are very bad days for me: but we ought to be able to arrange something if I'm still wanted.

Yours respectfully,
GILBERT HARDING

CHAPTER

FIVE

GILBERT HARDING'S MENTION OF A BROADCAST FROM LEEDS CATHEDRAL
refers to a Pontifical High Mass televised from St. Anne's Cathedral
on 10th January of that year (1954). Although it was the occasion of
very little controversy it was in the true sense of the word an historic
broadcast. It was the first time Mass had been shown on television in
this country. At that time the ecumenical movement was still in its
infancy. Traditional rivalries between Christians were growing less
painful. But vociferous sects still attacked the Church of Rome and,
with much greater vehemence, all Romanising tendencies in the Church
of England. When it was announced that Mass would be televised
there was an outcry from members of the Protestant Alliance. They
were pioneers in the campaign against pollution of the atmosphere.
They objected to the pure air of England being sullied by Papist ritual
and regarded it as treasonable to allow the Mass, a blasphemous superstition, to enter the homes of innocent citizens. They did not predict
that people would actually be murdered in their beds but made it clear
that the wrath of God must eventually fall on a country which defied
Him so outrageously. It is a psychological problem that a televised
Mass should arouse fury while no protest was heard about the Mass on
sound radio. Possibly it was the actual sight of the altar, the host and
chalice, and, above all, the priest in vestments which alarmed the
zealots of the Reformation.

The Queen's coronation was the most spectacular programme ever
shown on television in this country. It would have been even more
magnificent if colour television had then been available. The corona-

tion had everything required for successful television—the incomparable beauty of the setting, the grace and elegance of the chief character, the unique sense of occasion shared by all viewers. Despite these advantages the spectacle would have failed if all taking part had not been meticulously rehearsed. The Duke of Norfolk who, as Earl Marshal of England, is responsible for such royal occasions, has the reputation of being a perfectionist if not a slave driver. I recalled this after I had agreed to celebrate a televised Mass in Leeds cathedral and resolved that all taking part must be carefully rehearsed. The cathedral Master of Ceremonies selected an excellent team of priests and altar servers, the choir was practised to concert pitch and even the seating in the cathedral was arranged so that a roving camera would pick up a richly varied congregation—nurses, babies, scouts, Girl Guides, schoolchildren, soldiers and Knights of St. Columba. ("The congregation was improbably male" wrote the cynical television correspondent of *The Tablet.*)

We had one apparently insoluble problem. The administrator of St. Anne's Cathedral was an old canon with very definite ideas about how the affairs of the cathedral ought to be conducted. He was tetchy because he had not been given a place among the officiating clergy. This had been impossible because he would not have submitted to rehearsals—and even after rehearsal his movements would have been unpredictable. He was wandering round the sanctuary just before the Mass was due to start and we were afraid that he might decide to direct proceedings after transmission had begun. At the last moment one of the producers, Father Agnellus Andrew, had an inspiration. He asked the Canon to join the B.B.C. van outside the cathedral to assist the engineer. He explained that a priest would be useful in forewarning the technicians of the movements to be made by the ministers during Mass. The day was saved. The Canon was delighted to be doing something really useful. A shy man, he was very content to be out of sight.

The broadcast took place on the Sunday after Epiphany, the Feast of the Holy Family. In preparing my sermon I had two objectives in mind. The first was to explain the ritual which was very complex before the liturgical reforms of the Council. Today a Sunday Mass on television might attract an audience of only a few thousand but in 1954 television was still a novelty. Hours of viewing were by comparison with today few and therefore precious. For this reason it was certain that this programme would be watched by many who would not normally be interested in religious services. They were likely to be confused if not repelled by the ceremonial of a Pontifical Mass. Since the coronation had made such an impact on viewers I decided to make it a point of reference to explain the liturgy. My second objective was to appeal in the name of the Holy Family of Nazareth for families to adopt or foster children without parents. I was not greatly concerned with the congregation inside the cathedral. I had mainly in mind the viewers for whom a Mass would be a new experience:

I address myself to you whom I cannot see. I suppose that for most of you this is your first experience of a bishop's Mass—a Pontifical High Mass we call it. If so, you are probably finding it rather bewildering.

I don't wonder. I well remember the first time I saw a Mass like this. I was a boy in the school chapel. I didn't like it very much—and it was not only because the ceremony itself was hard to follow. What I didn't like was all the bowing and kneeling to the bishop. Somehow it didn't seem right. I said in my own mind: "People ought to kneel only to God". In fact, now I come to think of it, I felt rather angry with the bishop. Poor man! He has been dead for years—and by a coincidence, though my school was not in Yorkshire, that bishop was one of my predecessors, Dr. Cowgill, Bishop of Leeds.

Naturally, I understand these things much better now. At least I know exactly how a bishop feels. He does not for a moment regard the homage as being paid to him personally. Far from feeling proud when people kneel before him and kiss his hand, he feels very small and humble. When people show him reverence, he thinks of the words of St. Paul: "Let a man so account of us as of the ministers of Christ and the dispensers of the mysteries of God" (1 Cor. 14:1). He knows his own unworthiness. He is, it is true, a vessel of election. But he knows only too well that he is a vessel of clay.

I don't suppose you are as puzzled this morning as I was in my school chapel. You have had the advantage of seeing what a coronation looks like. In the old days the coronation ceremony was part of a Pontifical High Mass like the one you are seeing now. I am sure you will already have noticed certain points of resemblance. The instruments given to the Queen are not very different from those carried by the bishop—her ring, sceptre and crown, for example, are like this ring of mine, this pastoral staff and the mitre on my head. When people knelt before the Queen and kissed her hand, they were paying homage to her royal office not to the Queen's personal qualities.

So it is at a bishop's Mass. The authority of God and the holiness of the priesthood of Jesus Christ are honoured in the minister and his insignia. The man himself is unimportant. This ring is to remind me and my people that I am wedded to the diocese of Leeds. I must love my flock like a father. I must serve all God's children here in the West Riding of Yorkshire—even those who owe me no obedience and do not share my faith.

This crozier, or pastoral staff, is the symbol of my duty to rule my clergy and people with justice and mercy in God's name.

This mitre is like a crown adorning my head. It is a token of my obligation to teach the pure doctrine of the Son of God.

So the bishop is the head of a great family. It happens that today we are keeping the Feast of another Family—the Holy Family of Nazareth: Jesus, Mary and Joseph. This family is the model for all families. Jesus was subject to Mary and Joseph. All of them were obedient to Almighty God. The Child never saw or heard anything unworthy in the home. Let parents among you always remember that. There is no school so important as the home. Every home, indeed, should be a school for the training of saints. Now the binding force which united this family was the love of God. Nothing was allowed to disturb their peace. Bad times didn't make them quarrelsome—and they had plenty of experience of bad times. They were so poor that, as you know, they were reduced to a stable for the birth of the Child. They even tasted the hard lot of refugees and had to leave their own country. But they remained serene. They didn't round on God and complain because He hadn't arranged things better for them. They knew that the secret of peace of soul is the glad acceptance of God's holy will. This does not mean a sort of paralysis of resignation. On the contrary, it means an active determination to work and pray that God's will may be done.

God's will, notice, means God's will—not our version of it. Today's Gospel gives us a good example of what I mean. The Holy Family, you remember, went up to Jerusalem to worship. They might have said: "It's a long way to the Temple. Let's stay at home. We are just as good as those who go." They didn't talk like that. They knew that God has always required His people to worship Him. Even pagan governments know the value of ritual. It shows the authority of law. So when God demands our worship He helps us to understand His own holiness, beauty and authority.

So the Holy Family went up to the Temple. But, once again, things went wrong. They lost Jesus in the crowd. If you have ever lost your child for an hour or two, you will know the agony of Mary and Joseph when the Child was missing for three whole days.

Yes, the Holy Family suffered the same kind of sorrows and hardships as we do today. That is why the Church tells us to study this Family at the beginning of each New Year. Their secret was to love God and do His will.

I want to give you a last thought. It's about St. Joseph. This man made a home for a Child not his own. How many of you could do that? There are thousands of children all over the country whose home is an institution. We call them deprived children. Death or perhaps the sin of their parents has deprived them of their homes. It would be a wonderful way of thanking God for the love and security of your own home to give a home to Christ who lives in each of these children. Even if you have a child of your own couldn't you find room for one more? You may not feel able to manage a small baby. But, after all, Jesus was twelve years old when He was lost. Children of all ages are looking for a foster father like Joseph and a mother like Mary. What about you?

Now we must resume our Holy Mass which is the sacrifice of Jesus Christ on Calvary. Unite your prayers with ours in the Cathedral. Ask the Son of God to make the homes of England like the home of Nazareth—free from the voice of anger, free from sullen silence and full of God's love.

May God bless us all and grant peace in our homes, peace within this country and peace between the nations of the world.

Although I realised that the Mass had made television history I was astonished by the volume of correspondence which resulted. Telegrams began to arrive an hour or two after Mass. Letters poured in the next morning and throughout the following week. I was accustomed to the so-called 'fan mail' from the many B.B.C. programmes in which I had taken part during the previous decade but I had never received correspondence so large and varied as this. The most surprising features of the correspondence were the absence of criticism and the number of appreciative letters from non-Catholic viewers. There were, in fact, only two abusive letters. One came from Watford and the other from Belfast. The Watford critic was terse:

Dr. John Heenan,
What a travesty of religion your television of Holy Communion in St. Anne's Cathedral Leeds. '*Absolutely blasphemy*' and pure dupery. May God have mercy on your wretched soul. England does not want your Roman dope. Keep it in the Vatican.

The Belfast Christian was more expansive:

Sir
Such a bit of foolery never was performed as your service of the television on Sunday. You and your church is from Hell and going to Hell *a foreign cult* in England. If Martin Luther or John Huss appeared at your tomfoolery you would all have dropped dead, when the stench of burning flesh was all over London by Bloody Mary for the protestant faith good men burning at the stake but never mind your time is fast coming and your rotten church and pope will get what is coming to them. God is slow but sure to move, and popery will get their deserts sooner or later and your old hat so often off and on yesterday will be in the dust some of these days. What about Christ and the money changers?

It would not be of any interest to give the text of the many letters which came from Catholics. Cardinal Griffin and several bishops expressed their approval. The Duke of Norfolk, who had been responsible for the coronation, must have watched with an especially critical eye but the programme met with his approval and he sent me a letter of warm congratulation. Priests and laity from all parts of Britain found it a thrilling experience to see the Mass on their screens—especially as house Masses had not yet been introduced to this country. I had not anticipated the emotion devout Catholics would feel when television for the first time brought the Mass into their own homes. Most of the letters from non-Catholics were eloquent and touching. They came from people of widely differing education who wrote simply to express gratitude. Here is a typical letter. It was written by a viewer in Glasgow:

Dear Dr. Heenan,

Perhaps this is not the correct way to address you but I trust you will overlook it as no harm is meant by it, on the contrary I am writing to let you know how much I was impressed by your very lovely and dignified yet homely service.

Father Andrew was very good in describing in detail the procedure. The music was wonderful, your explanation of the service was truly magnificent.

As you will no doubt by this time have realized I am not one of your faith but I just had to write you and let you know how much I was impressed and to thank you for a really glorious Sunday and hoping it won't be too long until you are back once more.

A slightly different emphasis was given in a letter from the south of England:

Dear Sir,

I do trust you will not mind me writing to you, I just felt I must. It is the very first time I have seen a service like the one you conducted on Sun. Jan. 10th by television, and I hope it will not be the last. I am not a Catholic, but my eldest girl is. Perhaps I can best explain my admiration and interest in your most sincere address, when I tell you I sat in one position and never moved during the whole of the service. I was so enthralled. Your words to the *seeing* public I shall never forget, thank you so much, and may God bless you in your work.

Two more letters, the first from Cheshire and the second from Liverpool, aptly illustrate the general attitude of correspondents:
From Cheshire:

Most Reverend Father,

Although a non-Catholic may I express my gratitude to you for the most beautiful and moving service of High Mass broadcast in television from your Cathedral church of Saint Anne. For we who have found it hard to believe, your service came as an inspiration yet shattering in its impact. It seemed to reveal a great truth so long hidden from us. God bless you Father for the light you have shown us.

[85]

From Liverpool:

My Lord Bishop,

Your sermon, Sir, delivered in the language of the common people, and, so openly frank, contained a message which must have touched the hearts of thousands, as it did mine. The concluding allegory was so simple in understanding—yet its construction was the work of a master. I feel sure that to any Christian listening the appeal could not be denied.

Enlightenment of ritual dealt with by you was to me, and I feel sure to many, most helpful.

I trust, Sir, you will forgive the liberty I have taken in writing to you. *Dominus vobiscum.*

I was not surprised to hear from High Anglicans that they had been delighted to see Mass on television. It was more unexpected that Evangelicals and Nonconformists also took the trouble to write. Here is a short extract from a long letter:

You will not need to be informed that there has been quite a deal of controversy respecting the featuring of High Mass at St. Anne's Cathedral, Leeds last Sunday.

Naturally those of the Roman Catholic faith would appreciate it beyond measure. However, I write as Methodist, 67 years of age, grounded in my faith, and can only say that having seen it right through I fail to understand anything objectionable in it—in fact some parts were very moving—although naturally I do not agree with much of it.

Your sermon was one that I could listen to (excuse the grammar!) without my feelings being ruffled in any way, and if I felt inclined to criticise at all—which would be out of place in my instance—it is that it was rather too long.

Whether I am right or wrong I cannot say, but I am so strongly impressed with the need of Christianity throughout the world that the different interpretations of the Faith do not occupy much of my time. I joined in prayer for the persecuted Catholic clergy in the Communist countries, including Yugoslavia, as earnestly as yourselves, and shall continue to do so.

To my astonishment and joy I also received letters of thanks from a number of Jews. I have chosen two as typical of the rest. The first came from Lancashire:

[86]

Your Grace,

I saw, on Sunday last, the celebration of High Mass, and feel that I must write to thank you for the pleasure I derived therefrom.

This was the first time I had seen or heard a service of another denomination. I am Jewish, but that fact served only to enhance my appreciation and enjoyment of such a beautiful service.

May I also tender thanks for your sermon, which must have touched thousands of hearts as it indeed did mine.

I would like to hear that the service will again be televised in the near future, as it must surely be the means of bringing home to mankind just how beautiful life can be if people would only accept faith, no matter the denomination. I do not imagine that those near and dear to me would understand or appreciate my feelings on this subject.

The other letter from three Jewish old age pensioners was the most touching I have ever received after a broadcast. This letter came from a village not far from Bradford:

My Dear Bishop Father,

I feel I must write strait away and let you know how my husband, sister and I enjoyed your most wonderful service. How lucky your People of Leeds are, to possess such a Grand Father you most certainly have captured our hearts. Although we are Jewish evacues from London, who arrived in Yorkshire in 1940 thanks to God we are happily settled here. Enclosed you will find a small cheque, we sent it you with God's blessing strait from our hearts. We are three old aged pensioners whom thank you for a wonderful hour and a half T.V. which we never expected God bless you and your children and all who enters your cathedral.

Fortunately I have kept a copy of my reply to these generous old people:

I do not know how to thank you for your kindness in writing and your generosity in sending a donation to help poor children.

I am so glad that the High Mass gave you joy. I have many Jewish friends and I always feel that Catholics are very close to your people. You were not the only Jews who wrote after the television.

[87]

If you ever come to Leeds, I hope that you will take advantage of my Open Day on Fridays. You could come then without an appointment and I should be very happy to meet you.

Wishing you every blessing,

JOHN C. HEENAN
Bishop of Leeds.

One man wrote who had an experience which he attributed to divine providence. His television set which was out of order suddenly came to life:

My Lord Bishop,

I am not a Roman Catholic but as a boy I attended a nuns school. On Sunday last (10/1/54) I desired to watch the Mass; on television but was unable to do so because of trouble with our receiver. We have no vision, only sound. So I sat down to listen to the service on sound only. The service progressed until about 12.30 p.m. when for no reason that I can think of the picture appeared. I saw you deliver your sermon and indeed I saw the remainder of the service, and the picture was good too. At the end of the service, when we came to the part where the announcer tells the viewer that the transmission is closing down until evening the picture failed again.

And in the evening, when my daughter aged almost eight years, wanted to see children's T.V. the picture remained off. I can only say that I was meant to see or view your Service, call it the Lord's doing if you will and I like to think of it in this way.

I can vouch for what I have written, my wife saw the picture my daughter did also.

The set is now in the M.B.E. workshops. No doubt they would verify that there is a fault, and it was not possible to get a picture.

You can use this letter if you like or investigate it. I don't expect a reply either.

A letter which gave me great pleasure was from a retired civil servant who had been a colleague of my father in the Patent Office. I had heard my father speak of Mr. Morley but I did not know that he had seen me when as a boy I used to go to the Patent Office in Chancery Lane to meet my father. The date of this letter is 11th January, 1954. If my father had still been alive he would have been ninety years of age:

Reverend Sir,

As I watched the televising of High Mass on Sunday last, my mind went back to the time when a colleague and I contacted Logie Baird the co-inventor of television. It was in the Patent Office Library when Baird and his wife were searching the archives of inventions for their work. I don't think Baird realised to what wonderful results his labours would lead.

My colleague was a Catholic and he had a son studying for the priesthood. With me he used to share his hopes of the future. His son eventually went to the English College in Rome and then one memorable day took ordination. The happy father gave me a memorial card of the event.

Yes, watching the televising of the Service brought back memories. Old men live in memories, and I am 81 years of age

In my mind's eye I can see a young man coming to see his father. Could the father have known what the future would bring forth how happy he would have been.

Again the father of that young aspirant and I were discussing the work of Father Thurston and that of the Curé d'Ars to give the world some evidence of the survival of great souls!

Watching the Service I could not help wondering if that father would in some transcendental way know of the results of Logie Baird's work?

Anyway, thank you Reverend Father for the joy of bringing back pleasant memories of the past.

Then, again, I love ritual though I am not a Catholic. It is wonderful to know that the day of materialism is passing.

So please accept this small tribute of appreciation, even from a non-Catholic who loves ritual.

I write because you may receive many condemnatory letters and I would assure you that many like myself appreciated the solemn beauty of the Service. I know your correspondence will be heavy so please do not trouble to acknowledge this.

Please accept my thanks.

Yours faithfully,

GEORGE MORLEY.

A friend working in the B.B.C. was on duty that day and was so full of enthusiasm that he could not wait until he reached home and wrote from Broadcasting House:

I can't stop myself writing this note. This morning's televised Mass and sermon must mark a turning point. The whole thing was moving and magnificent in the extreme. No doubt others have told you so already, but I feel I must join them. It's no small light thing to have watched the great action of the Mass, to have felt suddenly the utter reality of its drama, to have known that at least a million pagans, many of them good but dense, were following it for the first time, too.

Father Agnellus' commentary, being a strict, exact account, must have made the ceremony meaningful as well as beautiful. And Colehan's camera production could hardly have been bettered.

A lot of superlatives in one paragraph, but then it was high time you were vindicated in your logical view that Catholic ritual needs no watering down on the BBC. What thundering vindication this was!

My best friends meanwhile were keeping a watchful eye on me:

Marvellous television today. The whole ceremony beautifully ordered and astonishingly well conducted for the Church. I was with non-Catholics who were most impressed. Sermon, of course, up to standard. Commentary convincing.

I know you don't mind a small criticism from me. During your sermon, I was a trifle distracted by your left thumb, which waggled far too frequently from side to side abaft the nob of the crozier: carping criticism perhaps, but somewhat noticeable because it was a close-up.

There were also letters from children. They tended to arrive in packets ("Please Miss, can we write to our bishop?"). I have kept a few of these letters. They bring to a conclusion this account of the first Mass to be televised in England.

From Mary:
I saw High Mass on Sunday morning. I was not in for the connecation (consecration). But I was in for your blessing. Mummy and Daddy saw it all. I saw the beginning and end. On Sunday it was the feast of the Holy Family. Dr. Moroney watched it in his office. Mummy says you look older than you are. I hope a lot of

people take in your little babies. You asked them very nicely. It is a pity you can not come to our party. You are a very nice Bishop and we hope you shall stay a long time with us. When I grow up I would like to be a nun. I pray for you every night.

Love,

MARY.

From another Mary:

I saw you preach High Mass on television. And two altar boys came with lighted candles. The choir was beautiful. Your prayers were beautiful. Mass is the best thing in the world. Why had you no flowers on the altar?

From Peter:

I saw you on T.V. at 11 a.m. That night I saw Hunpty Dunpty on ice there were a Witch she laughs funny. At childrens T.V. I saw a puppet Theatre at night. You looked better than Hunpty Dunpty. Did the Pope see you?

From John:

I saw you saying Mass in Leeds Cathedral on the television. We are having a party tomorrow. We will have a good time. At the party my Father is showing some films. Catherine was four two day. I remember when you blessed her. When I am big I would like to be a priest and then I could be a Bishop like you but not so clever.

A very different kind of programme was shown on B.B.C. television during the Christmas season two years later. The religious division decided to attempt a completely novel approach. Until that time all Christmas broadcasts had been in the nature of carol services. It was now suggested that since Christmas by tradition is a family celebration the usual studio service should be abandoned in favour of taking the cameras into a home to see how a Christian family celebrates Christmas. I was invited to devise a programme in which I would spend half-an-hour with a Yorkshire Catholic family. The first problem, as Mrs. Beaton might have said, was to find the family. The programme demanded a family with young children but children however lively in normal circumstances are liable to become shy under television lights. After much searching I decided to invite the Harkin family of Batley.

They had received so much publicity during the preceding year that they would probably be able to withstand the terrors of television.

In 1955 Jim Harkin, a prominent figure in the local Labour Party had been elected mayor of Batley. Being a bachelor he had asked his sister-in-law, Mrs. Harkin, to be his mayoress. Mrs. Harkin being a home-loving mother of a large family declined the honour. Uncle Jim therefore invited Mary, his fourteen-year-old niece, to be mayoress of Batley. The national press carried the story together with pictures of Mary, the schoolgirl mayoress. Mary, in addition to her beauty and great personal charm, had the hard head of a Yorkshire lass. She was not prepared to let her social duties as First Lady of Batley ruin her chances of good results in her O levels the following year. She performed her civic duties with great distinction but sent her deputy to the banquets and other late night functions. Because of the novelty of the situation reporters and photographers haunted the Harkins' home during the early months of Uncle Jim's term of office. No family in Yorkshire could have been more capable of coolness under bombardment by television cameras than the Harkins. Having met them all on my visits to the parish of St. Mary of the Angels I felt that they would be willing to do the programme with me. To my delight the parents accepted at once. Although they were retiring by nature (the mother, as I have said, refused to become mayoress) they were delighted that their children had been chosen to be stars of a show of which the bishop was the impresario. The Harkins belonged to that large body of Catholics who are ready to make any sacrifices when asked by the priest.

The programme, due to be shown on the last Sunday of the year, promised to be the most difficult I had yet undertaken. So, in the end, it proved to be. The only television appearance I found more taxing was a programme called "Press Conference" to which I shall refer later. There were several problems about a programme designed to be more like a play than a conversation. Today it would probably be called a 'documentary'. We were all to play parts but they were our roles in real life. The geatest risks were the youngest children. To rehearse their movements or give them words to recite would rob the performance of spontaneity. The success of the programme depended on giving viewers the impression of a pastoral visit to a typical Catholic home. In addition to Mother, Father and Uncle Jim there were seven children: Mary fifteen, Cecilia thirteen, Brigid twelve, Francis ten, Christine nine, Carmel seven and Aidan three.

[92]

The producer, Roy Lakeland, called on the Harkins to survey their living room and decide where to place his cameras. The Harkins' house provided our first problem. With a cast of eleven and the need, as in a play, to create movement (entrances and exits) a whole battery of cameras was needed. It became obvious that it would be impossible to accommodate all the necessary equipment in one living room. Roy Lakeland made a bold decision. He would construct an exact replica of the Harkin home in the Manchester studios of the B.B.C. It had to be an exact reconstruction or the youngest children would not feel really at home. Then they would be neither natural nor articulate. Painstakingly an inventory was compiled. Pictures, ornaments and small items of furniture were transported to Manchester. The rest of the furniture was mocked-up by B.B.C. craftsmen.

This ingenious solution led to our second problem. It would have been in order to mount the programme in the Harkins' home but the transfer to the studios led to legal difficulties. Child performers are rightly protected by law. Without permission of the Lord Chamberlain children under twelve years of age may not provide public entertainment. In the view of the B.B.C.'s legal advisers, by taking our programme to the studios we had brought it into the prohibited category. Fortunately this obstacle was easily overcome.

We were now able to begin more detailed planning. One evening I went to Batley for a conference with Mr. and Mrs. Harkin and the children. We discussed the shape of the programme and began the delicate process of creating enthusiasm in little Carmel and three-year-old Aidan. Our great fear was lest Aidan would become bored or fractious—it was a risk we had to take. The following morning I put the scheme we had devised together in a letter to the Harkins. There were still six weeks to go before we had to do the programme. Mrs. Harkin was fairly confident that this would give her all the time she needed to drill the little ones in their parts. I had decided that it would be a mistake to let the children see me too often before the night of the broadcast.

> Bishop's House,
> Leeds.
> 15th November, 1956.

My dear Mr. and Mrs. Harkin,

I write to thank you most sincerely for the kind way you received the B.B.C. people and myself last night. The living room is just what I had hoped for and I have no doubt that we are going to make a successful telecast. You must pray for its success every night in your family prayers because we may touch many hearts on December 30th.

I thought it would be a good idea to let you know at once the kind of thing I had in mind so that you can talk it over and perhaps think of some good ideas of your own.

The object of the programme is to show that the Faith is the foundation of your happy family life. This is so obviously true that there will be no need to do any acting to prove it. I know what your religion means to you and that is why I chose your family for this programme.

The ideal would be not to have to prepare anything. It would be best if I could just walk into the room and we could start talking. But experience shows that things never work out right if they are left to chance. That is why we must have definite plans of what we are going to say and do. The exact way we act and speak must be left to the actual night otherwise everything will sound false. I want to tell you how the programme is forming in my mind. It is still very vague but the sooner the children know what is expected of them the more likely we are to produce something first class.

A minute or two before we go on the air I shall be talking to Mary about the time she was Mayoress. The T.V. will, so to speak, catch me out. The first thing the public will hear will be something like this: ". . . That is very interesting Mary. I would like you to tell me more about that in a minute or two." The camera meanwhile will have picked me out alone. The public will not know where I am or to whom I am talking. Then I shall face the viewers and tell them what I am doing and where I am. The object of starting with Mary is to explain how it is that I happen to be with the Harkin family. I shall explain that most of my visits are to the sick and old and that I know your family because of the time when Uncle Jim was Mayor.

We shall then talk about Christmas and the children can tell me what they are doing. Those who went to midnight Mass can tell me about that. Then the small ones can tell me about their Christmas presents.

It might be a good idea if Aidan were lucky enough to have been given a Davy Crockett outfit which he could be wearing.

That would make an excellent start. Either Christine or Carmel might have been given a nurse's outfit. If one of the little ones—or even both—were dressed in that way it would enable them to tell me about their auntie the nun. Brigid could run to get her photograph off the sideboard. This would give Mother a chance to tell us about her sister winning the gold medal at the hospital as the nurse of the year.

At some point about here Aidan might say, "We've got a crib". Then all the children could come over to the crib with me and the small ones can point out Our Lord, Our Lady and St. Joseph and so on. When we have sat down again I will turn my attention to Cecilia and Brigid and ask them what they think the lesson of the crib is supposed to be. Cecilia will tell me how Bethelehem shows the love of Our Blessed Lord. He came down to show us the meaning of the love of God. At this point Brigid will tell me that she has a statue of the Sacred Heart. Mother will tell her to go and get it.

At this point I shall be able to talk for a couple of minutes to camera while waiting for Brigid to come back with the statue. I shall look up to the crucifix on the mantelpiece and explain that it is really the same love of God shown to us in the crib and on the cross. When Brigid comes back with the statue I shall look at it. Francis can ask me why the heart is showing. He will say something like, "Why does it have the heart outside where you can see it?" (He will, of course, put it into his own words.) I shall explain about the heart being the sign of love.

While I am doing this Father will interrupt and tell me about the very first wedding present you had and point to the picture of the Holy Family. He will also say that you have a lovely picture of Our Lord and then we can talk about the certificate of consecration which he will take off the wall and hand to me. This will give me another minute or two to explain the effect of devotion to the Sacred Heart on a Catholic family. I shall show how the Sacred Heart and the cross and the crib are all made real to us in the Holy Mass. This will enable me to ask Francis if he is a Mass server. I shall ask him to say some little thing in Latin. For example, the first answer—"*Ad Deum qui laetificat . . .*" Then I might ask why it is in Latin. This is where Mary will chip in and explain that the Church is world-wide and that is why there is this common language. Then I shall ask them who have made their first Holy Communion. Carmel will tell me that she has made it this year. Perhaps Sister at school could teach Carmel a little piece of poetry about Holy Communion. Or she could learn a couple of verses of a First Communion hymn to recite for me. I am sure that the Sisters at school will be able to produce something short and exactly right for the occasion. Her father could mention here that he once served Mass for Bishop Cowgill at Lourdes. At this point I shall suddenly remember that Mary was telling me about her time as mayoress. I might ask her what was her proudest moment. When she has told her story I can turn my attention to Uncle Jim and ask him why he is in politics.

Uncle Jim (I hope!) will be able to tell me he is interested in politics not for their own sake but for what good he can do by being on the Council. I can ask him too what was his proudest moment when he was mayor. The idea here is to show that it is precisely because of their Christian conviction that people like Uncle Jim want to do public work.

Until we time all this it is not possible to know what other things I can bring in. I might speak of Confirmation and the children I have confirmed can mention the fact. These details we can work out later. I shall say a word about your family prayers and towards the end we shall all kneel round the crib and say some short prayers. An Our Father, a Hail Mary, a Gloria, "Sweet Heart of Jesus I implore the grace to love Thee more and more" or "Mary conceived without sin pray for us who have recourse to thee". Then I shall give you my blessing. We shall fade out on this scene.

I am not quite sure what the children should wear. I am wondering if the bigger girls would be best in their school uniform? It is most attractive but perhaps it is not the natural thing for them to be wearing on a Sunday afternoon! The B.B.C. can advise us about that. I am sending a copy of this letter to the B.B.C. for their comments.

I shall be writing to you early in December and I shall fix a Saturday afternoon for us to have a rehearsal. The outline I have given is still vague. Any new ideas the children have of what they would like to say or do will be very acceptable. I am sure that the blessing of God will rest on this programme and on the family so that we may bring many who watch the programme to increase their desire to love Our Lord.

It is hardly necessary to say that the actual broadcast did not include half the topics mentioned in the letter. An unscripted programme takes its own direction. The star of the show was Aidan, the one performer about whom I had any doubts. He was very proud of his Davy Crockett suit and chatted at length about his Christmas presents. He knew that at some time he was expected to say, "We've got a crib." After waiting impatiently for five minutes he felt that it was time to speak up. He said his piece and led me to the crib. He then climbed on to his mother's knee and fell asleep. Aidan was not acting. By this time he was quite unaware that he was on show.

An unrehearsed conversation took place which turned out to be the best remembered part of the broadcast. After I had asked the children what they had done on Christmas night one of them unexpectedly asked me what I had done. I had in fact spent part of the evening with the Moorhouse family whose soldier son had recently died in tragic circumstances during the ill-fated occupation of Suez. He had been taken prisoner by the Egyptians and whether by accident or design was suffocated. As parish priest of Manor Park, it had been my custom on Christmas Day to visit the families bereaved during the preceding year. Their homes were especially sad at Christmas and if the loss were fairly recent they usually felt disinclined for Christmas festivity. They were consoled that the Church remembered them. The thought of my Christmas Days in Manor Park led me to visit the Moorhouse family. The broadcast ended not as planned round the crib but in front of the crucifix where we all knelt to pray for the repose of the young soldier and the consolation of his stricken family. As a premeditated finale this would have been in the worst possible taste. As a spontaneous reaction to the mention of the death of a friend it was a perfectly natural end to a pastoral visit to a Catholic family.

Some years earlier a brief but violent controversy had arisen from an address given by Pope Pius XII to an international congress of Catholic midwives. Press reports suggested that the Pope had bluntly told midwives to save babies and let mothers die. The Pope in fact had merely repeated the common teaching that it is wrong to kill one person directly and deliberately as a means of saving another. In the process of saving the mother's life the doctor may be unable to keep the child alive. Medical as well as Christian ethics require him to do his best to save both mother and child. Pope Pius was not saying anything new. Moralists have always posed hypothetical questions about life saving.

A favourite moral conundrum is to decide which person to save from drowning if there is room for only one more in the life-boat and your wife, your child and your mother-in-law are all struggling in the water. (This example is used not only by waggish professors of moral theology but also by comedians.) In his address the Pope had merely expanded the terse reply given in the last century by the Holy Office when asked whether in a medical emergency mother or child should be given preference: *"Consulenda vita et matris et prolis"* (Look after the life of both mother and child).

The actual words of the Pope were these:

> Every human being, even the child in its mother's womb, has the right to life *immediately* from God, not from the parents or any human society or authority. Hence there is no man, no human authority, no science, no 'indication' of a medical, eugenic, social, economic, or moral order that can offer or give a valid juridical title to a *direct* deliberate disposing of an innocent human life—that is to say, a disposal that aims at its destruction, whether as an end in itself or as a means to another end that is, perhaps, in no way illicit in itself. Thus, for instance, to save the life of the mother is a most noble end; but the *direct* killing of the child as a means to that end is not lawful.

A few days later (26th November, 1951) in view of the misinterpretation of his message in secular newspapers the Pope issued a clarification in an address to the Christian Family Front:

> Innocent human life, in whatsoever condition it is found, is withdrawn, from the very first moment of its existence, from any direct deliberate attack . . . This principle holds good for the life of the child as well as for that of the mother. Never and in no case has the Church taught that the life of the child must be preferred to that of the mother. It is erroneous to put the question with this alternative: either the life of the child or that of the mother. No, neither the life of the mother nor that of the child may be subjected to an act of direct suppression. In the one case as in the other, there can be but one obligation: to make every effort to save the lives of both.

The exact meaning of the Pope's words was explained and vindicated by a non-Catholic mother: In a letter to *The Star*, a London evening newspaper, Lady Rhy-Williams made a plea for good sense:

> Sir,—I write as a Protestant to deplore the tragic misunderstandings which are developing with regard to the recent Papal statement about midwifery practice.
>
> Roman Catholic doctors and midwives are already being caused much unhappiness through the loss of confidence of their patients, following the past week's sensational discussion of the Pope's address. This unfortunate development is only one of the many bad things which will happen if indignation continues to be worked up without proper understanding of the situation.
>
> The truth is that, if the doctor or midwife understand their business, and provide proper ante-natal care for their patients (as the free Health Service in Britain enables them to do so without counting the sometimes heavy cost involved) the much-publicised dilemma concerning the sacrifice of either mother or child during childbirth can never arise.
>
> The operation of Caesarian section is now so perfectly performed and so safe that risks are never taken with the mother's life by forcing her to face a dangerous confinement. If anything could go wrong she is sent to hospital, and the life of both the mother and baby is safeguarded by modern surgery.
>
> The patients of Catholic doctors and midwives are not only quite as safe as any others, but very possibly more so, inasmuch as the Catholic practitioner will be likely to take even more care than his Protestant colleague to avoid a dilemma which he must naturally dread, and which he knows he can avoid by the careful examination and ante-natal treatment of his patient.
>
> Behind the present outbreak of criticism of the Roman Catholic position concerning the sanctity of all human life lies the rather unattractive spectre of Dr. Malthus, the originator of the belief that everyone now living would be richer if fewer children had to be supported.

While the controversy was still boiling the B.B.C. invited me to appear in 'Press Conference'. This was a weekly programme in which a public figure was interrogated on his attitude towards some event currently in the news. The regular team of questioners included three formidable journalists—Francis Williams (later ennobled in recognition of his service to the press), Geoffrey—later Sir Geoffrey—Cox of the *News Chronicle* and Henry Fairlie of *The Spectator*. Whenever I had seen this team in action I had felt strong sympathy for the victims of their pitiless cross-examination. Alarmed by the prospect of submitting myself to a similar ordeal I declined the B.B.C.'s invitation to 'Press Conference'. I said quite frankly that the risk was too great. I would have been happy simply to defend the Pope's position in the mother and child debate but the ensuing programme might range over any number of controversies for which I would be unprepared. We were still in the early days of television. I had not yet become experienced in the use of this medium which is so much more treacherous than sound radio for the novice. Catholics would not like to see one of their bishops being made to look foolish by these scintillating performers.

The B.B.C. had traced me to the small Northumberland village of Bellingham where I was staying with the parish priest, Father Dick Delaney. He had a second guest, Father Patsy Redmond of Newcastle-on-Tyne, one of the most brilliant priests of our day. Close friends since student days we three always spent a few days together during the Christmas season. After answering the B.B.C. call I told Dick and Patsy that I had refused to appear on the programme. Far from approving my decision they accused me of neglecting an opportunity to defend the Faith. What I had regarded as prudence they called cowardice. They were still denouncing me when the telephone bell rang again. It was once more the B.B.C. This time the spokesman was Father Agnellus Andrew, a member of staff at Broadcasting House who had been pressed into service to persuade me to change my mind. With the abuse of Delaney and Redmond ringing in my ears I had little option but to give in. After two days spent framing answers to countless imaginary questions I went lamb-like to London to present myself before my shearers. In the event the programme was astonishingly untraumatic. Henry Fairlie, of whom I stood particularly in awe, turned out to be easy to handle. He told me after the programme that he had been quite terrified of meeting a Catholic bishop in theological argument.

The panel began with the topical question. In reply I gave the substance of the Pope's words and his later clarification to the Christian Family Front. There was obviously nothing more to be said on the subject. Within two minutes the panel began to broach the other questions they had prepared for my discomfiture. If I had ever doubted the efficacy of prayer my experience that night would have reassured me. During the previous two days I had solicited the prayers of children and contemplative nuns. This must have been why the panel chose subjects about which I had uncannily up-to-date knowledge. The strategy on which they had apparently agreed was to take me on a tour of the world to show that whatever fair reputation it might enjoy in England, the Catholic Church abroad was sinister. Geoffrey Cox questioned me about the Movement. This was a pressure group in Australia which had split the Labour Party and threatened to divide the Catholics of Victoria and New South Wales. A month before the Movement would not have been even a name to me but only a few days earlier I had been in correspondence with a sociologist friend in Sydney. He had given me a graphic description of the goings on in the Australian Labour Party and contrasted the Movement with the organisation of Catholic trade unionists in Western Germany. Astonished by my knowledge of the Australian scene the panel quickly moved to the Rhineland to question me about the Church's impact on industrial relations in Germany. Thanks to my Australian friend I was once again at ease. We became so involved in the problem of Catholic political parties on the continent that time ran out before any difficult question had been reached. Next morning the television critic of the *Daily Mail* protested that a professedly impromptu discussion had been rigged for the benefit of a Roman Catholic bishop. That is some indication of my good fortune—all due to prayer and my friend in the antipodes.

While I was Bishop of Leeds I did not appear with any frequency on television. At that time the names of Malcolm Muggeridge, Robin Day and David Frost were still unknown in television circles. I was destined to appear with these and other celebrities of the small screen in later years both in Liverpool and Westminster.

CHAPTER
SIX

WHEN I MET CARDINAL GILROY IN BARCELONA I ACCEPTED HIS INVITATION
to speak at the Sydney Eucharistic Congress in the spring of 1953 on
condition that by that time I would have completed the visitation of
all the parishes of the diocese. I was not yet fifty years of age and found
little difficulty in undertaking a very strenuous programme. There was
no doubt that I could finish my rounds but I was not altogether happy
at the prospect of going all the way to Australia merely to give two or
three lectures. I had no doubt that there were better speakers among
the priests and bishops in Australia but, as the Gospel warns us, local
prophets are without honour. A man from the other side of the world
is more attractive provided he has been in the news. Inglorious Miltons
must remain mute. To go ten thousand miles to give a couple of talks
seemed a reckless expenditure of money, although the money would
not be mine.

I resolved the problem by applying to the War Office for a temporary
assignment to the armed forces. At that time there were two wars in
progress in the Far East—one in the Malayan jungle, the other in Korea
where the United States and Commonwealth forces were fighting a
largely Chinese communist army. There were Koreans on both sides
but all the arms and most of the men were supplied by the great powers.
Since I had to go to Singapore on my way to Australia I offered to make
a detour to visit all the British and Commonwealth troops in Malaya,
Korea, China (Hong Kong and the New Territories) and Japan. Thus
I sought to make my journey worthwhile. Almost by return of post my
offer was gladly accepted. It was thought that the young Catholic

[102]

National Service men would be encouraged by the sight of a bishop from home. The army accepted responsibility for my lodging and travel during the whole time I would be with Farelf (Far Eastern Land Forces). The Royal Air Force or the Royal Navy undertook to supply any transport or hospitality the army could not provide. This gave a new interest to my journey. It would obviously justify the Australian visit if I could also visit the comparatively forgotten forces in the Far East. My only experience with the military had been with airmen and soldiers who were looking after barrage balloons and anti-aircraft guns in my parish of Manor Park. The service people I had met were mostly civilians in uniform for the duration of war. In the Far East there would be many professionals and I looked forward to meeting real men-at-arms.

Catholics in Australia are more involved in politics than their British co-religionists and their number is large—the percentage of Catholics in the population is three times as great as in England. The majority of Catholic workers belonged to the A.L.P. (Australian Labour Party) which had been infiltrated by communists. Socialists, whether Marxist or Fabian, tended to be anti-Catholic as a result of their materialistic creed. I was briefed to give a vast gathering of Catholic men a summary of the Church's teaching on social justice together with an exposure of communist strategy. The text of my address was required six weeks in advance. I did not have enough time to finish it before leaving Leeds but sent it from Rome where I spent a few days on my outward journey.

While I was in Rome I said Mass at the Regina Coeli prison. As I have already said, I had a special interest in prisons and I wanted to compare the Italian prisons with their English, Spanish and American equivalents. This building, euphoniously described as *carcere iudiziario*, reminded me of Barcelona. Since all unshaved Italians look like Al Capone my first impression of Regina Coeli was daunting but after Mass I found that despite their looks most of the prisoners were no more than petty thieves. The prisoners bore with serenity the imperfect Italian of my short sermon and were obviously pleased to see me. Before leaving Rome I was received in audience by Pope Pius XII. I told him of my coming visit to the British and Commonwealth forces and he graciously commissioned me to give the papal blessing to all the service men and women of whatever nationality I was to encounter on my travels in the Far East.

I was a passenger on a Comet, a jet aircraft which was still a rarity on passenger routes. It was exhilarating to be pulled against gravity in an almost perpendicular thrust and to surmount the clouds within five minutes. As soon as we reached maximum height we lost all sensation of movement. The Comet was a novelty and passengers balanced pencils on the meal trays to test the motionlessness of which B.O.A.C. boasted. Unfortunately, after three successive accidents in each of which the machine disintegrated with total loss of passengers and crew the planes had to have modifications. We stopped to re-fuel half-way from Rome to Karachi at Bahrein in the Persian Gulf at about one a.m. I had never experienced such heat as came off the tarmac. Bahrein, for all I know, may be one of the most delightful spots in the Near East but my stay in Bahrein airport did nothing to lead me to think so. The few off-duty men in the lounge where we were put to wait nearly all seemed to be in an alcoholic haze which may have helped to deaden their pain. We had to stay some hours in Bahrein because of fog in Karachi where we were later to land. In those days pilots flying jets were forbidden to take off unless they knew that flying conditions at the next stopping point were favourable.

One of the luxuries Catholics now enjoy is being allowed to receive Holy Communion without fasting from midnight. In 1953 the full eucharistic fast was still in force. The long delay at Bahrein therefore imposed extra hardship since I could not have so much as a cup of tea to fortify me for the long hop to Karachi which we would not reach until ten o'clock. The Archbishop of Karachi who met the plane had thoughtfully arranged for me to say Mass immediately on arrival in a little chapel near the airport. This thoughtfulness was as much appreciated as the cup of tea which I swallowed as soon as I had taken off my vestments. My clothes already felt unbearably heavy so at Archbishop's House after a cold shower I put on a white cassock provided by the archbishop who was of my own height and build. Wearing a white cassock made me look (but not feel) like the Pope. Cool and refreshed I sat down to sort out my impressions. Scenes in the East are startlingly different from anything a European has ever seen. The drive from the airport took an hour. The twelve-mile route from the military airport (where we landed because the civil airport was under repair) was lined with the miserable encampments of Moslem Indians who were refugees from Hindu persecution.

I had already seen misery in the *barracas* of Barcelona and was destined in years to come to see worse squalor in Hong Kong, Palestine and Peru but this was my first sight of vast, concentrated human degradation. The Moslems had fled to Karachi to avoid massacre after the partition of the sub-continent. These refugees will do almost any thing for a living but the 'almost' is significant. Although officially there is no longer a caste system in operation there are certain chores which no self-respecting Hindu or Moslem will do. Filthy work must be left to the Sweepers who are regarded as sub-human. I discovered that many of these outcasts are Catholics. It went some way towards lifting my depression to know that the Church had provided refuge for the Sweepers. Later I discovered the reason. These outcasts had nothing to lose by becoming Christians. In this they were unlike the Moslems who in Pakistan really practise their religion and gain strength from it. In addition to the advantage of exchanging superstition for the faith the Sweepers had nothing to lose socially. They gained by becoming members of a community in which they were accepted as equal children of God by priests, nuns and fellow Catholic laymen.

There had been a riot in Karachi on the morning of my arrival. As we drove through the city we saw everywhere police carrying long sticks. The explosive political situation was bedevilled—if that is not an incongruous expression—by religious agitators. I made some notes at the time in an attempt to understand what was happening. For what is is worth this is what I wrote:

A fanatical set of Moslems led by intransigent Mullahs are demanding government action against the nationalist Moslems (Ahmadiyya). The Foreign Minister Sir M. Zalfrullah Khan is a member of the Ahmadiyya. Hence the political significance of the dispute. The dissidents come from East Punjab. They oppose not only the Ahmadiyya but also all forms of Christianity. They maintain that Christ was not crucified. He died quietly in Kashmir.

I sensed enough of the atmosphere after the riot in Karachi that day to appreciate many years later something of the difficulties between Pakistan and India and between East and West Pakistan. Occasionally one meets fanatical Christians but fanaticism in the name of the Prophet, endemic wherever Mohammedanism is taken seriously, is far fiercer. Religion is capable of generating more passionate emotion than race or sex. Hindu and Moslem, Jew and Arab, Protestant and Catholic (in Northern Ireland) inherit mutual hostility in the name of the God of love and provide a powerful argument for atheism.

After a short rest I set out to explore the city of Karachi. It is less European than Tokyo which I was to visit later in the tour. The most distinctive feature of the Orient is its smell. I have not been able to

[105]

diagnose this smell but I have sampled it in towns as far apart as Jerusalem and Singapore. It is a musky sort of smell. If, as the geography books tell us, musk is found only in the glands of the small hornless ruminants of Central Asia these secretions have extraordinary power. They pervade the whole of the Middle and Far East. Perhaps camels, spices, ordure and dirt combine to give the East its characteristic smell. I merely record that I found the smells more impressive than the sights and sounds. My first visit was naturally made to the cathedral. Like other cathedral churches in the East, including Bombay, it has St. Patrick for patron. These churches were built by the Spanish Jesuits who might have been expected to choose their own St. Francis Xavier but since the money came mostly from Irish soldiers, at that time building the British Empire, St. Patrick carried off the title. In the cathedral compound were schools and colleges and an impressive hospital. A new wing of the hospital was due to open three months later but the rest of the planned building had to be postponed indefinitely because a refugee family was occupying part of the site. It was unthinkable to move a refugee Moslem family even to enable the Christian community to take possession of its own land. The hospital when finished would be staffed by American Medical Missionaries from Missouri. Since those days there has been such a decline in the numbers of American Sisters that today the hospital is no doubt run by native nuns.

On the same evening I called at the convent of the Franciscan Missionaries of Mary to see Christine Holden (Sister Thomas More). I had received Christine into the Church when I was parish priest of Manor Park and she was a teacher. Apart from the joy of seeing her again there was a special reason for my visit. Christine was the only daughter of a Nonconformist minister. I had broken my journey in Karachi so as to be able to bring back a reassuring report to her parents. The next morning I paid a longer visit to the Franciscan Missionaries to inspect the orphanage and high school. It is not unusual for nuns to run schools of different status. The object, as here in Karachi, is to use the fees to provide free places for poor children and orphans. The Notre Dame Sisters, the best known teaching nuns, have a rule never to open a fee-paying school without also providing free education for poor children.

Archbishop Miltenburg, a Dutch Franciscan, was in the odd position of being both Archbishop of Karachi and Inter-nuncio to the State of Pakistan. It is hard to understand why a small State maintains embassies (or for that matter nunciatures) throughout the world. In these days of instant communication, the Queen's Courier carrying the diplomatic bag appears vaguely anachronistic. In times of crisis embassies come into their own and this presumably is what justifies the enormous expense of their permanent presence. It was hard to see what advantage to souls came from the archbishop's activities as inter-nuncio. During my short stay in Karachi I saw how his pastoral work suffered from his diplomatic functions. Archbishop Miltenburg, a Dutchman with all the teutonic virtues, took his work seriously. (This is not a subtle way of calling him humourless. He was an amusing and charming host without a trace of self-importance.) He regarded the duties of inter-nuncio with deadly earnestness. One of these duties was to be at the airport to greet important members of the government whenever they were leaving the country or returning from abroad. His presence was required for this purpose with fair regularity—several times during my short stay. When I remonstrated at the waste of time he explained that the Pakistani politicians were still novices needing the bolster of protocol. As orientals they felt that they would lose face if the diplomats did not greet their comings and goings. If Miltenburg did not appear the Holy See, in turn, would lose face. It was all rather puzzling to a non-diplomat. Today the Archbishop of Karachi has no diplomatic status. No protocol now forces him to leave his flock to spend hours at airports or at parties.

The British High Commissioner, like many in the service of the commonwealth, was an Irish Catholic. He came to lunch accompanied by Colonel Archer Shee the military attaché, also a Catholic and already known to me. Hearing of my interest in prison welfare the High Commissioner promised to arrange for me to visit the Karachi prison. He telephoned the same evening to say that the prison governor would be expecting me at three p.m. the following day. The archbishop, who had never seen the prison, said he would come with me. The next day when the time was nearly half-past two I began to feel anxious. I did not know how long it would take to reach the prison but to be on the safe side I asked the archbishop if we were running the risk of being late. He was much amused at my question and remarked how typical it was of an Englishman to worry about being punctual. "There are two kinds of time here," he said, "we call one English time and the other Pakistani time." He then explained that in Pakistan it was under stood that everyone would arrive half-an-hour after the appointed time. To arrive early—i.e. on time—would cause confusion.

So we arrived at the prison gates not at three o'clock but at three thirty p.m. The governor and his staff in full uniform were awaiting us. After a curt greeting from the governor the tour of the prison began. As we walked along the governor answered my questions politely but coldly. Although he was not actually rude it was clear something was wrong. I wondered if as a Moslem he disliked playing host to two Catholic bishops. It was even possible that as an ex-colonial he was still resentful of the British. I summoned up courage to ask him what was wrong. It turned out that he was suffering from that most insufferable of all oriental misfortunes—loss of face. Given the chance he expounded his grievance with eloquent passion. Few of the young prison officers, he said, had any idea of keeping time but he had been in the prison service in the time of the British Raj. (In his view, he told me later, the British had left too soon.) He was always telling his men that the only way to run the prison was on British lines. When my visit had been arranged he was overjoyed. He paraded his men at a quarter to three and told them that this British bishop would arrive outside the prison at about two minutes to the hour. The car would then proceed slowly up the driveway. At three p.m. precisely the Bishop of Leeds would alight from his car. I explained to the disconsolate governor that I had wanted to arrive exactly at three p.m. but had been prevented from doing so on the grounds that in Karachi three o'clock meant three thirty. The governor was somewhat mollified by my excuse and agreed that unfortunately it was valid. He undertook to tell his men that it was their habit of bad time-keeping which had led me, much against my will, to come late. Thus his face and the British reputation for punctuality would be saved.

The Karachi prison is quite unlike an English prison. It is bright, clean and airy and, at least in the daytime, pleasant. I refer to the building. I doubt if the treatment of prisoners is as pleasant as that in an English prison. It is impossible to make strict comparisons because the caste system, allegedly non-existent in India and Pakistan, survives even in prison. There are three classes of prisoner —A, B and C. These, so far as I could judge, are social divisions. Class A prisoners wear their own clothes and have good food. Class B wear prison uniform but enjoy the same diet as class A. Class C are the lowest types. Living conditions are, if possible, worse than in their own homes. Not surprisingly the governor tried to dissuade me from visiting class C. Herded in huge pens these men are more to be pitied than the inmates of our own over-crowded, unhygienic prisons. They look cowed although there was no evidence of violence (no bruises, black-eyes or cut heads). I had no reason to suspect any official brutality. The men work an eight-hour day during which they are treated like normal workers. Once work is over they are locked up in their unlit pens where they must observe strict silence until the rising bell at six o'clock the next morning. This may seem harsh but until recently silence was the rule in prisons throughout the world. Prisoners had to keep at a distance from each other when taking exercise precisely to prevent conversation. The reason was that the authorities feared that prisoners in association would organise revolts and plan future crimes.

The governor, as I have said, was not disposed to take me to see the class C prisoners. Although it was not really late he explained that they were already locked up for the night. Only after entreaty on my part did he at last agree to let me see these men. In the large pen there were far too many bodies for any sort of comfort. There was no furniture at all—not a chair, stool or bed. It was most depressing. The emaciated bodies of the cowering prisoners completed a picture of unrelieved gloom. I might have been less depressed if at that time I had seen living conditions in the slums and villages of Asia. I was to become accustomed to the sight of stark poverty. In the lives of saints we read of the heroic virtue which led them to subsist by day on crusts and to spend their nights on the bare ground. What the saints in the West did for the love of God the poor in the East do as a way of life.

Finding the equivalent of a caste system in prison would have been less of a shock if I had known more about the customs and folk-lore of the Indian peninsula. It would have been unthinkable to put a man of high caste with the uncivilised men in class C—who also had their standards. They would dust a room but they would never clean a lavatory block. This could be done only by the Sweepers. Class C men might be criminals but they were not pariahs. It helps to measure the distance between East and West to imagine cleaners coming in from outside to clean lavatories in Parkhurst prison because such a task would be offensive to the dignity of men doing time for robbery with violence. My bewilderment in Karachi gaol was profound but after a few more days I began to understand something of the social outlook of the East.

Caste (which is not part of their tradition) is found among Moslems only where, as in India, they have absorbed the tribal customs of their neighbours. Caste began as calculated snobbery. Regarding themselves as uniquely pure-blooded—caste originally meant chaste—Top People kept aloof from lower mortals. No social disease is more contagious than snobbery (social distinctions are rigorously observed below stairs) hence the caste system easily spread from Brahmins to the lesser breeds. To the scrupulous Hindu life can become burdensome through social restrictions and ritual washings. If, for example, the shadow of an untouchable falls upon him he is made unclean. The orient is prolific in complicated rules of behaviour. We had to go to the Polynesians for the word 'taboo'. Hinduism is as much a social system as a religion in our sense of the word. It is polytheistic but none of its gods is God. Hindus have a sense of the supernatural but do not worship God after the fashion of Christians or Moslems. The Hindu religion, in other words, is more a code than a creed. There is no Hindu act of faith. Despite the lack of what we call religion the sub-continent of India is more spiritual than materialistic in outlook. To the newly arrived European the orient is bound to be mysterious but it was made more puzzling for me by the caste system in gaol.

The Y.P.s (young prisoners) are kept under rigid discipline. Until shortly before the time of my visit they had not been separated from the older men but a recent incident involving a man and a boy had led to segregation. Despite severe flogging for homosexual offences they were as difficult to stamp out here as in any prison in the world. At the time of my visit a high wall was being built to separate the Y.P.s from the men. In the East punishment is acknowledged to be the main purpose of prisons. Deterrence, of course, has its place but even for the young rehabilitation has no high priority. Oriental penologists reason simply that if prison is made really unpleasant criminals will not want to return. There were twelve condemned cells of which only five were occupied. The prisoners, due to be hanged during the next few days, were in single cells bereft of furniture. Although none was a Christian all these unfortunate men were glad to talk to me. They seemed pathetically grateful not to have been left out. One man with a beautiful voice began chanting his Moslem prayers as we left. The governor was not impressed with this show of piety. The man he said, had committed a savage murder and would be hanged as soon as possible. When I asked why no material comforts were available to the condemned the governor was genuinely puzzled. He replied as if to a backward child: "You don't provide comforts for men you are about to put to death." The east wind is chilly.

Among the prisoners were some mullahs who had been sentenced for organising the recent riots in Karachi. At first they were not disposed to talk to me. Being very anti-establishment they were ostentatiously unreceptive of my greetings. After I had explained that as a bishop I was also a kind of mullah and therefore a fellow man-of-God they dropped their antagonism and began to talk. The Archbishop of Karachi, who regarded them as a gang of political rascals, did not join the conversation. To me they appeared to be splendid fanatics. The most eloquent mullah happened to be also the best looking with a flowing black beard and flashing white teeth. He explained their religious stand. They were ineluctably pledged to fight for the removal of the Ahmadiyyas from power on the grounds that they are heretics. Their heresy is to hold that Mohammed is not the only Prophet. In the view of these mullahs the Ahmadiyyas deserved to be treated in the same way as Hindus, Christians, Parsees or any other infidels. Ahmadiyyas, the mullahs said, had all the best jobs and were the real power behind the politicians.

I next visited the prison hospital. Its atmosphere shocked me because I had not yet visited any of Karachi's civilian hospitals. This I was to do the following day in tragic circumstances. The prison hospital was an improvement on the civilian hospitals which are not only over-crowded with patients but also overrun by relatives who must share in the nursing if the patient is to receive proper attention. When they are able to leave their beds patients do not wear prison clothes but this seemed to be the only concession made to sick prisoners. The wards were squalid. An all male staff rarely manages to create a bright atmosphere even in well-endowed hospitals in the West. There is magic in a woman's touch but there was no such touch and, indeed, no suggestion of any other kind of magic in this infirmary. The doctor was unkempt and looked villainous. I wondered if he were a prisoner but obviously I could not ask. There is a surplus of doctors in many cities in the East. There, as in Latin America, native doctors are reluctant to go to remote areas where they are urgently needed. I did not expect to find Pakistan's finest doctors in a prison but I was depressed by what I saw.

The last stage of my prison visit took me to the women's block. The building was of the same type but the atmosphere was entirely different. This was interesting because the atmosphere of Holloway, the women's prison in London, is not notably different from that of Pentonville the neighbouring men's prison. It is a sociological fact that where religion is practised women criminals are few. Here in Karachi the whole female prison population of Pakistan was confined. There were only eleven prisoners of whom four were mentally defectives. The officer in charge was a Catholic woman who was enthusiastic about the improvements the governor had introduced into the women's section of the prison. Before his time the women enjoyed no more privacy than the men. They were not allowed even to wash and bathe in private. As a result of his reforms time spent in prison was no longer degrading to these women of whom none was a criminal. All had been convicted only of misdemeanours and would soon be released.

The women's block of Karachi prison underlined what I had learned in other prisons serving communities where religion is a feature of national life. One such prison was in the Irish Republic. I had visited Mountjoy prison during Holy Week 1950 while preaching the annual retreat in Newman's chapel at St. Stephen's Green, Dublin. There were only three women in custody of whom two had been sentenced for minor offences and would be discharged before the week was out. The other had the doubtful distinction of being the only convicted criminal among the women of the Republic of Ireland. Many years after this tour of the Far East I visited Malta to preach at the celebrations of the centenary of St. Paul's shipwreck. During my short stay in Malta I happened to visit on the same morning the old people's home of the Little Sisters of the Poor and the prison. In the women's section of the prison I found only three people. Two were Sisters of Mercy and the other a prisoner. She was an old lady convicted of persistent begging. Later that day I sent a note to the Governor of Malta suggesting that in honour of St. Paul the old lady might be transferred from the prison to the Little Sisters' Home where she would not need to beg. The Little Sisters readily agreed to receive her and the next day the splendid governor, Sir Maurice Dorman, exercised his clemency. Catholic Malta is a long cry from Moslem Pakistan but the principle is the same. Religion refines whether God is called Lord or Allah. Without religion to refine them women easily sink to the level of men. It would make a doctoral thesis for an enterprising sociologist to contrast female crime in Northern and Southern Europe or in North and Latin America.

I left the prison to the melodious sound of prisoners chanting their evening prayers. This was not done to impress me. The prisoners could not see me and did not know when I was due to leave the prison. Moslems would not pray merely to impress onlookers. They seem to lack that weakness which Catholics call 'human respect' (the petty cowardice which, for example, inhibits us from confessing our faith in the company of unbelievers). I noticed on more than one occasion that Moslems of every social class observe the times for prayer in public places without apparent self-consciousness. It made me recall my first visit to Ireland as a boy of fourteen when I was amazed to see everyone stop work in the fields to pray when the Angelus bell rang at twelve o'clock. I wonder if that custom has survived in a land more renowned for physical than moral courage.

On the way home from prison the archbishop took me to see some Pakistani Sisters who had offered their services to the local authorities to nurse the sick poor. They had been given charge of a maternity home which they ran with great efficiency and compassion. The expectant mothers, mostly Moslems, were obviously well content to be cared for by nuns. The small religious congregation to which these Sisters belong is a native foundation. This is a sign of the times—a sign of which congregations with headquarters in Europe have had to take note. In every former colony the spirit of independence is reaching religious organisations. It is now anachronistic to have white superiors in convents of predominantly coloured Sisters. I saw here and elsewhere evidence that the time has come to replace European ecclesiastical superiors—including bishops—with indigenous candidates. India had already begun to prohibit entrance of foreign missionaries. Before long in this Moslem nation Christians will survive only if they can claim the rights of citizenship. Whatever future there may be for Christian communities in Pakistan lies with native institutions or international communities with native superiors. These Pakistani Sisters were missionaries in their own land. Beloved by their patients they were respected by the civic authorities. Most of the mothers were in poor physical condition owing to malnutrition and, in about half the cases, venereal disease. The incidence of v.d. was extremely high in Karachi— probably as high as it was to become in Britain when youth became liberated from sexual "taboos".

Next morning during breakfast I received an alarming message from the High Commissioner. A Comet aircraft, not yet in commission for passengers, had blown up taking off from Karachi airport. It was being flown to Australia by a Canadian air crew and six de Havilland engineers. I made at once for the hospital to which the injured would be taken. I arrived at the hospital within half-an-hour to find that the matron had not even heard of the crash. I rang up the airport from the hospital to be given the grim news that there was nothing left of the crew. The aircraft failing to clear a low wall at the edge of the airport had exploded with such force that almost nothing remained of this newest and fastest Comet. There was no point in waiting at the hospital but out of courtesy I visited one or two wards before driving to the airport. This hospital was not notably different from the prison infirmary except that the wards were more over-crowded. There were no sheets on the beds, the whole place was grimy, the atmosphere was disheartening. There were people everywhere. In the East families move in with their sick relatives to make sure that they do not die of starvation or neglect. The older nurses were listless and to Western eyes slatternly though the younger ones were clean and tidy. One nurse, spotless in her white uniform, hurried to greet me and to my surprise knelt to kiss my ring. A convert to the faith she had been instructed by the Dutch priests. She must have learned hygiene as well as religion from the Dutch. Cleanliness was evidently part of her godliness.

Going from the hospital to the airport I called at St. Patrick's Cathedral to make tentative arrangements for some sort of memorial service for the victims of the crash. A Requiem Mass might be inappropriate as nobody knew if any of the dead were Catholics. I felt it my duty to go out to the airport in order to express sympathy to someone. I arrived at the air terminal at exactly the same moment as the High Commissioner. He felt that although we could do nothing we ought to show the flag, so to speak, on behalf of the relatives of the British and Commonwealth airmen. We walked to the scene of the crash but little remained beyond scorched earth and minute fragments of the Comet. We were joined by the Canadian travel representative. His function was to be the someone to whom we could express sympathy. We told him there would be a memorial service in the cathedral that afternoon. For those pre-ecumenical days we were doing rather well—the High Commissioner and Canadian were both Catholics yet none of us suggested a Requiem Mass. We devised a memorial service which included singing by the boys of the high school. The parish priest went from the cathedral to the local cemetery where, with the Anglican archdeacon, he committed token remains to a common grave.

In the evening I went to the parish church of St. Francis known as the slaughter house church because it is built next door to the city's abattoir. This is the dormitory suburb of the Sweepers and outcasts of whom many are Catholics. Their hovels are degrading but they spend most of their time in the streets. They are driven indoors only by the need to eat and sleep. On alighting from the archbishop's car we were immediately surrounded by hordes of half-naked urchins with their ragged parents. Like the poor almost everywhere these people obviously love their priests. Whether Dutch or Pakistani the priests were equally acceptable. Though a stranger I was taken at once to their hearts: "*Salaam, padri-gi!*" *Padri*, I learned, is the Urdu for father. (Hence the army term for chaplain.) The 'gi' is the diminutive of respect (like the Russian 'little father'). The stench in the slaughter house area was worse than the normal Karachi smell which it reinforced. After only two days I had learned to live with the smell but I hoped I would never become insensitive to the misery and squalor. The chapel boy who took us in charge guided us to little shrines in houses and to the tawdry chapel. The crowds of Sweepers and their children followed us in swelling numbers. The chapel boy said that most of them went regularly to Mass on Sundays. He was not telling lies but merely saving face. It would not have done for the English bishop to go away with a low opinion of the poor Sweepers.

Later the parish priest told me that few of his people go to Mass every Sunday but they say their prayers regularly and send for the priest in time of trouble. I am sure they do all that God requires of them. These despised Sweepers still haunt me after twenty years. I wince mentally when I recall them. Men and women for ever bent down scouring, cleaning, sweeping. Like the publican in the Gospel they do not dare lift up their heads. They are ignored or looked down on as little more than animals. Despite the words of the psalmist[1] they must come to regard themselves not as little lower than the angels but as little higher than the beasts. I have often thought how wonderful it would be to organise a Sweepers' strike throughout the Indian peninsula. If they all refused to be scavengers the rest of the population would have to do its own dirty work. Many a missionary must have longed to preach mutiny to the lower castes and outcasts but in this fiercely Moslem country that would spell the end of Christianity. As in most revolutions an uprising would bring terrible suffering to the humblest people. It is a source of pride to the Christians that nobody is too lowly to be cherished by the Church. If the Christian religion were set aside the poor Sweepers would lose their only source of consolation. The Church alone treats them as men and women made in God's image. The dilemma is that for their sake the Church cannot rouse them to rebel but left to themselves they may never find the spirit to rise from misery. Communists would not hesitate to set these down-trodden people against their exploiters. Unfortunately if communists became the masters the people would only be exchanging old chains for new—as the Catholics of Kerala were to learn a few years later.

[1] "Thou hast made him a little less than the angels" (Ps. viii: 5).

CHAPTER
SEVEN

THIS WAS MY LAST NIGHT IN KARACHI UNTIL I RETURNED THERE AS Archbishop of Westminster on my way to the Eucharistic Congress in Bombay ten years later. The Comet was due to leave for Singapore early in the morning. The memory of what had happened to the last Comet to take off from Karachi was uncomfortably fresh in my mind. If I had foreseen that in due course the Comet I was to board would also disintegrate in flight I would have been even more uneasy. I slept until four o'clock, said Mass and waited for the call to board the aircraft. It came at ten thirty a.m. By the time it reached Singapore it was exactly twenty-four hours overdue.

The Royal Air Force has a saying:
> If you've time to spare go by air.
I reflected when landing in Singapore:
> There's a worse fate than arriving late.
The time in Singapore was three a.m.

Although a day late it made no difference to the programme which had been arranged by the service chiefs. The first day had thoughtfully been left free for me to adapt to tropical conditions. From Changi, the R.A.F. airport, passengers were taken by bus to the civil airport at which the Comet had been expected to land. Despite the early hour Colonel Davey who was to be my host throughout my stay in Singapore, was awaiting me with Father Tobin, the senior Catholic chaplain. Although they had been waiting since midnight they made light of their lost sleep. I was to discover as the weeks went by that not only Catholics but all people in the services irrespective of religious affiliation took immense trouble to make my visit pleasant.

We arrived at the army barracks at five a.m. Colonel Davey took me at once to the garrison chapel and insisted on serving my Mass although by this time he must have been exhausted. Immediately after Mass I went to bed and despite the humid heat managed to sleep for a couple of hours. When I awoke the thoughtful Father Tobin was waiting in the next room with a white cotton cassock to replace my heavy black suit. With the help of a huge fan attached to the ceiling of the room like the propeller of an aircraft I began to find the heat bearable. Hilda, the efficient and gracious wife of the colonel, gave us all coffee and by eight o'clock with energy restored I was ready to face the first day of my tour of duty. Father Tobin had worked out every hour of the days ahead and had anticipated my personal needs in remarkable detail. He took me to a spare room where I found Tong Heng, the tailor, waiting with tape measure in hand. Tong Heng, one of Father Tobin's flock, had already made me a light cassock guessing my measurements from a photograph Father Tobin had cut out of an English newspaper. It was a perfect fit. Tong undertook to have two more cassocks ready by the next morning. It was not extravagant to order three cassocks because in the Singapore heat it is desirable to change at least twice a day. That is the ideal but my programme often allowed no time to change before hurrying from one engagement to the next.

My official duties began with a visit to the R.A.F. station at Changi —a name with fearsome recollections for prisoners of war under the Japanese. I then began what was to become a routine daily performance for the next five or six weeks. Those arranging the details of my tour had clearly honoured the principle that time is money. The cost of aircraft, motor transport, escorts, food and lodgings on a journey which took me to Malaya, Japan, China and Korea must have amounted to thousands of pounds. The service people thought the exercise worthwhile as a boost to morale but they rightly determined not to waste public money. They filled every moment of each day with an engagement. The time-table was often absurdly exacting but I did not feel disposed to complain. It was, after all, splendid that the War Office should have been willing to spend so much money to bring their bishop to the Catholic soldiers, sailors and airmen. Meals were part of the official programme and proved useful in establishing contact with the people who could 'lay on' (service jargon) the transport to enable me to visit the largest possible number of troops. The first lunch at the

R.A.F. Officers' Mess in Changi was a model of the rest. Weeks earlier it had been arranged for every Catholic officer to be free of other duties to join the other officers in the mess.

There was still a number of official calls to make before settling down to pastoral work among the service men and women. The first afternoon in Singapore was devoted to making formal calls on the mighty. The chiefs-of-staff of all three services had to be waited on in turn. These calls, although formal, were by means a waste of time. The service chiefs naturally wanted to meet the person who was going to spend several weeks moving among their men and giving them talks. It was also useful for me to meet the men at the top not only to gather information and views but to become acquainted personally in case I should need to approach them again at the end of my tour.

My last formal call was on Sir John Nicholl at Government House. Despite his reputation—probably undeserved—of being unfriendly to Catholics he received me most kindly. The governor was civil without being effusive. I was, in fact, only half conscious of the man because his room was air-conditioned and the contrast between its cold, dry atmosphere and the torrid, humid air outside brought on nausea together with a pain in the stomach. I was much relieved that the interview with Sir John was not only formal but brief. Father Tobin who acted as the equivalent of an aide-de-camp on these visits was slightly aggrieved that we were not offered any hospitality. The service chiefs had each invited me to return for luncheon or dinner at the end of the tour. Father Tobin felt that the governor might have produced at least a cup of tea. Last of all, I saw Bishop Olçomendy of the Missions Etrangères de Paris who had been in Malaya for thirty-five years. His welcome was typically French in its warmth and courtesy. He spoke in the highest terms of the behaviour of the British service personnel and invited me to lunch with him on Easter Sunday at the end of my tour. The day ended with a private dinner given by the commander-in-chief, Air Marshal Sanderson. He informed me that the R.A.F. would put at my disposal a flying boat for the duration of my tour to take me to Japan, Hong Kong and Korea. This was impressive evidence that the visit was officially regarded as useful. It is likely that Cardinal Spellman's spectacularly successful Christmas visits to the American troops in Korea inspired our authorities to show that the Commonwealth was no less interested in the spiritual works of mercy.

On the following day, 6th March, 1953, my pastoral visitation of the troops began. I left Singapore after a very early Mass served, as usual, by the zealous Colonel Davey. I was to be accompanied by Father Smith and Father MacMillan, whom I found awaiting me at the Singapore boundary where the Jahore jungle begins. My rather alarming escort comprised a scout car with telescopes mounted on the roof together with a large armoured car. One of these juggernauts preceded and the other followed the saloon car in which I sat with the chaplains and an armed guard. The officer in charge of the escort, apologising for its warlike appearance, explained that it was necessary to take these precautions as we would be in dense jungle until we reached Malacca at night-fall. I smilingly wondered if he would care to take my comfortable seat in the saloon and let me have a hard but safe seat in his armoured car. He saw the point when I said—rather less jocosely—that it might be safer for the fast saloon car to make its way alone instead of in a miniature cavalcade which proclaimed the presence of a V.I.P. My first experience of the jungle was all the more exciting for the spice of danger. Communist guerillas sniped at the soldiers during the day and massacred civilians in the villages by night. The notes I took in the jungle faithfully reproduce the atmosphere.

6th March: My first experience of a jungle. No doubt at all why the favourite description is 'impenetrable' (which, of course, it isn't). We kept to the main road until we reached areas in which army units were encamped. Then we followed tracks in the jungle until we located the camp. At intervals of a few hours we made four calls.

H.Q. 17 Gurkha Inf. Div. in Majidee barracks: A good muster of men considering the numbers who were out on bandit operations. The commanding officer, Brigadier Bourke, is an excellent Catholic and gave us a cordial reception. The troops here, as everywhere, were very pleased to see me but slightly nervous because they are not used to bishops. The chaplains collected their home addresses so that I shall be able to write to their mothers or wives when I return to England.

R.A.S.C. Coy. Sendai: A remarkably large number of Catholic soldiers. It was a sign of great goodwill that the C.O. (non-Catholic) had kept so many men at home to see me. A most amusing adjutant here had an unending flow of stories, filtered, he said, to be fit for my clerical ears. The C.O. is very proud of his men and their record. They drive about in 'soft nosed' cars not in armoured cars. They have a long list of kills and, of course, casualties. There is a nest of bandits some ten miles up the road. Only a few days ago they killed an officer and three men of this group.

Met the first Battalion at Batu Pahat: A grand experience. Most but not all the officers are New Zealanders. About twenty-four Catholics among the troops who are all from Fiji. The Methodists were the first Christian missionaries in Fiji. I addressed the troops, gave them the Pope's blessing and promised to talk of them to their bishop (Bishop Foley) whom I am to meet in Sydney. They have two accomplishments—rugby football and singing. They sang the Fiji version of 'Faith of our Fathers' with natural harmony. The officer in charge was from Fiji; the brigadier, a New Zealander, was away in the jungle. This Fijian major is a wonderful man. Educated at Oxford he is socially the most important citizen in his home town. For the benefit of the M.O. from Glasgow he boasted of his Scots' blood acquired through his grandfather, a cannibal who, he said, made a habit of eating Scots missionaries. Fijian soldiers, splendid looking men, were our escort on the second part of the journey. Their list of kills is long but fortunately they were not called upon to defend us. At the ferry we were met by an armoured car from the Gordon Highlanders. It would not start so we went alone over the ferry and through the dreaded jungle. The C.O. insisted on our taking an escort, a very young soldier whose weapon was the most alarming feature of the day. I persuaded him to put his sub-machine gun on the floor fearing that it might go off in his hand.

Malacca: We slept at a government rest house—very comfortably. Seven a.m. Mass in the convent of St. Maur. The small orphans were allowed 'as a treat' to stay for my Mass. I tried to send them away by asking them if they would rather have breakfast or a second Mass. They chose Mass. At nine a.m. the Gordons' armoured car collected me. At ten a.m. I addressed the troops in the Garrison chapel—they were paraded and all spit and polish but we made it as informal as possible. This grand set of boys were mainly from Aberdeen. Here we met Mr. Pitt, brother of Father Pitt, the naval chaplain. He took us to his house and showed us round his rubber plantation. Returned to Malacca for late lunch with De La Salle Brothers (with a very tired-looking superior) and went with a local Portuguese priest to see his compatriots. Visited the empty tomb of St. Francis Xavier, high above the town. Over the ruined church a beacon flashes each night to warn shipping. Then to the airfield where a very smart Valetta aircraft (V.I.P. Special) awaited us. Throughout the day a delightful and intelligent young captain (adjutant of the Gordons) remained with us and answered a variety of questions about local customs. We saw a funeral. He explained that since spirits are unable to turn right angles an empty coffin is taken out of the front door while the corpse is carried

[120]

in another coffin through a side door specially designed in every house for the purpose. This attractive and efficient soldier refused to leave us until we were air-borne lest we might need him again. I understood him to be the son of the Rev. D. Oliphant of Yateley, to whom I wrote later. The vicar was delighted but replied that the soldier was not in fact his son but he loved him like a son and was delighted to have news of him.

Arrived four p.m. at Seletar: Met by Air Commodore McDonald, the A.O.C., who took me home to Diana, his delightful wife, a tremendously friendly non-Catholic. I thought of Hilda, Colonel Davey's wife, also a non-Catholic and a most gracious hostess. Tea and then a rest till dinner when I met several senior R.A.F. officers and wives. A pleasant party.

9th March Singapore Garrison: Nine a.m. addressed all ranks (about 300) a most attentive audience. Spoke for longer than usual and gave a quasi-mission sermon. Later I was told that the talk was much appreciated by the soldiers (preachers rarely hear the truth). At ten a.m. I waited on the C.-in-C., General Sir Charles Keightley, a most impressive person genuinely anxious for the moral welfare of his young soldiers. It was in no formal fashion that he promised to consider any suggestions I might have at the end of my tour to help these boys to keep straight while on active service. Ten thirty a.m. to twelve thirty p.m. visited the garrison schools. Excellent buildings, a goodly proportion of Catholic teachers and a very pleasant atmosphere. The colonel in charge of education accompanied me throughout. The Catholic children were eager and very well instructed (they complained to their parents that evening that I asked no hard questions). Then to the hospital where I was taken round by Colonel Franklin, Chief M.O. (whom I was to meet again in Korea) and Lieutenant Colonel Fava, a tremendously keen Catholic. There were many Catholics among the patients who were mainly casualties from attack by bandits. For some reason many have caught bullets in the mouth and will require extensive plastic surgery. I was taken through the 'Asiatic ward'—all Moslem women. A girl greeted me Indian fashion with joined hands—the *namaste*—and in my ignorance I thought she must be a Catholic and patted her head. Dr. Franklin later told me that this fatherly gesture would not be welcomed by a Moslem.

12th March: This is being written in the air near Hong Kong at two a.m. on Thursday 12th March, St. Gregory's Day, the second anniversary of my consecration as bishop. Our aircraft has been diverted

[121]

owing to bad weather. A signal was sent to Hong Kong to inform those responsible for the day's programme that we should be arriving late, if at all. When it is misty it is impossible to make a landing in Hong Kong because the entrance between the hills is narrow and treacherous. It was obvious that whatever happened we would not be landing in Hong Kong in time for Mass so I decided to celebrate Mass at once. It was thrilling to say Mass in a flying-boat. I wondered if it had been done before—Pat Henry, the R.A.F. chaplain, could not recall an instance. It was much easier than saying Mass at sea because the flying-boat was completely steady. The navigator, a keen Catholic, served the Mass at which I was assisted by Father Henry and Father Tobin. It was well that we decided not to postpone Mass because soon after Mass another signal was received directing us to proceed to Sangley Point, the U.S. naval base in the Philippines. Several hours later we reached Sangley Point where we were most hospitably received by the U.S. navy. Admiral Cruzen insisted on my staying in his lovely, air-conditioned house. His wife was a most charming hostess. To her credit this charm was apparent long before she discovered that we were fellow Catholics. Unaware that there were any Catholic bishops in England she had assumed that I was an Anglican. The admiral sent his chaplain, a Southern Baptist, with his launch to show us the city of Manila. I visited the old church of St. Augustine which had been the scene of brutal massacres of civilians during the war. The Japanese are credited with such atrocities that it is thought impossible for a Japanese ever again to visit these islands. These things are said confidently but time heals all wounds—Germans are now welcomed in Israel.

We toured Manila and saw the President's palace with its striking chandeliers. Then we went into the suburbs to see the famous bamboo organ in an old mission church. The nun who played it for us was a French Canadian, the priest a Dutchman. I saw a school song written on the blackboard in the choir loft. 'Hail to our dear school today.' This is also the school song of St. Angela's, Upton, to which our senior girls went in the carefree days when I was parish priest of Manor Park. I wondered if some old Brownie (St. Angela's girl) turned missionary had nostalgically taught her old school song to the young Filipinos.

Returned to the admiral's house to find a beautiful dinner awaiting me. I was told to invite Father Henry and Father Tobin who had been billeted nearby. In a pre-prandial chat the admiral's wife, who had to accompany her husband to a party, consulted me about a spiritual problem. She had given up drink for Lent but was going to find it difficult the following week when she had to entertain three admirals from U.S.A. I solved her problem by telling her to anticipate Laetare Sunday by a few days. (Laetare Sunday comes in the middle of Lent. The priest wears rose instead of purple vestments at Mass, the organ plays and Catholics relax their lenten mortifications.) We went early to bed and next morning a U.S. chaplain, Father Broadhurst, S. J., came from Manila with altar kit and stayed to serve my Mass at seven a.m. The admiral's wife had warned all her friends about the Mass so we had a large congregation. The other priests were invited to breakfast and the admiral saw us off to Hong Kong. This visit was one more proof of the amazing kindness of Americans. They could not have been more hospitable had we been U.S. citizens. They fully expected us to have to return again as the weather in Hong Kong was uncertain at this season and they almost persuaded us that they would like us back. This time the flying-boat made the precarious entry to Hong Kong without difficulty. At the pier Wing-Commander Devas awaited us with a number of Jesuit Fathers. We went for tea to Wah Yan, a splendid new Jesuit college designed by the professor of architecture of Hong Kong university. A Chinese Buddhist, he became a Catholic while on the job. We were a day behind schedule and therefore had to abandon the tour of the New Territories (the hinterland of Hong Kong). We had missed the dinner arranged by the Catholic officers to welcome me. According to report it had been a very grand affair at which Father Sheridan, S.J., had deputised for me in a speech which excelled in wit. The dinner was evidently a great success largely by reason of the chief guest's absence. My late arrival had also prevented my attending the official luncheon in my honour given by the governor. I was able to make some small amends because the U.S. admiral's wife had given me a box of mangoes to deliver to the governor's wife who was also an American.

My first engagement in Hong Kong was a luncheon at Flagstaff House the residence of the Commander-in-Chief. The company was very mixed. I could find no topic for conversation with the delightful young ladies seated on either side of me but when they had retired I had a long talk with the C.-in-C. This chat would have been more interesting but for the too frequent interventions of a civilian who spoke English self-consciously well and, like most Chinese, was called Li. He was immensely proud of his command of the language and of his Oxford degree. He spoke volubly of Chiang Kai-shek who, he alleged, would soon return to liberate the unhappy mainland. Next morning an early start from Wah Yan to make good the missed visit to the New Territories. We were greeted by a large gathering of troops under the care of Father Madden, a young Irish priest. The brigadier, a most courteous man, took me up to the frontier where we saw Chinese awaiting a train for China. I regret to have to confess that they seemed very happy to be going back to China. All had bicycles which the police, tapping their noses, said would be confiscated by the communists as soon as they had reached the first town. No missionaries were due to come out of Red China that day. A few months earlier Bishop Bianchi of Hong Kong, a saintly Italian, had come through dressed as a coolie. He was still in very poor health. Missionaries arrive regularly and all are miserably thin and ill-clad. Soon all European missionaries except those undergoing life imprisonment will have been expelled. The Chinese clergy and nuns have been heroic. Few remain alive and free but bishops, priests and religious have all refused to make any sort of compromise. They are much loved by the poor people and it is said that for this reason the communists dare not harm them in public. Other 'foreign devils' are openly attacked and ill-treated. The people are conditioned by atrocity stories which are readily believed by simple pagans and lead inevitably to outrages.

Late that afternoon I arrived with great joy at Sheko, John Keswick's house. His wife, Clare, sister of my old friend Val Elwes, was awaiting me looking radiant but, like myself, much greyer than during the war when we used to meet regularly. Maggie was also at home, leggy, friendly, no longer a baby but with Nannie nevertheless still in attendance. Johnny came home soon after my arrival and we had a wonderful evening. Johnny, who does not look a year older, is much more forthcoming than in the old days. He was vastly amusing and most informative. There must be few Westerners who know more about China. He does not air his knowledge but, on the contrary, pretends to know nothing. His dissimulation makes his contributions all the more valuable and attractive (he has published a book *All I Know About China* which contains only blank pages).

Said Mass next morning in the drawing-room—served by Clare and Maggie—Nannie also insisted on coming despite her Scots Presbyterian upbringing. The next morning at nine a.m. I went to Stanley barracks to address all the soldiers and R.A.F. units. Lunch with G.O.C. was most diverting. He was evidently not used to being contradicted. I could not resist giving him the experience. We disagreed on many things but mainly about books. We reached this topic because von Papen's memoirs had just been published. After a shaky start (I failed to agree with some of his views) we quickly came to like each other. He became so friendly that thereafter he made me use his own car for every trip and pressed me to stay in his house. On to Wah Yan College (the same name but not the same institution as the one in Kowloon). Dinner at the Catholic Centre given by warrant officers and sergeants. They kindly included the officers and wives who had been disappointed when I failed to arrive for their dinner on the night of my arrival in Hong Kong. To preside at this dinner they invited Colonel Cotton, a fighting Catholic who to everyone's sorrow goes home tomorrow.

Mass at six forty-five on John's desk. The congregation for Mass included three Catholic girls who were staying with Clare. Set off at eight a.m. with Johnny in his car (general's car following) to visit the troops I had missed on the first day when I had failed to arrive in Hong Kong. As always the C.O. was most gracious. Visited an army school which was not nearly so nice as the Singapore schools but had a simply charming headmistress. My next visit was to the hospital. On my way I looked in at St. Teresa's church and caught a glimpse of the grand work the Italian clergy are doing in Hong Kong. American nuns (Maryknoll) were rehearsing catechumens about to be baptised. Other Sisters were instructing groups of children. Between two and three thousand Chinese are received into the Church each year in Hong Kong. They are mostly refugees from Red China who have had their fill of atheism. This church alone had thirteen hundred baptisms last year. Went to Maryknoll for dinner with sixty missionaries of all orders and nations. Bishop Bianchi, the Bishop of Hong Kong, and an American Maryknoll bishop were also present at this impressive gathering of men who had suffered for the faith.

Nine a.m. St. Patrick's Day: Mass for over 300 Royal Ulster Rifles in a cinema in the new territories. After Mass I listened to a military band while the officers entertained the sergeants in their mess. Lunch with Brigadier Stirling and a most charming group of officers of whom none was Catholic. Sandy, the adjutant, was anti-Catholic in an amusing sort of way but in a battle of wits he proved rather slow. All in all the table chat was most entertaining and conversation with Brigadier Stirling was instructive. Back to Marina House where I met Clare and went window shopping. Returned to an early dinner to which several people from Jardine Matheson (John Keswick's firm) had been invited. To bed at Wah Yan college by eleven p.m. Mass at four a.m. next day was served by a young Jesuit scholastic. Seen off by Father Pat Henry,

Father Tobin and Father O'Dwyer, S.J., the rector of the college. I found the same flying-boat and crew waiting to take me to Japan. I had enjoyed every moment in Hong Kong. The Keswicks had often told me of the great beauty of this city but I had not expected ever to visit it. It was a great stroke of luck to find myself in Hong Kong at the same time as Clare and Johnny.

CHAPTER
EIGHT

I ARRIVED IN JAPAN ON 18TH MARCH AND WAS MET BY FATHER RYAN, Father Reid and a Canadian chaplain. A fast motor launch took us from Iwakuni to Kure where I was met at the landing stage by the Chief of Staff, Brigadier Dalton, and Brigadier O'Meara, senior medical officer, who was to be my host. He introduced himself by telling me that he had been in charge of Millbank Hospital London when my nephew, Brian Reynolds, was a house surgeon there.

19th March: Mass at Sacred Heart church. Paid a formal call on the Chief of Staff who told me of the good morale and bad morals of the troops. His report was later substantiated by senior officers of the many nationalities of the commonwealth. Briefly the problem is that the Japanese in order to exploit the soldiers financially do everything possible to trap them through the gentle Japanese women. It is commonly alleged of the Japanese that in matters of sex they have no moral sense. This most unlikely story is supported by commonly held myths such as that poor Japanese parents gladly see their daughters become prostitutes. The origin of these myths may be that immediately after the Japanese defeat these girls sold their bodies to buy food for their families—similar behaviour was common in Vienna after the first world war when the Austrians were starving. It is alleged that in Japan having followed the oldest profession does not debar a girl from a good marriage. I was told that while the mere street girl is despised the professional prostitute is quite respectable. This is an unlikely story. The geisha system (not to be confused with a call-girl service or any other form of prostitution) gives a well-educated girl training to enable her to converse with gentlemen but not to cater for their sexual desires. It need hardly be added that the women who entertain troops are not the expensively trained geishas but the poor girls hired by beer hall proprietors to exploit the lust of young men far from home. The scourge of venereal disease is menacing. The curve of v.d. cases on the graphs I was shown disclosed that the incidence of v.d. is proportionate to the scale of pay—with North Americans an easy first. The British are quite often the object of pity to other troops because they receive much less money than many other U.N. troops. However, from the health point of view it is evidently fortunate that the U.K. troops are so poor. They frequent beer halls rather than brothels and hence contract v.d. less often. The well-paid service men from the dominions stationed in Japan (not just on leave) regularly keep Japanese mistresses. A Protestant chaplain with the Australians told me that ninety per cent of the men on his station have mistresses. These girls are regarded as common law wives and not infrequently marry their men and return with them to Australia.

At nine thirty the Chief of Staff took me to the Commander-in-Chief, a most impressive Australian with whom I am due to stay later in Korea. The incidence of v.d. was yet again a topic of discussion. Senior officers easily become obsessed by the problem because altogether apart from ethical considerations this disease can seriously affect the fighting capacity of their men. A Japanese priest in Kure one day remarked that the Christian soldiers had put back the conversion of the Japanese indefinitely. If this is true the story of Japanese indifference to sexual morality is obviously false.

The rest of the morning I spent in the Britcom General Hospital. The doctor in charge was Colonel Meneces, a much decorated soldier and an authority on tropical medicine. The hospital chaplain told me that the colonel is an exemplary Catholic who, like St. Thomas More, prizes Mass above all other daily duties. I visited Red Cross head-quarters and Tenno wing (reserved for v.d. and skin diseases). The blunt M.O. in charge of this department was convinced that P.A.C. (Prophylactic Centres) are a strategic error because they encourage young men to believe they can fornicate with impunity. They give an official blessing to promiscuity by fitting out the boys for their escapades but, in fact, no prophylactic is safe. Because it is such a scourge the question of v.d. is frequently discussed by officers of all the allied nations —Australian, New Zealand, Canadian and American. The view of the chaplains is that most officers are concerned only with the health (i.e.

[128]

Hiroshima: Peace Memorial Hall.

Hiroshima: Where the bomb fell.

Whitby Abbey: Centenary Mass: celebrant Bishop Brunner.

the fighting efficiency) of their men and give no thought to the moral aspect. I am not sure that I share the chaplains' view. Speaking to a bishop officers may express rather more concern than they feel over the moral issues but I am sure that many officers—especially the married men—were really troubled by the moral implications of the prevailing sexual licence. British officers were particularly frustrated at being prevented from taking sterner measures because of the complications of the multi-national high command. Later, in Korea, I was given statistics which again showed the ratio of infection to be exactly that of pay—Canadians the highest, British the lowest. I saw no American figures but from their chaplains I gathered that absolutely and proportionately their v.d. figures are the highest of all. It would, however, be cynical to assume that the British are more moral only for financial reasons. The fact is that the British national service men are notably younger and more disciplined than most of the others. In the estimation of all—especially of their own officers—the chief craving these boys have for women is for their mothers. They were the best behaved of all troops and if more provision could have been made by the Y.M.C.A., the Catholic Women's League and other voluntary societies for them to drink their beer away from army supervision they would not have wanted to visit the beer halls which in Tokyo are ante-rooms to brothels.

The chaplains thought that at least for the young national service men discipline should be more rigorously enforced and respectable beer halls provided by the army. Only approved beer halls should be on-limits and these ought to be policed to make sure that the boys go home after drinking. The rival establishments set up by army authorities (Commonwealth Club, Stars and Stripes, King of Clubs) had already ruined trade for the Japanese beer halls which mushroom at the door of each army camp. It must be added in defence of the authorities that whereas the Japanese police are most co-operative in all other directions they will do nothing whatever to impede the exploitation of U.N. troops by beer hall proprietors, pimps and prostitutes. The explanation offered by the army people is that since this is the largest source of revenue the government has instructed the police to be non-co-operative.

21st March: I presided and gave the commentary at Mass in the cinema at Haramura, H.Q. of the First Commonwealth Division Battle School. The men here are at the final stage of training for action in Korea. It is very tough. All exercises are carried out with live ammunition. Accidents are inevitable—there was a near-fatal shooting while I was watching. It is essential, I was told, to make this last exercise as realistic as possible because training under realistic conditions saves casualties when the troops go into action in Korea. The casualty this morning turned out to be a soldier hit by the recoil of a gun. The driver of the tank released the pedal before the gunner was ready; the result was severe concussion and perhaps internal head injuries.

Returned to Kure and inspected N.A.A.F.I. headquarters. This old naval college is a magnificent setting for a canteen and club. Here I saw the mechanical cow designed by one of the officers. The machine contains frozen milk which it liquefies. I drank a glass and found it impossible to distinguish it from ordinary milk (but I can't tell Stork from butter). My next call was to the Military Corrective Establishment which is run on strict but humane grounds by Major Davies. I addressed the men—mostly Canadian and British—and found them in good heart. The regime (unlike that of the Field Punishment Unit run by the Canadians in Korea—of which more later) allows a certain minimum relaxation e.g. a cigarette after dinner and occasional conversation but is by no means a Butlin's holiday camp. Men, though unlikely to want to return here, do not leave embittered. Dinner with the Australian officers who were most friendly. The C.O., a non-Catholic, said he would like to attend my Mass on Sunday. One shy-looking officer was being congratulated on his majority. He is obviously a much admired and beloved character. He was, in fact, only visiting this mess where as brigadier he had once been the senior officer. The story is that when the Korean war broke out he attempted to re-enlist but was rejected on grounds of age. He therefore changed his name and enlisted with the army as a private. Today he has climbed back to major. Some hope that one day he will be C.-in-C.

22nd March: eight thirty a.m. Mass and sermon at Sacred Heart garrison church, Kure. Ten thirty a.m. gave a running commentary and preached at Missa Cantata sung by Father Reid, the Australian senior chaplain. The Mass, which was broadcast, was accompanied by a Japanese choir brought from the School of Music, Hiroshima, by a Belgian Jesuit. The server at Mass was young Michael Shead whom I taught to serve Mass in Manor Park. I was invited to the weekly army lunch in the officers' mess as the guest of Brigadier Dalton. I had been warned that Dalton was a very establishment sort of person and probably disliked having to play host to an R.C. bishop. In the unlikely event of this being true the brigadier must be a splendid actor. His personal courtesy and the efficiency with which he arranged every detail of my tour were beyond praise. Brigadier Dalton struck me as typical of the traditional British officer—unemotional and utterly devoted to the welfare of his men.

Immediately after lunch I left by fast launch (the same one as had met my flying-boat to Iwakuni) for Eta Jima. This former Japanese Dartmouth is a most impressive set of buildings. I preached and gave Benediction to a congregation of American soldiers and their wives. Quite a few of the senior officers are Catholics and a reception in the hall after Benediction was very well attended. There were endless photographs—I was among Americans—and these young men were obviously as pleased to see me as the British had been. They accepted my offer to write to their mothers. One boy said it was his happiest afternoon since leaving home. Later the American C.O. gave a cocktail party in my honour at his headquarters to which all Catholic officers and wives were invited. The officer in charge of all sport and social activities for the Far East—a very enthusiastic Catholic—showed me round this splendid place. It is a special school for all trades and crafts. The amenities are wonderfully good—including facilities to telephone home once a week for a few dollars. To protect them from v.d. these men are allowed into the local village only on a Sunday afternoon and are permitted to visit Kure only once during their whole stay. The army is concerned with its own efficiency not the men's morals.

23rd March: Hiroshima. Called at the Jesuit school of Music—an excellent building with a new church nearing completion. At eleven o'clock I was conducted over the atomic bomb research station by the deputy superintendent, Dr. McCarthy, with whom I had previously had a meal in Kure. He and his wife are friends of Cardinal Cushing of Boston. In this research station the doctors collect every conceivable variety of data relating to the victims of the atomic bomb, to be digested by a mechanical brain. The operations of the computer were demonstrated for me with sample tests. Despite its accurate calculations, the computer, in the words of its operator (a Ph.D. from Harvard) "hasn't the brains of a glow-worm". There is nothing complicated or mysterious about the way it works. Like all machines it depends on human judgment (i.e. the minds which choose the data) for its infallibility. The research going on here is thorough and exhaustively cross-checked. All relatives of casualties in the atomic attack are examined and told to present themselves for a medical examination at half-yearly intervals. At first the people were grateful and co-operative but they have now become bored. Mothers may be bored, too, but they willingly bring their babies. This enables doctors to assess the effects of the bomb on descendants of those living in Hiroshima at the time. Genetics rather than medical care has become the most important aspect of this project. To avoid giving offence to the Japanese doctors nobody is treated here and there is full co-operation between general practitioners and their American colleagues. Very few of the local doctors are skilful because medical training for many years after the war was little more than a glorified first-aid course lasting about eighteen months. The Harvard man assured me that all effort in pre-war Japan had been directed to preparation for war either directly or through industry. The Japanese, renowned for imitation, followed the Nazis in curtailing professional training for the sake of the war effort.

After Mass next day I left for Korea by Australian transport plane. Arrived in Seoul at ten o'clock after a flight of under three hours. From the airport I went straight to the cathedral where I was greeted by Father Jim Petry whose parents have been my friends since childhood in Ilford. The Korean bishops were holding their annual meeting. I called in to greet them and Monsignor Furstenberg, the inter-Nuncio from Japan, who was presiding. I was surprised to find that the cathedral was not badly damaged. The chaplains were proud of the new statue of St. Teresa, replacing the one destroyed by the communists, donated (a word they have picked up from the Americans) by the British troops who helped to liberate the city. The huge shrine of Our Lady at the entrance to the cathedral had been left untouched by the communists. One curious feature of the cathedral is a double set of Stations of the Cross—one for the men, the other for women. Later I called on the Protestant bishop, Dr. Chadwell, a pleasant man who dresses not in purple like an Anglican but in piped cassock like us. News had just come through that Malenkov was to advise the release of a number of English missionaries, including the Protestant Bishop of Seoul for whom Bishop Chadwell is supplying. I called at the residence of the C.-in-C., General Wells, to leave my bags. I was greeted by the colonel, a Downside boy. With him were an Australian officer and a young British A.D.C. They combined with the sergeant and the general's batman to make me feel at home. The sergeant and batman took complete charge with customary Australian efficiency and friendliness. After a wash I was taken in charge by a captain who looked, sounded and acted like an old-time regimental sergeant major. Everyone called him Mike and that is probably why I forgot to write down his surname but I think it was Turner. He is an utterly unspoiled product of a Lancashire Catholic village with only two loyalties—the Catholic Church and the British army. Mike took us to the outfitting department called the Kat Comm of which he is quartermaster. We watched him 'kitting-up' the Koreans joining the British forces. They had happy faces which glowed more and more as Mike's men filled their kit bags with new equipment. They reminded me of myself as a child when taken shopping. I used to pretend that shoes fitted me in case my right size might not be available and I would have no new shoes. It was impressive to watch Mike moving rapidly down a long line of men shouting the required sizes. His men would produce shorts, vests, caps and socks which fitted each recruit. Mike, having been a quartermaster through two wars, could in the literal sense size up a man at a glance without the aid of a tape measure.

I asked Mike if these Korean recruits were really happy to be joining the British or if they would not prefer an American detachment with its higher pay and better equipment. Before replying Mike shouted out something in Korean and all the boys grinned and shouted back. Mike told me that he had said, "Are the British O.K.?" To which the Koreans had shouted back "British are best." Nobody looking at Mike's gnarled and honest face could deny that the British must be best. I had lunch with the colonel and two men from the British embassy of whom the senior, said to be an excellent Catholic, is holding the fort for the Minister who lives in Pusan to which Rhee's government has been evacuated. This Mr. Humphreys told me that he had just received a letter from his father saying that there had been dense but completely silent crowds in the streets for Tito's reception in London. Nobody waved.

I then paid a visit to the 25th Canadian Detention Barrack—a visit which had repercussions throughout the rest of my tour of Korea. As I arrived the men carrying full packs were being drilled by roaring N.C.O.s. I was glad that these unfortunates would gain a respite while they had a talk from me. I decided to make it a long talk knowing that for once I would have an audience which would be happier the longer I spoke. The C.O., a Canadian major, instructed a raucous sergeant to halt the drill and 'fall-out' the R.C.s. While they were assembling I studied a notice giving the daily routine. Twice a day they had to scale a hill in full kit. Another two hours were devoted to physical exercises in full kit. An obstacle course had to be run each day. For any apparent slackness the normal punishment was to repeat the obstacle course 'at

[133]

the double'. There was no smoking, talking or reading during the whole period of detention which might last from twenty-eight days to six months. Most of the prisoners were Canadian but all Commonwealth troops except Australians were represented. After my talk to the prisoners I spoke to each man individually. I had never seen young men so utterly exhausted. On my way out of the camp I saw groups of two or three men being given individual treatment by shouting N.C.O.s. Presumably they had been slack in drill and were now being made to do extra exercises—press-ups, packing and unpacking kit-bags while the sergeant relentlessly bawled at them to go faster. I was appalled. With me were the senior chaplain and Mike. The latter, a tough old soldier, was no less disgusted. He said that such methods had been abandoned thirty years ago by the British army as being suitable only for morons who could understand no appeal to reason. The chaplain, Father Ryan from Essex, maintained that the 'glass house' (detention barracks) in Colchester, was just as tough but he had not observed all the incidents I had noted. Prisons and prisoners had, after all, been a special care of mine for many years. I felt that I could distinguish discipline from brutality.

I then visited the orphanage near the cathedral. Here delightful and happy children sang Korean songs and Latin hymns for me. They were tenderly cared for by diminutive Korean nuns. The atmosphere was unlike that of any orphanage I had seen anywhere in the world. The Sisters said they had no more rules than any other family. There were no bells even for meals. Elsewhere superiors might be worried by such an ostentatious lack of regulations. Seeing the joy in the faces of the orphans and Sisters I remarked to Mike (who was in tears) that we were as near Nazareth as ever we were likely to be on earth.

This visit went some way to relieving the depression created by the detention centre. My next visit—to the Columban Fathers—completed the cure. A large notice at the entrance read: 'Abandon rank when you enter here. Resume it when leaving.' Officers, men and chaplains cease to be soldiers while in this house. I was impressed but not surprised to learn that as many as fifty chaplains of various nationalities assemble here for a day's retreat every few weeks. The Columbans, the original Maynooth Mission to China, were famous for their personal self-discipline and the austerity of their religious life. Prayer and spiritual exercises were the foundation of their missionary work.

That evening I spent in the house of the Commander-in-Chief, General Wells (an Australian), where I bathed in the smallest bath I had ever seen. It was a concrete box three feet by two. I had a long chat with the general and his A.D.C. before dinner. We ranged over many topics including the much discussed moral danger for young soldiers on leave in Japan. I brought up the detention barracks in the course of conversation. I was very frank and did not hesitate to describe the regime as sadistic. The general had not yet been to the prison though it was on his list for a visit after he had inspected the fighting troops. When he heard my strictures he thought that they were the natural reaction of a cleric unacquainted with the wicked world of delinquents. When I told him that I was familiar with prisons in many countries he decided to take my criticism more seriously. He told his A.D.C. to alter the next day's programme so that the detention centre would be the first call of the day. At the risk of being thought fanatical on the question I pressed him to make the prison not the first but the last call of the day. Otherwise, I pointed out, it would not be possible to gain any impression of the utter exhaustion of the prisoners after a day's treatment at the hands of the Canadian military police who staffed the institution. The general asked my opinion of the field punishment block in Kure which he had visited. I replied that I thought it strict but in no sense brutal. In a war it was obviously necessary for detention quarters to be very unattractive indeed if soldiers were not to prefer them to the field of battle.

The general, impressed because I had not been shocked by the severity of the Kure centre, now promised to visit the prisoners at the end of the next day and instructed his A.D.C. accordingly. He then revealed that as an Australian he had little use for punishment depots in a theatre of war. He said that they provide temptation for men to commit petty crime in order to be withdrawn from the fighting zone. He was against the brutal treatment of detained men but still more opposed to the whole principle of detention. There were no Australians detained. This, the general said, was not because Australian soldiers were more disciplined but because they knew what happened to them if they were delinquent. Rough justice was administered to Australians by sending them on suicidal missions. Detention is a minor punishment by comparison.

On the following morning which was Lady Day, 25th March, I offered Mass for the first time in Korea. I said Mass for the repose of the soul of Jack Courchaine, a young friend of mine from New Rochelle U.S.A. who had been killed in Korea a year earlier. He was the only son of Helen and John Courchaine who had been close friends for many years. I first met them, like so many of my friends, when travelling. Not the least advantage of clerical dress is to be a passport to friendship with strangers. Before the war on board ship I met a Jewish couple, Camille and Beatrice Stamm of Philadelphia. They are dead but first their children and later their grand-children regarded me as one of their family.

Outside Seoul the roads became almost impassable. This territory had been much fought over and the city changed hands more than once. I had never seen roads to compare with those leading from the city to the front lines. It was difficult to know if a vehicle was on or off the road because the surface was broken with holes so treacherous and deep that a truck would overturn or be submerged without warning. Appeals for careful driving were everywhere displayed but there was no need to tell drivers to go slowly. Even with the special four wheel drive battle wagon which had been put at my disposal it was not physically possible to drive at more than two or three miles an hour, stopping every three or four yards. The system for controlling traffic was by colour. After rain (which is frequent) all roads were red. A red road might not be used without written permission from the commanding officer. When roads were amber a permit could be granted by an officer of lower rank. Only when roads were green could drivers use them without permits. During my days in Korea rain was incessant and all roads were red.

My programme had been worked out to include a visit to every sector. The permit from the commander-in-chief gave me maximum priority to use the roads at any time. It was sometimes impossible to make the tires bite on the soft shoulders of the roads. In one of these soft shoulders our truck became so firmly imbedded that it seemed we could never be extricated. Fortunately an American sergeant working nearby with a team of Koreans came to our rescue. With chains and shovels they managed at last to put us back on a firm piece of road. When I thanked him he told me that his mother was born in Ireland. I promised to write to St. Louis Missouri to tell her that her son had got a bishop out of a nasty hole. Rarely have I seen a man so grateful for so small a favour. As my mission was to British and Commonwealth troops he was one of the few Americans to whose family I wrote on my return to England.

Although our progress was dauntingly slow the programme had been planned with the state of the roads in mind. In the event we arrived at each mess or camp exactly on time. The army may not always know how to win battles but it is superb at organising tours. I ended the day in a caravan at the headquarters of General Wells, commander of the British Commonwealth Division. He was on leave most of the time but he had made arrangements for me to use H.Q. facilities as a centre for my visitations of units at the front. The second-in-command who took over the duties of host was Brigadier McConnell, a soldier highly popular with all ranks. It was an example of his thoughtfulness that he personally made sure that every Catholic soldier would be relieved of other duties at the time of my visit to his unit. Detailed care for the other ranks is a sure sign of a great officer.

In the programme worked out by the chaplains and the War Office the procedure was always the same. I was taken first to the Commanding Officer who, in fact, usually contrived to be awaiting me at the entrance to the camp. For a few minutes the C.O. would brief me in his tent and then conduct me to where the Catholic officers and men were assembled. This might be in the chapel-tent, cinema-tent or, if the numbers were very large, in the open air. I wore a cassock all the time. It was sometimes quite cold but I thought the soldiers would like me to look like a bishop. The army offered to fit me out with warm clothing but this would have made me indistinguishable from an army officer. It is worth the personal inconvenience for clergy and religious to be seen for what they are. Our dress is not only for ourselves but for our people.

In my address I encouraged them to make their Easter duties and unite their Holy Communion with that of their families at home. I promised to write to the parents or wives of those who left their address with one of the chaplains. Apart from that bare outline the Talk varied according to the report on his men given to me by each chaplain. Some groups had an excellent record of Mass attendance and a high percentage had made their Easter duties. These were accorded praise and encouragement. Others had a poor record. The Londoners had the worst record but Liverpool was also one of the black spots. Their chaplains told me that they had not seen most of them at Mass before. This was probably a result of the abolition of church parades. These boys had been paraded to see me but they would probably have come in any case. A bishop was an unusual visitor and gave them something to write home about. The Yorkshire boys, in particular, were delighted to see the Bishop of Leeds. Their record as Catholics was good but the best by far were the Scots. From time to time I met boys from my old parishes of Barking and Manor Park. It was particularly encouraging to see Michael Shead, whom I had trained at the age of seven as an altar boy in Barking, still serving Mass with all his old enthusiasm and young Crispin, the chimney-sweep's son, whom I had last seen when I rescued him and most of his twelve brothers and sisters from the rubble of their home in Walton Road, Manor Park, after a land mine had fallen. There were boys from St. Ignatius' College, Stamford Hill, very proud of their *alma mater* and a credit to their Jesuit masters.

Rivalry among commonwealth units was friendly. Such co-operation at all levels between nations with diverse traditions calls for diagnosis. It may sound far fetched but the most likely explanation was the shared pride in the young Queen. Men fighting a war thousands of miles from home can become sentimental. This was no doubt increased in Korea by the fact that the Queen made a most attractive picture. The favourite one was of the Queen as a colonel-in-chief riding a horse side-saddle. I saw it everywhere in Korea. Her picture banished less worthy pin-ups in commonwealth barrack rooms and messes. Envious American chaplains wished that their G.I.s had a queen to substitute for the curvaceous nudes which adorned the walls of the U.S.A. barracks.

The most memorable of my visits was to the Duke's Own which is a regiment based on Leeds. Understandably I was given an especially enthusiastic reception by the men from Yorkshire. There were probably many Leeds lads who became Catholics for the day in order to greet someone from home. After the routine sermon and prayers there was an unusually prolonged session of photography. All the young soldiers wanted pictures to send to their mothers. If I had ever doubted the value of making this tour of the fighting forces I would have been reassured by the enthusiasm of these national service men from Leeds, Barnsley, Bradford, Halifax and Huddersfield. From the army point of view the expense of my tour was justified as a morale-booster. It was not only soldiers from Yorkshire or even from England who were heartened. My visit to the Black Watch was greeted with demonstrative joy. These big Scots with the red hackle in their bonnets are reckoned to be the toughest of the U.K. forces. They certainly looked tough and it was easy to accept their reputation as the fiercest fighters in Korea. Many of them are Catholics. It was inspiring to see the fervour with which they recited their prayers. The fact that I had preached and lectured in Scotland made me one of their own.

The Tank Corps was well forward within sound and range of the enemy. The proportion of officers to men is unusually high and to my surprise the percentage of Catholics well above average. There were

[138]

ten Catholic officers and I gathered from their chaplain that without exception they were exemplary in the practice of the faith. All were from Catholic schools. For some reason the percentage of Catholics among the other ranks was also exceptionally high and they, too, were all keen on their religion and a source of pride to their chaplain. I wondered if it was more than coincidence that so many Catholics are adventurous. Is there something about danger which Catholic men find attractive? I had found the same in Malaya. The most hazardous job in the jungle was being done by the parachute troops where again there was an unusually large number of Catholics. None was a national service man. All were volunteers and about half of them came from Tipperary, Cork or Dublin. Perhaps Irish blood has more to do with it than creed or patriotism.

Since there were far too many Catholics to fit into a tent we had an outdoor parade on three sides of a square. The scene was impressive and inspiring. These men are drawn together by constant sharing of danger. After the usual service I went to the officers' tent for tea. It was a lavish spread completely unexpected in the front line. The explanation was simple—all the cooks were Catholics. They had spent the whole morning making cakes. During this high tea the most moving incident of my whole tour took place. The soldier who served at the colonel's table where, for the occasion, the Catholic officers all sat was a nineteen-year-old boy who told me that he came from Middleton near Manchester. He did not mention that he was a Catholic but just before the end of the meal he pushed his way through the crowd of officers, knelt down and asked for a blessing. It was a noble example of moral courage. After giving him a blessing I took him outside the tent and one of the chaplains took our picture together for his mother. Then the lad told me that the other boys in the cookhouse were Catholics. They were sent for, given a blessing and each one had a picture taken with me to send home to mother.

After I had taken leave of the C.O. the Catholic officers took me up to Castle Hill where we could view the Chinese positions. I was given an eye-witness account of the epic defence by the Gloucesters in this place now known as Gloucester Valley. In this terrible battle the regiment was surrounded, outnumbered and completely cut off from supporting troops. Many men were killed but there was still an unknown number of prisoners with the Chinese. Our artillery was in action at the time of my visit but there was little return fire. On the next hill a mile away there were frequent bursts of fire. "They are being beastly to each other," someone remarked. Soldiers usually speak in this unemotional way about the enemy. Hate does not come into it. They seem to keep as detached from the objectives of their operations as surgeons do from theirs.

It was late when I returned to my caravan to prepare for dinner with General West. It was late but not late enough. There was still over an hour to wait because most of the officers were at a concert during which the draw for the Grand National Sweepstake was to take place. Eventually they arrived together with members of the concert party. These were pleasant Jews from London whose clean show, I was told later, was most popular with the troops. Contrary to the general opinion, soldiers prefer clean fun.

Next morning I said Mass in the tent to which, as usual, I was guided by the friendly Anglican chaplain. After breakfast I took leave of my host to make a visitation of the Canadian Forces. I talked with Brigadier Bogert about conditions in the detention camp. He did not bring up the subject (as I had been warned he would) but since I knew that the C.-in-C. had reported my criticism it seemed diplomatic to repeat my complaints to him personally. He admitted the danger of sadism and said that the officer in charge was not of the calibre of his predecessors. I imagine that he had no first hand experience of conditions but he promised to look into my allegations. He probably regarded me as an interfering cleric—which, of course, I am.

I talked to the English-speaking Canadians in a large theatre tent quite inadequate for the numbers. I gave the usual talk and blessing. Then I went to the famous 'Van-Dooze'. This was a memorable experience. The regiment is almost entirely Catholic and nothing would satisfy them but a full scale parade. At the gate I was met by a guard of honour. All ranks were drawn up in review order. Having been planted on the bonnet of a jeep I addressed the regiment in flawless French. This flawless French lasted about twenty seconds. It consisted of the words 'Mes amis' and the opening remarks which I remembered from the excellent sermonette which my bi-lingual brother had written for me many weeks before and which I had tried to commit to memory on the bumpy jeep en route. Despite my inability to remember the sermon I managed to speak in halting French for five or six minutes. I saw nobody wince though the sermon must have added to the horrors of war for the vingt-douze. What I said was apparently intelligible and the chaplain assured me afterwards that even if the soldiers had not understood a word they would still have been grateful that I had taken the trouble to speak to them in their own language. He also told me that almost all officers and men had made their Easter duties. This report was very different from that of the British chaplains on their troops.

This was my last visit. I went to a nearby air strip and took a tiny monoplane to Seoul. The pilot was married to a nursing sister whom I had met in a hospital near Sheffield. She had warned her husband to look out for me. In Seoul I had lunch at the staff mess. Immediately afterwards I left for U.S. Airhead K. 16. On the way to the airfield I visited a brave little Italian hospital where building was progressing with great speed. This hospital was for Korean children suffering from diseases caused by malnutrition and neglect. The Italians were not yet accepted as members of the United Nations and therefore did not qualify for dollar aid. There was a large Italian staff of doctors and nurses, all practising Catholics. The chaplain was a keen sympathetic Franciscan. It was good to see a fine piece of relief work being carried on despite total lack of encouragement from the authorities.

CHAPTER
NINE

I LEFT SEOUL IN THE LARGEST PLANE I HAD EVER SEEN. A GLOBEMASTER is able to carry a hundred and twenty soldiers with full equipment. It is fitted with lifts (I should say 'elevators') and entry is through the rear of the plane. An ambulance or lorry (I mean truck) can be driven straight on to the aircraft. The crew were very friendly. Soon after take-off I was invited up to the flight deck where I was given a great deal of interesting information about this vast machine. The pilots were quite relaxed as they sat smoking cigars, chatting and reading. Their task was to take off and land the aircraft. When cruising altitude is reached they leave the piloting to one or two men sitting in a sort of alcove. A charming Catholic boy from New York made me some coffee and told me about life in the U.S. Forces. On board was Father Molloy, a U.S. chaplain who, like our own chaplains, felt that the authorities were not doing enough to give moral protection to the young service men.

At about eight o'clock we arrived at Tachikawa, the military airport of Tokyo. We were met by an Australian army car which took nearly two hours to reach our destination because the driver lost his way. My home for the night was the E.T.A. leave hotel EBISU (whether this is a suburb or an hieroglyphic I cannot say). Here I was met by Monsignor Knox, the quiet kindly Australian secretary to the Internuncio. Many years later he became Archbishop of Melbourne and a cardinal. The next morning I called on General Shoosmith with whom I had a long and cordial talk. He is an old comrade-in-arms of my friend Father Ryan, a chaplain for whom he had a great respect. The general agreed that much more needs to be done to provide congenial recreation quarters for troops on leave in Tokyo and Kure. We went to lunch at the British Embassy. The ambassador was exceptionally well-informed on Japanese culture. Born in Japan he had spent most of his life in the Far East. Despite his knowledge and intelligence I was not wholly convinced by his views because I always suspect generalisations about people of any nation. The Japanese, he said (as everyone said) are complete materialists. I wonder. It is well known to missionaries that the Japanese become exemplary Christians once they are brought to a knowledge of the faith. From the embassy I went to the nunciature where Monsignor Knox awaited me. With him I visited the Jesuit university and several convents. The German Jesuits are providing the same kind of higher education as their Irish colleagues in Hong Kong. It is impossible not to be impressed by the dedication of these Jesuit Fathers. The director was an alert man with a brilliant mind. He had been there since Cardinal Hinsley secured his release from internment during the second world war. The Jesuits have built a magnificent library. All their buildings, like those in Hong Kong, are modern and impressive.

The rest of the afternoon was spent visiting convents where Europeans live. I met Commander O'Brien-Twohig's sister, a witty and holy nun who has given the best years of her life to the education of Japanese children. I paid a short formal call on the Bishop of Tokyo who soon afterwards with several priests and a missionary bishop joined me for dinner at the nunciature. The Nuncio himself was still in Korea. I stayed the night with Monsignor Knox and said Mass the next day at the leave centre where I preached to a very varied congregation. Among those present were Brigadier O'Meara who had been my host in Kure and the doctor who is to take over from him as senior medical officer of the U.K. forces in the Far East. I spent the afternoon resting and writing letters. To lunch came Father Molloy to lay before me the problems of a chaplain's life in the Far East. Later I had dinner with Monsignor Knox and just as I was leaving for the airport the Nuncio returned from Korea. Soon after midnight I arrived at the Tokyo civil airport for the return trip to Hong Kong.

My baggage and tickets had been looked after most efficiently by the transport officer and Father Ryan. I had a pleasant journey via Formosa to Hong Kong where I was met at about midday by a new chaplain, Father Joseph Gardner of the Westminster diocese. Being free of military duties I was able to spend a few hours with John

[143]

Keswick. For the first hour he gave me a fascinating account of his recent meeting with Adlai Stevenson. He had told the American states-man that the U.S. policy of breaking off trade with China (and forcing others to do likewise) was illogical and mistaken. It was obviously illogical since there is no justification for having diplomatic and trade relations with Moscow if Peking must be isolated. It is mistaken because the great hope of avoiding a crushingly powerful Soviet/Chinese bloc is to make the Western connection more attractive to the Chinese than that of the Soviets. Furthermore North China, racially distinct and traditionally hostile to the South, could be wooed with the object of fostering better relations between China and the West. This strategy is more sensible than hostility and a possible war which even if won (by no means certain) would leave the non-communist world ruined and atomised.

While we were talking a friend of John's, sent by Christopher Chancellor to inspect Reuters in the Far East, looked in for a drink. He asked me to give an interview at the airport next morning to make public what I had said privately about the splendid work being done by the Indian Field Ambulance. India, he said, felt hurt that no credit is ever given to it. This I agreed to do and in return he undertook to see that the people at home would be told of the need for more social amenities for the troops in Japan to offset the hazards to their physical and moral health. Next day, my plane to Singapore was routed through Saigon. A cable was sent to Bill Cunningham, a secretary at the U.S. embassy whom I had met on a boat some years earlier and with whom I had kept in touch. The pilot, an Australian Catholic, invited me to make the journey in his cabin. He gave me a great deal of information about the engines which was boring but he also let me hear the radio communications which came in continually and were of the greatest interest. Safety precautions are remarkably detailed. I learned that the height of the plane is constantly controlled so that even in poor visibility the possibility of a collision is almost nil. Bill Cunningham was awaiting me at the airport where we were due to tarry for an hour. He had received the cable from Hong Kong and, in addition, had been warned by the air-attaché of the British embassy of my impending arrival. He would therefore have been there to meet me even without my cable. I was amazed that our embassy had to be told that I was being routed through their territory. I was met in Singapore about eight thirty p.m. by Father Tobin who took me to Air Commodore McDonald at Seletar to stay the night. Colonel Davey,

[144]

my usual host, was away but since I had to leave early next morning for Ipoh and Kuala Lumpur it was more convenient to stay near the airport. Diana and Bill McDonald were out at a concert so I retired early to bed. Next morning I said Mass in the sitting-room served by the chaplain.

On 1st April at nine a.m. I flew with Father Tobin to Kuala Lumpur. It was a special plane which I shared with the newly appointed commander-in-chief R.N. Far East. This most charming man regretted that he would be away when I visited the navy the following week. We had a long talk and he spoke of the rather absurd arrangements by which a sailor receives less money when on active service at sea than when he is at home. He said he would arrange for an expert to give precise details about conditions and pay when I went to the naval base. He would be infinitely obliged if I would put the sailors' case to the authorities when I was back in London. He told me he was to be met by a guard of honour at Kuala Lumpur and invited me to inspect it with him. Naturally I refused. I was glad I had done so when I saw the size of the guard of honour. Not knowing the form I would have been completely out of place in episcopal regalia at a purely military exercise.

Father Henry, the senior R.A.F. chaplain (who had been in my class at school) was among the group awaiting the arrival of the aircraft. We all stood by respectfully while the admiral inspected the guard of honour. Immediately the ceremony was over I was introduced to General Stockwell and other senior officers whom I was later to meet on their own ground. Father Henry had the Catholics of this station assembled in a little room. I addressed them in the usual way, prayed with them and gave a blessing. After chatting for a little while and collecting the addresses of their wives or parents I was taken to the house of Chief Justice Mathew with whom I was to stay. I was shown to my room, given a cup of tea and immediately afterwards taken to call on the G.O.C. of this region. By the time all the formalities were completed it was time for lunch.

My host at lunch was General Templer. I found him interesting, energetic and enigmatic. It struck me that he has exceptional flair rather than text-book military learning. A resolute man, he sees with piercing certainty that the way to win the jungle war is to create social conditions likely to tempt bandits from the jungle into the 'new villages' he has created. I had a slight argument with him during lunch when he repeated what he had been told by some reporters. Their story had been that the G.I.s are soured and refuse even to fraternise with Korean civilians. "When they come out of the line," he quoted, "they just sigh for Wyoming or Nebraska and refuse even to smile at the Korean children." Recalling the generous way in which the G.I.s have clothed and looked after the Korean orphans I suggested that these reporters must have thought it would please an Englishman to be told how much kinder British Tommies are than American G.I.s. He took my criticism kindly. Before the day was out he sent a personal letter by messenger thanking me for coming to the Far East to visit the troops and especially for expressing my views on Korea. If true greatness is shown by small courtesies this was one more proof of the stature of the future Field Marshal.

That night the Catholic officers gave a dinner in my honour to which General Stockwell came and made a magnificent speech. The next day I flew to Bentong to talk to the King's African Rifles. After that I flew to a spot in the jungle occupied by the Royal West Kents. In the evening I had dinner privately with General Stockwell who is, if possible, even more impressive in private than as commander of the Malayan forces. The following day I addressed all staff officers at the request of General Stockwell. I had a large and attentive audience. I sat up late that night to make sure that the speech was well prepared. I gave my (superficial) impressions of the jungle war, communism and the situation in Korea.

Immediately after the talk I flew to Ipoh to visit the Manchesters, Worcesters and Lancers. After lunch I visited all the patients in the large hospital where the chief medical officer, as often, was a Catholic. On my return I gave the Stations of the Cross in the garrison church in Kuala Lumpur. Father Smith had erected a marquee in the grounds and there was a reception. Dinner that night at Chief Justice Mathew's house was beautifully cooked and served by his boy Ar See. The judge had formed the view that since it was Good Friday it would be improper to invite Catholic officers to bring their non-Catholic wives. I did not ask him to explain the theological reason for this view.

The next day I was due to leave for Singapore. Since I had no foreign money throughout my tour with the troops my host had to give me money to tip his own servant. This kind of thing can hardly make men anxious to entertain bishops. Ar See is a Moslem and probably would not have thanked me for my blessing if I had left him with nothing more. The judge had smiled too obviously when first introducing me to his man. "My man," he said, "is Ar See." I unkindly denied him his joke by asking: "Is that his name or his religion?" My first stop on the return journey to Singapore was at Segamat. I flew on the smallest aeroplane it has ever been my misfortune to use. It had been hired by the chaplains from the Malayan Airways as no R.A.F. craft small enough to land on the tiny grass airstrip in the jungle was available that day. I was met at the clearing in the jungle at Segamat by the usual scout and armoured car. We drove about ten miles to the H.Q. of the Cameronians. The Catholic soldiers were all assembled in the church—a small mission church with a delightful Chinese priest who regarded this visit as being primarily to his tiny flock rather than to the troops. He played the organ and sang the '*Sacerdos et Pontifex*' on my entry making the little ceremony as impressive as if I had been the Pope entering St. Peter's in Holy Year. I spoke to the soldiers and blessed them and afterwards they clustered around and took pictures. I then discovered that they were about to leave for home. They had been due to go the day before but had insisted on putting off their journey for my coming. Faith and loyalty can hardly be better proved than by postponing home leave even for an hour. The Scots are wonderful Catholics. I told the chaplain not to bother to take their home addresses since they would be home before me. At the close of the visit he nevertheless handed me a long list. The men did not see why their wives and mothers should be deprived of a letter because their men had got home first. The soldiers, in fact, looked forward to being home to receive the letter. After talking to the soldiers I went into the Chinese priest's house to drink lemonade. He was very young and keen and had a devoted little flock most of whom brought children to be blessed.

I had a long talk with the C.O. who had just attained fame by a realistic performance in which an enterprising B.B.C. reporter broadcast while an ambush battle was actually in progress. This dour officer was most appreciative of the chaplains who were all ready to go with the soldiers into the jungle for action. He had especially nice things to say about Father Smith, the R.C. padre.

After lunch I returned with my escort to the airstrip in the jungle. I woke up the pilot and we took off in thundery weather. Soon after we were airborne a tremendous storm broke out. Although it was mid-afternoon the blackness was almost complete. It was broken only by flashes of lightning. The thunder was deafening and the tiny plane was thrown about in the air like a piece of cardboard. We strapped ourselves in tightly but it would still have been hard to keep our seats unless the pilot had clung to his joystick and I to the side of the plane. We both felt shaken. Perhaps I should speak only for myself but the pilot certainly looked shaken. He may, of course, have felt as calm as I tried to look. Suddenly we came out of the storm into bright sunshine with the jungle looking peaceful and attractive five thousand feet below. At that moment any land would have looked attractive to me. "That wasn't so good," said the pilot with a relieved smile. The relief didn't last long. As he spoke a great thunder cloud swallowed us up and the pitching started all over again. I shall not attempt a description but the second storm was considerably worse than the first. It really did seem unlikely that this small craft could weather it. The experience was too unpleasant to allow me to feel any sensation—even fear. I imagine that if my blood pressure had been taken at that moment I would have been ordered six months' rest. Again without warning we came into beautiful weather and found ourselves over Singapore. We made a grateful landing. I felt sure that the pilot shared my feelings. The poor fellow then had to take his tiny craft back to the jungle base.

Father Tobin was at the airport to meet me and we went at once to the Good Shepherd convent where the team I had chosen for the Easter broadcast was assembled. Colonel Davey, his daughter and some service people together with two chaplains were waiting to rehearse the scripture readings. The girls' choir was anxious for me to hear their singing. It was to be a feature broadcast on the resurrection and I had to put in a great deal of work with the readers. The choir was almost perfect but I gave them the impression that they could do better. With the co-operation of the nun choir-mistress (an excellent musician who had no suspicion of my musical ignorance) a superlatively good performance was produced. After nearly two hours the programme took shape and I was optimistic for the next day's broadcast.

On Easter morning I said Mass at the hospital and preached a very short sermon so as to be in time to preside and preach at High Mass in Tanglin. A large congregation was assembled and girls from the Good Shepherd convent sang beautifully. These young girls—mainly Chinese —have been rescued from the streets. After Mass I gave special praise to them and the soldier servers who had rehearsed the ceremonies with great care. After Mass Reverend Mother mentioned an ex-chaplain living in Singapore who had left his religious order and was working with the British Council. She thought that a visit from me might prepare the way for him to be reconciled to his superiors. I arranged to call on him in his office before leaving Singapore.

I had lunch with the bishop who lives near his cathedral. There was a large gathering of clergy mostly French but also some Chinese who had been expelled from China. It was a happy gathering and the bishop made a long and graceful speech to which I replied with less grace but more brevity. In private conversation he told me that he and his clergy had been seriously misrepresented by articles in the *Tablet* accusing them of being un-enterprising and anti-British. I promised that when opportunity served I would speak to Douglas Woodruff, the editor, and try to remedy any harmful views current in England. He and his clergy, the bishop explained, were in no way anti-British but happened to be French. The bishop is a shy man and, surrounded by service brass-hats, probably does not play the same part in public life as an English bishop would in his place. The whole of Malaya is under the ecclesiastical care of the Missionary Society of Paris. Since the country is a British protectorate (Singapore was still a British colony) some thought it might have been an advantage for the Church to have been in the care of English clergy. It was not a matter of great importance since the people are Malayan and Chinese and the services have their own chaplains from home. There was no reason to think that if Malaya were independent the Church would be best served by the British. The bishop told me of the wonderful work being done by the Sisters of St. Maur, the Sisters of the Good Shepherd, the Little Sisters of the Poor and all the nuns. Here, as everywhere in the East, the Sisters are a great power for good. More vocations to the missions would yield rich spiritual dividends.

In the afternoon I repaired to the radio station and met my team of performers. We had a long rehearsal in an air-conditioned studio which was ice-cold and rather too much of a contrast to the furnace atmosphere outside. The girls were in tremendous voice and the reciters were by now *so* scared of me that they were in that highly nervous state which is so desirable for a first class broadcast. The professional singer who was to sing extracts from *The Messiah* was terrible when she first ran through her score but I gave her the treatment. She, too, fortunately remained unaware of my total musical incompetence and submitted to some high-pressure tuition. It had its effect for she stopped being casual (apparently she broadcasts regularly) and to my relief became as twitchy as the rest of the cast. Having reduced everyone to nervous wrecks I sent them out to the furnace to relax but only after assuring them that their performance was now truly remarkable. I had no doubt that the broadcast would be a complete success. They had precisely five minutes to take draughts of hot air. The professional singer demanded a nice cup of tea and it was clear that she needed it. There was nothing casual about her now. Then it was my turn for a shock. As soon as the studio was empty I began to put my papers in order. I then made a terrible discovery. In all the excitement I had quite forgotten to write any script for myself. I had been so anxious to make everyone else perfect in their parts that I had done nothing about my own. I had not even written my sermon—much less what in the trade is called the continuity. So now we were all nervous. The service started on time, the singing was superb, the reading of the scripture magnificent and the professional was on her mettle. When sermon time came I pretended to read as I improvised. I was afraid that if the people I had bullied were to realise I was preaching impromptu they would be tempted to assassinate me in the studio.

Dinner that night with Father Tobin at the Graysons, a magnificent Catholic family. Colonel Grayson, the Provost Marshal, is a convert who had to overcome great opposition to become a Catholic. His wife, a Holy Child girl, is a veritable rock of Peter. The girls Mary and Angela are keen Catholics and the little lad is splendid. A very happy evening.

Next morning after Mass I put the final polish on a speech due next day and had lunch with the medical officer of the hospital, Colonel Fava, an old boy of Fort Augustus. He had just heard that his youngest boy was not going to be accepted in their prep. school despite a promise by a former headmaster. I promised to write to the Abbot of Fort Augustus on my return. This fortunately I remembered to do and subsequently learned that all was well. The baby boy in the house who had spent the week rehearsing how to kiss my ring and say "Good morning, my Lord", lost nerve as I approached and disappeared in a sea of tears from which it took me fifteen minutes to extract him. But all ended happily. When he grows up he will be both a bishop and a doctor so as to follow in his father's footsteps and mine.

A terrible thunderstorm broke out during lunch and must have caught some of the children who were on their way to the Confirmation due that afternoon. The garrison church was too small to accommodate the congregation but as there are no windows everyone standing round the church could follow the service. The ceremony was beautifully accompanied by the Good Shepherd choir and the children had a wonderful tea after Benediction. In preparation for a garden party a marquee had been erected but a storm swamped the field. The party had to be held in the neighbouring drill hall and the children's sports abandoned. We had some fine rowdy party games in the hall to make up for it. Between items I met soldiers, civilians and wives. Despite the weather most Catholics arrived and I shook many a hand and signed untold numbers of autograph books, prayer books, holy pictures as well as cigarette packets and dirty pieces of paper eagerly offered by children who doubtless lost them before nightfall.

I was entertained, inevitably, at the Raffles Hotel. My hosts were the service chaplains (of all three services) stationed in Singapore and Malaya. We were about a dozen and they presented me with a beautiful gold watch suitably inscribed. Short speeches were made on behalf of the army, R.A.F. and navy. Making allowance for conventional compliments I was persuaded that my visit had heartened all Catholics and especially the chaplains. They pointed out the obvious lesson that a Bishop-in-Ordinary to the Forces would be of great value. I promised to report to the hierarchy and the Holy See their strong desire for a bishop of their own to whose support, they said, all chaplains would be happy to contribute. Considerate as ever the chaplains released me early for a much needed night's sleep. I kept my promise on my return and they soon had their own bishop.

On 7th April I gave the War Room Talk to a hall full of staff officers. This was in some ways the most rewarding of all my ventures. I was, of course, more than usually nervous. The title of the talk was 'Impressions of the Far East' but after five weeks in the area I felt it intolerable to inflict my views on an audience of whom many had spent years in the Far East. I talked instead of Korea (which few had seen) as a preamble to a review of world communism. I drew on a fairly wide knowledge of communist literature and techniques as well as my brief tour of Soviet Russia to show that what they were attempting by military means the Catholic Church had been and was still doing with the sword of the spirit. The talk was in no way provocative. I made no attempt to boost the Catholc Church but called for a realisation that false doctrine is conquered not by force but by true doctrine.

This War Room Talk was routine procedure at the end of a visit. The V.I.P.s are usually top military or political people. The only other clerical performer had been Dr. Garbett, Archbishop of York, several years earlier. He was a gifted speaker and a famous public figure. I was unknown to all but the Catholic officers and my invitation to speak was due to the courtesy of the commander-in-chief who thought that failure to invite me might be interpreted as a slight to the Catholic Church. My own nervousness was probably equalled by that of the senior chaplains and Catholic officers. When I learned that attendance at War

Room Talk was compulsory my nervousness increased. It would have been bad enough to talk to senior officers (only those who had attained their majority were allowed to attend) who had come freely. I felt almost sick with fear at the thought of a hall full of restless colonels forced to listen to me. I decided to assure them at once that I did not regard myself as capable of teaching them anything about the Far East.

I began by comparing my position with that of the commander of a prisoner of war camp for British officers in Germany during the recent war. He knew that the prisoners were planning to escape but not the details of their plan. He therefore tried to bluff them into abandoning their attempt. He paraded the prisoners and addressed them in what he thought were colloquial terms. "You think," he said, "that I know damn nothing about your plans. Let me tell you, my friends, I know damn all." That, I explained to my audience, was a fair description of my own knowledge of the Far East. I would therefore need their indulgence as I gave my brief address. This they willingly accorded me. I have rarely had a more attentive audience. My words were enthusiastically listened to and the discussion which followed was intelligent and prolonged. I heard later that the officers were immensely surprised that my talk had been interesting. I had been unwontedly frightened of speaking because I knew that I was talking to the best brains in Farelf on their own subject. The chaplains were relieved that they would not have to live me down.

At midday I went to the naval base. An invitation to lunch had been received only that morning. The officer in charge, a captain or an admiral (I was not familiar with naval uniforms) was stiff. The commander-in-chief had evidently expressed displeasure at the lack of naval hospitality. The priest rightly refused to cancel the lunch he had asked a lowly civilian from the admiralty to provide for me. This excellent Catholic offered to stand down when the tardy invitation to lunch had been received. I talked to the Catholic sailors in chapel and had tea with the station commander, a man of great charm and warmth. On the instructions of the C.-in-C. I was furnished with figures relating to pay and allowances. I promised to campaign on my return for the removal of the anomaly which made it more expensive for married men to go on active service abroad than remain in port at home.

At eight p.m. the Catholic Officers' Association gave me dinner. My kindly host, Colonel Davey, as president was in the chair. On my left was Diana McDonald, the non-Catholic wife of the Air Officer Commanding, who had been my hostess on more than one occasion when I was visiting the R.A.F. The dinner was excellent and the attendance large. At my request there were few speeches though an unscheduled speech by Mrs. Swan, president of the English Catholic Women's League on her way to Australia for the Congress, was permitted. During my brief remarks I thanked all who had been my hosts and praised the magnificent spirit of all the service personnel I had met during the whole course of my tour.

8th April was a quiet day. After Mass I went in search of the ex-chaplain. On my way the Grayson family took me shopping, not to buy anything but just to see a bazaar. I found my priest and had a long talk. He was friendly and co-operative. We agreed to say a daily rosary for each other and he promised to let me know if and when he was ready to be reconciled to his religious superiors. I never heard of him again.

I had lunch with the Australian Redemptorist missioners. A grand set of men. Among other duties they look after Catholic broadcasts on Radio Malaya. After lunch I addressed the local Legion of Mary which had gathered at short notice in impressive numbers. In the late afternoon the Daveys gave a cocktail party for their non-Catholic friends who had not had any chance to meet me informally. Among them were two brigadiers who were most anxious to carry on discussion arising from the War Room Talk. They came early for this specific object but others came early too. We had to leave most of the problems of the Far East unsolved.

My last social function was a dinner given by Catholic civilians (mainly civil service and business men) at the Singapore Club. We had a very pleasant dinner and, of course, more speeches. Here I met an old lawyer whose lapsed son had just been released from prison where he had been held without trial on the suspicion of being a communist. I asked the father to send his son to me next morning if he would like a chat. This should have been my last night in Singapore but the B.O.A.C. plane lost a propeller in India and the flight was twenty-four hours delayed. The young man came and we had a long talk. He sounded bitter at first but I think I was able to help him. The rest of the day I spent writing letters and making calls. In the evening I saw the two brigadiers who had been defrauded of their discussion the day before. Incidentally, I had my first meal with the Daveys. Although their house had been my headquarters I had been booked every night for some official engagement. We had a lovely early night. I had to rise at three a.m. next morning. The splendid colonel served my Mass at four o'clock. I returned to the house to say good-bye to the colonel's wife and daughter. Nobody ever had more charming hosts. The colonel and Father Tobin drove me to the airport where I met Cardinals Gracias and Agagianian en route for the Sydney Congress. The Bishop of Malacca was there to see us off. So was Mary Grayson who works part time for the civil airlines. This typical kindness which involved rising in the early hours was the last of a series of acts of courtesy.

CHAPTER

TEN

FOR THE FIRST TIME IN SIX WEEKS I WAS ABLE TO TURN MY THOUGHTS
to the Eucharistic Congress which was the chief reason for my being
so far from home. I realised that I was not really enthusiastic about
this or any other congress. The reason why I had offered to visit the
British and Commonwealth Forces in the Far East was the need to
justify my journey. To travel half-way round the world just to give two
or three talks took a great deal of justifying but the tour of the forces
had been so rewarding that I had no regrets. Now I needed to work
up some enthusiasm for what was awaiting me in Australia.

One task which brooked no postponement was the re-writing of the
chief speech I was to give at the peak of the congress. On the Saturday
afternoon I was due to address the men's rally on the show grounds in
Sydney. Australia by reason of its geographical position was far more
conscious than Europe of the communist threat. The Catholics of
Australia were doubly aware of the danger because of the persecution
of the Catholic Church in Soviet-controlled countries. That is why I
had been asked to address the rally on social justice and the communist
threat to Christianity. I had complied with the request to send a copy
of my speech two months in advance and this was now an embarrassment. Events had overtaken me and rendered my speech useless. In
what I thought to be a brilliantly original approach to the subject I
had contrasted Stalin, the current personification of Soviet power, and
Christ, the symbol of divine power. In graphic terms I had pictured
Stalin then at the height of his despotic might lying dead in a tomb
next to Lenin's mausoleum in Red Square. Stalin's power would vanish

at his death while Christ became still more glorious when He rose from the tomb. While my back was turned Stalin had actually died. Thus the speech had become pointless. I had to re-write it taking as my point of departure not the living but the dead dictator. This was before the famous Khrushchev relations in which the Soviets admitted—what all but fellow-travellers knew—that the Stalin era was a reign of terror.

The Australian Eucharistic Congress was so perfectly organised that although the priest responsible for all arrangements was struck with a fatal illness just as the congress was due to open, everything took place in faultless order. Visiting bishops had been booked into hotels while the more fortunate priests were lodged in presbyteries and convents. My plane was met by Monsignor Wallis, a remarkable man who was officially in charge of hospitality but ended up in control of everyone from Cardinal Gilroy to the youngest altar server. He saw how I envied the clergy their presbyteries and invited me to sleep in my hotel but make my home in his parish of Darlinghurst. In the event after two days he managed to find me a bed in his own presbytery. This made the congress an outstanding success for me personally. All the New Zealand bishops and no small number of the Australian hierarchy managed to find their way to Darlinghurst at the end of each day's ceremonies. No *maître d'hotel* in Sydney dispensed more generous hospitality than Monsignor Wallis. His genius as an organiser was equalled by his virtuosity as a host. I had never experienced such comradeship with strangers or, to be more exact, new friends. Of those whom I met daily in Darlinghurst I had previously met only two—Bishop Goody with whom I had been a student in Rome and Bishop Young who had visited me in the Mission House in London.

At the close of the Sydney Congress I went to Canberra with Bishop Young to address the Catholic Society of the University which, like the city itself, was in the chrysalis stage of development. It was fascinating to visit a place in which everything was so new. Canberra was planned to be the capital city of a great nation. There were other cities which could have served but presumably the rivalry of the city fathers in Sydney and Melbourne made it politically desirable to construct an entirely new capital. There is something both touching and exhilarating about Australia. It has the look and feel of the new world but passionately desires the culture of the old. While being attached to American plumbing it is nostalgic for the mother country.

It is difficult to describe the outlook of the Australian people. It will become even more difficult with the increase of New Australians i.e.

those who have been encouraged to immigrate to populate the sub-continent with whites. The New Australians will supply the needs of industrial and agricultural development and will presumably produce manpower to attempt to defend the country if uncomfortably-crowded Japan seeks an outlet. The yellow peril which was a source of anxiety to the England of my boyhood is hardly mentioned in Australia. At the time of my visit Japan was still a topic of conversation because the war was still a recent memory. Since then the Chinese have emerged as a nuclear power. Traditionally the yellow races have been mutually hostile but communism is a busy bridge-builder. Before the end of the twentieth century Japan and China may have formed a political alliance and the yellow peril may again become a preoccupation. Such thoughts must be at least in the sub-conscious minds of Australians. Although the country is vast the population of Australia at the time of my visit was not much more than that of London. Yet the Australians have made an international mark in literature, music, science and, of course, in sport. We are not surprised when Australian sportsmen carry off the prizes since they can always find sunshine somewhere in their country and so presumably they practise their sporting skill at all times. Weather alone cannot explain the cultural and intellectual eminence of such a disproportionately large percentage of its citizens.

During my evening with the teachers, students and bureaucrats of this new city I sensed an effervescent enthusiasm for high standards. The questioning by the undergraduates after my lecture was penetrating and original. Their reactions were less naïve than those of audiences with similarly modest academic attainment in the United States. Nor did the undergraduates try to demonstrate their intellectual superiority over the lecturer as we have always done in student circles in England. Impressions left after one evening with the students of Canberra do not establish for all time that Australians are brighter and better mannered than Catholics elsewhere. I merely record the extraordinary effect this less than half-built city had on me. For all I know Canberra may now be as unenterprising as any other city but it gave me the unforgettable experience of meeting young Catholic enthusiasts determined to reach the top of the academic ladder and to spread knowledge of Christ and the Church throughout their country. There were doubtless plenty of cynics among the undergraduates but they happened not to appear at my meeting. To judge from the many Australians I have met subsequently the proportion of cynics in the Australian Church remains astonishingly low.

[157]

From Canberra I went to Melbourne to lecture in the city hall under the auspices of the Legion of Mary. I was the guest of Archbishop Mannix. The chance to meet this renowned warrior would alone have attracted me to Melbourne. To an earlier generation his name had been the symbol of Catholic resistance to the Protestant Establishment. Mannix had been called from his chair of theology at Maynooth near Dublin to join the mainly Irish hierarchy of Australia in 1912. He was already a recognised Irish patriot when war broke out in 1914. His powerful advocacy of resistance to conscription was heard in every village in Ireland. At the height of the Anglo-Irish troubles Dr. Mannix was summoned home to Ireland where his mother was dying. The British government, reluctant to allow him to land in Ireland, caused his liner to be intercepted by a destroyer. Mannix was taken on board and brought to England where he was forbidden to reside within thirty miles of the coast. International Catholic sympathy for Mannix was immense. When to his love of Ireland was added a son's love for his mother on her deathbed the emotional mixture was potent indeed.

For me this was no more than a childhood memory but it made the prospect of meeting Dr. Mannix the more attractive. The silver-haired archbishop with the refined beauty of his countenance made it hard to think of him as a warrior. He was destined to live until a few months before his hundredth birthday but I met him when he was not yet ninety years of age. He was a host of quite exceptional charm. All good hosts care for the comfort of their guests but Mannix conveyed the impression of deep personal feeling. The following morning the old man insisted on serving my Mass. He knelt down at his own prie-dieu and showed me the inscription on the fly-leaf of his prayer book. It was in the handwriting of my predecessor in Leeds, Bishop Cowgill. The book had been presented together with a silver chalice by the priests and people of Yorkshire to Archbishop Mannix during his exile. The British government had forbidden him to visit Liverpool where the largely Irish population was anxious to cherish him. Leeds was as near as he was allowed to approach.

That night Archbishop Mannix introduced me graciously to the crowded city hall. He had no intention, he said, of referring to "far off unhappy things and battles long ago" which in retrospect seemed more amusing than tragic. He nevertheless was glad to have an opportunity of publicly showing courtesy to a bishop from Leeds. He spoke of the welcome he had received from the Catholics of Yorkshire at a time when he was forbidden to be the guest of the larger Catholic communities in Liverpool and Glasgow. He refrained from telling the dramatic story of his encounter with the British government thirty years earlier when the I.R.A. (Irish Republican Army) was fighting for the independence of Ireland. These were the days of the Sinn Fein movement of which the I.R.A. was the military wing. Although responsible for the murder of fellow Irishmen in the police force (R.I.C.) the I.R.A. of that time were regarded as genuine patriots. The clergy and people of Ireland were behind them. The hierarchy of Ireland had issued a proclamation in January 1920 which said: "The legitimate demand of Ireland to choose her own government has not only been denied her but every organ for the expression of her national life has been ruthlessly suppressed and her people subjected to an iron rule as cruel and unjust as it is ill-advised and out of date."

It must be remembered that the hierarchy was speaking at the height of the reign of terror by the notorious Black and Tans. These were mainly unemployed ex-service men hastily recruited and armed to subdue the rebel Irish. This improvised army wore the black trousers of the R.I.C. but their jackets were made from surplus army khaki material. Hence the nickname 'Black and Tans' or 'the Tans'. It was at this time that Archbishop Mannix was summoned to the death-bed of his old mother whom he had not seen since before the war. He was destined never to see her again because Lloyd George, the British prime minister, feared that if Mannix were allowed to visit Ireland he would give such heart to his fellow countrymen that they would redouble their fight against the army and the Black and Tans. Unfortunately he chose to return to Ireland via the U.S.A. where he conducted a coast-to-coast lecture tour. Whether or not by chance, his tour coincided with that of Eamonn de Valera who had been elected President of the Irish Republic after his escape from an English gaol. Daniel Mannix was an impressive orator. He did not raise his voice or wave his arms but he chose precise and emotive words. "All that Ireland asks of England is this," he told Americans. "Take one of your hands off my throat and the other out of my pocket."

Such expressions were culled from his speeches and headlined in the press of Australia and the United Kingdom. They caused grave disquiet and the prime minister told the House of Commons that "in view of his disloyal utterances" in the United States Dr. Mannix would not be allowed to set foot in Ireland. When the *Baltic* in which Mannix was travelling drew near the Irish coast it was shadowed by British destroyers. When the liner came within sight of Queenstown (Cobh) two of the destroyers closed in and remained within hailing distance. When darkness fell the searchlights of the naval escorts kept the ship under observation. At midnight it was ordered to heave to. Before transferring Mannix to a destroyer detectives from Scotland Yard warned him that he was to be taken to England by order of Sir Henry Wilson C.I.G.S. (later assassinated by two Anglo-Irish ex-servicemen). He would not be allowed to visit Liverpool, Manchester or Glasgow where the Irish lived in great numbers. The *Baltic* was then sent on its way while the destroyer H.M.S. *Wyvern* took its explosive cargo to Penzance. Not surprisingly the archbishop was thereafter known as the Pirate of Penzance.

On my way home from Australia my first stop was in Auckland, New Zealand. My chief object in making that city a port of call was to visit an old friend who was superior of the Little Sisters of the Poor. Sister Constance had been a friend since I was a student in Rome. She had kept in touch with me by letter from many parts of the world but I had not expected ever to see her again. Archbishop Liston of Auckland, a devoted friend of Sister Constance, did everything in his power to make my visit memorable. He arranged for all the New Zealand bishops to stay the week-end in Auckland where he organised a rally in the town hall and a High Mass in the cathedral. I was not in the country long enough to come to any firm decision but I felt that New Zealanders are gentler than their Australian neighbours and rather more enthusiastic about the mother country. When Captain Cook annexed this territory in the eighteenth century his action was solemnly disavowed by the government of the day. It was not until 1840 that H.M. government directed the Union Jack to be hoisted by Captain Hobson, R.N.

Since a return ticket to New Zealand allows a trip round the world for the same price I chose not to retrace my steps. I was nevertheless impatient to be back in Leeds. I did not regret the time I had spent with the forces in the Far East but like most men on their travels I had begun to yearn for home. I therefore made few stops on the way back but I was sorry afterwards that I had not stayed in Fiji. Such regrets are futile. It is useless to delay in foreign places when your heart is already half-way home. Sight-seeing under such conditions becomes a torture. The only overnight stay on my journey to America was in Honolulu, a city of astonishing beauty. Honolulu and Hong Kong are rivals for the title of the most attractively illuminated city in the world. (For the record my award went to Hong Kong.) I wanted to stop here because

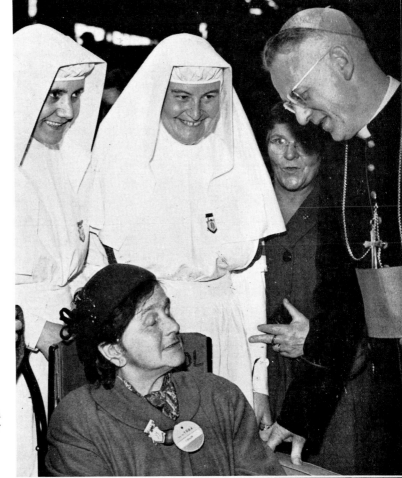

rdes: with the Poor
ants and sick pilgrim.

evision discussion with
rbara Ward (Lady
kson)

St. Nicholas Pro-Cathedral 16th July 1957: Enthronement as Archbishop of Liverpool.

Pearl Harbour played such a decisive role in the history of our times. If the Japanese had not made the treacherous attack which virtually annihilated the U.S. Pacific fleet the Americans might not have entered the second world war until the axis powers had conquered the old world.

Honolulu and, indeed, all Hawaii is as unreal as a picture postcard. Sky and sea are azure, the waters opalescent and the vegetation exotic. Although a pleasure ground for the wealthy—Waikiki beach frequently features in the literature of luxury—Honolulu takes care to avoid all ostentation in catering for rich tourists. Hoardings—bill boards in the American idiom—have been banished in the interest of the landscape while the city centre itself is a spacious park. The vegetation has been enriched by the introduction of Chinese banyans, Norfolk pines, African tulip trees, Australian ironwoods as well as palms, vines and flame trees —anything in fact will grow in this fertile soil. The city resembles a botanical garden. In some miraculous fashion this has all been achieved without vulgarity. Some tourists do their best to degrade this lovely city but it remains a triumph of nature and planning. Much as I wanted to be home I would willingly have stayed longer in such surroundings.

From Honolulu I flew to San Francisco where I was met by Father Wallace. An Irishman ordained for the diocese of Los Angeles, he had been prevented by the war from taking up duty. He had joined the British army as a chaplain but was soon discharged as unsuitable. He was an organist of genius and hyper-sensitive as musicians often are. This was the chief reason why he always managed to fall out with every superior. He was neither rebellious nor wayward but he took offence at the slightest opposition or rebuke. In himself he was gentle and lovable. When eventually he reached Los Angeles he became depressed, felt harshly treated and soon returned to Ireland. I had first met him when he was doing duty as a curate in Ilford where my mother lived. Having two sons priests she always kept open house for the clergy. Young priests far from home found in her a willing substitute for their own mothers. She was just what Peter Wallace needed when, inevitably, he fell out with the bishop, parish priest and all the local clergy. After a scene he would go to my mother's house, play the piano, have a cup of tea and calm down. All this time he was worried because he knew that his proper place was in Los Angeles, the diocese to which canonically he was bound (incardinated). The difficulty was that the diocese of Los Angeles refused to have him back.

In the summer of 1947 I had gone to the United States before taking up my work with the Catholic Missionary Society. While I was in New York Cardinal Griffin had come from England to see Cardinal Spellman. I was invited to lunch at Archbishop's House where I met one of the New York auxiliary bishops named McIntyre. In the course of conversation I told Bishop McIntyre of the plight of Peter Wallace. I explained that he was a good zealous priest but a victim of his musician's temperament. I asked if he would make a plea for Peter when next he wrote to his friend, the Archbishop of Los Angeles. He kept his word but the Archbishop died before he had the chance of replying. The successor who was appointed with unaccustomed speed was none other than Bishop McIntyre. As Cardinal McIntyre he became well known after the Vatican Council for his efforts to save nuns from destroying themselves by abandoning their vows, constitutions and religious habits. This was regarded by the liberal press as unpardonable interference with religious freedom. Bishop McIntyre was no more successful in saving Peter Wallace than in his later attempt to save his nuns. Peter, of course, was invited back by the new archbishop. Fellow priests in the Catholic Missionary Society helped me to buy Peter a ticket to Los Angeles. He was so grateful that not only did he repay the money but all during the severe post-war rationing he used to send food parcels to the Mission House in Hampstead. It was this same feeling of indebtedness which led Peter to come all the way from Los Angeles to meet me in San Francisco. Unfortunately by this time he had begun to fall out with his brother clergy again. Not long after this visit I lost touch with him. He left the Church some years before it became fashionable to do so. No doubt God who created the angelic choirs will judge a musician with special indulgence.

I had no appointments in San Francisco to which I went only because there was no direct flight from Honolulu to Los Angeles. Peter had booked rooms in a small hotel where we had supper together. I remembered that San Francisco was the home town of Allie Adams whom I had met in Moscow in 1936. Seventeen years had passed since we had been in correspondence and I had no idea of her address. I looked at the telephone directory to find that, although there were several entries under Adams, there was only one Mrs. Adams. Not very hopefully I dialled the number. The lady who answered the phone said that Mrs. Adams was not at home but if I left the number she would ask her to call me. Not without embarrassment I explained that I could hardly give her that trouble unless she were the Mrs. Adams for whom I was looking. I asked if this Mrs. Adams had ever been in Russia. Yes, I was told, she had been there nearly twenty years earlier. I left my number and rang off. Within seconds Alice was on the phone. She had not been out but never spoke to strangers on the phone. Her house, she said, was only a few blocks away and she would be round within five minutes. We had a great re-union and for old times sake Allie came to Mass the next morning as she used to do in Moscow.

The rest of the story of my journey round the world is soon told. In Los Angeles I stayed with Monsignor George Scott once my fellow student at Ushaw. His brother Pat who had been my special friend had recently died. It was chiefly to visit George and to console his parents that I had arranged my itinerary to include the city of the angels. Joseph Scott, the father, was also an Ushaw man. He had enjoyed a formidable reputation in the courts. He was the most famous advocate on the west coast and during my two days in Los Angeles he recounted some of the notable trials in which he had taken part.

George Scott showed me enough of Hollywood to make me glad to be returning to England. There was an opulence and artificiality about the town which I found most unattractive. The only bright spot in my tour was a visit to Barbara Clark to whom as a little girl in Barking I had given First Holy Communion. She was entirely unspoiled by the glamour of filmland. It was in Los Angeles that I had my first experience of Cinerama. We were taken for a simulated ride on a roller coaster (giant dipper). It was so realistic that I began to feel sick and had to leave the cinema hurriedly. George then took me to Forest Lawn, the cemetery which makes burial a pleasure. Evelyn Waugh in *The Loved Ones* has satirised this institution and it is indeed hard to write of it without appearing cynical. I brought away with me from Forest Lawn a sample of the book-marks given to mourners to tell them the number of the page of the register on which their sleeping friend's name is recorded. ("This little gift marks the page in your Book of Friendship which bears the name of N.N.")

> Tis but a simple marker,
> Yet your place 'twill always keep,
> And show the place where you left off
> Where you . . . dozed . . . off . . . to . . . sleep.

The Forest Lawn mortuary ("The Kindlier More Reverend Way") is a highly successful enterprise. The promoters are not necromancers or religious fanatics but astute business operators. Every word of their

[163]

advertising is calculated to extract money from the bereaved. The vulgarity is breath-taking. You can have a memorial service in one of three churches ("not chapels but regularly dedicated churches. Organist supplied without charge. Hearing aids available.") One of these is called "Wee Kirk of the Heather, an exact reproduction of the Kirk where Annie Laurie worshipped". The words used by the morticians are presumably not calculated insults to their clients' intelligence but they would not deceive the most unsophisticated English widow:

> At Forest Lawn there is positive protection for the precious departed. Built to resist fire, earthquake and time itself, here is positive protection for the precious departed which brings a sense of security to families in the hour of grief... Forest Lawn Memorial advisers are as humanly interested as a doctor or lawyer. They devote unlimited time and attention to assure that the final tribute will be fitting, economical and complete in every detail.

Forest Lawn has not only the best but the largest religious painting in the world. It is the picture of the Crucifixion which is so big that a special hall had to be built to house it. That, size apart, this is no ordinary masterpiece is made clear in the brochure:

> For the subject of this tremendous composition Jan Styka chose the portentous last moments just before Jesus was nailed to the cross.

Nor was the artist content merely to study guide books of Palestine before beginning to paint.

> In order to gain first-hand knowledge of the countryside he undertook a pilgrimage to the Holy Sepulcher and traversed the banks of the Jordan and the Dead Sea. He was determined to give the world the greatest interpretation of Christ at the cross that had ever been or ever will be painted. Pope Leo XIII called him to the Vatican and blessed the palette on which he planned to mix his colors.

With such preparation it is no wonder that the greatest masterpiece of all time was produced. Los Angeles is not America. Millions of Americans are no less amused (or nauseated) than Evelyn Waugh by

[164]

Forest Lawn. It is, however, arguable that this phenomenon could not have appeared in Europe. Enough people are found in the U.S.A. to make a cosmetology service for the dead worthwhile. "Why not the best when it costs so little?" asks Forest Lawn and gives samples of its service.

Protection:
We have the only Class A fireproof mortuary building in Los Angeles.
Use of Private Slumber Room:
Where the departed loved one rests in utmost privacy, seclusion and safety during the interval before the funeral.
Uniformed Casket (coffin) *bearers:*
Another service exclusive with Forest Lawn.
Hospital Cleanliness:
White tile preparation rooms where cosmetology is conducted gleam with hospital cleanliness.

Americans are more church-going than the English. That is probably why the Catholic Church in pre-conciliar America seemed so strong. At the time of my visit to Forest Lawn the churches were crowded, priests with distinctive black silk stock revealing a small square of clerical collar were ubiquitous, convents were being re-built to accommodate the burgeoning number of novices. Smiling Bing Crosby (*Going my Way, The Bells of St. Mary's*) was taken (wrongly) to be typical of the popular and beloved American Catholic priest. Today clerical dress is regarded by many priests as an embarrassment rather than a witness of priesthood. Sisters who used to regard themselves as dead to this world have, like the Forest Lawn corpses, become painted and coiffured.

From Los Angeles I went to Denver, Colorado, to revisit my faithful friends Marney and Wilfred Eyre. The journey was remarkable only because it took us over the Rocky Mountains. I don't know if it is a routine performance or if I was especially privileged but our pilot took us down to within a few hundred feet of the Grand Canyon. The experience was not unlike seeing Cinerama but this time I did not feel sick. Nor, in fact, did I feel frightened but it did occur to me that if an engine were to develop a fault at so low an altitude it would have been impossible to land on those inhospitable rocks. Some months later an air liner did, in fact, crash in the Rockies with the loss of all lives. I wonder if the pilot had been demonstrating the rugged beauty of the mountains when the accident took place.

I did not delay long in Denver which I knew well from previous visits. The only object of my call was to give myself the pleasure of revisiting my old friends. Whenever I went to Denver I lectured at Loreto Heights College. This college and its more famous sister college, Webster Groves, in St. Louis Missouri, had impressed me on my first lecture tour soon after the war. We have nothing in the Catholic Church in England to compare with the American Catholic colleges. It is difficult, in fact, to say what an American college would represent in English terms. The great colleges correspond to our universities. The academic standards of Yale and Harvard are roughly equivalent to those of Oxford and Cambridge.

The smaller American colleges of which many are religious foundations have no counterpart in England. They are hardly comparable to the new British universities. We do not yet know how our new universities will compete with the old. How does Warwick compare with Durham? Will Essex or Sussex develop in the same way as Manchester and London? The answer depends mainly on the quality of the teachers. Chairs are not normally awarded to incompetents but thousands of lecturers had to be found quickly to fill posts in the new universities. It would be remarkable if among them there were not a fair proportion of second-rate teachers. My impression of minor American colleges is that the first two years (freshmen and sophomores in the American idiom) would be equivalent to second and third year sixth in an English public school. There was a network of Catholic colleges throughout America. (I am speaking of the year 1953 when the Church in U.S.A. was at its peak.) The parochial school system was also flourishing because the schools were staffed almost exclusively by Sisters who were paid only a nominal salary. The Greeley-Rossi survey of Catholic education which was highly regarded by Americans suggested that parochial schools were like the Rocky Mountains in being one of the indestructible facts of life. I doubt if these sociologists would still make that claim. Without Sisters there can be no free education outside of public schools (our public schools are really private schools). At the time of which I am writing the desirability of education in a Catholic school was almost an article of faith. Hence the popularity of Catholic colleges. Parents felt that in addition to giving academic training these colleges would safeguard the faith and morals of their sons and daughters. The college scene has now completely changed. Catholic colleges which mushroomed after the war have now closed or passed into secular hands. It would no longer be taken for granted in America that entrusting adolescent Catholics to the care of priests and nuns carries any reliable spiritual insurance.

My visits to Denver and St. Louis all took place at a time when the Chuch in America was peaceful and happy (or complacent and self-satisfied). Webster Groves was a favourite haunt in my lecturing days. The president was Sister Mariella who was adored by her students. Academic standards were not astronomically high but the girls received a grounding in Catholic philosophy in addition to their specialist training. American citizens feel deprived without some kind of degree but at Webster Groves a degree was not the ultimate object of education. The aim of the college was to produce balanced young women who would be leaders of the Catholic community. On one of my earliest visits to St. Louis the city had been in something of an uproar because the archbishop had just decreed that racial segregation must end in all Catholic schools and colleges. It had already been abolished in parochial schools but not in high schools and colleges. St. Louis is on the Mason-Dixon line and has a large negro population. It also has an unusual number of rich white Catholics. In America there are many millionaire Catholic families apart from the Kennedy clan of Boston. There is a concentration of such families in St. Louis, Missouri.

From earlier visits to St. Louis I knew that the rich Catholics were not indifferent to social justice. The town of St. Anne is about ten miles outside St. Louis. This town had been created as an experiment in Christian economics by a rich Catholic. The whole town was planned and built with the sole object of fostering Christian family life. It was, of course, paternalistic but since it brought security and comfort to thousands of working people they were not affronted. In any case the word paternalistic had not been coined in the 1930s. The town was laid out not only with homes, shops and playing fields but library, cinema, schools and churches both Protestant and Catholic. The houses all had central heating and air conditioning. The roads, like the town itself, each bore the name of a saint. The most remarkable feature of St. Anne's Town was its system of payment for homes. There was no fixed sum payable off the mortgage. Payment varied according to family circumstances. A man contributed according to his income and the size of his family. A well-employed man with a wife and two children might pay a hundred dollars a month. His neighbour with the same kind of house but with a family of five might have to pay only fifty dollars.

Further down the road a man unemployed or sick would pay nothing. When I first heard of St. Anne's Town I was sceptical. I was really convinced of the existence of this utopian city only when I visited it in the company of the man who had created it. He took me through the town and answered all my questions. It transpired that what had begun as an experiment in social justice with no intention of making money had already become a commercial success. Honesty is not always the worst policy.

A story which belongs to an earlier visit is worth relating here. The rich Catholics of St. Louis were angry with their archbishop because he had not consulted them before de-segregating all Catholic schools. They were wise before their time. The days of consultation came only with the Second Vatican Council. They held that if they had been consulted they would have put up enough money to provide high schools and colleges for the black Catholics of St. Louis. The archbishop, they alleged, was acting illegally in desegregating all Catholic institutions. If he persisted in his policy to integrate all Catholic schools they threatened to take him to law. The archbishop's reaction would probably cause a schism in any properly 'structured' diocese today. He threatened the rebels with excommunication. Quoting canon law he warned them that by taking their archbishop to law they would incur ecclesiastical censure. They were at liberty to denounce their archbishop to the Pope but not to the civil authorities. The rich Catholics were wise enough to know that an appeal to the Holy See would have been rejected unconditionally. The Pope could hardly have become a champion of racial segregation. No more was heard of a civil action against the archbishop. Nor was any Catholic high school or college for negroes built.

During the week following the declaration of the archbishop (read from every pulpit in St. Louis) I found myself addressing an open forum at Webster Groves. In those pre-television days a lecture from an international speaker produced a packed hall. (Although I was often introduced as an 'international' speaker I never learned the precise meaning of the term. It made me feel like a tramp flying a Liberian flag.) After the lecture questions began, inevitably, with one on colour. I refused to answer or even give an opinion on the grounds that an English visitor lacked knowledge of the domestic situation. I contented myself—and, as it happened, the audience—with the fictitious account of a bridegroom who confessed to his bride on their wedding night that he had deceived her. "Darling," he said, "I hadn't the courage to tell you in case you refused to marry me but I've got an incurable disease: I'm colour blind." His pretty bride was unperturbed. She replied, "I knew you was colour blind, honey, I'm a little black girl."

From St. Louis I went to New York for a few days. I stayed with my Dominican cousins in the convent at Blauvelt and turned my thoughts towards England. I had been away for more than three months and was anxious to return to Leeds which had become home to me although I had lived there for only two years. The Yorkshire people are blunt but they are also faithful and affectionate. They had been without a bishop for a year when I was appointed. That was the chief reason why they cherished their new bishop. I felt like a father who had been too long away from his family. I was anxious not to delay in New York despite the number of relatives and friends I had there. So I took the first aircraft B.O.A.C. had to offer. I learned on boarding the aircraft that it was coronation day. As soon as we had crossed the coast the captain made a short speech and invited all passengers to toast the new Queen in champagne. The bar would remain open throughout the voyage and passengers were to help themselves at the expense of B.O.A.C. I was relieved to notice that the captain drank the toast in orange juice. Despite all temptation the crew drank no wine or spirits but three American passengers showed the depth of their attachment to royalty by emptying the whole contents of the bar before the end of the journey.

Even if the hospitality of B.O.A.C. had not made coronation day memorable the graciousness of H.M. Customs would have ensured that the day would never be forgotten by me. It is essential to keep down the weight of baggage when travelling by air because excess weight has to be paid for at a phenomenally high rate. I had therefore collected as little extra baggage as possible in the course of my travels. The only acquisition of value was the beautiful gold watch which had been presented to me by the chaplains in the Far East at the end of my tour. Suitably inscribed it was a very handsome ornament. I had very little money left at the end of my travels and wondered if I would be able to afford the customs duty on this expensive gift. I declared the watch but was unable to give the customs officer any idea of its cost. He took it to his superior officer who studied the inscription with great interest. The watch was returned to me with the compliments of the chief customs officer who said that on coronation day it would be indelicate to impose duty on a warrior returning from Her Majesty's Forces.

CHAPTER
ELEVEN

BACK IN LEEDS I WAS ABLE TO TAKE A FRESH LOOK AT THE DIOCESE.
From March 1951 when I was consecrated bishop until my departure
for the Far East I had completed my first visitation of the parishes. Thus
I now had personal experience of all the very different types of parish
in the West Riding of Yorkshire. Leeds and Bradford are now so linked
by buildings as to form one continuous mass but each town retains a
quite distinctive civic consciousness. Their people are as different from
each other as both are from those of south Yorkshire. Sheffield, Barnsley and Rotherham produce a breed quite unlike that of the Leeds/
Bradford area. It is exaggerated in fun but in fact Yorkshire is unique
among English counties. It is more than just refusing any but native
Yorkshiremen for the county cricket team. When asked where they
come from, other Englishmen name their town, Yorkshiremen their
county. Their celebrated bluntness is a real quality. It can, of course,
sometimes be sheer arrogance but usually it is a genuine expression of
honesty. Integrity is admirable even when manifested without finesse
of language. It is the Yorkshire way to express disapproval with crude
directness. This can be embarrassing and even bruising but when the
newcomer has learned that such bluntness is without malice he is grateful. Nobody is left in doubt about what a typical Yorkshireman is
thinking. The Oxford dictionary gives 'tyke' as the sobriquet for Yorkshiremen (regrettably it gives 'cur' as the alternative) and this breed
has a fine pedigree.

The Catholic teachers in Yorkshire like their colleagues throughout
the country were nearly all active workers in their parishes. Only the

insensitive teach in a church school without taking some part in its wider spiritual activities. In parishes where teachers and clergy really know the children and their parents great results are achieved. Only excessively stupid parents refuse to take an interest in their children's education if both teacher and priest show enthusiasm. Having visited all the Catholic schools in the West Riding I knew the teachers and found many of them willing to give their free time to review the whole field of religious education. After regional meetings (Leeds, Bradford, Halifax, Sheffield) the teachers divided into groups according to their qualifications—Infants, Juniors, Seniors, Sixth-Formers. We had in mind ultimately to produce new text-books for Christian doctrine but the immediate intention was to revise the catechism which was in urgent need of re-writing. Even in 1954 we were not so unenlightened as to regard the catechism as the ideal handbook for catechetics but while new text-books were in course of preparation—we thought it might take ten or twelve years—the catechism could be modernised. It had remained unrevised since the last century.

Apart from nuns—notably the Notre Dame Sisters Mary John and Monica—the team included many lay teachers whose love of the faith was palpable. Mr. Jim Brannigan was senior master at St. Bede's College, Bradford, and exercised an invigorating influence on religious education throughout the country. Among the women was Miss O'Donnell, the most remarkable teacher I have ever known. Her twin sister was a Carmelite nun and must have devoted her life of contemplation and self-denial to praying for her sister's apostolate. The influence for good of this one teacher bordered on the miraculous. She was quite old when I went to Leeds but she had the energy of an adolescent. When she was forced to resign the headship of her school on reaching retiring age she sold her house in Barnsley and went to teach black children in South Africa. Meg O'Donnell was a woman of one idea. She was convinced that if children learned to value the Mass they would never lapse from the faith. In her small school at Worsborough Bridge she taught her children to know and love the Mass. They knew every action and the history and meaning of the rubrics. Understanding children Meg based her teaching on their love for the things with which they were familiar. Small children will not tolerate the slightest deviation from traditional stories and rhymes. She was relentlessly opposed to the experts who said that the shape of the Mass must be constantly changed to retain the interest of the young. Meg's seven-year-olds were fascinated by the dialogue Mass to which they knew the Latin responses by heart but I have no doubt that she would have been a great supporter of the vernacular Mass.

For nearly three years the teachers of Leeds diocese gave up their Saturdays and holidays to work on the old catechism and new text-books. Some groups even took their vacations together in order to hasten the work. What had begun as a private initiative in Leeds soon attracted the attention and interest of the Catholic community in England. I agreed to put our research at the disposal of the whole country and the hierarchy appointed Bishop Beck of Salford (later Archbishop of Liverpool) and Bishop Rudderham of Clifton to join me in this catechetical work.

This was a step towards the eventual production of an entirely new book on the lines of the German Catechism which was then thought by catechists to be the ideal work. Today it is a catechetical relic. To me as chairman of the committee this meant extending the work I had begun with the Leeds teachers in 1954. Three groups used to meet at week-ends to discuss material for religious text-books for infants, juniors and seniors. Subsequent publication of three of my books, *My Faith* (infants), *My Lord and My God* (juniors) and *Our Faith* (seniors), owed much to these devoted teachers. The nature of our work did not, however, lend itself to the catechism revision which the bishops were demanding. It was therefore necessary to recruit more teachers and to seek them from all over the country.

The original group had been formed to produce not a catechism but a set of books for the various age groups. The bishops knew that this would take several years. That is why they asked for an interim revision of the catechism which would be ready within two or three years. The major work of producing religion books would meanwhile continue. Consultations over the comparatively minor task of revising the existing catechism were held with catechists in every diocese. The result was a mass of documents which were not needed for the catechism and, in fact, were eventually handed to the national catechetical centre. The first (and, as it happened, the last) version of the *Revised Catechism of Christian Doctrine* was published (for private circulation only) in the autumn of 1958. It was used in selected secondary modern, grammar and public schools in various parts of England.

I have said that Bishop's House, Leeds was rather seigniorial. It had been bought at a time when mansions were sold for far less than modest houses. That was before property developers began to buy large houses to tear down and convert into flats. Bishop's House, Leeds, had been bought for the modest sum of six thousand pounds but it had an opulent air. I decided to move to the cathedral in the centre of the city which would provide a centre for a more intimate ministry. It seemed clear at the time that both clergy and people would benefit by my move. Looking back I now think that my move was an unconscious act of self-indulgence. I now believe that I went to Cathedral House because I had not reconciled myself to not being a parish priest. A bishop has to do his work for souls mainly at one remove. His people are all members of parishes and their own priests provide for their pastoral needs. Theoretically a bishop is parish priest of his own cathedral parish. That is why the priest-in-charge is called not a parish priest but administrator. My move was made possible because by 1954 the former Leeds Seminary near the cathedral had at last been released by the Army Pay Corps to become the diocesan curial offices. In changing residence I did not therefore have to transfer diocesan papers and business to the Cathedral House.

For some months I blissfully carried out the duties of parish priest without suspecting that my work as bishop of the diocese might suffer. I took my turn at ceremonies, hearing Confessions and preaching. Whenever I was free from other duties I visited the homes of the people, prepared children for First Holy Communion and took Holy Communion to the sick. The priests on the staff were men of outstanding zeal. At the time I did not appreciate that they needed also to be men of angelic patience. They never complained but my presence in the parish must have been a serious embarrassment. Since episcopal duties did not leave me enough time to administer a large parish efficiently I had to put many burdens on the other priests. To be in a parish once again gave me great personal satisfaction but the move was a serious error of judgment. The falsity of my position became apparent to me one day through the chance remark of a teacher. I was presenting prizes on sports day when the teacher, the coach of the winning team, sympathised with me for having to present the cup to a parish not my own! I replied that all parishes were equally dear to me but for the first time I saw the danger of what I had been attempting to do. I decided to give up the parish with the least possible delay.

It is proverbially easy to be wise after events. It is clear enough now that I ought never to have attempted to resume parochial work but I was blinded by self-interest. Nobody but a priest can understand the joy of a pastor of souls. It is more than a figure of speech to call him father. Nothing can ever replace the parish priest in the pastoral strategy of the Church. The true pastor knows his people and his people know him. They look to him in time of sorrow and joy. Academic exponents of pastoral theology suggest the abolition of territorial parishes in favour of a central body of priests trained for different sections of the people. In theory one priest will care for the young, another for the old. There will be a priest for the sick and one for the strong. The educated and the workers will each have their chaplain. In fact people want the priest they know. No matter how many specialists are appointed the men always in demand are the general practitioners. Through the regular visiting of his people the priest in a parish forms a precious relationship with families as well as individuals. This is what I missed as a bishop. It was not until I had tried and failed to combine parochial with diocesan responsibility that I resigned myself to being just a bishop.

I came to know many of the people in the cathedral parish through their children. While preparing children for first Holy Communion I would visit the parents and was often able to persuade them to return to their religious duties. Careless Catholic parents who nevertheless value their religion enough to send their children to Catholic schools are often brought back to the practice of the Faith through the school. The influence of a Catholic school on the life of a parish is an added reason for the tenacity with which Catholics hold on to their schools. It was stimulating to teach Christian doctrine to the sixth-formers of Notre Dame High School whose pupils came from every parish in the city. Even though I was mistaken in appointing myself parish priest the experience of routine pastoral work in a northern city ultimately proved helpful to my work in the diocese.

Once it became clear that I must give up the cathedral parish I had to look for a new home. The house in Weetwood Lane had by now become a junior and infants' school under the care of the Notre Dame Sisters. It was more properly occupied by three hundred children than by one bishop. The garage was so spacious that it was easily converted into a dining-hall for the whole school. My search for a house was soon successful. Canon McShane, a native of Glasgow, in addition to being diocesan financial secretary was a wise adviser in questions of property. Within a few days of my decision to leave the cathedral he discovered a modest house in a Leeds suburb only a quarter-of-an-hour's drive from the cathedral and curial office. Father Bernard Keegan had been my secretary (chaplain) from my first weeks in the diocese. He gladly agreed to combine secretarial duties with those of curate when I left

Bishop's House for the cathedral. When I left the cathedral parish I did not have the heart to ask him to move yet again. It did not take long to recapture the rhythm of normal episcopal life. I resumed visitation of parishes and found that the second round of visitations was even more interesting than the first. I now knew people and places. I was able to judge to what extent the redistribution of clergy had been beneficial to themselves and their people. There was no doubt that most parishes had been revitalised. The only drawback was that many priests and parishioners were afraid that my second round of visitations would renew the state of flux. I had to show that I was not an ecclesiastical Heraclitus.

During the years which followed I became well acquainted with both priests and laity. The wags no longer talked of 'the cruel see'. I continued to devote a great deal of my time to new approaches to Christian doctrine and in the 'fifties there was renewed interest in catechetics throughout the Church. The word still justified its etymological meaning of teaching through questions and answers but the age-old system of learning hundreds of answers by heart was beginning to be rejected. Many teachers besides those working with me on catechism revision were seeking new methods of instruction. The effects of the upheaval of the second world war, immeasurably greater than that of the first, were appearing in the schools. Young parents whose childhood had been disturbed by evacuation or air raids were less docile and more in need of reassurance. Teachers were aware that children required fresh styles in pedagogy. Physically the post-war child was bigger and healthier but nobody knew or even suspected the considerable psychological and sociological changes which were impending.

CHAPTER
TWELVE

IN THE EARLY 1950S THE AUTHENTIC PATTERN OF POST-WAR BRITAIN
began to emerge. Among the first signs of change was the influx of
commonwealth citizens from the West Indies, Africa, India and Pakistan. By the year 1956 the flow of immigrants from the Caribbean was
steadily growing but many came ill-prepared for conditions in an over-
crowded industrial country with a cold climate. I proposed that the
bishops of this country should send me officially to the West Indies to
tell prospective emigrants what they must expect to find on taking up
residence in the United Kingdom. (This country is always called the
U.K. by citizens of the commonwealth.) I also hoped to establish
communication between Churches in the West Indies with the object
of arranging for immigrants of every religion to be welcomed by
members of their own Church. If information were made available to
religious bodies in this country I thought it would be possible for them
to meet young people and mothers with children on arrival in this
country. At that time there were far fewer agencies interested in the
welfare of immigrants and the West Indians had not yet formed
organisations to help themselves. The bishops agreed to my proposal
and I left Leeds for Jamaica on 6th May, 1956. The following pages
contain extracts from the diary I kept on my journey. To preserve the
flavour of the period I have refrained from undue editing.

Tuesday 7th May: Arrived Kingston Airport in the early evening.
Awaiting me were Bishop McEleney and my American cousin, Sister
Cornelia Marie O.P., Matron of St. Joseph's Hospital. Sir Hugh Foot, the
governor, was also there but he had come to meet his schoolboy son.

Wednesday 8th: Spent all day at Bishop's House, Kingston. Various press interviews including one for *Manchester Guardian*. I said that the important point for Jamaicans to grasp is that British reserve is not British hostility. Even in church it is not customary for strangers to be approached. I said that as yet immigration had not created any great problem beyond that of housing. The real problem would arise should unemployment come. Then the trade union rule 'last in, first out' will operate and Jamaicans will almost certainly think themselves victims of colour prejudice. In the event of a depression all newly arrived workers (Irish and Poles no less than Jamaicans) will be dismissed.

That evening Bishop McEleney took me to dine with a Catholic family. Husband eighty-five, wife a young seventy. Millionaire, self-made, uneducated, first-class financier. Having been born on 8th December, Our Lady's feast-day, he said he had been guided in all his financial transactions. He simply couldn't help making money (for which, he alleged, he had no use). I later gathered from the clergy that this had not led him to divert unwanted cash in their direction. The house is huge but has so much furniture and so many pictures that it only just misses being a junk shop.

Thursday 9th: Nine thirty a.m. waited on the governor, Sir Hugh Foot, at King's House. He seemed smooth and friendly. He introduced himself as the right Foot of his family. Certain facts emerged. The first is that the number of emigrants was far higher and much more constant than anyone had originally expected. Judging from the number of pass-port applications and passage bookings, it was expected that the current quarter, July–September, would reach the record of 10,000. This meant that if the present trend continued something like 40,000 per annum would go to England from Jamaica. Among the worries of the British government was what would happen if there were unemployment. Would they be forced by H.M.G. to repatriate the workless? Would discontented unemployed B.W.I.s form a group of dangerous anti-socials in Britain?

Sir Hugh seemed to think that the major problem would be financial. Neither government would feel called upon to pay return passages for those who failed to find employment or could not settle down in the U.K. I suggested that the odd million or so involved in paying for repatriation would represent a saving on unemployment insurance, sickness benefit and pensions. The governor—incredibly surely?—did not appear to have looked at the problem from this angle. In any case this was all speculative. They might all find work and fit in admirably.

Now came my big question: would the Jamaican government be willing to include, either in the passport application or other documents necessary for emigrants, a note about the religious denomination of the applicant? He saw at once the value of this. I pointed out that any social group or voluntary body—especially a religious body—would help integration. It might save much trouble to the civic authorities at both ends if ministers of religion and social workers were to visit and help these people on arrival. If they felt themselves to be among friends they would be more willing to join the community.

The objection raised by the governor was that some people might object to filling in such details. He agreed that he was not thinking of emigrants but Jamaican business men. I suggested that this particular part of the form might be permissive. Thus in bold type some such phrase as: IT IS IN YOUR INTEREST TO FILL IN THE FOLLOWING.

After leaving the governor we returned to Bishop's House for an iced lemonade. Father Heffernan was waiting to take me for a tour of the interior. On the winding road which was narrow and necessitated frequent stops for other vehicles I was struck by the extreme politeness of Jamaicans. Drivers and pedestrians were equally forthcoming and friendly. We stopped for lunch in St. Anne's Bay at a luxury hotel owned by Catholics of Syrian stock. The hotel is called Town Isle and is one of the many springing up to cater for the rapidly expanding tourist trade, mainly American. Jamaica is becoming the not-so-wealthy-man's Miami. The hotel guests were dressed with startling informality. The women mostly wore swimming suits and short coats even in the dining-room. It takes great humility or stupidity for faded, obese women to appear so scantily covered. Most of them looked pathetic rather than immodest. After lunch—which was not charged for—we had a bathe. Thence to St. Anne's (to which we were to return next day and of which more later) and on to a convent of Servite Sisters recently out from England. We stayed only a few minutes but arranged to say Mass there the following morning.

Supper at the rectory of Father Charles Judah, S.J., a Jamaican of Jewish stock whose older brother Sydney is also a Jesuit. Father Charles was a boy at my old school, Stamford Hill, before the first war. An interesting evening was spent mostly discussing Catholic writers including Graham Greene who had once stayed in this rectory. Again, as so often in conversation with chaplains, the moral outlook and attitudes of the Jamaicans were discussed. This priest being a Jamaican could speak authoritatively. He said that there is no sense of shame about unmarried motherhood nor any stigma attached to the illegitimate. This is obvious from the high rate of illegitimacy.

The reason for the casualness of Jamaicans regarding marriage is complex. First, it is a relic of slave-days when marriage was impossible. Second, marriage itself even among the poorest is an expensive undertaking. If they cannot marry in style they don't marry at all. A stylish marriage costs more than most of them have. Again there is a reluctance among both men and women to tie themselves to life-long unions. They treat each other with more respect when either is free to walk out. Illegitimacy is in no sense a sign of promiscuity. Common Law marriages are the rule. Men and women live together, have large families but will still refuse to marry. There are, of course, girls who are promiscuous and others who have changed partners. But although the children have different fathers there seems to be no disunity in the family.

Friday 10th: At seven a.m. to the Servite convent for Mass. These English Sisters have been in Jamaica less than two years but already have a flourishing boarding school. They did not come to do this kind of work but to open small mission schools. The bishop decided that at the moment this was a greater need in Jamaica. The educational picture is interesting. The Jesuits have St. George's, a magnificent grammar school whose pupils are mainly Catholic. Over the years this school and the evening classes for adults have led to many conversions. Some of the keenest Catholics are Chinese. They have been here for only two generations and are converted in large numbers. They represent the greatest hope for the conversion of Jamaica. Industrious and successful they make splendid Catholics. The Syrians too are mostly Catholics. They are successful and rich but are not of the same religious calibre as the Chinese.

The great obstacle to social and religious advance in Jamaica is lack of family life. This is one result of the lack of stability in marriage. Jamaica is a matriarchy. Grandmother takes charge of the children while mother goes her own way, works and contributes perhaps five shillings a week for each child. There is often no man about the house and children more or less bring themselves up with a nod in the direction of grandmama. Many do not attend school and, indeed, there are not nearly enough schools for the children to attend. Religious instruction corrects promiscuity to some extent but even Catholics are slow to marry.

After leaving the convent we went back to St. Anne's Bay where Father O'Donoghue would now be at home. The national shrine to Columbus is in this parish. It is also said to be the site of the first Catholic church on the island near the spot where Columbus landed. I arrived at a moment when the priest was interviewing a young lady about to migrate to England. In the room were three children. I asked if she were taking them. No, she wasn't. Was she married? No. After her departure I was shown their baptismal certificates. She was their mother but each had a different father. The girl had been a Catholic only three years and since that time had lived an exemplary life. She was not living with any man. Her mother would take care of the children until she had made a home for them in the U.K.

This girl had no shame about her illegitimate children but I was to discover later that Catholics living together do realise that they ought to marry. I heard from their own lips that they were prevented mainly by the tradition of an expensive wedding (irrespective of social class). The expression 'living in sin' would be meaningless here. They are not living in sin but usually living in hope of saving enough money to have champagne with their wedding breakfast.

We arrived back hot, dizzy and late to the convent where Sister Cornelia had lunch waiting. We had delayed on the way to visit Bamboo where Father Ray Sullivan had started a brave but not very successful project called the Holy Name Homesteads to provide decent homes for a hundred Catholic families. The theory is that good family life is impossible under the conditions in which poor Jamaicans live. These homesteads are family houses of at least four rooms (most poor families in the towns live in one room or even share with another family). Nearby is a lime factory which is supposed to provide employment for these families. In addition each homestead has an acre or so of land. The rent is small and is regarded as payment of a mortgage. The theory is that within twenty years each family will have its own house and land. In practice people find the place too dull and remote. Few men relish the hard work in the factory. Two or three of the homesteads were empty and the atmosphere was depressing. I visited a home at random where I found a nice young mother with several children who did not seem very happy. She and her husband would like to move. Where to?—The U.K. of course.

In the evening I went to dinner with Bishop McEleney, Father Heffernan, Father Tobin (Superior) and the leader of the rural Catholic programme and the Vatican Representative at the World Agricultural

Organisation. After the meal I was taken to the house of Mr. and Mrs. Shann. He is in an oil company being taken over by U.S.A. (Trinidad Oil). Awaiting us was Meg, a delightful fifteen-year-old daughter on holiday from an English convent school. We discussed *Frost in May*, a novel about a convent school which the Sacred Heart nuns had confiscated when they found Meg reading it.

Saturday 11th: A day of comparative rest. Sister Cornelia popped in and out of my room in the intervals between duty. We have not talked a great deal but I have given her a potted history of Leeds. She was very busy in the operating theatre and cheering up patients in the wards. She radiates happiness and holiness. Everyone here loves her—especially the blacks.

Sunday 12th: A car came at seven o'clock to take me to Holy Cross church where I said Mass for the people. After breakfast the parish priest of St. Anne's—the poorest parish in the city—came to collect me. We called at the hospital so that I could exchange my cassock for a light suit. I had asked to be taken to the homes of the really poor people.

Nobody knew who I was so people behaved naturally. I was just a new priest learning the job, not a bishop from the U.K. The conditions under which people live in this part of Kingston are difficult to describe credibly. We visited a number of houses—a misleading term—in Rose Lane off Oxford Street. Rose Lane had as much in common with roses as Oxford Street had to the London thoroughfare of the same name. All down the street were wooden gates leading to yards. In each yard there were roughly a dozen shacks. These reminded me of the *barracas* in the insanitary encampments near Barcelona. Usually the shacks were of two storeys. Each storey had only one room but each room usually had more than one family. Writing this down it seems like a traveller's horror story. Unfortunately it is a true horror story.

I must refer again to the marriage-shyness of the Jamaicans. In most homes there was a mother, grandmother and several children. Sometimes there was also a man but in this dreadful slum the mother's children were in no instance all fathered by the same man. We did not encounter any married mothers except one very sick lady who had not seen her husband for years and whose children were not his. She was not a Catholic but was anxious to be instructed. Her children all attend the Catholic school.

In less than two hours' visiting in most intense heat we came across many unbaptised children who nevertheless go to Catholic schools. The mothers were all anxious for their children to be baptised. The priest either wrote them notes of introduction to Sister or told them to see Sister and have the children enrolled in the instruction class. Many Catholic children had not been confirmed and the mothers were anxious for them to be put in the confirmation class. This outlook towards the Church and the sacraments is similar to that of ignorant Catholics in our own cities. The people are feckless, stupid, lovable and full of good will and intentions. These poor children are more regular at Mass than the children of the English poor because they are given far more encouragement by their parents. I imagine that the Society for the Prevention of Cruelty to Children would find no clients in Jamaica.

I now saw what partly confirmed and partly corrected my impressions about the Jamaican attitude to marriage. These women did hang their heads when admitting that they were not married and were easily induced to promise to seek the blessing of God on their unions if likely to be permanent. Naturally it was their priest not I who raised the question of marriage. I cannot say to what extent they were merely giving answers to please Father. They are so childlike and friendly that they were willing to give the same answer to contradictory questions.

Q. Would you like to go to the U.K.?
A. Yes, I like to go to the U.K.
Q. But you're better off here in the country. You don't really want to go, do you?
A. No, I don't want to go to the U.K.

I had evidence in one house of the truth that quite stable unions are not blessed simply because the couple want to marry in style. A girl with a permanent partner said that she was saving up to marry. To her and several other girls the priest made the offer of a quiet marriage at five or six a.m. The girls all agreed to call on him during the week. I feel certain that no calls were made. One girl with three small children said that she and her man were saving up for their marriage which would take place as soon as the children were old enough to enjoy it.

The direct manner of approach of this priest embarrassed me at first but not for long. I soon saw that the people were not at all put out. The lapsed were told that they would go to hell if they didn't reform and women were upbraided for living in sin. Questioned about their common law husbands and various boy friends they showed no sign of distress. Towards the end of our visiting the priest tried another approach (I had told him that an English priest would be unwilling and unable to make the direct attack he so successfully launched). He

[182]

became quiet spoken and appealing and to his great surprise this proved more effective.

I went to bed early. I was always glad to do so because the heat was exhausting and sleep not easy to come by. I had to be up at four thirty each day to say the community Mass at five thirty after which I took Holy Communion to the sick. I had said a private Mass for the first few days while I was recovering from the journey and growing used to the heat.

At the time of my visit the ecclesiastical status of Jamaica was about to be upgraded. Jamaica was now to become a diocese with Kingston as the cathedral town. On the principle *Omne ignotum pro magnifico* (which in loose translation means that the grass on the other side of the hill is always greener) I had been invited to enthrone John McEleney as first Bishop of Kingston.

Monday 13th: Spent a quiet morning writing my sermon for the enthronement. It was very hard work in this tremendous heat. Despite several visitors during the morning I managed to finish writing the sermon. I read it out to Sister Cornelia to see if she thought it would be intelligible to my audience—this was my first sermon in Jamaica. Sister thought that the sermon was just right but she would think that of any sermon of mine. I would not be a hero to my valet but I am to my cousin.

Just before three o'clock the bishop came to collect me and take me to see Mr. Glasspole, Minister of Labour. He proved to be a most intelligent and charming man. The bishop and I had no sort of difficulty in soliciting his aid in helping Jamaican emigrants to Britain. I told him that the chief problem would be to find their names and addresses. He said that if I drafted a form he would circulate it to steamship companies and airlines. No compulsion could be used but he thought that all would co-operate. Every sensible person sees that it is worthwhile for voluntary organisations—above all religious bodies—to take an interest in these strangers and help them to settle down. In the event of unemployment West Indians will become a big political problem. The Minister sent for the permanent Under-Secretary who was even more helpful. After an hour we reached agreement, as they say, on all points:

(1) no compulsion
(2) no attempt to gain information about religion through the passport officer
(3) co-operation with transport companies.

After two attempts I drafted a satisfactory form and sent it with a letter of thanks to Mr. Glasspole.

In the evening Pam Lindo, an English friend of the bishop, called to take me to dinner at her lovely home. Roy, her husband, a convert Jew, is an attractive man and, I was told, most efficient in business. To dinner also came the local superintendent of Barclays Bank with an American wife. Both excellent Catholics. After dinner when the men were alone I got down to business with Roy. I asked him to soften up the travel people against my official approach and to arrange for me to broadcast to intending emigrants. Pam, meanwhile, kept fussing to take me home because Sister Cornelia had told her to have me back by nine forty-five as I was tired, overworked etc. etc. Being English Pam took her promise very seriously so that I was out of the house in less than two hours. A valuable two hours they would prove to have been.

Tuesday 14th: Mass at five thirty. At eight thirty Radio Jamaica was on the phone to offer me facilities. Roy had phoned Douglas Judah, Chairman of the Board, and one of the most respected and influential citizens of Jamaica. He is a member of the Senate. The following day Roy called for me promptly at ten o'clock. On the journey he told me that he had already been in touch with B.O.A.C., P.A.A., and the chief shipping companies. All were perfectly willing to co-operate. On arrival at Roy's house he asked if there were anything else to which he might apply his restless energy on my behalf. On an inspiration I asked him how much it would cost to air condition the operating theatre at St. Joseph's hospital. At once he was on the phone seeking details. Meanwhile he undertook to defray half the expenses whatever they were. This must be partly his Jewish blood—Jews are always moved by suffering and most generous in relieving it. Roy had been touched by the death of a friend, Mrs. Kennedy, mother of four small children, who was dying on the night of my arrival in Kingston. In fact I had gone with the bishop to pray with her and bless her a few minutes after my arrival. She died three days later. I told Roy that I had been appalled by the state of the Sisters coming from the operating theatre bathed in sweat. A Jesuit, Father O'Sullivan, had been operated on a few nights previously and I was with him in the anaesthetic room. During the operation a priest with him had fainted. Roy promised to see to everything.

August 15th: The great day. I was taken by the nuns' friend, Henry Haegy, to Broadcasting House at nine a.m. I duly recorded my talk for transmission at nine thirty-five after the government announcements tonight. I went home via the bishop's office and told him of Roy Lindo's activities with shipping and air people. The bishop had decided to open an Emigrants Bureau in his own office building and pay a secretary to run it. Awaiting me was a letter from the Jesuit Provincial in Boston turning down my request to send Father Carter, S.J., a Jamaican priest, to England. He is booked to take a special course of study. The bishop was surprised and disappointed but said that a new provincial was about to be appointed and might alter this ruling. He was determined that a Jamaican priest should come to England. To do him credit the Jesuit provincial also wants to oblige but not with Father Carter. The rest of the morning I spent trying to learn my sermon. But I was interrupted continually. Somehow or other I managed to commit it to memory. At almost the last moment I decided to write another small page referring to the bishop's courage in opening a seminary "in a setting of unrivalled beauty, for the training of Jamaica's native sons in the sacred ministry". This particular passage gave especial pleasure. The Holy Ghost who was obviously at work knows that Jamaicans love pompous prose.

After a struggle with my lower self I decided at four fifteen to put on all my purple and feeling like a martyr set out for the cathedral with Father Barry. We were half-an-hour early which I spent rehearsing my warm words. I was so warm that I wondered if I could survive the ceremony long enough to speak. Very promptly at five p.m. the procession moved into the cathedral. Within the building were Sir Hugh and Lady Foot, various distinguished service people and local parish presidents (mayors to us).

The choir greeted the bishop's entrance with the '*Ecce Sacerdos*'. This and all subsequent singing was of a very high order. The ceremony, despite the fact that almost all taking part were Jesuits, was perfect. The Papal Bulls were read by one of the few secular priests, Monsignor Gladstone Wilson. I knew him as a student and thought he looked rather faded, even the blackness which used to shine was softened by grey. He probably thought that I was pretty faded too.

My part in the function was not taxing. I merely had to lead the bishop to his throne, hand him the crozier, bow and retire. Unfortunately I had to retire to the pulpit. My memory played no tricks and I was able to fit in the new sentences without doing violence to logic or rhetoric. The bishop thought—he told me later—that only an Englishman could have preached that sermon. He meant that I was able to praise his loyalty to H.M. Government, and at the same time give warning that he would show unflinching resistance to "any act or legislation, however eminently supported, which ran counter to God's law . . .".

Dripping with sweat I returned with Father Barry to St. Joseph's to change back into a white cassock. The Lindos called on their way home from the cathedral to say good-bye. Roy hopes to see me in Leeds in November. I had a sandwich and a cool drink with Father Barry. Soon a car came to take me to dinner at the home of a Syrian millionaire. Joe, our host, is president of the St. Vincent de Paul Society. I was introduced to a vast collection of Kingston's rich Catholics with a few ambassadors (Lebanon, for example) thrown in. I spoke to Douglas Judah and obtained his co-operation in the scheme for air conditioning St. Joseph's operating theatre. He and one of the many Issa brothers promised to see to the other half of Roy's gift. I arrived at seven thirty but dinner had still not been announced at nine p.m. Sister Cornelia had, as usual, been busy. The bishop had promised to have me home by nine thirty. He kept his word and I was excused dinner. On Joe Issa's insistence I blessed the table before leaving. I begged the assembled guests to support the bishop's native seminary and—need I say?—the air conditioning of St. Joseph's. All enthusiastically agreed. I hope they will redeem the promises they so readily made. Home to Sister who had thoughtfully provided a much needed sandwich (I had not tasted dinner) with ginger ale. It was most welcome. We listened to my recorded broadcast at nine thirty-five and said the rosary.

Thursday 16th: I rose without enthusiasm soon after four o'clock to spend my last day in Jamaica. Community Mass at five thirty and Holy Communion to the sick. Sister Cornelia was soon in my room putting the finishing touches to the packing. We said the rosary together and agreed that the visit had been grand.

THIRTEEN

TO MEET ME AT THE AIRPORT IN TRINIDAD WERE ARCHBISHOP RYAN AND —incredibly—a Father Heenan, O.P.! He is quite sure that we are related. He is strikingly like my cousins, the Heenans of Clareen. The archbishop who is shrewd, humorous and cultured, gave me a rather cautious welcome. I don't think he liked my grey suit. He put Father Heenan next to me in the taxi and sat with the driver. On the drive to the city the archbishop said his rosary with his fingers but his mind was busy weighing me up. When we alighted I changed into my cassock and soon the conversation became more animated and I think he took to me. I was lodged with the delightful Irish Dominicans at Cathedral House. The archbishop explained that he had no facilities in his house and thought I would be happier 'in the centre of things'. He stayed to supper and the evening passed pleasantly.

Friday 17th: It had been decided to do my business as soon as possible to leave time for seeing people. In the morning I had the usual press conference (reporters all Catholics) and interview with representatives of Radio Trinidad. It was a repetition of Jamaica but I had to be careful not to refer to Jamaica. I made it clear that Jamaica had been given priority in my tour only by reason of its preponderance of emigrants to the U.K. (I had learned always to refer to England as the U.K.) In the afternoon I went to Archbishop's House for a long interview with Dr. Ryan and the Attorney General. Our business was quickly done because emigration is no great problem. Most Trinidadians who go to the U.K. are students, apprentices or nurses. Manual workers are too few to attract government interest. The main thing, I was told repeatedly, was not to lump Trinidadians in U.K. public opinion with Jamaicans. I decided that the best plan here would be to leave the Legion of Mary to see the travel agencies and steamship companies and sell them the idea of filling in the form I had composed.

Saturday 18th: After breakfast I had to record two broadcasts. One will go out at one p.m. on Saturday in the weekly Catholic hour ('The Catholic Church in the U.K.') the other at eight p.m. in government time ('West Indians in Britain'). Because the engineers were fussy and the studios are not sound-proof I had to make a number of attempts before the tapes were acceptable. Everyone was pleasant and—eventually—pleased. At eleven o'clock I picked up the archbishop (and borrowed some purple as I had no time to return from Radio Trinidad to the presbytery to dress) to interview the governor. Apart from being an act of courtesy the visit was not rewarding. The governor is in some ways typical of British officials in under-developed lands. He likes 'these chaps' and has a respectful but cautious regard for the archbishop. He was courteous and friendly. He thought my coming was a jolly good idea, was all for it and so on. He sent for the Colonial Secretary, a Chinese of high intelligence who happens to be a very keen Catholic. His name sounded like Ho Choy. On his arrival the two of us went to another room for discussion. The archbishop wanted to talk privately with the governor—doubtless to discuss the elections. The archbishop is politically well informed. Apart from his Irish penchant for politics he has two brothers in the British diplomatic service. He loves political crises. Eminently level-headed he is most unlikely ever to say a word out of place in public.

My talk with the Colonial Secretary was brief but clear. Nothing needed to be done beyond what I had agreed with the archbishop. If the unlikely happens and Trinidadians should go in large numbers to the U.K. there should be no difficulty in adopting measures similar to those in Jamaica. The archbishop came back to lunch at the presbytery. We had plenty of laughing and joke-telling. He is an expert raconteur. In the afternoon I went to the Holy Cross College, a magnificent building designed by one of the fathers. Here I met Father O'Dwyer, brother of Michael O'Dwyer with whom I had fought the Blitz in Manor Park.

Sunday 19th: Up around four o'clock to say the five o'clock Mass. It was a most impressive experience. The cathedral holds about 1,200 people and there was not a vacant place. The people were poor. Mass-missers give the valid excuse of not having any decent clothes but any-

[188]

thing will do for this early Mass. The market opens at about four o'clock and they do their shopping before or after Mass. Priests began to distribute Holy Communion at four forty-five and stopped at five o'clock for Mass. No Holy Communion during Mass. The remainder receive after Mass. I preached a ten-minute sermon on the obvious topic—the world-wide Church. This Mass will be one of my happiest recollections of the West Indies.

For the rest of the morning—which, naturally, after such an early start seemed terribly long—I wrote these notes. I would have gone to other Masses but I simply could not face the heat (at least, I didn't). By appointment Roger Fulford came after the seven o'clock Mass. He has just arrived to edit a weekly journal which though owned by a Catholic is not a specifically Catholic paper. It is a poor man's *Tablet*. I gave him some facts about my tour for the English press. In the afternoon I put on a Dominican habit and visited the homes of the poor people I had seen at Mass in the morning. I guessed that I would more easily make contact dressed as a friar than a bishop.

Visiting here was similar to Jamaica yet curiously different. The first part of the visitation was to normal homes. They seemed less crowded than the Jamaican ones though also grossly overcrowded. The people seemed more 'on terms' with Father Devell, O.P., who accompanied me than the Jamaicans had been with the American Jesuit. One reason for the slightly but distinctly better relationship may be that here Catholics are much more numerous and more sure of themselves. One or two families had married parents but most were not married. There was the same ignorance but occasionally parents as well as children had been to Mass that morning. The priest made appointments for people to arrange baptisms. One Hindu married to a Catholic—or, rather, living with him and willing to marry—was anxious for her twins to be baptised though not keen on being converted. She had arranged for godparents. This is a fair example of the slightly more hopeful religious state of these people. The reception was always friendly. We were called to the house of a blind man who is anxious to become a Catholic.

The second part of our visit was to 'Shanty Town'. We approached it via the city's rubbish dump thick with flies and black with vultures. Here physical conditions were worse than in Kingston's slums. We met no married couple and spoke to an apostate who had found Jesus and the True Church with the help of (I think) the Seventh Day Adventists. We saw people constructing their hovels. Because the weather is mild these people suffer less than squatters in Europe. Furthermore, they spend little time indoors except to sleep. No houses have lights. People are less conscious of their squalor than a visitor would be. Since they have never known good sanitation the worst feature of their misery does not depress them. Many of the negroes are workless and hungry but the Indians are better off. They are clannish and hard working. All these slums will soon be cleared and already there are blocks of small, well-built flats in demolished areas. I returned rather less depressed than in Jamaica but with the thought that the desperately poor are much the same in the West Indies as in Spain, India or anywhere else. The standard of morality here is different. Stealing is regarded as reprehensible mainly because it is punished severely (Law and Order). Provided no harm is done to another it does not occur to West Indians that there can be real sin. God is not imagined as angry if a girl does a perfectly natural thing like 'making a baby'. As people rise socially the respectability of marriage is accepted but what we think of as immoral behaviour is not even a peccadillo here. Housing conditions, as well as history, are responsible. Since there is no privacy in the crowded rooms children become familiar with what are called the facts of life.

Monday 20th: At about ten a.m. Father Heenan and Father Fitzgerald drove me to the oil fields and pitch-lake at La Brea and Point Fortin. The road was the celebrated Churchill-Roosevelt Highway built by U.S.A. troops during the war. The two-hour drive was full of interest. Most of the villages we passed through are Indian with few Christians. The Asians are not trusted and they, in turn, despise the negroes. We went to lunch with Canon McNamara, a delightful man whose staff had prepared a magnificent meal. There we met one of the few other secular priests, a native Trinidadian of French origin. After lunch the canon took us to the oil refineries. Here we were courteously received and the whole process was explained to us. It was so hot that keeping awake was an effort. Less from any desire for information than to keep awake and be polite I asked a series of unintelligent questions which were accorded incomprehensible answers. After an hour during which an oil barrel was constructed *ab initio* for our benefit I left with little addition to my knowledge but with my grey suit liberally spotted with oil which, however refined, will still ruin my only suit. In this town Catholics are in the majority and a new church is being built. We returned via the Shell oil refineries which I did not have time (or inclination) to inspect. Father Heenan was growing anxious about his Rosary Confraternity but we returned in excellent time and I preached to a crowded congregation in the cathedral. Radio Trinidad recorded the service to be broadcast on Catholic Hour next month.

Tuesday 21st: During Monday night thieves broke into my room while I was asleep and stole my watch. The programme for Tuesday morning was therefore complicated by police who came with an alsatian dog which walked round the grounds in a purposeful manner but was more interested in shrubs than clues. Various people called during the morning to consult me about relatives in the U.K. or about emigrating to the U.K.

In the evening I addressed an overflowing meeting at the Holy Name Hall at which the archbishop presided. A remarkably attentive audience followed the talk with questions. My reference to the archbishop's pastoral letters (Father Leahy made me read them during the afternoon so that I would not contradict Archbishop Ryan) was well received. I told my audience that these same pastoral letters could be read in Leeds cathedral without changing a word but I admitted that Leeds was unused to such deathless prose (next day's paper called it depthless prose). "You will never know," the archbishop said after the meeting, "what good your reference to my pastorals will do." He had been criticised by anti-Catholics and accused of interfering with politics. The public would now know from the independent witness of a stranger that Archbishop Ryan's pastorals contained the common teaching of the Church.

Wednesday 22nd: Said Mass five a.m. and caught the plane to George-town, British Guiana. Met at airport by Bishop Guilly, S.J., and Father Smith in the governor's splendid car. A long and bad road into town. Awaiting me were my old school friends, now Jesuit priests, Terry O'Brien and Tommy Lynch. The presbytery is across the road from the cathedral and college. It is remarkable how Jesuits manage to make all their houses look the same. Apart from the heat I might have been in the Jesuit house in Stamford Hill or Leeds—everything musty and untidy, everyone friendly and self-contained. My bag had not come off the plane (it had been taken on to Barbados) but kindly Jesuits each contributed items—a comb, a razor, a shirt, a set of pyjamas. These were deposited in my room by the benefactors and I was left alone to rest. Dinner was at twelve, preceded by a rum drink with bitters and sugar and lime—the mixture all churned up with a swizzle stick. The result was so comforting that in the afternoon I took a siesta. About three thirty the bishop took Fathers O'Brien and Lynch and me for a drive. He said he would leave us to talk 'shop' (meaning Stamford Hill) but forgot to do so. Not that it mattered since there is no long-lost-brother stuff about Jesuit old boys. Only much later and practically under duress were the Ilford Jesuits induced to talk of their family and friends at home. We visited the Sisters of Mercy hospital. I promised to ask my nephew Brian, a doctor in London, to find an English surgeon looking for a job. At six o'clock I met some local Catholic Actionists in Bishop's House where we had iced drinks and discussed the Church in British Guiana. We looked in at the Catholic club where men were playing billiards and women enduring a social evening. The Church is uniform as well as universal.

Thursday 23rd: Said Mass for the Ursulines where Winnie Rowntree —Mother Xavier—is superior. She is still like the pretty girl I knew at school. Her cheeks are so rosy that the orphans (Ursulines here run the orphanage as well as a first-class grammar school) are told to eat their food if they want cheeks like Reverend Mother. Since they are all black the outlook is bleak. Returned at ten o'clock to Bishop's House for a meeting with the Bishop's Council—all Jesuits. We went into the question of what organisation should be set up for fact-finding and decided that the bishop's office will be the information centre. Ladies of Charity, St. Vincent de Paul Brothers and members of the Sword of the Spirit will help clergy to find names and addresses. The bishop's office will send lists of emigrants to the Legion of Mary in London.

In the afternoon the bishop took me to a mission in the country where Father Brian Scannell was staying on vacation. He is headmaster of the college. The parish priest is a calm, good-humoured man. As always the atmosphere is typical of any Jesuit house. The sanitary conditions are, strangely, a great advance on the primitive Brickdam Presbytery in Georgetown itself. I delivered a letter which I had brought for Father Scannell from Barry Scannell, a parish priest in Leeds, one of five priest brothers.

In the evening I addressed an immense mixed audience in Queen's College Hall. The town hall had been booked originally but proved too small for the numbers wanting tickets. They do not have many visiting speakers in British Guiana. The main impression I retain of the meeting was its tense silence. I imagine that the people here were used only to political harangues and a simple statement of Catholic doctrine more or less paralysed them. The result was that the question time produced only more silence. The speech was widely reported in the local press. One paper serialised it in three consecutive numbers. I cannot imagine a speech of mine being accorded that treatment in England—I mean the U.K.

[192]

Friday 24th: Said Mass in the cathedral and was served with much rubrical exactitude by Terry O'Brien. I did some writing and, my bag having arrived from Barbados, changed into a cassock that fits. Bishop Guilly whose cassock I had borrowed is four inches taller than me. Later in the morning Tommy Lynch took me round the college. It is sad that these gifted men are teaching in such inadequate premises. Apart from the few Jesuits there are lay-masters who are not teachers much more than in name. Their educational standard is that of sixth form boys in England. The salaries paid are absurdly small so a graduate is not likely to be attracted. Most masters leave after a year or so for further study or go to England to earn more money as bus conductors.

In the afternoon we took the ferry across the Demerara River to visit the Scarboro Fathers, who were being given a retreat by Father Quinlan, S.J., of Jamaica. We had tea and I gave a brief conference. In the evening we had dinner with the governor, a charming man who had come here from British Honduras. His wife, Lady Renison, is a delightful mixture of Scots and Yorkshire. After dinner when his wife and school-girlish daughter Anne had retired Renison spoke of the situation. Like most governors he has a high regard for Jamaica's Dr. Manley.

Saturday 25th: The kindly governor again sent his car to take Bishop Guilly and me to the airport. Father Quinlan was with us en route for Barbados to preach another retreat. We landed at Trinidad about one p.m. Fathers Heenan and Fitzgerald were waiting with the archbishop. We had lunch in an air-conditioned restaurant where the Catholic proprietor refused any payment. The archbishop was in splendid form. Obviously he was pleased (and relieved) at the results of my visit. He told us once again that the speech (which had been a revamped version of the Vatican v Kremlin speech of Mission House days) had been much talked of in town and the identification of Archbishop Ryan's pastorals with those of bishops everywhere else in the Catholic Church had helped to refute his critics' allegations that Ryan did not speak with the true voice of the Church.

As I was to wait until three thirty for my onward plane, I prevailed on the archbishop to go home. I said I had plenty to read and write as I waited in the airport. At this moment Father Leahy made his appearance. We talked for an hour and then I prevailed also on him to go about his duties (he was giving a retreat out of town). Events showed me to have been unwisely considerate. We were summoned to our plane and sat in it for half-an-hour but it would not start. We were therefore decanted and had to stay another night in Trinidad. I knew that Mass and sermon had been arranged in Grenada but I was delighted to have the excuse of spending another night with the hospitable Irish Dominicans. I had no transport, but a friendly Catholic, who like everyone in town had heard of the theft of my watch, offered me a lift into town. I had been unable to phone from the airport and found on my arrival that the Fathers were all hearing Confessions in the cathedral. They drifted in from the cathedral and successfully concealed their chagrin at my reappearance and, in fact, gave me a real Irish *cead mile failte*. We had a lively and fascinating session before going late to bed. The subject this time was Our Lady of Fatima. The general thesis was the undesirability of ballyhoo about localised devotions and the need for a return to the veneration of Our Lady, simply as Mother of God. The usual clerical exaggerations stimulated our discussion.

Sunday 26th: Father Barry drove me to the airport to catch a plane to Grenada. Father Field, O.P., was there to meet me. Much confusion had been caused by my failure to arrive the day before. My non-arrival and the death of Cardinal Griffin in London had both been announced. Meanwhile the nomination of the first bishop of Grenada was daily expected.[1] I had been advertised as saying Mass at the magnificent church at Beaulieu designed by Father Field. When the faithful were told that my plane had not arrived the day before there had been much weeping. They thought that I had crashed because the death of Cardinal Griffin had been taken as my own. Later still many took me for their new bishop. It was all very puzzling but quite delightful.

Father Field took a long route home to show me the beauties of this outstandingly attractive island. We stopped at Beaulieu where they rang bells and I blessed a few people who were waiting hopefully outside church. We arrived at the Vicariate in St. George and it was soon time for an excellent lunch. I was hungry and ate my first full West Indian meal. At lunch were the two curates, Father Bernard, an energetic Czech (a wonderful priest who is pessimistic about the state of family life and morals in Grenada) and a magnificent negro priest on loan from Trinidad. After a siesta we went to the beach at Grand Anse where a little school is being rebuilt after last year's terrible hurricane. Last week some Carmelite nuns had arrived from Trinidad with their Mother General who is English. They are installed in a small house. We had a bathe and had a word with the Sisters and children

[1] Father Field, O.P., was nominated first bishop of Grenada a few months later.

attending the catechism class. Back at the Vicariate I prepared my sermon for the evening. Meanwhile Father John, O.P., arrived to be deacon at Mass. We had a wonderful Dominican Solemn High Mass *coram episcopo* with a markedly devout and attentive congregation. The church was full to the doors. I preached on the catholicity of the Church with a bit about emigrants thrown in. It was reported by the local press.

Monday 27th: Mass at the tiny beach chapel at Grand Anse. An enthusiastic congregation including many of the children of the catechism class. Fairly easy morning, during which I interviewed the labour officers of the Leeward and Windward Islands who are both Catholics. They are about to print a booklet of information and will hold up the proofs for my suggestions. I inserted several Catholic addresses including the Legion of Mary in London. In the afternoon a bathe, a visit to a leper colony, recordings at Radio Windward Isles and tea with the governor and his outstandingly gracious wife and two adolescent sons. He is a friendly and humorous man, a native of Dublin.

In the evening I presided and preached at Grand Anse. The people who had been disappointed on Sunday were promised sight of me at this special Mass and the church was overflowing. This represented enormous sacrifice—hundreds of men and women had come several miles down from the mountainside. This large church, despite its size and the number of faithful, has no resident priest. There is a flourishing Legion of Mary. I preached very simply on the Mass, the richest treasure of the Catholic Church, and the faithful seemed to follow me. I told them their new church is more beautiful than all the new churches built in Leeds during the last five years but asked them not to report me if they went to Leeds. They promised—in chorus—not to tell the people in Leeds what I had said. After Mass they presented me with vegetables and eggs. Home in the driving rain and early to bed after a happy, consoling day.

Tuesday 28th: Mass at six o'clock in the cathedral assisted by the Dominican priest from Trinidad. After breakfast a bathe and a tour of the island. Our first call was to Ionyave—Father Kevin Clarke, O.P. He was out but we examined his church which had been almost completely destroyed in last year's hurricane. The courage and skill of these Dominicans is beyond praise. Father Field had re-designed the building and in various ingenious ways—e.g. criss-cross roofing so as to use every piece of wood—is keeping down costs. On to Victoria where a priest in worker's shorts and shirt was rebuilding his church and building a presbytery. My dig in *The People's Priest*[1] at priests too busy to do pastoral work because they are 'building' a church has no place here. The stones are brought up from the river by children and, after dark, by men and women. The adults don't like doing such menial tasks by daylight. This is probably a relic of slave days. The children were very keen and very undressed.

Next to Santems for lunch with Father Raymond Devas whom I had last seen when he gave a mission for my children in Barking twenty years ago. He is unbelievably young, active, amusing and well informed. After lunch he took us to see some of the local beauty spots and, despite the heat, insisted on being dropped at the last point to walk home. On to Tivoli where Father Pyke talked to us about his hurricane damage. It reminded me of the London blitz when each man's bomb was bigger than the other fellow's. Finally, as night drew on, to another part of the island, to see Mount St. Urbans with a Yorkshire parish priest, Father Gabriel Wyle, and a Tyneside curate, Father Dowling. For my benefit an elderly man climbed an eighty foot coconut palm tree. It was a sight worth seeing. I drank some milk from the nut and ate some of the rind: not unpleasant. At last to St. David's where an enthusiastic Maltese, Father Paul Dimayo, had his Legionaries waiting and the bells were set ringing. He is a real apostle. Tireless and interested in everyone and everything—including current affairs. What a pity more Maltese are not persuaded to leave their little island for the missions. Our last call was to Perd Mon Temps. The priest, Father John Cowley (sub-deacon at Sunday's Mass), had just gone out. We looked at his church and then returned, tired and happy, to the Vicariate.

Tuesday 28th: This was unexpected extra time. I had wrongly thought that I was due to go this morning. Father Bernard took me inland. We went first to the one parish we had left out the day before—Birchgrove where the parish priest is a grand Scotsman, Father Andrew Anderson. His church is fairly new (and unpaid for). These missionaries really have to count the pennies to live. Having now seen them all I am impressed by their high quality and spirit. We had intended to visit some homes but the weather made that impossible. The rain was quite literally torrential. It would have been impossible to go from house-to-house but we did visit one poor girl who has been in bed for ten years with spinal trouble.

After the rain had cleared we had a delightfully free afternoon. I had a bathe and went with Father Field to see the nuns, newly arrived to

[1] Sheed and Ward, London, 1951.

form a community of native nuns. Then we called on a community of Anglican Sisters who were happy to welcome us. Father Field had called earlier to ask if they would like me to call. It was a pleasant but pathetic visit. They were self-conscious and seemed unsure of themselves. I am sure that they are exemplary religious but in this very Roman Catholic area they felt very Anglo-Catholic. Perhaps the fact that Father Field is a convert from Anglicanism embarrasses them a little. From here I went straight to the airport.

I was met at the Barbados airport by the Jesuit rector and one of his parishioners. This island is West Indian with a difference. It had the air of prosperity and, I was to learn, is called Little England. The Church of England is strong here and the Mirfield Fathers are numerous. The Catholic Church has made small impression on this Protestant island which is soon to be handed over to the care of the Dominicans. The Jesuits have used it as a rest home for missionaries retired in old age from British Guiana. There has been no growth because the old priests are very old indeed. There is only one young priest, Father Pearson, who is full of energy.

I was taken, via the parishioner's house, to the presbytery which is dilapidated without and within. The house with the now familiar Jesuit atmosphere of disorder is friendly and pleasant. Old copies of the *Month* and ancient photographs are lying about everywhere. One old Jesuit brought me a book—the history of Barbados—within minutes of my arrival. Then I was left alone—sensibly and kindly—until swizzle time before lunch. Father Pearson was out with friends who were spending a few hours in Barbados on a cruise but came in early in the afternoon and took me for a swim. Needless to say nothing had been arranged here but the radio station was to be given my recording. Father Pearson phoned the governor and I was bidden to lunch next day. In the evening we returned to the swimming pool where a polo match was to be played between the police and the army. To my delight the police were defeated. (I am going through an anti-police phase having been fined for alleged speeding shortly before my departure for the West Indies.)

Thursday 30th: Mass at the Ursuline convent where building is in progress on a large scale. The nuns were very pleased to see me not only because I am an old friend of the Reverend Mother but also they were in retreat and my visit gave them an excuse to talk. Father Pearson came to collect me and we saw something of the town. In the afternoon we had a siesta and a swim from a different beach. We changed in the house of friends of his from Trinidad.

After supper I went with Father Pearson and Father Quinn to the prison. Here my object was to renew acquaintance with the prison governor whom I had met at Wakefield when he was doing a course of prison administration. He was formerly in charge of Grenada prison. He and his wife are keen Catholics. She hates the snobbery of Barbados and longs for the friendliness and faith of Grenada. We spent a most interesting hour or two and I learned more about the colour situation and saw his enlightened treatment of his prisoners who were all very friendly.

Saturday 1st September: Mass at the Jesuit Church and a peaceful morning. At twelve thirty the car was ready to take me to lunch with the governor. It was a quiet and interesting occasion. H.E. is charming and has a wife who very ably shares the white man's burden. They had been in Grenada and had a deep affection for the Dominicans who had used their house as a second home. I was most impressed by this couple and felt that although Protestants they were as devoted to the Dominicans as any Catholic could be.

At six o'clock there was a private reception in the house of the man who had met me at the airport. All the European Catholics on the island were invited. Most of them came—including a young Irish doctor and his wife whom I had known as a child at the Ursuline convent, Upton. A lovely couple. She was within hours of giving birth to their first child.

Sunday 2nd September: Mass at six o'clock. Crowded congregation. Many Communions. The parishioner (whose name I never really learned) came with his wife at eight thirty to take me to the airport. I was put next to Rosen, a film director who was in the West Indies to shoot Alec Waugh's novel *Island in the Sun*. He had also directed *Alexander the Great*. We had a long and interesting discussion on many things including communism (he is ex-Party). He promised to phone me when he comes to England to finish shooting the film. It was about seven p.m. when we arrived at New York airport where most of my family and friends were waiting.

I did not realise that the events of the summer of 1956 would result in my departure from the diocese of Leeds. Cardinal Griffin, Archbishop of Westminster, had been in failing health for some years. He suffered two strokes over a period of years and had his last and fatal attack on 20th August, 1956 while I was in the West Indies. In

December of the same year William Godfrey, despite his sixty-seven years, was translated from Liverpool to succeed Cardinal Griffin. In May of the following year I was translated from Leeds to Liverpool. The best part of a year elapsed between my return from the West Indies and my departure for Liverpool. During that time a black priest from Jamaica came to live in Leeds. His compatriots were glad to see him but at that time there were very few immigrants from the West Indies in Leeds. In the neighbouring city of Bradford the number of immigrants was rising but most of them were Asians. After a few weeks the Jamaican priest decided to make London his headquarters.

CHAPTER
FOURTEEN

CATHOLIC ECUMENISM WAS STILL ESOTERIC IN THE 'FIFTIES BUT THE movement towards Christian unity which began during the war was showing signs of growth. It was urgently necessary to show that Catholics were not interested only in their own affairs. Whenever possible I accepted invitations to address non-Catholic audiences and take part in community affairs. I have given examples of speeches which caused friction but it would be wrong to give the impression that I never mounted a platform without creating controversy. During my six years in Leeds I engaged in few battles but they were all given great publicity. Most of my speaking was done in churches during parish visitations or on special occasions such as centenaries and jubilees. I also spoke at prize-givings in schools and hospitals. There were two universities in the diocese—one in Leeds and the other in Sheffield. I took a very personal interest in the students and with the help of an enthusiastic body of laity established a Catholic chaplaincy in both universities.

In the autumn of 1953 I was invited to give the inaugural lecture for the academic year at the University of Leeds. By tradition this lecture is given in the medical school but it is attended by all faculties. This was a particularly welcome invitation because my predecessor Bishop Poskitt had not been able to take a very prominent part in public life. My only difficulty was to find a subject which would have some reference to medicine without requiring any specialist knowledge on the part of my hearers or myself. At about this time there was great interest in the theories of the Soviet biologist Lysenko who had been highly praised by Stalin and Russian scientists but unanimously condemned by all non-communist scholars. I therefore decided to use Lysenko as a peg on which to hang a lecture on Academic Freedom. The following extracts will show the kind of approach thought proper in the 1950s. Its interest lies chiefly in showing how easily freedom is destroyed if the State is allowed to become too powerful.

You must not imagine that the persecution of scholars belongs to the forgotten, unhappy past. You know, or you will learn in the course of your studies, what the world owes to Mendel, the father of modern biology. The greatest names in that branch of learning are Mendel, Weismann and Morgan. It has been decreed by the Supreme Soviet that it is no longer permissible for communist biologists to accept their views. The rest of the world perversely clings to Mendelism only through senseless hostility to Marxist dogma. The spokesman for the new learning in Soviet Russia is Lysenko who says: "Mendelism represents an attempt of clerical reactionary elements to displace the materialistic biological system of Darwin by a veiled form of idealism." It must not be thought that the Lysenko controversy is a domestic quarrel between rival schools of biology in the field of genetics. The controversy is not over genes and chromosomes but over freedom of scholarship and political dogmatism. What Lysenko is saying is that when nature does not fit your theories you must alter nature. This is how Langdon-Davies sums up Lysenkoism:

> This very remarkable man
> Commends a most practical plan;
>   You can do what you want
>   If you don't think you can't
> So don't think you can't; think you can.

It would be complacent to suggest that all threat to academic freedom comes from the Soviet Union and her satellites. It is impossible to ignore the new American doctrine 'McCarthyism'. I am not at all sure that we have heard the full story of this phenomenon which has made the United States look so foolish in the eyes of the whole world. Who could have imagined that intelligent Americans would destroy books in embassy libraries simply because of their political doctrine? The theory is that communism can best be defeated by reading nothing about it except from its enemies. A worse feature of American policy is the current fear of citizens being suspected of un-American activities. A man faces indictment if a copy of the *Daily Worker* is found on his desk. . . .

. . . When you have forgotten the smell of dissecting rooms and exchanged orderly wards for the often squalid sick rooms of your patients, you will discover that medicine is only part of the art you will be called upon to practise. You are destined to be not only healers of bodies but directors of souls. Doctors are increasingly taking the part of clergy as spiritual advisers. At least three-quarters of the men and women of this country have no contact with clergy except on the more or less social occasions of baptisms, weddings and funerals. In the Middle Ages and for long afterwards the priest was the only educated man English people knew. He wrote their letters and advised them in all their domestic problems. In every town and village he was the person who mattered most—hence the word 'parson'.

Today the doctor is the parson—the only educated man to whom everyone has ready access. As you feel the pulses of your patients you will receive all sorts of confidences which have nothing to do with medicine. You will be called upon to advise in the complex human problems of birth, education and marriage. I beg you to regard your profession as a calling. You will often be responsible for the moral as well as the physical health of your patients.

You will begin your practice of medicine at a moment when the realities of God's law are often ignored or denied. The Hippocratic oath is now regarded cynically by some doctors. The time may come when legislation will tell you to kill the incurably sick. You are already expected by impatient relatives to give over-doses of drugs to bring on the end more quickly. Remember the doctor's pledge not to harm his patients nor murder the unborn infant in the womb. Abortion does not become right by being called therapeutic. In the whole field of medicine you must be aware of your responsibilities to the law of God.

It is no longer unusual for clergy of different denominations to occupy each other's pulpits. In the early 1950s we had not advanced so far but it was not uncommon to be invited to give a talk to members of another creed. On more than one occasion I spoke to mixed audiences in parishes. We did not use the word 'ecumenical' but we were already thinking and talking in terms of Christian Unity. Looking at the text of talks I gave in those years I discern a defensiveness which would be absent today. This is well illustrated in the following passage from a talk given in the union at Sheffield University at the request of the Student Christian Movement during my last year as Bishop of Leeds.

> To a Protestant the Catholic attitude is insufferable and wrong. In a short talk I cannot prove that it is not wrong but I hope to show that it is not insufferable. It is not charitable to mislead and it would be misleading for me to pretend that frank discussion can lead to a compromise doctrine to which in good conscience Catholic and Protestant could subscribe. Let me give the facts as they appear to me while assuring you of my respect for sincere believers of whatever creed. There are holier and better men than I on the bench of Anglican bishops and among the superintendents of Methodist circuits. The fact that my theology is true will not take me to heaven but I would lose my soul if I were to pretend that it is false.

I cannot imagine that I would speak that way today. It is a pity that ecumenism, which is essentially an exercise in Christian charity, has been saddled with a name which suggests a purely intellectual exercise. This restricts the work for Christian Unity to clergy and those laymen not frightened by Greek words. Ecumenism has been successful at the top. Church leaders have altered their outlook and have achieved mutual goodwill which is completely genuine. The theory that the laity desire unity but are prevented by prelates is sheer fantasy. Sectarianism is disappearing among all denominations. The reason is not that believers are huddling together as survivors from the wreck of Christianity but that there has been a change of heart among Christians. The change has been greatest among Roman Catholics and Orthodox Catholics. It was much easier for Anglicans to become ecumenists because they were used to comprehensiveness within their own communion. The Anglo-Catholic party included papalists while among Evangelicals there were fundamentalists. The great difficulty of Roman and Orthodox Catholics was to have discussions with other Christians (or with each other) except with conversion in view.

The Catholic ecumenist believes that reunion will come about in God's good time and in God's own way without any dogma of the Church being discarded. That may seem to rule out dialogue but the

Anglican or Methodist must also look forward to reunion without sacrifice of essential truths. The explanation of the paradox reveals the true nature of ecumenism. The deeper the analysis the more clear become the fundamental points of agreement. The great lesson of ecumenism is that without sacrifice of principle Christians of traditions hitherto regarded as irreconcilable discover an identity of belief. Where direct contradictions exist error must give way to truth. Contradictory doctrines cannot both be true. Dialogue means the sifting of evidence and the separation of doctrine from semantics. That is why the work of Christian Unity calls for tolerance, patience and learning. Ecumenism has already produced unity among Christians which is perhaps more important than the reunion of Christians.

At the end of 1956 I took part in the meeting of the North of England Education Conference at Harrogate. This conference takes place each year in a different town in the north of England. Attended by directors of education, chairmen of education committees and H.M.I.s (Her Majesty's Inspectors of Schools) it is a prestigious occasion. In 1956 religious education was on the agenda and despite the fact that voluntary schools were not under consideration I was invited to address the meeting. Dr. Wilson, the Anglican Bishop of Birmingham, and Dr. Roberts, the Methodist theologian, had been asked to give their views on the religious provisions of the 1946 Education Act. This laid down an act of worship and religious instruction in county schools (i.e. schools other than non-provided (church) schools). What I remember best about the meeting was the personality of Dr. Wilson. Of his words from the platform I can remember only his amusing introduction. He alleged that he alone of our trio was really qualified to address an audience of such distinguished educationists. Only he among us had ever actually been a schoolmaster. He had not only been a teacher, he added, but a teacher of outstanding ability. He did not ask us to accept his word for this but read out a brief testimonial written by his former headmaster: "Dr. Wilson has taught at this school for a year and has been fired with enthusiasm."

During the luncheon interval I invited the bishop to come for a walk and it was now that I was given a glimpse of the depth of character of this remarkable man. He had been taken prisoner by the Japanese in Singapore. He was held in the notorious Changi gaol and subjected to interrogation with violence. At no time did he feel fear even though threats of execution were made each time he refused to answer questions likely to incriminate others in captivity. At the beginning of each session of torture he composed himself to meditate on the passion of Christ. Thus he was able to retain peace of mind whatever punishment his captors inflicted. He had no bitterness in his heart and was able even to feel gratitude to the Japanese for what he had learned under torture. The years of captivity transformed him and gave him a new understanding of Christ as Saviour. He told me that for the first time he realised the literal truth of the words of St. Paul: "I can do all things in Him who strengthens me" (Phil. IV: 13). Dr. Wilson came back to Leeds with me that afternoon and we continued our conversation in Bishop's House. This was the beginning of a friendship which lasted until his death. We used to sit together at Broadcasting House at meetings of C.R.A.C. (Central Religious Advisory Council). My admiration and affection continued to grow.

My contribution to the education conference was that of an outsider. Religious education in Catholic schools was not on the agenda. It was a mark of courtesy and a sign of the growing co-operation between Christians that I was asked to give my views on the place of religion in county schools. The problems of religious education have increased largely because of a general decline in belief. Since the proportion of active church members among teachers has dropped sharply in recent years my words in 1956 are even more apposite today. Here are some excerpts from my short speech:

While we were fighting a war, as we said, in defence of Christian civilisation the evacuation of school children from our cities took place. The public was alarmed at their ignorance of the elements of religion. One country parson discovered that twenty out of thirty children—two-thirds—had no idea who was born on Christmas Day and died on Good Friday. You may recall the famous *Times* leading article "Religion and National Life". "The grim fact is," it said, "that in a country professedly Christian, and a country which at the moment is staking its all in defence of Christian principles, there is a system of national education which allows the citizens of the future to have a purely heathen upbringing." So it was decided to christianise education. . . .

. . . Religious education is to be sought not in the school but in the home. But this Conference is dealing not with homes but with schools. With the object of providing topics for debate let me therefore throw out one or two lines of discussion.

(1) *The morning assembly and act of worship:* Would it not be a good thing for these to be treated as separate? If a headmaster is

not a convinced Christian is it likely that his conduct of the act of worship will nourish the spiritual life of the children? He will not want to forego the presidency of the school assembly. That is why the act of worship should be distinct from the assembly and be led by an active member of a worshipping community. There is no reason why the two exercises should not take place successively.

(2) *Teaching of religion* should be entrusted only to believing Christians. This does not mean that the teacher should teach the doctrines of his own denomination. That would be to cheat the law. It means that fundamental Christian truths would be taught from conviction and so would be more likely to carry weight with intelligent boys and girls.

(3) The idea of 'reserved' teachers in a controlled school might be extended to other schools. At the moment there is no reason why in a county school the act of worship should not be conducted by a communist or doctrine be taught by an atheist.

This was one of the last speeches I made as Bishop of Leeds. There was much speculation as to who would be asked to go to Liverpool. For some reason it was taken for granted that the Holy See would translate a bishop rather than appoint a priest to the vacancy. This was the more surprising since the two previous archbishops had both been Liverpool priests although Dr. Godfrey had been the Apostolic Delegate at the time of his appointment.

What in secular professions would be looked on as promotion is not necessarily so regarded in the priesthood. Candidates do not opt for higher office and have little more than notional freedom to refuse it when offered. Becoming an archbishop involves a man in heavier responsibilities but does not change what has come to be called his life style. An archbishop is not responsible for the dioceses in his province though as Metropolitan he presides at provincial meetings. Theoretically he is also an ecclesiastical ombudsman for the priests and people under the jurisdiction of his suffragan bishops. The only significant prerogative of an archbishop is that as spokesman for the province he is listened to with attention. This is particularly true of Liverpool which has a greater proportion of Catholics than any other province in England. Not only by their numbers but also by their enthusiasm Liverpool Catholics have traditionally given their archbishop a prestige which makes him an impressive champion of good causes. When I was asked to leave Leeds for Liverpool I was aware that it would give me increased opportunities of working for the Church and the whole community. I did not have the same misgivings about accepting as when I had been asked to become a bishop. As Bishop of Leeds I had asked many priests to move. I could hardly complain when asked to move myself.

The announcement of my appointment as fifth Archbishop of Liverpool was made on 7th May, 1957. The last of my public appointments was to lead the diocesan pilgrimage to Lourdes. I did not return with the pilgrims but went on to Rome to make a retreat and consider some of the problems which I already knew would be awaiting me in Liverpool. One great problem would be the Metropolitan Cathedral of which the crypt was half constructed. Ought the building of the Lutyens cathedral to go on or should the whole scheme be rejected? I wanted to consider this and other problems before arriving in Liverpool. That was one reason for deciding to postpone my departure from Yorkshire until I had been to Rome. Pope Pius XII was most encouraging and promised to write a letter to the people of the North which could be read out on the day I took possession of my new see. He spoke with great affection of England and of the thousands of British soldiers he had welcomed to the Vatican during the war. One of the greatest of modern popes his stature has been reduced by the immense popularity of the beloved Pope John. The reputation of Pope Pius XII has also suffered from the allegation that he did not do enough for the Jews persecuted by Hitler. There has never been any real evidence to support the attack. Having been Papal Nuncio in Germany and Cardinal Secretary of State in the Vatican Pius XII knew very well how best to deal with Hitler and the Nazis. It would doubtless have given him intense personal satisfaction to have attacked Hitler for his treatment of the Jews. Had he done so Hitler would certainly have vented his anger on the Jews. The Pope chose to protect the Jews in other ways. He encouraged religious houses to provide refuge for the persecuted Jews and to give shelter to their children. The most eloquent answer to those who allege that Pope Pius XII failed the Jews was given by the Chief Rabbi of Rome. After the war he became a Catholic.

I returned from Rome as Archbishop-elect of Liverpool to take leave of Leeds. The newspaper articles show that in the late 'fifties it was not yet unfashionable to speak kindly of bishops. Without suggesting that the reporting was accurate I give samples of the way the contemporary press treated my translation from Leeds to Liverpool.

The first is from the *Sheffield Telegraph*:

Very far from mere platitude is it to say that the new Archbishop of Liverpool, Dr. J. C. Heenan, Bishop of Leeds for the past six years, is held in the deepest affection among his 25,000 Church people in Sheffield and the many thousands more in the surrounding region. For them, it is difficult indeed to realise that the period in which he moved among them, so frequently and so graciously, is one of only six years. Bishop Heenan is the sort of man one feels one has known much longer than actually is the case. For this Essex-born, Cardinal Hinsley-trained prelate combines an extraordinary radiance of personality with all the innate dignity associated with high ecclesiastical office. Serenity, deep spirituality, patent sincerity, warm friendliness, a concern for the spiritual well-being of all, whatever denomination, are combined, in Dr. John Carmel Heenan, with a loving and charitable regard when speaking of Christians of all other Communions.

In Leeds the *Yorkshire Post* was no more sparing in its tribute of affection.

Dr. John Carmel Heenan became Bishop of Leeds in February 1951. Since that time he has endeared himself to all who have come in contact with him, whatever their religious convictions or lack of them. Since he was consecrated, Dr. Heenan has achieved much, by his work for the Catholic schools, his establishment of full-time chaplaincies at the universities of Leeds and Sheffield, and of new parishes, and his encouragement of all Christian activities, to make the Leeds diocese the home of a living faith. But he will be remembered best by the people of Leeds as the people's Bishop—a sincere man with a lively personality and a sense of fun.

The *Yorkshire Post* also marked the occasion with a leading article from my friend, Sir Linton Andrews:

Our pleasure at the news that Bishop Heenan, the sixth Roman Catholic Bishop of Leeds, has been appointed Archbishop of Liverpool is mixed with regret that one so greatly admired among us for his zeal, courageous outspokenness and humanity is to leave Yorkshire. Monsignor Heenan is a much-loved personality among those of his own faith and among many others also. He is much more than a forceful, and sometimes controversial, speaker. To a multitude of people he is a warm, sympathetic friend.

I hoped that the Catholics of Yorkshire would be sorry to see me go but I was quite unprepared for the stream of good wishes both public and private which came from non-Catholics and non-Christians in the West Riding. I issued a short statement which was published in the press of both Yorkshire and Lancashire. It was farewell and hail:

It is always sad for a shepherd to bid goodbye to his flock. But the will of God is made known to us through the authority of the Church. At the request of the Pope I leave the diocese of Leeds, which I love, for the archdiocese of Liverpool, to which I shall give myself without reserve. From both priests and people of the diocese of Leeds I have received nothing but loyalty. I can never thank them enough for the warmth of their affection.

I am also grateful to my non-Catholic and Jewish neighbours in the West Riding for their kindness and for so constantly inviting me to share their social interests. During six years in Yorkshire I can recall no unpleasant word or incident between Catholics and those of other faiths. In Liverpool, with God's help, I hope to be a true friend and father to my priests and a good shepherd of the faithful. I know how much they miss their great archbishop, Dr. Godfrey. I shall try to imitate him in his calm and prudent zeal. I beg the prayers of all my friends in Yorkshire and Lancashire that God will guide and bless me as I accept the heavy task given to me by the Vicar of Christ.

Before saying good-bye to the priests and people of the diocese I had an engagement of long standing to fulfil. I had promised to preach at High Mass in the ruins of Whitby Abbey on the thirteenth centenary of its foundation. It was a great Yorkshire occasion which attracted over ten thousand Catholics from all parts of the north. The event was made especially impressive by the presence of the monks of Ampleforth Abbey whose forbears had been expelled from this very abbey of St. Hilda in the sixteenth century. In my short sermon I reminded the enthusiastic Catholic congregation that nostalgia can be dangerous. If we dwell too much in the past, I told them, we shall halt progress toward Christian Unity. It is useless to argue whether the Archbishop

[209]

of Canterbury is the legitimate successor of St. Augustine or the Archbishop of York of St. Wilfrid. What now matters is their utter sincerity in claiming these titles. If we accept the sincerity of our fellow Christians we shall show our love and thus promote Christian Unity. In those pre-ecumenical days the sermon had an unexpectedly beneficial effect. It gave particular pleasure to Dr. Fisher who at that time was Archbishop of Canterbury and President of the British Council of Churches. A few days later (16th July which happened to be the day of my enthronement in Liverpool) Dr. Fisher made reference to my sermon in a speech at the Mansion House in London while presiding over a meeting of the British Council of Churches:

> The Roman Catholic Archbishop of Liverpool has said that it is no good going on bickering as to whether the Archbishop of Canterbury is right in saying he is descended from St. Augustine but that the most important thing is to love one another until we come to the real truth. I regard this as the most hopeful utterance that has come from the Roman Catholic Church in Britain for a very long time. If that can be followed up in our relations with the Church of Rome, as it is in the British Council of Churches, a new epoch would arise of hope and promise for the Christian Church as a whole in this land.

My formal leave-taking of the diocese took place on the evening of Sunday 30th June, 1957 in the Town Hall, Leeds. Since the cathedral would not have been big enough the organisers boldly sought permission to use the town hall as an improvised cathedral. The authorities gladly gave leave for Mass to be celebrated in the town hall. To allow for extra crowds the neighbouring assize court rooms were connected to the main hall by loud speakers. Mass was celebrated by Monsignor Thompson, Vicar General of the diocese. A presentation from the laity was made by a child from an orphanage. The child was so excited by the applause that she handed me the gift and ran back to her place. Then remembering that she had forgotten something she hurried back to the platform and made this pretty speech: "It is my privilege to present you with this gift from the Catholics of this diocese. We thank you for all you have done for us as our bishop during the past six years. We will continue to pray for you when you leave us to be Archbishop of Liverpool."

In my farewell speech to the priests and people I stressed the fair treatment Catholics receive from all the civic authorities in Yorkshire and paid tribute to the lack of religious bigotry in the county. Because of the large percentage of Jews in the city of Leeds I gave them special mention: "In this city of Leeds where so many Jews reside I think it right to express my great joy that the relationship between Christians and Jews is so very good. My prayer is that the friendly feelings between Protestant and Catholic, Christian and Jew may deepen and grow greater. God is best served when his children—we are all his children— love each other like brothers."

A few days earlier the indefatigable Sheffield Council of Catholic Action had organised a rally in the City Hall. The Lord Mayor invited the aldermen and councillors to a farewell tea-party before the evening rally. This was typical of the generous attitude of the non-Catholics of Sheffield. The steel city has a reputation for producing flint-hearted citizens but there are no more warm-hearted people in all Yorkshire. Elsewhere they are merely more demonstrative. The priests joined the laity in these two gatherings but also invited me to an entirely clerical party at St. Bede's School, Bradford. To my great surprise the clergy gave me a generous cheque which enabled me to buy new episcopal robes. The purple cassock which I had inherited from Bishop Poskitt six years earlier was showing signs of wear. Although I would not have encouraged a collection if I had been consulted I was glad to have the means of buying the clothes I needed without having to ask my new diocese to pay the bill as soon as I had arrived. I possessed no money of my own. The priests were most gracious and Monsignor Thompson was their spokesman. He was able to refer good-humouredly to the upsets and alarms of the early days of the 'cruel see' and assure me that all was forgiven if not forgotten. The diocese had been calm for three years and by now the priests all knew me personally. It would be too much to say that they were in tears at the prospect of losing me but at least they were not rejoicing at my departure.

So I had to change the white rose of Yorkshire for the red rose of Lancashire. It does not take long to cross the Pennines but each side produces a very different kind of citizen. It is as foolish to compare people as to evaluate colours. White is neither better nor worse than red. The Yorkshire type is not inferior or superior to Lancastrian. It was nevertheless permissible to reflect as I left the diocese of Leeds that I would have a long road to travel before finding anyone more loyal and loving than the sturdy Catholics of the West Riding.

PART II—LIVERPOOL

1957 — 1963

FIFTEEN

"YOU'VE LEFT IT TOO LATE THIS TIME, FATHER. YOU HAVEN'T A DOG'S chance of getting in," said the police sergeant on duty near the Liverpool pro-cathedral on the morning of 16th July, 1957. The master of ceremonies had begged me not to arrive a moment before eleven o'clock for the enthronement. I had therefore instructed my driver to wait in a side street round the corner until three minutes to eleven so as to arrive at exactly eleven a.m. I was half-a-minute late as a result of having to persuade the sergeant that I had quite a good chance of getting into the pro-cathedral if only he would let me pass. The old 'Pro' was pitifully inadequate for a great function. After places had been found for officials, clergy and nuns there was room for no more than two representatives from each parish. The reporter from the *Daily Telegraph* under the heading "A poor backdrop for pomp" made a plea for speed in the building the new cathedral.

A good many of those who waited patiently outside Liverpool's Roman Catholic pro-cathedral on Copperas Hill yesterday while Archbishop Heenan was enthroned must have tried to envisage how different the scene would have been were the Metropolitan Cathedral already built. Instead of the wide flight of steps and spacious forecourt which such a ceremony demands, the pro-cathedral can only offer a narrow cobbled street and a flight of steps necessarily turned sideways to come within the building line. Opposite there is a dingy hotel yard, flanked by a wall topped with barbed wire and broken glass; on the next corner there is the noisy clatter and chink of a dairy. All around are blitzed sites and rusting sheets of corrugated iron; and looming above the whole scene, and quite dwarfing the pro-cathedral are the messy hindquarters of the Adelphi hotel.

The pro-cathedral is very close to the city it serves and has done its work well. But there is precious little room for pomp in such a setting; and I imagine that those who love spectacle will be heartily glad when the new cathedral however scaled down, rises to dominate Brownlow Hill.

A few days before the ceremony I had presented the papal bull of appointment to the chapter of canons. It had been a private occasion followed by a meal in the presbytery of Monsignor Adamson, the Vicar General of the diocese. It was one of the most gay and friendly luncheon parties I ever attended. It set the pattern for many a clerical gathering I was to enjoy during the six years which followed. Each diocese has its own feel. It is hard to define what is distinctive but no two dioceses have quite the same ethos. Liverpool was alive with ebullient friendliness and religious fervour. It is renowned for demonstrative faith and the love of the laity for their clergy. This is due in some measure to the religious history of the diocese. In the early years of the century friction between Protestants and Catholics in Liverpool was constant and bitter. The city presented a scene of sectarian strife traditionally associated with Northern Ireland. In no other English city was a colour bar maintained between orange and green. Politics and religion were so identified that in the city council there was a party actually called the Protestant Party. Even so short a time ago as the 1940s anti-Catholic feelings were so deep that a special Liverpool bill had to be passed by Parliament to implement the Education Act in its provisions for Catholic schools. The bigotry was almost dead by the time I came to Liverpool but, as will appear in the course of the narrative, the embers were not quite cold.

My first meeting with the canons established such a cordial relationship that when, during the ceremony of enthronement, each member of the chapter came to salute me it was a meeting of old friends. I was to discover that the warmth of the older priests reflected the traditional loyalty of Liverpool priests for their archbishop. The joy of the enthronement was lessened for me because the Provost, Bishop Halsall, a fellow student at the English College in Rome, was sick and unable to take a leading part in the ceremony. While still comparatively young he had

[218]

suffered a stroke and was now scarcely able to walk. He bravely continued his duties as Auxiliary Bishop but on that day he seemed close to death. He died less than a year later.

On the evening of the enthronement the B.B.C. gave recorded extracts of the ceremony to which I added a few words which closely followed the lines of my address when introducing myself to the people of Yorkshire on the day of my consecration as Bishop of Leeds. I had not forgotten that, to my immense advantage, a request for prayers on that occasion had been taken seriously by listeners both Catholic and non-Catholic:

From the extracts you have just heard you will have some idea of the sacred character of a bishop's enthronement. The man told to rule a diocese is left in no doubt about the nature of his task. The beauty of the ceremony and the marks of honour paid to him do not mislead him. He knows that a heavy burden has been placed upon him. When the rich vestments are put away and the sounds of music stilled, he is left alone. He has time to reflect. I want to tell you briefly what my thoughts are as I take up my duties as Archbishop of Liverpool. First, I recall the words of my old friend and master, Cardinal Hinsley—God rest his great soul! One day he picked up a mitre, turned to me with a wry sort of smile and said: "Young man, when you wear a mitre you will discover that it's a crown of thorns." That's a solemn thought—too solemn, you may think, for this festive day. But what is solemn need not be sad. After all, to wear a crown of thorns is to be like Our Lord. That's just what a bishop must try to be. As shepherd of the flock he must model himself on the Good Shepherd.

It's impossible, of course, for any of us to be quite like Him. Left to myself I would not dare to try. But God never refuses grace to those who ask. "Ask and you shall receive," He said. I shall ask constantly. The Holy Mass I offered this morning was a plea for grace. I begged Almighty God to guide me in my work for Him. I sought grace for all the souls entrusted to my pastoral care.

Now let me tell you why I wanted to speak to you as soon as possible after my enthronement. I want your help. No, I'm not asking for a subscription for the Metropolitan Cathedral—though, of course, donations will be welcome. No, I want your prayers. Help me to obtain the grace to be a good shepherd. Ask God to give me the courage to wear the mitre—even if it should prove to be a crown of thorns.

I want the prayers of you *all*. My priests speak to God of me by name at Holy Mass each morning. Please say a prayer for me each day. A Christian family should kneel together for a few moments each night before the youngest child goes to bed. At your family prayers please mention me. I don't ask for long prayers. If you say "God bless our Archbishop", I shall be satisfied.

I ask especially for the prayers of the sick and the house-bound. You often feel helpless and useless. Well, you can be of great help and use to me. Give me a share of your prayers and of your pains. Your prayers and those of innocent children have great power with God.

I am bold enough to ask also for the prayers of those who are not Catholics or Christians. If you believe in God and in the value of prayer, you, too, can help me.

I pray for you all every day of my life. I cherish every soul in this great archdiocese and want to prove myself a friend and father to you all.

Six years ago, coming from the south to be Bishop of Leeds, I asked my flock to adopt me as a Yorkshireman. I hope they will not think me fickle if I now change the white rose for the red. That white rose will not be discarded. It will be kept fragrant to match my memories of Yorkshire.

And now I must say "Good-night and God bless you." I leave you with a sincere message of good will. Even if you do not share my Faith I wish you well. No words of bitterness or rancour will fall from my lips. On this feast of Mary, the Immaculate Mother of God, I pledge myself to serve the people of the North in peace, in justice and in love.

My first engagements were a series of meetings with the Liverpool clergy. I invited priests to meet me either at Atlantic House, the seamen's hostel in Liverpool, or in Wigan at the other end of the diocese. A third meeting was held on the Isle of Man which is under the jurisdiction of Liverpool. Despite its distance from Liverpool Douglas, capital of the Isle of Man, is more quickly reached than Chorley or Wigan because of the excellent service from the Liverpool airport which is only about a mile from Archbishop's House. These meetings with the priests were most valuable. I felt that I owed them some reassurance. The recollection of 'the cruel see' had not yet been entirely erased. In Leeds itself the expression had long ceased to be used even as a joke, but good news travels slowly. Many Liverpool priests must have felt some misgivings lest I repeat the Leeds pattern by signalising my arrival in Liverpool with a general post. I was determined to calm their fears. I pointed out that a bishop taking over a fresh diocese is bound to have learned from experience in his former diocese. In these talks I made it clear that they need not fear any upheaval. "I give you my promise," I told them. "I shall not repeat the mistakes I made in my early days in Leeds. I undertake not to make the same mistakes again. I shall make entirely new ones." Reassuring as these meetings were to the clergy they were even more reassuring to me. It was evident that the Liverpool priests were going to judge me by my performance not on my record.

The depth of Liverpool loyalty to its archbishop is unique. Priests and people have inherited and maintain a quite remarkable veneration for their chief pastor. Universally referred to as 'the Arch' he is a shepherd beloved by the whole flock. Demonstrative affection is not limited to children—who will love any bishop or priest who takes the trouble to know them. The Catholics of Liverpool, practising and lapsed, educated and unlettered, share this esteem for their archbishop. It has little to do with the personality of the holder of the office. The explanation for this outstanding loyalty is found in the early history of Catholicism in the north-west. It is personified in Thomas Whiteside the first Archbishop of Liverpool who died in 1921 after a reign of nearly thirty years.

Ethnically the diocese is heterogeneous. In Liverpool, Bootle and St. Helens where the proportion of Catholics is two or three times greater than the national average, many are of Irish origin. At the time of the Irish famine (1846) there was a massive exodus from the stricken Irish villages to the cities of England. Liverpool was the first port of call and tens of thousands among the immigrants went no further. Starving, impoverished and often disease-ridden they lacked the strength to journey any further in search of food and work. But there are plenty of Catholics who are not Irish. Until 1924 the whole of Lancashire was in the diocese of Liverpool and most truly Lancastrian Catholics can trace their family tree beyond the Reformation. Not a few of them claim ancestors among the martyrs. Parishioners of Preston, Chorley and, to a lesser extent, Wigan were often of English stock. There are even small enclaves in Lancashire which the change of religion scarcely touched. Even in my time in Liverpool the village of Little Crosby had an entirely Catholic population.

Liverpool is associated in the public mind with the Liverpool Irish.

Until recently the Liverpool Irish, for most of whom the closest contact with Ireland was through their grand-parents, lived in Protestant and Catholic ghettoes. The poorest section of the city was divided between the Green and the Orange. We shall return to the sociological effects of this partition which is one of the reasons for the exceptionally close relationship between the people and their priests. Religious intolerance was a feature of social life in Liverpool until the second world war. Archbishop Whiteside was a hated figure among illiterate Protestants and was regarded by the Catholic poor as saint and hero. Protestant antagonism bred a defiant unity among the Catholic clergy and people. There was widespread unemployment, malnutrition and disease among the Catholic poor. Led by their pastors—Bishops Goss and O'Reilly were the heroes before Thomas Whiteside became archbishop—the priests of Liverpool gave heroic service to their flocks. With such renowned bishops and clergy it is not surprising that the Catholics of Liverpool became fiercely attached to their priests.

The enthronement took place on the Feast of Our Lady of Mount Carmel, 16th July, 1958. Since there was room for so few in the pro-cathedral an open air service was held on the following Sunday at Brownlow Hill on the site of the future metropolitan cathedral. Liverpool being a strike-prone city it surprised nobody when a bus strike was announced for that very week-end. It is perhaps unnecessary to say that the strike was not a demonstration against the new archbishop. Demonstrations had not yet become fashionable outside dictatorship countries. We were afraid that only people with cars would be able to make their way to the cathedral site and that the great rally would be no more than an outdoor service for a few neighbouring parishes. We need not have worried. The papers said that over forty thousand people 'beat the strike'. Thousands unable to gain admission to the grounds gathered in the surrounding streets. It was a magnificent demonstration of faith which filled me with courage at the beginning of my new task. This was a period of intense zeal in the Catholic Church. The popularity of the beloved Pope John has made many forget the achievements of his predecessor, Pope Pius XII, who inaugurated many of the liturgical reforms in an era of renewed eucharistic fervour. He relaxed the fast before Holy Communion and encouraged the celebration of Mass in the evening. A message addressed to me but intended for the priests and people of Liverpool from the Cardinal Secretary of State was read at the rally by Monsignor Adamson, the Vicar General.

The Holy Father expresses the prayerful hope that your zealous apostolic activity will reap an even more abundant harvest of spiritual fruits among the flock now entrusted to your pastoral care. The reputation which the Catholics of the Metropolitan See of Liverpool have won for themselves gives every reason to hope that Your Grace's ministry among them will be fruitful. The people of Liverpool, and especially the workers, have always been noted for their living faith and unswerving loyalty to the Catholic Church. For this reason they have ever been particularly dear to the heart of the Vicar of Christ. The Pontiff's purpose in relaxing the regulations for the Eucharistic fast and in giving permission for evening Masses was to enable workers to attend Mass regularly and receive Holy Communion more frequently. He feels confident that the working people of Liverpool will prove anew their loyalty to the Church by availing of these facilities and by renewing and intensifying their devotion to the Mass and the Blessed Sacrament.

After this rather spectacular introduction to my flock I quickly settled down to the routine work of the diocese. I did not have to face problems like those I had found in Leeds which had been without a bishop for over a year when I was appointed. There had been no great delay in making the appointment to the vacant see of Liverpool. Less than six months elapsed between the translation of Archbishop Godfrey to Westminster and my own to Liverpool. I found a diocese in splendid order both spiritually and materially. The visitation of parishes proved to be a far more strenuous exercise in Lancashire than in Yorkshire because of the greater density of the Catholic population. In some city parishes all households were at least nominally Catholic. In such parishes the visitation was made into a gala for the whole neighbourhood. Houses were decorated and streets were closed while I made my visits to the sick. In keeping with Liverpool tradition slogans were painted on walls or printed on banners slung across the streets. "God bless our Archbishop" was the most popular. By now the colours were fading because the same banners had done duty for Archbishops Whiteside, Keating, Downey and Godfrey before my turn came round. Another common slogan was "God bless our parish priest" and, inevitably, the banner with a strange device: "God bless the Sacred Heart".

Apart from seeing the sick the most rewarding part of the visitation was meeting the children in the schools. Nearly half the children of

[223]

school age in Liverpool and Bootle were Catholic. The task of visiting schools was therefore quite formidable. Including schools in a parish visitation was a recent innovation and children were excited by the prospect of the very first visit of an archbishop to their school. The younger children are the more they enjoy showing their paces. They said their prayers, sang hymns and took delight in bowing low to greet me with the carefully rehearsed formula: "Good morning, Your Grace". They practised the greeting many times before I was due to arrive. One class of infants in Wavertree though well-drilled had been kept waiting so long that the teacher thought it wise to refresh their memory before I entered the classroom: "Don't forget to say Your Grace," she said. It being nearly dinner time I was greeted with the words of the grace before meals, "Bless us, O Lord, and these thy gifts which we are to receive from thy bounty".

On these occasions there was little time to speak to the staff. I was introduced to each teacher but real discussion was possible only at the teachers' meetings which I held in various parts of the diocese. In addition to communications sent to the priests (called *ad clerum* letters) there were also occasional messages to teachers. Many ideas which are now commonplace in Catholic schools were then so new as to seem revolutionary. It seems incredible that so short a time ago there was great opposition to any change in the system of school inspection. It required perseverance and tact to persuade teachers that chaplains would be useful in schools. During my early months in the diocese I addressed teachers at five meetings during which lively discussions took place. I then sent to each teacher in the diocese a letter of which the following is an extract.

My dear Teacher,
Much as I enjoy meeting you, I cannot ask teachers to give up an evening to attend a meeting each time I have something to tell you. That is why I am sending you this letter.

1. *Religious Inspection*
The present system of religious inspection has remained more or less unaltered since the days when few Catholic teachers were properly trained. The Church in those days was grateful to accept the services of any zealous person willing to teach Catholic children. Many of the teachers were young and untrained. It was necessary, therefore, for inspections to be more in the nature of

Crowded but happy occasion in Liverpool.

During a parish visitation.
Liverpool University: receiving honorary doctorate from the Chancellor
(Lord Salisbury).

examinations if the bishops were to have detailed knowledge of the doctrine being taught in the schools. Today our teachers, trained in college, are well equipped to give religious instruction. For this reason it now seems desirable to alter the system of religious inspection. In future it will be conducted on a deanery basis. Each inspector will be responsible for the schools in his deanery. From time to time a full-scale inspection may be helpful but annual inspection will be less formal than in the past. Priests will arrange with you the most suitable times to call. They will visit a class with the object not of examining the children but of advising the teacher about the syllabus and methods of instruction.

The priests who will inspect schools have been with me to Hopwood Hall for a short course during the summer. They will keep in touch with the training college in order to be better able to advise teachers in their work. I have suggested that when visiting a school they should first see the head teacher to be given a general view of the work being done in the school. They will then go round the classes and, finally, hold a Staff meeting. In this way there can be a free interchange of ideas and the inspections will be more fruitful . . .

2. *School Chaplains*

A common drawback of inter-parochial schools is lack of contact between the priest and the children. For this reason I have decided to appoint a chaplain to secondary schools both grammar and modern. In some parts of the country a priest is a regular member of staff appointed as a specialist in divinity. These priests must have a degree or a teacher's certificate. Whether or not this arrangement is desirable, it is out of the question in the Archdiocese of Liverpool for many years to come. But a chaplain can bring many advantages to a school without being on the staff.

I do not propose to make any detailed regulations concerning the duties of the chaplain. He can make out a programme which will benefit not only religious instruction itself but the whole spiritual and moral tone of the school. It will be for the priest and teachers to consult together about the syllabus, methods and spiritual exercises of the children. I know that I can rely on the good will of the teachers to make this experiment worthwhile.

A month after my enthronement I was invited to take part in a controversial television programme. It was one of the first of many encounters with Mr. Malcolm Muggeridge who eventually became a cherished friend. At the time of this broadcast and for many years afterwards he was an unbeliever. "I see the happiness of those who believe in Christianity," he told a reporter, "but I haven't got it." At that time he was editor of *Punch* and had not yet made his name as a broadcaster. In this programme he was chairman of a panel of not very high calibre. Maurice Richardson, the T.V. critic of the *Observer*, evidently did not think that their performance was worthy either of the chairman or myself. "The Archbishop," he wrote, "played a brilliant dialectical innings but the bowling was so loose and half-hearted that Muggeridge as umpire was obviously tempted to signal no-ball and take over himself. Rationalists must learn to be forceful and articulate in controversy and not be afraid of flaunting the banner of scientific humanism: the moment they falter the trained cleric runs incense rings round them." One of the opponents (whom I later discovered to be a former priest) accused the Roman Catholic Church of upholding sanctity in order to give virgins to the Church. I had to point out that his quarrel was not with the Church of Rome but with St. Paul who preached the excellence of virginal chastity.

Later that month I went to the Somerset village of Mells to take leave of Monsignor Ronnie Knox who was dying of cancer. We had never been close friends but rather more than acquaintances. He was perhaps the greatest figure in the Church of the twentieth century. As a writer he was admired not only by his fellow Catholics and former colleagues of the Anglican Church but by all connoisseurs of stylish prose. His greatest contribution to literature was his translation of the bible into contemporary English. To this monumental task he brought not only his wide learning but an extraordinary capacity for assembling critical views of his draft translation to enable him to produce a final polished version. A notoriously shy man he might have been expected to work in scholarly solitude but he sought the help of the widest possible range of students, young and old, famous and obscure. All were invited to give their criticisms and suggestions. He was overwhelmed by the number of those who offered advice. After the publication of his translation he thanked all those who had written. Then (typically) he could not forbear to thank 'still more' those who did not proffer help. Although renowned as a preacher and scholar his real greatness lay in his holiness of life. He was very near death when I visited him but he received me with great courtesy and thanked me for coming to take leave of him. Being a genuine intellectual he had an essentially simple faith. He was what we now call an old-fashioned Catholic. He loved the Imitation of Christ of which he left an excellent but unfinished translation (published posthumously).

In September 1957 an incident occurred which today would pass unremarked but in those days when the first faltering ecumenical steps were being taken, it received headlines in the national press. The occasion was an international congress of scripture scholars at Oxford. I had accepted an invitation to take the chair at a lecture by Dr. Michael Ramsey who was still Archbishop of York. Shortly before, he had succeeded Dr. Garbett, and I wrote to welcome him to my diocese. (Bishopthorpe, the residence of the Archbishop of York, is just within the boundary of the Catholic diocese of Leeds). We were acquainted but had not yet become close friends. At this meeting our demeanour no less than our words received close scrutiny. It was evidently a matter for speculation among reporters which of us would sit down first. "Problem of Precedence" was the headline in the *Yorkshire Post*. "Archbishops give example of Charity" said the *Belfast Telegraph*. "No problem for Archbishops" proclaimed the *Manchester Guardian*. "No scoring" the *Daily Telegraph* reported. *The Times* gave the following account under the sober heading "Shared Platform":

> The Archbishop of York, Dr. Ramsey, and the Archbishop of Liverpool, Dr. Heenan, shared the platform to-night at the international congress in Oxford on "The Four Gospels in 1957". They settled the question of precedence by approaching their seats together, bowing to each other, and sitting down together amid a storm of applause from more than 600 delegates from all parts of the world.
>
> Dr. Heenan, who was in the chair, in introducing Dr. Ramsey, said "In some ways this is an historic occasion. It is not every day that the Catholic Metropolitan of the North has the honour of presiding at a meeting addressed by the Primate of England ... I regard it as a very great honour indeed. I am particularly pleased because Catholics and Protestants are assembled here, not to score points off each other, not to show how wrong the other is, but to demonstrate for all with eyes to see that we regard charity as the greatest of all virtues."
>
> Replying, Dr. Ramsey said: "When, a little over a year ago, I migrated from Durham to York, I found myself residing in what was then Your Grace's diocese. Then, all too soon afterwards, in

[227]

your departure for Liverpool and for your present great office, Yorkshire lost a man of charity, friendship, and of unselfish service to the good of the people. I have now escaped the privilege of residing in Your Grace's diocese, but you have not escaped the privilege of living in my province," he said amid laughter.

Dr. Ramsey then delivered his address on "The Gospel and the Gospels".

CHAPTER
SIXTEEN

THERE IS NO ENGLISH CITY IN WHICH THE WAY TO CHRISTIAN UNITY HAS been so strewn with obstacles as Liverpool. The most patent cause is the traditional division of the city's poor into Orange and Green. Their simmering bitterness used to burst into flame annually on 12th July, the day of the orange parade. As the century progressed these demonstrations became less lethal. By the middle 'fifties orange parades had become no more than colourful processions of beautifully-dressed children accompanied by adoring mothers. In earlier years the procession had been a politico-religious protest march during which the windows of Catholic churches and schools in Everton were ritually broken. Catholics were well advised to keep off the streets on Orange Day. For the rest of the year both sides preserved a kind of neutrality which although unbenevolent and unchristian was at least non-violent. This was not the full explanation of the intolerance which until after the war was found even among the better educated. There can be no doubt that rivalry between Protestants and Catholics was fostered by segregation. Catholics avoided close contacts with Protestants through fear of mixed marriages. This was the common outlook of Catholics everywhere in Britain but in Liverpool abhorrence of mixed marriages was obsessive.

Opposition to mixed marriages was intense among Protestants (and Jews) as well as Catholics. Protestants contracting marriage with Catholics were guilty of a double fault in the eyes of their families. In addition to an act of religious disloyalty they committed a social solecism. A Protestant was far more likely than a Catholic to be ostracised after a mixed marriage. It is easy to see why the Liverpool Catholic community had such a horror of mixed marriages. The archbishops had taken more stringent measures to discourage mixed marriages than bishops in other dioceses. Until the death of Archbishop Whiteside in 1921 it was virtually impossible for Catholics to obtain dispensations to marry Protestants. They had to resort to the subterfuge of crossing the river Mersey for a few days to acquire canonical domicile outside Liverpool. They could then apply for a dispensation to the Bishop of Shrewsbury in whose diocese milder regulations were in force. After Archbishop Whiteside's death dispensations were less difficult to obtain but mixed marriages were still regarded in the words of the old catechism as 'unlawful and pernicious'. Such strong words had been warranted while legalised intolerance prevailed (Catholic Emancipation was passed in 1829 but anti-Catholic attitudes continued until the first world war). It is not suggested that only in Liverpool were mixed marriages deplored. In the Ilford of my childhood I often heard Canon Palmer, the parish priest, denounce mixed marriages intemperately. Many years later when I was curate in the neighbouring parish of Barking I found that his uncompromising attitude persisted. He assured me that he had seen such unhappiness and so much lapsing from the faith because of mixed marriages that if he were a bishop he would not grant any dispensations. Archbishop Whiteside was one of his greatest heroes. Canon Palmer was kindly and tolerant in all his other dealings with his flock but there was thunder in his voice when speaking to any unfortunate who had come to arrange a mixed marriage. On the occasion of a mixed marriage he would keep the bridal couple waiting up to half-an-hour. The ceremony would be brief, brusque and cheerless. Yet no priest was more popular with non-Catholics. He made many converts but he must have repelled many partners of mixed marriages by his regular tirades at Sunday Mass. His opposition to mixed marriages was total. The Liverpool attitude was by no means confined to the diocese.

Today opposition to mixed marriages has softened. This is an effect both of ecumenism and of pastoral experience. If the majority of those whom Catholics meet socially are not Catholics it is obvious that mixed marriages will be frequent. Mixed marriages are less common among immigrants (Irish, Poles, Italians, Spaniards) precisely because they seek companionship among their compatriots. However ecumenical they are, pastors of souls have to admit that even today differences of religion can hazard loving relationships. People who fall in love are not looking for obstacles to their union and tend to make light of the problems likely to arise from a mixed marriage. Those closely attached to their Church may see the dangers ahead and even break off the engagement, but they are exceptional. Religious controversy is usually provoked not by the young couple but by their relatives. This is especially true when parents on either side have strong links with the local church or chapel. Emotions are so easily aroused over this issue that parents who have not attended a religious service since their own marriage can become passionately hostile when any of their children propose to marry a person of another faith.

After the second world war it became easier for Liverpool Catholics to obtain a dispensation for a mixed marriage but there was little relaxation of the restrictions imposed on the ceremony itself. The marriage had to take place at a side altar, the organ was not played, no singing was permitted, the candles were not lit and the whole atmosphere was chilly. Priests would beg favours in special circumstances—for example if the Catholic were a convert and the relatives on both sides Protestants. Sometimes a couple would appeal to me personally for leave to be married before the high altar or to have the organ played. I found it difficult to uphold the prevailing custom. Knowing the devotion of the priests to the memory of Archbishop Whiteside I did not set aside the old rules immediately on arrival in the diocese but in the New Year of 1958—six months after my enthronement—I addressed a letter to the clergy of which the following is an extract:

I am convinced that once a dispensation is granted the marriage should be performed in such a way that the couple and their families will not feel slighted. A bride, in particular, sets great store by all the details surrounding her wedding. She feels affronted if she has to be married at a small altar obscurely sited. The organ has an exaggerated importance in the estimation of the bridal couple, their family and friends. The fact is that to have been married at the side altar and to have been denied the organ can become an abiding source of contention after marriage. The Catholic sometimes becomes bitter and the non-Catholic hostile to the Church and disinclined to keep the promises.

Such unhappy results do not always follow as a result of a sombre ceremony at a mixed marriage but even practising Catholics (who admittedly have less excuse for contracting a mixed marriage) find

[231]

a ceremony stripped of joy a source of resentment against the Church. Some priests whose opinions I value greatly may deplore any relaxation of the present regulations. While respecting their views I must act according to my conscience. I have therefore decided to allow mixed marriages to take place at the High Altar and the organ to be played before and after the ceremony. This ruling supersedes Appendix V of the last Synod. The Chapter knows that this is not a hasty decision. I raised the question with the canons in July and for six months I have given it prayerful consideration. Having hitherto refused to make any exceptions I now find it impossible to continue to deny privileges which, despite the obvious risks, I believe to be for the greater good of souls. I have no other motive in this matter.

This is an excellent example of what Catholics took for granted until ecumenism altered our thinking regarding ourselves and our fellow Christians. Apart from its contention that mixed marriages should no longer be lugubrious the tone of the letter would not commend itself today. A pamphlet I once wrote on mixed marriages was withdrawn at my request by the Catholic Truth Society after the Council. The reason is of great significance. It is true that mixed marriages by their nature involve difficulties. When a family is divided on such a fundamental matter as religion their unity is obviously less than perfect. The ideal is for husband and wife to be united in everything affecting the unity of the family. No intelligent person, Catholic, Protestant, Jew or Atheist will advocate mixed marriages. Mixed marriages have not become desirable since the Council but the Catholic Church has made a serious effort to reduce the causes of friction. In 1958 Catholics thought of mixed marriage problems almost exclusively from the viewpoint of the Catholic partner. Because non-Catholic partners of a mixed marriage are rarely active members of any church their religious views were discounted. Those who were practising members of the Church of England or the Free Churches were thought to have surrendered their right to have a say in the religious upbringing of their children in exchange for the privilege of marrying a Catholic. This was not acceptable to thoughtful non-Catholics but it was taken for granted by most Catholics. Their line of reasoning was uncompromising. My children, the argument ran, have the right to inherit the Catholic religion. If you want to marry me you must guarantee my children's rights. It is easy to see why mixed marriages have been the cause of controversy. The problem is immeasurably greater if non-Catholic partners of a mixed marriage are Jewish or Moslem.

Since the Vatican Council decrees on ecumenism and religious liberty many grievances of non-Catholics have been met. Before the Council both partners of a mixed marriage had to sign promises regarding the Catholic upbringing of any children born of the marriage. Today only the Catholic is asked to make the promise. Even that promise is regarded by some as unfair. It is impossible to find any perfectly satisfactory solution to the problems involved in mixed marriages but progress has been possible through the good will of both Catholic and non-Catholic authorities.

The change of Catholic attitudes is illustrated by the following quotation from a small book, *They Made Me Sign*, published in 1948 when I was a member of the Catholic Missionary Society. It will be seen that the only alternative to signing the promises was to abandon the marriage. Addressing Protestants in a special preface I wrote:

> The nearest approach to an act of religion many people make in adult life is to scrawl the mystic letters C. of E. after their names when entering hospital. Then people blame the Church of England for having 'failed'. If I were an Anglican I should regard it as an impertinence for people to write themselves down as C. of E. without making any attempt to follow the teachings of the Church of England.
>
> But if you are a genuine Protestant about to marry a Catholic you have my full sympathy. For in order to be married to a Catholic you are required by the Catholic Church to sign a promise that any children born of your marriage will be brought up in the Catholic Faith. If you are a convinced Protestant you must not sign such a promise without a great deal of thought. . . . You may be tempted to say: "I am not going to sign away the rights of my children. They must decide for themselves." It is not a question of signing away rights but of accepting an inheritance. If before marriage you were asked to accept a legacy for your unborn children you would have no scruples about signing. There is no legacy as valuable as the legacy of the Catholic Faith. It is not that the Church sacrifices the rights of the unborn child. She protects them. She secures them.

To my relief my ruling removing most of the obstacles to a joyful and dignified celebration of mixed marriages met with almost universal approval from the Liverpool clergy and faithful. There were a few who feared that the new policy might lead to an increase of mixed marriages but most people were delighted to see the end of an embarrassing situation. Today it is taken for granted that a mixed marriage will take place with all the beauty of which the liturgy is capable. It has become common for mixed marriages to be solemnised at a Nuptial Mass. This development gave me particular satisfaction because at the Vatican Council I had made a plea for the abolition of the old restrictions. It is appropriate to jump a few years to mention here the debate on mixed marriage during the third session of the Council when I spoke of the pastoral opportunity a mixed marriage can present to a zealous priest. Here is an extract from a speech I made in St. Peter's on 19th November, 1964 (I had been Archbishop of Westminster for a year):

I am speaking on behalf of the whole hierarchy of England and Wales and for bishops from many other countries. We can say of this document on mixed marriage, what has been said in recent days in this hall about other schemata—it is excellent but much too brief . . . Some words of the document I would like to see written in letters of gold. "Pastors should treat the non-Catholic gently and with respect when a couple comes to arrange a mixed marriage. He must in due season warn the couple of the very real difficulties which arise in a mixed marriage not only for the parties themselves but also for their children." I say that such words as these should be written in letters of gold for two reasons. First, for the young couple this first meeting with the parish priest is of the utmost importance. If, as our schema urges, the priest is kind, understanding and full of charity the Church will appear as a real mother. The good will of the non-Catholic meeting a priest perhaps for the first time can easily be won or lost at this interview. The second reason is the schema does not hesitate to stress that by their very nature mixed marriages produce grave problems. These problems and difficulties are not less real because we are living in ecumenical days. Some ecumenists lead the faithful to think that there is no longer any real distinction of Jew or Greek, Catholic or Protestant but after marriage husbands and wives may learn that there are still important differences.
I am wholeheartedly in agreement with what is proposed for the celebration of mixed marriages. Until now in many places the

ceremonies for a mixed marriage were so stripped of solemnity and joy that they were more suitable for a funeral than a wedding. There was no blessing of the ring, no candles or flowers and—what used to make the bride burst into tears—there was no organ. It is perfectly clear that if the Church grants a dispensation she should do so graciously, magnanimously and in an openhanded way. The wedding day should be both beautiful and happy even though the marriage is a mixed marriage. Let the Church show herself as a real mother not only to the Catholic but to the non-Catholic as well.

Sectarian bitterness had almost entirely died out in Liverpool by the time I was appointed. Archbishop Downey, a scholarly man, had won the respect of the people of Lancashire and of the city of Liverpool. In demand on all public occasions he was especially highly regarded as a speaker at civic and university functions. In his diplomatic way he was probably more responsible than anyone for the improvement in the relationship between Protestants and Catholics. It is greatly to the credit of the citizens of Liverpool that they were able to break with a long and ugly tradition. At one time there was violent partisanship between the football clubs Liverpool and Everton similar to that between Rangers and Celtic in Glasgow. One was regarded as a Protestant team and the other as Catholic. (In both cities sectarianism among the players has long ceased to exist. Modern clubs are limited companies which engage players for athletic prowess irrespective of their religious persuasion.)

Despite the normally placid atmosphere of the Liverpool of the 1950s there was one outbreak of violence a few months after my arrival. It took place in Robsart Street just inside the Protestant sector of the city. (Most of these streets in the famous Scotland Road district have now been demolished.) The incident, despite great publicity in the national press, was of small significance but the graphic reports must have persuaded readers that the bad old days had returned to Liverpool.

"Archbishop Stoned. Screaming Women and Children Mob Dr. Heenan" were the headlines of one popular paper. The story was told in detail by the *Daily Mail* of 4th March, 1958:

The Archbishop of Liverpool, Dr. J. C. Heenan was stoned by screaming women and children in a Liverpool street yesterday. Some women, still in their aprons, wielded brooms. Children hurled stones at the Archbishop and his car. While it all went on, a paralysed woman, whom Dr. Heenan had been visiting, lay helpless on her sickbed, listening to the noise. A housewife said: "It was awful. Several stones just missed his head. Some hit his cloak. He put his hands over his head for protection." The incident took place in Robsart-street, off Great Homer-street, 'stronghold' of thousands of Orangemen (supporters of William of Orange, who on July 12th each year celebrate the Battle of the Boyne).

Police called

Dr. Heenan had driven up Clay Street to visit Mrs. Winifred Denson, 40 year old widow, who had been bedridden for 18 months. The archbishop chatted with her for nearly an hour, said a prayer, and blessed her. Then he left . . . and the commotion began outside. Said Mrs. Denson: "I could hear shouting and screaming. It was terrible to be just lying there and unable to do anything." Dr. Heenan fought his way to his car and drove off with stones bouncing off the roof and bonnet. The Orange supporters followed him down the street shouting and jeering. Policemen from nearby Rose Hill station dispersed the crowd. "No one was arrested as the Archbishop was not hurt," said a police official.

The facts were less dramatic than the reports. I had been visiting the sick in St. Anthony's parish, an overcrowded slum area now mostly demolished. The number of these house-bound parishioners was unusually large. Although I had begun my visits early in the day I was still calling at homes when the children (whom I had seen in their class-rooms that morning) came out of school. When they caught sight of the purple biretta they came rushing and cheering. A crowd of grown-ups accompanied me in typical Liverpool fashion as I walked from house to house. Swollen by the shouting children the informal procession took on the aspect of a parade. Hearing the noise the Protestant neighbours did, in fact, think that a Catholic demonstration was being mounted. When I went to visit a sick woman on the edge of the parish the Protestants put out their orange flags and armed themselves with missiles. The stones damaged the car but I was hit by nothing more lethal than a tomato. The Catholics began to sing "Faith of our Fathers" with more venom than fervour. The Protestants made no musical riposte but shouted descriptions of the Pope and myself unflattering to us and even more so to our parents.

I was not perturbed by the incident because I knew it resulted from

[236]

a genuine misunderstanding. The Catholics had not been demonstrating against their neighbours. The Protestants had merely reacted in what they regarded as self-defence. My only worry was lest the rumour might spread among Catholics that I had been the victim of an unprovoked attack. There might then be few windows (or heads) unbroken in Robsart Street when the Catholic dockers returned from work. I therefore asked the priests to visit every road in the district with a personal message from me that the Protestants had not been responsible for the affray. The men were asked to show their loyalty by taking no action. My wishes were respected but some men may have felt aggrieved at being denied the opportunity of professing their faith without actually going to church. The Catholic men of Scotland Road were ready to fight or die for their faith. They found it more difficult to go to Mass. That evening I gave a statement to the press which effectively lowered the temperature:

> It would be a great mistake to imagine that relations between Protestants and Catholics have suddenly grown bitter. On the contrary, they were never more genuinely cordial. To put the incident in perspective: It is my custom in making a visitation of a parish to visit the schools and then see the sick, the aged who are house-bound and the patients in hospital. On Monday I visited about fifty houses and the patients in the John Bagot Hospital. It took all day from nine a.m. till six p.m. After the school was closed many of the children saw me and joined me as I was visiting the sick. When we reached the Orange quarter there was quite a crowd. It is possible that the Protestants thought some kind of demonstration was being staged by the Catholics and took alarm. There was very little throwing of bricks and the only damage was to my car. There was a good deal of booing, but most of the shouting came from the children who were waving orange colours. I'm sure they were enjoying themselves. I imagine that when they come to know me in those streets, where I shall continue to visit the sick, we shall become friends.

Despite all trepidation the incident did nothing but good. When the Protestants learned what had really happened they regretted their reaction. A number of them telephoned the presbytery or sent messages to the local priests apologising for the stone-throwing. The shopkeepers who had feared reprisals were especially grateful for the restraint of the Catholics. The affair was soon forgotten. The police were anxious to provide me with an escort when making subsequent visitations in the Scotland Road area. Naturally I refused this courtesy and they soon realised that this was unnecessary and could have proved provocative. During my remaining years in Liverpool there was no repetition of fighting between Protestants and Catholics. In few cities is the relationship between religious bodies more cordial. I enjoyed a close friendship with Clifford Martin, the Anglican Bishop of Liverpool, and his saintly wife. The warm relations between clergy extended to their people and the civic authorities.

My years in Liverpool were singularly free of controversy. In television interviews and speeches on social questions I expressed opinions which were challenged but the ensuing public debate was always short lived. I began to avoid controversy in order to husband my energy to promote unity. Religious argument as opposed to ecumenical discussion is usually sterile. It took me more than half a lifetime to discover this simple truth. I used to regard it as a duty always to contradict those holding subversive views. I had seen Stalinism in the U.S.S.R. and like all civilised people I had been horrified by Soviet atrocities in Hungary and Czechoslovakia. For years I attempted to free dupes of communism from their mental chains but at last I came to recognise that rational argument is likely to make them only more obdurate.

Because of my growing distaste for controversy I became disenchanted with mock battles on television. Performers of the first rank who would attack me with simulated scorn on television were all subsequently my friends in real life. The viewing public thinks that a heated battle of words is real but professional interviewers are concerned only to provide lively entertainment. They do not mind if they are worsted in argument if the programme keeps flowing and viewers remain tuned to the right channel. Nevertheless every discussion I have had on T.V. has been quite genuine. What has kept interviews from becoming bogus is my rule never to be told what questions are to be put to me on radio or television. This practice is important to me for two reasons. First, if controversial points are discussed in advance it is difficult not to slant the questions or pre-package the answers, thus making the performance artificial if not actually dishonest. My second reason for refusing to rehearse programmes is to preserve spontaneity. If I have no idea of how an interview is going to be conducted I can give my full attention to the topic under consideration. If I knew what other points were to be raised my mind would (at least subconsciously) be moving on and away from the immediate issue. It is also a psychological gain to be nervous on television. This gives a certain electric quality which suggests sincerity. If you have no idea what line of attack the interviewer is going to follow you are nervous from the flashing red signal until that blessed moment when the lights fade and the whole studio team relaxes. Because I am frightened on television my mind works at great speed.

For a time I was successful in persuading ABC Television that speaking is more attractive without the intervention of an interviewer. Twice in a programme called "Living your Life" I was permitted to talk straight to camera for half-an-hour. "His second appearance was in part a compliment to his outstanding success in the same programme last May," one critic wrote. "Standing before a crucifix or sitting casually on the edge of a table the archbishop has an informality and ease of manner as satisfying as the sincerity of his words." Despite this tribute which was echoed by other critics, there was no third performance. So far as I know this technique has never been repeated in a religious programme. It was, however, used with great effectiveness by Professor A. J. P. Taylor when giving talks on history. There may be no cleric with Taylor's mastery of the spoken word but there are plenty of able religious speakers.

Unfortunately most producers think that anything so static as an uninterrupted talk is beyond the mental capacity of viewers. They are wrong. There is a powerful fascination in soliloquy. This truth is illustrated by the indignation so often directed against chairmen of panels or interviewers who switch a speaker to another subject just as he is beginning to develop his thought. In the second of my talks I spoke of the forgiveness of sins and the Catholic practice of Confession. "The cameras showed the archbishop from different angles as he spoke, but nothing broke the gentle yet concentrated course of his explanation of what confession is. This speaker seems to hold a silent colloquy with his listeners, so sensitively does he anticipate the next step in their thoughts. He dispels misconceptions and then passes on. It seemed impossible that twenty-five minutes had passed—it seemed more like ten. As a journalist I rarely hear a sermon. I was grateful to T.V. for letting me see and hear this." When there are more channels or when pop-singers, entertainers and current affairs commentators are unable to fill all the time available the straight talk may return.

So I had to return to the old routine of question and answer. I had a number of encounters with Mr. Malcolm Muggeridge in various studios in London and the provinces, on both independent and B.B.C.

television. On one occasion he asked me a rather complicated question (most of his questions were rather like anti-personnel bombs) to which I replied: "I don't know if you are serious in your enquiry about the existence of God, Mr. Muggeridge, but if you are I shall be glad to answer. It can't be done in half-an-hour on a T.V. programme. If you are really in earnest come to stay with me in Liverpool." It is surprising how many people in the following month wrote to one or other of us to enquire if the visit had ever materialised. It had.

Mr. Robin Day was also among my interlocutors. He was and has remained one of the most impressive T.V. pundits. With a well-stocked and legally-trained mind he prepared for each interview with the closest attention to detail. Master of what parliamentarians call the supplementary he gave the impression of a human ferret. This created in viewers a gratifying sympathy towards the hunted rabbit. The result was an exciting programme which pleased both performers and viewers. "Among the longest and liveliest interviews I have ever had," Mr. Day told reporters after his programme "The Roman Catholic mind". This interview was one hour-long session but it was broadcast in two transmissions. The programme would evoke little comment now that such subjects as contraception and abortion have become family table talk but at that time it was thought astonishing for such questions to be publicly discussed. The *Yorkshire Post* commentator was amazed but delighted. "As a piece of television," he wrote on 9th February, 1959, the day after one of the programmes was broadcast, "Dr. Heenan's discussion with Mr. Robin Day was momentous. It was a completely frank discussion. It broke the old rule of sound radio that religion and sex should not be discussed in any but the most circumstantial terms. When the B.B.C. had a monopoly there were often lively discussions but always they were cushioned by a knowledge that certain things should not be talked about. Last night's transmission was the culmination of a liberating process which has been pioneered by I.T.V. That this new frankness is a good thing there can be little doubt."

Appearance on platforms and on television creates the impression that the major part of a bishop's activities is conducted in public. In fact his most important pastoral work does not feature in the press or on television. Visits to parishes, religious houses, hospitals, schools and prisons are fortunately of no interest to reporters. An even larger part of a bishop's duty is the personal care of his flock—both priests and people. Hours each day are taken up with correspondence and purely administrative work. Most pastoral work is as unremarkable as the daily round of doctors, teachers or other public servants but though not newsworthy these routine activities are far more important than public appearances. They are not of interest to journalists and, indeed, would lose their value if they were reported.

Many enterprises are initiated by private approaches to a bishop. I was indebted, for example, to the Chief Constable of Liverpool for being made aware of the need for a new approach to youth work in the most deprived sections of the city. The day following my enthronement I had written to Sir Charles Martin to thank the police for their efficient and courteous handling of the crowds. I had not expected any reply but Sir Charles wrote at once asking if he might call on me as soon as possible. Before the week was out he came to tea. He said that as an archbishop I would never be allowed to see how people really behaved. Once established in the city I would be recognised wherever I went. All my visits would be official and people would always be prepared for my coming. Everything and everyone would be clean and tidy. He suggested that I ought to make an unofficial tour of the city before my face became too well known. He said that officers of discretion would be willing to take me to places I might never otherwise see.

The Chief Constable was immensely proud of his men whom he regarded as absolutely incorrupt. He declared that for a city of its size Liverpool was remarkably free of serious crime. It was at the bottom of the crime league table of England. The Scotland Road area widely regarded as a black spot had no real criminals. There was pilfering from the docks and drunken brawls on Saturday nights but burglary and robbery with violence were almost unknown in the area. He contended that most petty crime had its origin in poverty and deporable housing conditions. (By 1971 the Scotland Road area had been demolished.) Juvenile crime was on the increase but the police were receiving splendid co-operation from parents. There was no tradition of hostility between police and the families of those who had been 'in trouble'. The Liverpool police were pioneers of a scheme to keep young people out of borstal or prison. Young men and women of the force were released from normal police duties (taken off the beat) to work in their own way and at their own pace with the families of delinquents. Wearing no uniform they set out to make friends of parents and teachers in slum neighbourhoods. They visited homes frequently and their visit came to be welcomed as the visit of friends. The police never took first offenders to the juvenile court or had them put on probation. They employed the Nelson technique but made it very plain to both offenders and their parents that the police had all the information required to 'put them away'. They refrained from taking out warrants on the understanding that if parents suspected another offence was in prospect they would warn the police. Every night some of the plain clothes police called at the homes of potential delinquents. It was deliberate policy to be regular visitors because in this way they safeguarded the good name of the family in the eyes of neighbours. A visit from the police no longer meant that a member of the family was in trouble. This system proved so successful that it was being copied by police forces in other cities in the country.

Sir Charles told me that the young slum-dwellers were mostly Catholics but the Church was not doing enough to help them. He said that most Catholic youth clubs recruited members from respectable homes. This was understandable but it did not help the young people most in need. Shortly afterwards I made a tour of the youth clubs which catered for these unattached young people. Sir Charles gave his word that no advance warning of my visit would be given to the clubs nor would I be introduced as the archbishop. I would see these clubs in normal action. When I made these visits I was greatly impressed. Familiar with self-sacrificing social workers from the Church I had not hitherto met many volunteers belonging to no church or organisation. Those running youth clubs were simply public spirited men and women who had taken up the work without pressure and usually without encouragement. Unlike leaders in recognised youth clubs they were not given any subsidy by the local authority. They did not, therefore, attract young teachers who needed to supplement their meagre salaries by working after school hours in registered youth clubs. In most clubs I found members of the police force who, without remuneration, gave much of their free time to youth work. Most clubs catered only for games and were patronised mainly by boys. In almost all the clubs the second favourite sport was boxing. The first favourite was just sitting and talking. The problem of teaching young people to employ their leisure time usefully baffles most youth leaders. If young people do not take up music, crafts, religion or politics the evenings are too long to fill. Only the less intelligent—which does not mean only illiterates—are satisfied by an endless diet of pop and ping-pong.

By far the most impressive of the clubs I visited was the Rodney club, housed in a building about to be pulled down. The place was crowded with children of all ages. There seemed to be no rules and very little supervision. The premises were in a shocking condition but since they were condemned it would obviously have been a waste of time and money to restore them. Budding decorators and fresco artists had experimented in various rooms but surprisingly there were no graffiti. The atmosphere was more cheerful than in any of the other clubs and I felt sad that the place was destined to close so soon. I promised to press the Liverpool education committee to find alternative premises. The club leader was a man in late middle age who had learned the secret of commanding without appearing to rule. He was delighted to see me because he said that eighty per cent of those who used the club were Catholics. This was confirmed by the reception I received from the boys and girls. They had not been told who I was but their sharp little eyes penetrated my thin disguise at once. Exploring the city incognito I hoped to be taken for a local parish priest but so far as these youngsters were concerned I might just as well have been wearing a mitre. In this doomed club there were few helpers and no representatives of the teachers or police. The Rodney club was a fitting climax to my tour. It confirmed Sir Charles Martin's contention that too little was being done by the Catholic Church for young people unattracted by official youth organisations.

On my tour of the city, I had, in addition to police officers in plain clothes, Father George Waring, one of the most experienced priests in Liverpool. He was associated with Atlantic House the famous seamen's club, the biggest hostel for seafarers in the world. Although under the direction of the Apostleship of the Sea it is strictly non-sectarian. Nobody entering Atlantic House is questioned about religion. Whether they come for an evening's recreation or to find a bed for a few days while their ship is in port all are made welcome who can produce evidence that they are genuine seafarers. Soviet sailors have just as much right to the hospitality of Atlantic House as the Catholic Goans. Each night there is a dance attended by hostesses trained in the delicate art of being gracious to the sailors without encouraging familiarity. The hostesses are governed by strict rules. They do not drink with the guests and must not make appointments to meet them except at Atlantic House. The hostesses are unpaid. They are fervent Catholics who try to attend Mass on week-days as well as Sundays. The evening session ends with prayers (Mass or Benediction) in which nobody is pressed to join. In addition to hostesses there are men who visit the ships in Liverpool docks. George Waring was chiefly responsible for giving the Apostleship of the Sea the shape it has now assumed throughout the world. I took him with me to the clubs because I felt he would give

[243]

practical form to any solution I might propose after I had made my tour of inspection.

After this rapid round of clubs we decided to act without delay. Father Waring organised a course of training for leaders prepared to work in any youth club, official or independent, Catholic, Protestant or undenominational. I was especially anxious to train young Catholics to go into clubs of the Rodney type where there were so many rootless Catholic children and no Catholic leaders. The intensive course was taken by a hundred and fifty prospective leaders. Nearly three hundred applications were received of which a hundred were turned down by the interviewing panel. At a splendid ceremony held in Atlantic House three months later in the presence of Sir Charles and Lady Martin ninety-eight youth leaders were awarded certificates. Among them were nearly forty young teachers. No less than thirty priests helped with the course which included what has since become known as counselling. At the presentation ceremony I acknowledged that the drive to make Catholics more aware of their responsibility towards the young had come from the Chief Constable.

CHAPTER

SEVENTEEN

MR. HAROLD MAGNAY, DIRECTOR OF EDUCATION OF LIVERPOOL, WAS A brilliant speaker and a good scholar. A Tynesider he had no sympathy with the anti-Catholic bias he had found in Liverpool on taking up his appointment. Being a lay preacher of the Congregational Church he could not be accused of being under the influence of Rome. The religious atmosphere of Liverpool having now changed so completely it is hard to believe that just before the war (August 1939) an act of Parliament was needed to force the reluctant Liverpool city council to provide for the education of its Catholic children. Few have heard of the Liverpool Act which is a unique testimony to religious bigotry. One of the few good results of the war was to make such sectarianism absurd. The Liverpool Act was a dead letter almost as soon as it became law. Because this strange act of Parliament is virtually unknown it is worth giving its title and style:

Senior Public
Elementary Schools (Liverpool) Act, 1939.
CHAPTER 60
An Act to facilitate the provision in Liverpool of public
elementary school accommodation for senior children.
(4th August, 1939)

1.—(1) For the purpose of giving effect to the objects of certain proposals for the provision of new public elementary schools for senior children in the city of Liverpool, being proposals which were submitted to the local education authority of that city in accordance

Provision of senior non- provided schools

with, and within the time limited by, section eight of *
the Education Act, 1936, and towards the cost of carrying out which the authority might under that section
have made grants, the authority may themselves provide schoolhouses and grant leases thereof to such
persons interested in the submission of the original
proposals as they think fit upon such terms and conditions as the Board of Education may approve:

Mr. Magnay put the provisions of the Butler Act into operation with
imagination and courage. Seeing that the interests of Catholic children
had been neglected for generations he resolved to concentrate on
Catholic school building. At the end of the 1950s the building programme submitted for approval to the Ministry was mainly for Catholic
schools.

Harold Magnay gave me powerful support in a project so daring
that neither of us thought it could possibly succeed at the first attempt.
Studying statistics of higher education I found that Catholic boys were
far worse off than their sisters for grammar school education (this was
before the days of comprehensive schools). There were many convent
schools but few Catholic grammar schools for boys. A boy at a county
primary school had a one in five chance of qualifying for a place in a
grammar school. A boy at a Catholic primary school had only a one in
twelve chance of a place in a Catholic grammar school. This meant, of
course, that the mental calibre of boys entering Catholic grammar
schools was well above the city average but this was no consolation for
Catholic boys of grammar school standard for whom there were no
places. It happened that in Liverpool there was a huge derelict building
which had once been an orphanage. A team of eight architects under
Mr. Alfred Bullen set to work to discover how soon and at what cost
the premises could be converted into a four-form entry grammar school
for boys. They reported that, with the right contractor, the place could
be made ready within eight months. Since at that time there was no
question of receiving a government grant towards building a grammar
school I made no application to the Ministry of Education. Plans were
drawn up and the building put in hand without delay.

This would have been impossible without the co-operation—perhaps
I should say connivance—of Harold Magnay. The building itself was
the least part of the cost. The great expense would be the maintenance
of a school for nearly a thousand pupils. This burden would fall entirely

on the city. Without putting anything in writing Mr. Magnay undertook to convince the city education committee of the educational advantages of the scheme. It was for me to persuade the Ministry to allow it to go forward. Knowing the length of time government departments are bound to take before approving projects I realised that at least one year's intake of boys would be lost if the start of the building had to await the minister's approval. I decided, therefore, to proceed with the building and hope that the minister would accept with good grace a new grammar school which had not appeared in a building programme. The building went ahead with amazing speed and Mr. Magnay easily gained the approval of his committee. Only the Ministry remained. While I was still hesitating about the best means of winning over Whitehall Mr. Magnay telephoned to say that the minister was about to visit Liverpool to open a new school. He would arrange for me to be an official guest at the function and thus give me an easy opportunity of making a first unofficial approach. Harold Magnay subsequently not only introduced me to the minister but argued the case for me. He explained that I had presented the city with a school at no public expense whereas if I had waited a few years the building might attract a considerable grant. For my part I admitted that although technically it was out of order to have proceeded without ministerial sanction it would have been deplorable to deprive a hundred and twenty boys (a year's intake) of the opportunity of a grammar school education. The minister promised to give the proposal favourable consideration when it was officially presented. A nod is almost as good as the seal on an official document. Formal permission to open the school arrived while the first term was drawing to a close.

The new school was called the Cardinal Allen grammar school in memory of the Lancashire prelate who founded the English College at Douai for the education of priests for the English mission during penal days. Four diocesan priests were appointed to the staff with Canon Kieran as the first headmaster. The ceremonial opening was performed by Sir James Mountford, the vice-chancellor of the university, with Mr. Magnay in attendance. It was exactly eight months since the contractors had moved on to the site. "Seldom," said Harold Magnay "can so much building have been completed so quickly. This is the fastest piece of work in the history of education in the city of Liverpool." The director of education and the chairman of the education committee—Mrs. Wormald, a distinguished educationist—were both non-Catholics. They were determined to give Catholic children equal opportunities with all other children in the city. Catholic parents had no need to agitate nor was any pressure applied by Catholic councillors.

While the Cardinal Allen school was still under construction I found myself involved in much wider educational issues. In company with other bishops I was asked to discuss the whole question of grants for Catholic schools with Mr. Geoffrey Lloyd, the Minister of Education. He had agreed to receive a deputation of three bishops—Bishop Beck (Salford), Archbishop Grimshaw (Birmingham) and myself. Bishop Beck, chairman of the Catholic Education Council, had been nominated Auxiliary Bishop of Brentwood while still a headmaster. No bishop in recent years has been so well informed on the complicated legislation affecting non-provided schools. The Archbishop of Birmingham was included in the deputation chiefly because he lived in Geoffrey Lloyd's constituency and knew him well. I was invited because much of the numerical strength of the Catholic Church in England is in the north. It was felt that my words would carry particular weight because of the enormous burden borne by the Catholics of Liverpool in paying for their schools. Bishop Beck suggested that before we went down to Whitehall it would be wise for me to see Mr. Wilson, the member of parliament for Huyton near Liverpool. Harold Wilson, who was not yet leader of the Labour Party, had always taken an active interest in the Catholic schools in his constituency where the proportion of Catholics is high. He was well known to the local clergy especially to Canon O'Sullivan the parish priest of Huyton who had been given many proofs of the local member's support for Catholic schools. Canon O'Sullivan arranged for me to see Mr. Wilson and the interview proved most helpful. Mr. Wilson made it clear that neither his party nor the conservatives intended to play politics over Catholic schools. He said that whatever concession the government might offer would be acceptable to the Labour Party.

The following day the other two bishops came to Liverpool to discuss plans. My talk with Harold Wilson proved most useful in preparing our strategy for the meeting in Whitehall. Having no idea what the government was prepared to offer we intended to ask for a less complex system of grants for non-provided schools. As the law then stood some schools were totally excluded from grant, others were entitled to a percentage grant for a new school according to the number of pupils displaced from schools in other areas. New primary schools attracted no grant at all. Even the largest grants were inadequate to enable Catholics to make provision for all their children. By now it was recognised by all parties that the forecast of cost to Catholics made when R. A. Butler had introduced his Bill had been wildly erroneous. Despite the hierarchy's protests at the time the government had maintained that the cost of reorganisation of secondary education to the Catholic community would be under ten million pounds. When the Butler Act came to be implemented it was found that complete reorganisation in even one large diocese might involve expenditure of more than ten million pounds. The government was now ready to listen with more respect to the statistics prepared by the Catholic Education Council.

At our Liverpool discussion we tried to prepare ourselves for every eventuality. We rehearsed what we would reply to the various proposals Mr. Lloyd might make. Thanks to Mr. Wilson we knew that we would not be given the answer that although H.M. government was prepared to make generous grants it was politically impossible because of H.M. opposition. In the past this argument had been used with justification. The nonconformists had been inflexibly opposed to state aid to denominational schools. This was not due to anti-Catholic bias but to a conscientious objection to subsidising schools in which children would be taught a creed different from that of their parents. They had in mind specifically the hundreds of single school areas in which all schools belonged to the Church of England. The nonconformists had not been content with verbal protests. Early in the century some Welshmen had gone to prison rather than pay the education rate. The nonconformist conscience far from being a myth is, for many, a proud memory. Since the Labour Party had its origins in the chapels it was not mere political adroitness which had led conservatives to shelter behind the nonconformist conscience in refusing higher grants to church schools. Mr. Wilson had not been expressing a pious hope when he said that his party would not oppose further aid to church schools. He had discussed the whole question with his colleagues and especially with Mr. Griffiths, vice-chairman of the parliamentary party, a Welsh Nonconformist who agreed that circumstances had so completely changed that there need no longer be conscientious objections to aid for church schools.

On more than one occasion I have heard journalism coupled with politics as 'a dirty trade'. Yet if it is true that papers increase their output of salacious news only to increase circulation the reading public must be to blame. We attack the British press when it gives offence but we rarely recognise its virtues. Although I have sometimes deplored the apparent inability of editors to distinguish between important and trivial news, I have not experienced a single breach of confidence from journalists in all my years as a bishop. Admittedly a serious address which may have taken hours to prepare is likely to be dismissed in a sentence, while an off-the-cuff reply to a heckler will be given half a column. Good news is ignored while a parking fine imposed on a celebrity is prominently reported. This has the effect of giving important people unjustified immunity from prosecution. If the press magnifies beyond measure the small offences of the famous, police prefer not to take action. This shows the good sense of the police but suggests that sensationalism may defeat the cause of justice.

I had one notable experience of the integrity of a journalist during my last few months in Liverpool. I had been campaigning for over two years to secure compensation for victims of the Nazi concentration camps. Theoretically all victims were entitled to compensation but in practice the funds were administered in an unimaginative way by the German courts. Applicants for grants had to establish that they were genuine victims of Nazi cruelty. The courts refused to aid German nationals who had opposed the Fatherland or foreigners who could not prove that they were victims of the Nazis. It was almost impossible through lack of witnesses for stateless persons to prove the truth of their stories. Their advocacy—especially since they were speaking a foreign language—rarely prevailed against the German lawyers. The cause of these unfortunate people had been taken up by Sue Ryder and Leonard Cheshire more than ten years earlier (1948) but their indignant de-nunciations seemed only to harden the attitude of the German Federal Government. Through the Catholic Women's League Refugee Com-mittee I was able to gather precise details and furnish the German authorities with lists of people who had been refused compensation although clearly genuine victims from concentration camps. I asked the bishops to allow me to approach Herr Adenauer, the German Chancellor, in their name.

I wrote him a very personal letter. I knew that he was a keen Catholic and that one of his sons was a priest. Refraining from political argument I begged him to do his Christian duty to those still living in refugee camps, often on the very site of the concentration camps in which they had suffered their agony under a former German Chan-cellor. I was greatly helped by the German Ambassador in London, Herr von Herwarth, whose anti-Nazi record was unassailable since he was partly Jewish. I sent a copy of my letter to the Papal Nuncio in Bonn with a request that he would also press the cause of the refugees.

On Sunday, two days after I had written to the Chancellor, I was making a visitation of the parish of the Holy Family, Southport. At about eight p.m. I was called to the telephone to speak to a journalist from the Press Association. He wanted me to confirm that I had written a letter to Herr Adenauer. He asked me to give him the gist of its contents. I was dumbfounded. How could the P.A. possibly have heard of my personal letter of which even my own secretary was ignorant? It seemed unlikely, to say the least, that the West German Chancellor had given my letter to the press. I was in a dilemma. This was a perfect example of 'no comment' meaning confirmation.

I took the only possible course. I asked the P.A. man if I might speak to him 'off the record'. His answer and, indeed, our whole conversation I remember very clearly. "My pencil," he said, "is down." I then told him it was true that I had written to Dr. Adenauer but it was most unlikely that he could yet have received my letter. It was even more unlikely that he had released it to the press. A possible explanation was that an indiscreet or venal clerk in the German chancery or papal nunciature had spoken to a reporter. I pointed out that if next day's papers were to carry the story Adenauer would assume that I had given my personal letter to the press before giving him time to reply. In the event he would be very angry indeed and refuse my plea. The sufferers would be the unfortunate refugees. The P.A. man paused. Then he replied very firmly: "I shall kill this story stone dead. It will not appear in any British papers tomorrow morning and I'll have it killed abroad too."

Those who know the ways of the press will appreciate what it meant to a journalist to suppress a story of great human interest. The reporter did this for the sake of the poor people I was trying to help. If he had chosen to exercise his right to a scoop there would have been no hope of success for my approach. In the event I soon received a letter from the Chancellor, brought to Liverpool by the German Ambassador in person. Dr. Adenauer gave me the assurance that special funds would be made available to the victims of the Nazi concentration camps. The German government was not willing to accept my suggestion of handing over funds to an international body such as the U.N. Relief Organisation, the Red Cross or one of the religious relief services for distribution but lawyers were to be given instructions not to be obstructive. The war had become only a memory for us in England but not for the families homeless since they had fled before the invading armies. Many Poles preferred to trust the German enemy rather than await a kiss of death from the Soviet liberators. The misery of the war is still a present reality for many of its victims on the continent of Europe. They are like the survivors of gas attacks after the first war. Others might forget the 1914–18 war but not those old men coughing away their lives.

CHAPTER
EIGHTEEN

IT IS HARD TO REMEMBER THE GREATNESS OF A MAN ONCE HIS SUCCESSOR is well established. In England during Mr. Heath's first year as prime minister there were, in addition to his immediate predecessor Mr. Wilson, no less than three former prime ministers still alive—Sir Anthony Eden, Sir Harold Macmillan and Sir Alec Douglas Home. Such is the power of possession that irrespective of his or their merits the reigning premier outshone them all. Even the redoubtable Winston Churchill became a figure of pity in his declining years. He was resurrected only by death. Popes no less than premiers are usually dwarfed by those who follow them. This was dramatically true of Pope Pius XII who died during my years in Liverpool. His was such a formidable personality that he seemed certain to be the dominant pope of the century. A much travelled diplomat before his election he became better known than any pope before him. This was due to the war which brought to Rome combatants of both sides. This remarkable man was recognised as genuinely neutral even at the most bitter phases of the struggle. Although from experience of Nazi Germany (as nuncio he negotiated the futile concordat) he disliked Hitler, he never identified the Fuehrer with the German people. When Italy entered the war Pope Pius XII gave no support to Mussolini by word or gesture but, on the contrary, gave shelter in the Vatican to the British Minister to the Holy See and, when German troops occupied Rome, to all allied diplomats. He received in audience thousands of service men of all nations and creeds who found themselves in Rome during the war years.

Television made his face familiar to Europe and sound radio carried his voice to the ends of the earth. Not such an accomplished linguist as

[253]

his predecessor, Pius XI, he was a more experienced diplomat and more at home with science and technology. Even after allowance is made for the army of experts around him the scope of his pronouncements is astounding. Other leaders may often need merely to read a brief but the pope must not only master his brief but inspire it. Critics reasonably complain that Pope Pius XII was too encyclopaedic. Disquisitions on philately and bee-keeing, on which he was unlikely to be an authority, made his views on peace and medico-ethical problems less impressive. The influence of public figures is proportionate to the rarity of their utterances. The Pope had no ambition to pose as an oracle but seemed unable to refuse audience to anyone. Irrespective of their race or religion all were made welcome. The cardinals complained that they were denied regular audiences as heads of Congregations (departments of ecclesiastical affairs) and that the business of the Church was being sacrificed to tourists.

From the evidence of Roman prelates it appears that the Pope as he grew older became increasingly isolated from those around him. It is said that when his doctors insisted that he must talk to someone the Pope bought a parrot. It must be confessed that the credibility of this story is not enhanced by the fact that the same or a similar parrot appeared after the death of his predecessor. Perhaps it is a stock joke among Vatican monsignori. There is no doubt that Pius XII did concentrate great power in his own hands and in the end dispensed with a Cardinal Secretary of State. He was a giant among modern popes. It is therefore the more surprising that his fame so quickly vanished during the short reign of his successor. The reduction of his stature began while he was still in his death agony. His doctor published to the world the most intimate details of his physical condition. For this abuse of confidence he was struck off the roll by his medical colleagues.

I flew to Rome for the funeral of Pope Pius because I had a great personal affection for him. Many years earlier he had shown tenderness towards my sister for whom I sought a special blessing when she was mortally sick. He had appointed me both to Leeds and Liverpool and had always granted any request I made on behalf of the Catholics of Yorkshire or Lancashire. My presence at the obsequies—in those days papal funeral rites were spread over nine days—was a filial tribute to a much loved father.

On the evening of the Pope's death I broadcast a tribute in radio-newsreel. It is a corrective to the canard that the reign of the reactionary Pius XII was a disaster for the Church. Here is a brief extract:

. . . To the world at large, the Pope stood as a figure apart, speaking words of peace, invoking blessings upon a stricken world. But to Catholics he was naturally much more. His wisdom brought the practice of their faith into line with the stress of modern life. One of the most far reaching of his reforms was his entirely new approach to the discipline of fasting before receiving Holy Communion.

. . . His was always an original approach. Only recently, for example, he authorised bishops to arrange for the celebration of Mass in the evening as well as in the morning. Thousands of people who could never be at Mass except on Sundays are now able to enjoy the spiritual benefits of frequent Mass, and Holy Communion.

. . . He was not only original but courageous in his enterprise. To take one isolated example: he allowed a convert clergyman to be ordained priest, although a married man. Another example of his enterprise was his readiness to allow the age-old Latin texts to be translated in the administration of the Sacraments so that the people might understand better. Catholics, at least, will be anxious to know if the Pope's successor will allow experiments or return to conservative ways. One thing is certain, that any modern pope will follow the example of Pope Pius XII in thinking and speaking in a way which non-Catholics can appreciate. . . . The affection and respect which the late Pope won from millions who did not share his faith was the greatest triumph of his pontificate.

At the Requiem Mass for the Pope I was much distracted. Kneeling in the benches before me were most of the cardinals of the Sacred College which had been allowed to dwindle to half its normal complement. I was distracted because as my eyes ranged up and down the thinned ranks it was difficult to see any of them as *'papabilis'*. The superlative qualities of Pope Pius made all the cardinals seem undistinguished.

The appointment of a diocesan bishop can involve factors which have nothing to do with a candidate's character, such as political and racial considerations. Today, for example, it would be impossible to appoint a white priest to a see in Asia or Africa. Choosing a pope is more complicated. When Pope Pius XII died it was still taken for granted that the pope (who is also the Bishop of Rome) would be an Italian. In the past there have been Spaniards, Frenchmen and even one

[255]

Englishman, Adrian IV (Nicholas Breakspear). The difficulties a stranger to Rome would encounter in modern Italy, still a parvenu among nations, were regarded as insurmountable. The situation has now changed. Europe is politically more homogeneous and foreign cardinals are so frequently in Rome that they are as familiar with the ecclesiastical machine as the Italians themselves. The process of internationalising the curia begun by Pope Pius XII was completed by his pupil, Paul VI, who put all the Sacred Congregations into the hands of foreigners.

Other popes have described the Holy See as truly international but it was Pope Paul who made it so. To the Holy Office, supreme in authority among the Roman dicasteries, he appointed a Croat, Cardinal Seper. The French Cardinal Villot became Secretary of State. Another Frenchman, Cardinal Garrone, was put in charge of universities and seminaries. Cardinal Wright, an American, became Prefect of the Congregation of the Clergy. The Missions were put under the care of Cardinal Rossi from Latin America. The increasingly important Secretariat for Christian Unity was entrusted to the Dutch Cardinal Willebrands, former secretary to Cardinal Bea. Liturgy was put under the direction of Cardinal Gut, a German. All this, of course, was far in the future. At the time of the conclave after the death of Pius XII there was little sign of a truly international curia. The reality was still far away—Monsignor Montini, Archbishop of Milan, was not yet a cardinal. Looking at the kneeling cardinals I could see no candidate to compare with the Russian, Cardinal Agagianian. Although like Stalin he had been born in Georgia he had lived in Rome since boyhood and was as familiar as any native Roman with the curial scene. I did not give a second glance to Cardinal Roncalli, Patriarch of Venice. Old and fat he could not possibly be considered. Gravely distressed though it was by the death of the great Pius XII the Church was surely not in such a crisis that it would seek the next pope from among the septuagenarians.

I had scarcely arrived back in Liverpool when the election of Angelo Giuseppe Roncalli from the village of Sotto il Monte was announced. He had chosen the name of John XXIII. Whatever the reason for his choice the name proved perfect as a description of the ensuing pontificate. John was "the apostle whom Jesus loved" (John XIII : 23). There has never been a pope beloved by so many. It was not long before I went to Rome once more and was able to judge whether the election of this old man from under the mountain was likely to be a disaster.

Sir Frederick Gibberd
displays Cathedral model.

Inspecting the work of
the Cathedral builders.

View of the Metropolitan Cathedral of Christ the King, Liverpool.

My visit to Rome took place in the early months of Pope John's short reign before the world had really discovered him. It was appreciated that he was only a stop-gap filling the chair of St. Peter until the college of cardinals should contain someone of truly papal timber like Montini of Milan. (Papal stop-gaps have a way of making history. The last stop-gap had been Cardinal Pecci, nearly seventy years old at the time of his election. As Pope Leo XIII he became the greatest social reformer among modern popes. His encyclical *Rerum Novarum* is a yardstick. He died in 1903 at the age of ninety-three as much part of the world scene as Queen Victoria.)

I was received in audience by the new Pope soon after his coronation. I was more curious than elated as I waited outside his room. When I entered I observed that he was even smaller and fatter than I had supposed. An audience with Pope John was an anti-climax to anyone who had experienced the electric presence and luminous gaze of his predecessor. I felt myself wondering yet again why the Holy Spirit had guided the Church to a candidate of such little promise. Nobody at that time knew that the cardinals, however unwittingly, had chosen a saint. The Holy Father bade me sit down. He then recited what may have become a set piece when introducing himself to a bishop. Here is the substance of Pope John's talk from the notes I made immediately after the audience. The opening sentence startled me. It was as if the new Pope were something of a clairvoyant:

> Why [Pope John began] did God allow this to happen to His Church? I am unfit to be pope. I'm not a diplomat like Pius XII or a scholar like Pius XI. I keep asking Our Lord why He has put me in this position. What have I to offer? The more I think of it the more I feel that the only thing I can offer is myself. I can throw out my arms [he suited his gesture to the words] and tell people that I am the Common Father and that all are welcome in their father's house. There is no profit in controversy. The only way of winning people is by showing that you really love them. That at least I can do. There is a second thought which keeps returning to my mind. It seems to me that the Church undervalues the Precious Blood of Jesus Christ. The Protestants have something to teach us here. We have devotion to the Sacred Heart and the Blessed Sacrament but we rarely talk about the Precious Blood which is the price Jesus paid for our Redemption.

He spoke also of other things but these were the main topics. Pope

John did not make any notable efforts to introduce devotion to the Precious Blood beyond introducing an additional invocation into the Divine Praises (a prayer recited during Benediction of the Blessed Sacrament): "Blessed be His most Precious Blood". I assume that Pope John had intended to write an encyclical to introduce a cult of the Precious Blood akin to that of the Sacred Heart—a devotion of comparatively recent origin in the Church. The Second Vatican Council engulfed Pope John and gave him far more urgent problems to resolve. The Divine Praises are now rarely heard in parish churches because in most places the service of Benediction has given place to evening Mass. Popular devotions were unintentionally killed by liturgical experts familiar only with monastic traditions. Pope John's spiritual outlook was that of a pastor, not a monk. He told me that his bedside book was *All for Jesus* by Father Faber. Readers of Pope John's diary, *Journal of a Soul*, know that throughout his life he was guided by the old rules of prayer and self-discipline.

Looking back at the reign of Pope John we can see why he had such a hold over the hearts of people of all shades of political and religious belief. It is impossible to prove that any appointment is the direct result of God's guidance of His Church but certainly Angelo Roncalli's was a providential appointment. He began by making an extraordinary impression on the millions who saw the televised coronation. He was obviously ill at ease in the pontifical pageantry of St. Peter's. Viewers instinctively felt sorry for the old man and began to take him to their hearts. Soon after becoming Pope he went to visit the prisoners in Regina Coeli on the banks of the Tiber. It is only five minutes' drive from the Vatican but no other pope had thought of making the short journey. His behaviour inside the prison earned him extra marks. He told the men about his uncle who had been put in prison for poaching. That was Pope John's way of making himself one of them. He visited hospitals and called not only on dying cardinals but on old servants of the Vatican who were sick. What captured the attention of the world was the obvious fact that the new Pope loved everyone. They sensed that this was not a public relations stunt. Pope John was loving and lovable.

Once journalists decide on what they call a man's public image every event is made to fit. Anything regarded as out of character is ignored. They were not short of material to build up the Pope John image. There was, for example, his insistence that genuflecting whenever he appeared must cease. Those on duty in the Vatican were to salute him only on the first encounter of the day. The editor of the Vatican news-paper the *Osservatore Romano* was instructed to be more sparing of superlatives when reporting papal occasions. There was no need, Pope John said, to say the August Pontiff every time reference was made to himself. As happens to all great men Pope John had many unlikely stories fathered on him: "You have a big place here, Holy Father," an American pilgrim observed. "How many people work here?" "About half," Pope John is alleged to have replied.

The name of Pope John will always be associated with work for Christian Unity. I was involved as a member and, later, vice-president of the Secretariat for Promoting Christian Unity under Cardinal Bea. In September 1960 the names of ten members were announced. Although established at the same time as the various commissions to prepare for the Council (due to open in 1962) the Secretariat for Unity was not merely a part of the conciliar machinery. It was expected to carry on its work independently of the Council and to remain a per-manent department of the Holy See after the Council had disbanded. This is among those appointments—curate in Barking and parish priest of Manor Park are the others—which I welcomed with unmixed pleasure. It would have been compatible with custom if Cardinal Bea had asked Pope John to appoint a Belgian or French bishop as the authority on English religious affairs. It might have been assumed that none of the English hierarchy was capable of ecumenical ideas. Since the Malines conversations Anglicans, it was thought, had to cross the channel to find friendship or even Christian charity among Catholics. This is manifestly absurd today but even when the word 'ecumenism' was unfamiliar to English Catholics it was equally untrue. Readers of the previous volume will recall the close friendship I had with the Anglican Rector (H. Pink) and the Methodist Superintendent (A. Binks) when I was parish priest of Manor Park. This, of course, was not ecumenism but it fostered Christian Unity.

Continentals used to imagine that in England Catholics were hostile to all Protestants. When I first joined the Secretariat I was not surprised to find that apart from Cardinal Bea and Monsignor Willebrands few members understood the situation in England. One of the most brilliant men in the Secretariat was Emile de Smedt, Bishop of Bruges. Sub-sequently we became joint vice-presidents and close friends. He made a reputation as an orator during the Council and was the coiner of the word 'triumphalism' which has been employed assiduously ever since by critics of the old Church and, like many a coiner of words, has had reason to regret his invention. What he intended to condemn was the arrogance which led Catholics to speak as if they alone had the right to call themselves true Christians. Coming from Bruges, renowned for spectacular processions, he would not be likely to disapprove of pageantry. He can hardly have rejoiced when noble guards and papal trumpets in St. Peter's were abolished by pressure from post-conciliar puritans who wrongly regarded anything splendid as triumphalist.

The German and Dutch members of the Secretariat knew a great deal about practical ecumenism. Hitler had succeeded where Christian exhortations had often failed. He had compelled Protestants and Catholics to come together to protect each other and, to their credit, the persecuted Jews. This had not happened to the same extent in France where the Protestants are few and in Belgium where native Protestants scarcely exist. In the diocese of Bruges, for example, there is only a handful of Protestants among the Christian millions. I am not sure that Bishop de Smedt actually knew any Protestants in Bruges before joining the Secretariat for Unity. At first I found it hard to persuade fellow members that my accounts of the religious scene in England were objective. Even Pope John was ill-informed on the outlook of English Catholics during his early days at the Vatican. During a private audience he once said to me, "Tell me why do the Catholics in England remain bitter? Tell them to forgive the Protestants for what they did to the martyrs." I assured him that while the martyrs were a source of pride to English Catholics there was no trace of bitterness towards the separated brethren on their account.

It was hard work during the first months at the Secretariat to give an accurate picture of relations between Catholics and non-Catholics in Britain to men who had never lived in England. It was impossible to convey a true picture to those of my fellow members who had been in ecumenical contact only with Anglo-Catholics. It was difficult to correct the picture of Catholic clergy and people all anti-Anglican because they were either converts or Irish. They knew all about Newman and Manning but nothing of such typical English prelates as Vaughan, Bourne and Hinsley of Westminster; Ullathorne and Williams of Birmingham; Wilkinson, Cornthwaite, Gordon and Cowgill of the North, Bagshawe and Brindle in the Midlands. All were English. None was a convert. I had to explain that almost every English Catholic has non-Catholic relatives and non-Catholic friends. I assured them that apart from such special areas as Liverpool there are no longer any social or political divisions between Catholics and other citizens. The very expression non-Catholic has a different connotation here and abroad. A continental non-Catholic is likely to be a Socialist which, in turn, implies anti-clericalism. Few in this country know what anti-clericalism means. Anti-clericalism is not a question of being critical of the clergy (otherwise most of the laity would be anti-clericals). It means hating the clergy because they are doing God's work. True anti-clericalism is militant atheism. Old-fashioned bigotry was dying everywhere in England but was not quite dead in Liverpool. On the very day that news of the creation of a Secretariat for Unity was announced in the press Protestants in Liverpool collected a thousand signatures to prevent the infants and juniors of St. Malachy's Catholic school from using empty classrooms in Beaufort Street county school while their own school was being rebuilt. The city council had to drop the project for fear of violence. The Secretariat in Rome could be forgiven for thinking that such acts were still typical of Catholic-Protestant relations.

After a short experience of Secretariat meetings I felt need for the support of a second English bishop. At that time we had no bishop from Australia, New Zealand, Ireland, Canada or even the United States of America. A Dutch bishop from South Africa spoke English but was no substitute for an Englishman. His command of the English language was wrongly taken to be indicative of his understanding of the English mentality. He contradicted almost everything I said. I decided to ask Pope John to help me. I explained that other members of the Secretariat might not realise that my views were not personal. Although it might seem excessive to have a second English bishop on the Secretariat while so many countries were unrepresented, I thought that the importance of the Anglican Church in the ecumenical context justified my proposal. Pope John who at first had also been ill-informed about the religious situation in England at once saw the force of my argument. He asked me if I had any bishop in mind. I told him that I would prefer a bishop with wide experience of non-Catholics who was not a convert or of Irish stock. I have always regarded it as tactless to offer Anglicans an ex-Anglican as a Catholic spokesman. Catholics would feel affronted if Anglicans were to reciprocate by dealing with us through ex-priests. I gave the name of Thomas Holland who had recently been consecrated Co-adjutor Bishop of Portsmouth. Pope John acted with amazing speed. My audience was on Saturday afternoon and I was due to leave Rome on Sunday. On Saturday evening Archbishop (now Cardinal) Felici, Secretary General of the Committee preparing for the Council, asked me to visit him on my way to the airport the following morning. Pope

[261]

John had telephoned Monsignor Felici immediately after I left the Vatican. There must be no delay, he said, in appointing a second English bishop to the Secretariat for Unity. Archbishop Felici asked for more information about Bishop Holland's background and theological qualifications. Within a few days the appointment was made. The speed of the whole transaction is a tribute to both Pope John and Cardinal Bea.

On 31st October, 1960, the eve of the feast of All Saints, the momentous news of the visit of the Archbishop of Canterbury to Pope John was released. Nobody can estimate the full effects of Dr. Fisher's gesture on the history of ecumenism. It required immense courage and imagination for him to visit the Vatican. He was not a notably ecumenical figure. I had first met him twenty years earlier when, as Bishop of London, he was chairman of the Public Morality Council on which I represented the Archbishop of Westminster. He had always appeared to be a typical Protestant. He had an impatience amounting to contempt for papalistic Anglicans. "They need a sharp kick," he once said to me, "and if that kicks them out of the Anglican fold into the Roman so much the better for us—but not for you!" The initiative for this meeting of Canterbury and Rome came from Geoffrey Fisher. Two years later he told me how it had come about. "Like everyone else," he said, "I was impressed by the change of outlook in the Roman Church since John became pope. It struck me quite suddenly one day that if I was going to Jerusalem to see the Orthodox Patriarch and to Istanbul to meet the Ecumenical Patriarch why shouldn't I visit the Head of the Church of Rome?" It was a much more delicate business than in these days when ecumenical approaches carry little risk of rebuff or misunderstanding.

Geoffrey Fisher was a complex character. In no way devious his approach was often a combination of affection and censure. In his pre-ecumenical days he would not let me call on him at Lambeth Palace when I badly wanted to consult him before seeing the Minister of Education about school grants. He was addicted to giving advice to people in authority. It cannot have been only members of our bishops' bench who received letters of condemnation or approval after press reports of their speeches. He was a constant correspondent and his flow of letters to private persons and to newspapers did not noticeably diminish after his retirement. His successor at Canterbury, Dr. Ramsey, while wondering whether to write to *The Times*, must often have opened his paper to find a letter over the name of Fisher of Lambeth. He occasionally wrote me letters of commendation or dissent. Here is a fairly typical note sent on the occasion of my nomination to the See of Westminster some three years after the Archbishop's visit to Rome:

11th September, 1963.

My dear Archbishop,

May I write with a very full heart to welcome you to your new office. I will not congratulate you, because congratulation seems to me the wrong word. What comes to my mind is a text I preached from last Sunday where St. Paul says that we all have gifts differing according to the grace that is given to us and that we must all earnestly use those gifts according to the proportion of Faith. That like the rest of Romans Chapter 12 is a most alarming and inspiring truth: and I hope that you may find increasing joy in the working out of it in your high office. I know that you have in your heart the care of the Church of England as well as of the Church of Rome, and I hope that in your time you will be able to make a grand contribution to the drawing together of the gifts of grace entrusted to our two Churches—a task as perilous and as exhilarating as climbing Everest. You know how eagerly I shall support you in my prayers, and if I can be of any service to you please call on me. I would even ask that you would still allow me sometime if I feel moved to it, to write to you if I ever see barriers between our two churches being raised instead of lowered. You will know that I do it in humility and affection, so my dear Archbishop may the grace of God abound in your heart and make you perfect in all good works.

Yours sincerely,

FISHER OF LAMBETH.

The first hazard Dr. Fisher faced in deciding to visit the Pope was the disapproval of anti-Catholics among his own flock. To his astonishment it never came. He told me that all his correspondents except obvious cranks approved his action. To reduce risk of opposition he had taken pains to emphasise that his was a purely courtesy visit. When asked to comment I told the press, "Courtesy translated into the language of religion means charity. The Primate's visit to the Pope is significant because it shows that differences of theology need not prevent mutual respect and love." The result of this visit was far greater and more lasting than Archbishop Fisher foresaw. By seeking an audience with Pope John he healed a breach extending over four centuries. He set the seal on the trust and affection with which Pope John had come to be universally regarded. Pope John himself was unaffectedly delighted to welcome the Archbishop of Canterbury but some of the Vatican prelates were less enchanted. They had no protocol to guide them. Catholic ecumenism being still embryonic there was no question of a joint service. (By the time Dr. Ramsey made his visit to Pope Paul joint religious services were no novelty. The Pope and Archbishop were able to take part in an ecumenical act of worship without incurring any criticism.) At the time of Dr. Fisher's visit officialdom was unsure of itself. It was not clear about the correct manner of receiving the head of another Church. Caution was the prevailing guide. Even photography was strictly and needlessly rationed. The Archbishop of Canterbury had as the main object of his visit to reciprocate on behalf of Anglicans the goodwill so abundantly shown by Pope John.

Whatever else Dr. Fisher may have had in mind he can hardly have foreseen that a significant result of his papal visit would be to stimulate ecumenism among English Catholics. The courtesy done to the Holy Father deeply moved them. Their loyalty to the Holy See is perhaps greater and more emotional than that of Catholics anywhere else in the world, not excluding Italy. The reason is historical. Hostility between English monarchs and the Holy See began hundreds of years before the Protestant Reformation. Henry VIII was not the first King Henry to quarrel with a pope. Henry II as a young man had been regarded as one in mind and heart with Thomas Becket, his chancellor. The same Thomas was later ordained priest and consecrated Archbishop of Canterbury. Martyred by knights who thought his death would please the king St. Thomas became the most celebrated of English saints. Little less famous is the other Thomas who was chancellor to another Henry. Thomas More and John Fisher, Bishop of Rochester, died in defence of the pope's position as head of the Church on earth. The traditional devotion of English Catholics to Fisher and More has made them sensitive to any mark of honour paid to the Sovereign Pontiff. The English take their loyalties seriously. English Catholics love and revere both the monarch and the pope. The courtesy of Dr. Fisher warmed the hearts of every Catholic in Britain.

The reaction of Anglicans, Nonconformists and the religiously neutral was similar to that of Catholics. The news was regarded as important and splendid. Unbelievers are almost as exasperated as Christians by the spectacle of religious divisions. Everyone realises that vast resources of goodwill would be available if reunion were to become a reality.

The differences in outlook among those who regard God as their Father are of small significance compared with the gulf between them and those who regard man as essentially of one nature with the beasts and with no more hope of immortality. The whole world would benefit from unity between all who acknowledge God. The reunion of Christendom is only a first step. The visit of the Archbishop of Canterbury was seen to bring that first step nearer. Here is a short article from *Time and Tide* of 5th November, 1960. This weekly journal had no political or religious affiliation and may be taken as giving a typical non-sectarian view:

ROME AND CANTERBURY

Almost too good to be true

The visit of the Archbishop of Canterbury to the Pope is a bit of news that seems almost too good to be true as well as something that might well have happened long ago—like Mr. Macmillan's Capetown speech or the evidence about Lady Chatterley. In spite of a few 'spokesmen' telling us that of course nothing will come of it, it's quite a step for the heads of two branches of the Church to find themselves on speaking terms again after five hundred and sixty-three years—Archbishop Arundel visited the Vatican in 1437 —a length of estrangement that makes summit protagonists look as if they lived in each other's back gardens.

And of course nothing will come of it—except a nail the size of a crowbar in bigotry's coffin. Nowadays few people who hope for Church re-union expect that this can come by imposed uniformity: they hope that if churches and denominations live truly according to their own tenets, and love one another, then unity will grow in the way that matters. This involves simple courtesy: a quality Christians should possess, but often don't. Schisms perhaps start from matters of conscience and principle: but they often flourish on the principles of the showmanship of all-in wrestling—"the Catholic or the Protestant, the man you *love* to hate."

The signs of all this changing have been so thick recently that the hopeful must be breathless. First there were the Roman Catholic observers at the World Council of Churches: the other day there was the Roman Catholic Archbishop of Liverpool's letter in *The Observer* saying how splendid were Anglican and Non-Conformist clergymen: now the Archbishop of Canterbury is making his own move, and he has the gratitude of what must be the whole Church of England.

There is probably less anti-Roman bigotry now in England than at any time since Archbishop Arundel. But what is it that Anglicans still object to about Romans—apart from the sort of qualities they object to in themselves? It probably boils down to Papal Infallibility. And the answer to this (might not the Archbishop suggest it to the Pope? the Pope is said to be taking English lessons: The Archbishop is a very good schoolmaster: what a subject for semantics!) is for the Pope to make an infallible statement that he is fallible. This of course would be meaningless; but it would make everyone happy who wanted to be happy, and it would let the rest go on arguing about the meaning of the words until (as they themselves would put it) Kingdom Come.

The reference to my letter to *The Observer* will need clarification. At that time *The Observer* was running a series of articles by Paul Ferris entitled "A dog collar in the hostile sixties". It would be an understatement to call the article on parsons unflattering. It was grossly offensive. Short of accusing them of immorality it gave a picture of futile and feckless men doing needless tasks with consummate inefficiency. It was a difficult article for Protestant clergymen to counter. They could hardly write to the paper claiming to be efficient pastors, compassionate social workers and eloquent preachers. It occurred to me that only a Catholic priest could write a convincing defence on their behalf. I could praise them in all sincerity because I had worked with them for over twenty-five years. I therefore wrote to the editor of *The Observer*: My letter was published under the title "Friends under fire":

Sir,

I well understand if Anglicans and Free Churchmen are distressed by the articles of Mr. Paul Ferris. It is likely that readers with no religious affiliation would be confirmed in their view that the activities of Protestant clergy are only remotely related to the serious problems of life. Clergymen were represented as disillusioned men engaged in trivial and frustrating tasks, while being mainly preoccupied with thoughts of their own inadequate stipends.

I hope it will not be thought impertinent for a Catholic to comment. During the last thirty years I have known parsons and ministers in all parts of the country. As a body they are dedicated men. It is impossible not to be impressed by their frugal living and the alacrity with which they respond to calls on their compassion. The poor, the sick, the young, the worried and, indeed, the criminal turn to them as friends. The self-sacrifice and devoted charity of the wives of clergymen are everywhere recognised and admired.

I am sure that Mr. Ferris did not intend to bring the Protestant clergy into contempt. From the nature of his material it was impossible to give a true picture. As a reporter he could not be entrusted with full details of the pastoral life. The cure of souls does not lend itself to newspaper publicity. People fly to religion especially in time of trouble or sorrow. It follows that a clergyman's most valuable work must remain hidden. Without breach of confidence he cannot discuss his intimate spiritual and social apostolate.

This, I think, is the reason why the portrait of a clergyman seemed to many of us more like a caricature. It gave no comfort to Catholics to see their friends under fire.

The visit of the Archbishop of Canterbury to Pope John created interest far beyond ecclesiastical circles. England was naturally the centre of discussion. The Established Church may attract only a small percentage of citizens to active membership but it has loose allegiance from a majority of the population. This is probably due in part to the almost mystic English loyalty to the monarch who is the titular head of the Church of England. To the British public the grand tour of the Archbishop of Canterbury was of importance mainly because of its Roman climax. The friendship of Anglicans and Orientals has never moved the British people to anything approaching ecstasy. Relations with Rome fascinate even agnostics. It was a pity that television was not invited to record Dr. Fisher's visit to the Vatican. The full facts have not yet been fully disclosed. It is likely that some person or persons unknown, apprehensive of the results of the meeting, reduced ceremonial to a minimum and refused to allow television cameras past the bronze doors of the Vatican. Nobody was told if anything of importance was discussed by the two prelates. The cameras recorded the Archbishop's car crossing the piazza of St. Peter's. Dr. Fisher then disappeared within the walls of the Vatican: "Behind those walls," the frustrated television commentator was reduced to saying, "history is being made." The fact is that history was made by the very presence of the Anglican Archbishop in the Pope's apartments. The actual conversation might have added little to history.

"We talked," Dr. Fisher told reporters after the papal audience, "about everything and nothing. We exchanged trivialities, as you do in all conversations, but the theme was the drawing together of Christian peoples." Defrauded of a sight of the protagonists in conversation, B.B.C. television mounted a minor summit in the persons of the other Anglican Primate, Dr. Ramsey, Archbishop of York, and myself. On the first Sunday in December 1960 we took part in a programme with Kenneth Harris as chairman. It was a pleasant occasion. There was no need for Michael Ramsey and me to perform. We knew each other well enough to have a conversation without attempting to outwit each other. The Archbishop came to lunch in Liverpool a few days before we were due to go down to the television studios in London. We did not rehearse the actual conversation but discussed in broad outline which subjects of controversy to avoid. We realised that in a programme designed to draw attention to the Rome meeting as a step towards Christian Unity it would be inappropriate to concentrate on doctrinal differences between the Church of England and the Church of Rome. The television programme, like the meeting of the Pope and Archbishop, was significant simply because it took place. The content of the programme was of minor importance. The only passage in our conversation which I recall concerned our appearance. I asked Dr. Ramsey why he was wearing two crosses. He was doing so in the hope that he might use them to illustrate the good relations existing between Anglicans and the Orthodox. The second cross had been given to him in Moscow by the Russian Patriarch. "If," I said, "you are going to boast about your jewellery what about this ring of mine which belonged to Cardinal Pole, the last Catholic Archbishop of Canterbury?"

Here are two short reports on the broadcast from contemporary journalists. The first is from *John O'London's* (15th December, 1960):

> The Archbishop of York and the Roman Catholic Archbishop of Liverpool also seemed in excellent spirits a few days later when they met before the cameras to pick amiably over the bones of Christian controversy, to swop anecdotes over what they described as their 'jewellery', and stoutly to renounce any truck with bigotry; the one piece of good news in a week when all was floods, snarls over Central Africa, and speculation as to how to persuade young men to take up soldiering.

The second is from the *Yorkshire Post* (5th December, 1960):

Christian Meeting Point

The B.B.C. Television feature, Meeting Point, richly justified its title last night by bringing together two eminent men of the Anglican and Roman Catholic Churches, the Archbishop of York, Dr. A. M. Ramsey, and the Archbishop of Liverpool, Dr. J. C. Heenan. Christian viewers, noting the warm goodwill of these two and how manifestly they felt at ease with each other, must have rejoiced at this evidence that the spirit of love and charity is alive between the Churches. As the two Archbishops showed, it was alive long before the Archbishop of Canterbury paid his famous call upon Pope John in the Vatican last week.

But the exchange of courtesies between Pope and Primate has fixed attention on the desire which Christians of many denominations share to emphasise their common beliefs and their common allegiance rather than the differences that have kept them apart so long.

The broadcast stimulated papers to speculate on the extent to which my friendship with the Archbishop of York was a reflection of the relationship of our clergy and laity. Christopher Driver came to interview me on this subject for the *Manchester Guardian*. His article which appeared in the last issue of the *Weekly Guardian* in 1960 is of particular interest because it refers to a number of events I have already described. It is fascinating to compare what I have already described in Liverpool with the impressions of a non-Catholic reporter. Here, in part, is what Christopher Driver wrote:

Religious Divisions in a City

By their exchange of courtesies the Archbishop and the Pope recently demonstrated that the ecumenical movement is something about which the Church is serious. At humbler levels, what happens?

Liverpool is a hard case. Until recently, Catholic and Protestant lived in ghettoes. "Ah, you're in the Catholic quarter now," said a woman in Scotland Road. "No, I don't go to Mass, but I like to do something for me faith." Steep hills lead to Protestant Everton, and the gigantic blocks of flats called "The Braddocks" loom like Cunarders out of the fog, port-holes aglow. Not religion but position on the housing list decides who lives there, and some months ago a social caseworker calling on a Catholic family in the flats found the mother in a state of terror because a Protestant Party leaflet had been dropped through their letter-box, announcing that "The Braddocks" were "blotting out the Orange sun," and calling for a halt to "the Romanisation of Netherfield." On the Battle of the Boyne day, July 12, when members of Orange Lodges carry banners round the streets of Liverpool, this family stays indoors, and takes down its green curtains. It is a gesture to history rather than to any actual danger—but there were Protestant demonstrations when Mr. Gaitskell opened "The Braddocks" to the considerable astonishment of those members of the national press who were in attendance.

Moreover, the geographical and cultural 'apartheid' (both sides use the word) takes uglier forms than disagreement at the ballot boxes. Within the past three years the Roman Catholic Archbishop has been physically attacked on a visit to a house in a Protestant area; and a 1,000 strong opposition has been organised to stop Liverpool Education Committee accommodating some Roman Catholic schoolchildren in a State school while their own school, St. Malachy's, was being rebuilt. The project had to be abandoned.

The Roman Catholic Archbishop who presides over this cauldron is one of the three English members of the Pope's recently established Commission on Christian Unity. Dr. J. C. Heenan—a television 'natural', say his producers—is a courteous, crisply eirenic man; one receives a strong impression that he really likes his fellow-Christians. Certainly his relations with his Anglican counterpart in Liverpool, Dr. Clifford Martin, are on a basis of personal friendship previously inconceivable in the city.

Dr. Heenan is inclined to play down the more spectacular clashes between members of his own community and the Protestant ultras in the city. "The St. Malachy's school petition? It really surprised me, but I'm quite sure that it wasn't spontaneous—that some whipping-up was done. The attack on him in Robsart Street? That was an example of the ghetto mentality surviving when the need for it has gone. Everyone knew I was going to that house—the only Roman Catholic house in the street. Some of our people must have said: "Will they do anything to our Archbishop? We must protect him" because there were a couple of hundred Roman

Catholics in the street when I got there, before a brick was thrown. If they hadn't been there, it would have passed off without any incident at all."

Liverpool City Council refused to implement the 1936 Education Act, which empowered it to give grants for the building of denominational schools, and a special Liverpool Act had to be passed in 1939, after pressure had been brought to compel the city to fall in line with the rest of the country. But now shining new schools like St. Gregory's, Fox Street, with all its pupils in uniforms, offer a hope of erasing the smear beloved of Protestant propagandists in Liverpool, that Catholic children are delinquent children. And the Council's willingness to hasten the construction of Catholic schools has saved Dr. Heenan from having to invite controversy by agitating for them.

In autobiographical writing it is safer to quote than to give personal impressions. Apart from the sound principle that nobody should attempt to be judge in his own case (*nemo sibi iudex*) a Christian is inhibited from recording his own conduct with approval because he better than anyone knows how mixed his motives are even when he is doing good. In working for religious unity my outlook has always been simple. I feel much greater affinity with Jews, Moslems, Buddhists and Hindus than with those who reject God. Belief in God and man's eternal destiny is the most important of all religious truths. The Vatican Council talked of a hierarchy of truths. By this is meant not that some doctrines are less true but that some are less important than others. The Mass is more important than any other form of Catholic worship. The doctrine of the Blessed Trinity matters more than the dogma of the Assumption of the Virgin Mary. The unity of all men matters more than the unity of believers. The unity of all believers is more desirable than the reunion of Christians who make up less than half the human race. To think of reconciling only Protestants and Catholics is to lack faith, hope and imagination. It is also a waste of energy for Christians to concentrate on each other while the majority of their fellow citizens are no longer certain that Christ is God or, indeed, that God exists.

This will explain why as archbishop of a city once renowned for bigotry I tried to preach tolerance by word and example. In a series of articles entitled *Your City* Mr. Eglin, the best-known journalist in the north west, attempted to explain Liverpool to Liverpudlians. In an interview he drew from me what might be described as a declaration of intent. This is a very small part of the article in which he described my outlook and motives to the people of Liverpool. It was sub-titled "Old antagonisms are dead". Together with Mr. Driver's piece it gives an account which I could hardly write in the first person:

In Liverpool, religious intolerance has blazed more fiercely than in any other English city. In Liverpool pitched battles between Catholics and Protestants, men, women and children, have been fought. In Liverpool there is still a minister of religion and former Lord Mayor who says publicly that there is a case for apartheid in religion. In Liverpool the car of the Roman Catholic Archbishop was stoned when he went to comfort the sick. How strange it is— but how significant—that when the present Pope wanted an English priest to help him in the task of bridging the gap between different faiths and of furthering the cause of Christian unity it was to this same turbulent Liverpool where the gulf between the two great churches of the Western world has been widest that he turned.

Even more significant, the priest to whom Pope John sent his call was that same Archbishop at whom stones were thrown in Robsart Street, Liverpool, only two years ago—Dr. John Carmel Heenan, Metropolitan Archbishop in the city. Dr. Heenan came to his diocese less than four years ago but he has already made a great impact, not only on the people of his own faith but on those of what were once rival faiths who perceive the truth and wisdom that lie behind his maxim. "We must love one another until we come to see the same truth . . . we must stand to our principles and yet we must go on loving."

CHAPTER

NINETEEN

EARLY IN JANUARY 1961, DR. FISHER ANNOUNCED HIS RETIREMENT FROM
the See of Canterbury. He received many tributes from Catholics. His
later years as archbishop were marked by a growth of his understanding
of Christians outside the Anglican fold. Until near the end of his term
of office he did not seek contacts outside Britain and the Commonwealth. He was not enthusiastic about the approaches to continental
Catholics traditional in Anglo-Catholic circles. As he grew older he
softened in his references to Catholic teaching and practice. The asper-
ities which marked his earlier pronouncements were missing or had
become muted. When asked for a press comment on his retirement
from Canterbury I paid tribute to his great love of his Church: "He
never spared himself in his efforts to extend its influence in the world . . .
When we have forgotten any of his utterances which gave pain to his
Catholic friends, we shall remember his great goodwill and courage in
making a visit of courtesy to the Pope. This gesture has encouraged all
who strive for closer unity among Christians. He takes his leave in a
glow of charity."

It was not long before the expected news was announced of Dr.
Ramsey's succession. His place in York, we were told, would be taken
by Dr. Coggan, Bishop of Bradford. Michael Ramsey I already counted
among my friends and I had met Dr. Coggan while I was Bishop of
Leeds. I thought it would be an attractive ecumenical act to invite the
Anglican Archbishops and their wives to lunch at Archbishop's House.
I also invited the Bishop of Liverpool and Mrs. Martin. In order not
to make the party too one-sided I asked my neighbour John Murphy,
Bishop of Shrewsbury, to support me. It was one of the happiest

luncheon parties I have ever given. It would now be regarded as normal for clergy of different denominations to break bread together but even as recently as the early 1960s it was still novel to be host to three Anglican bishops and their wives. It was a purely social occasion to wish them well before they began their new tasks. Dr. Ramsey and his delightful wife, Joan, were particularly glad to visit Liverpool where the young Michael had been a curate. Everyone who has lived in Liverpool suffers nostalgia ever afterwards.

In Liverpool the archbishop is expected to provide leadership much more frequently than a Catholic bishop elsewhere in England. The reason is that in Liverpool there is a strong tradition of reliance on the guidance of the archbishop. Except at a time of national emergency a bishop's sermon rarely attracts interest outside his church. A pronouncement by the Archbishop of Liverpool commands such attention in the north that the rest of the country usually regards it as national news. Civic Sunday does not usually attract journalists to church except on Merseyside.

On the last Sunday of May 1961 the Lord Mayor of Liverpool, Alderman Peter McKernan, came officially to Mass. There had been nothing unusual about his election. It had been supported by the Conservative majority although he was a member of the Labour Party. The only opposition had come from the Protestant party of which the Rev. H. D. Longbottom, a rabid anti-Catholic, was the leader. The theme of my sermon was the duty of a city council to apply itself to the solution of local problems instead of dissipating its eloquence on national and international political issues.

Here is an extract from the report in the local paper:

> Unless more houses are built, the Roman Catholic Archbishop of Liverpool, Dr. John Heenan, fears that Britain will become "a nation of neurotics". He told councillors yesterday at a Lord Mayor's service: "The greatest single problem is the decent housing of our people. Do not fritter away your talents and your time in the council chamber in the discussion of national and international problems you are powerless to resolve. Concentrate irrespective of party on providing homes for families. The splendid schools now being built will fail in their purpose if scholars have to return from classrooms to squalid, overcrowded homes. We shall breed a nation of neurotics if young husbands and wives continue to be unable to find the blessed privacy of their own hearths."

The sermon was not brilliant but the publicity accorded it made its message memorable to the city councillors. They expected the Archbishop of Liverpool to offer advice and they were ready to listen. In place of a text from the bible I had taken words reported to have been said a few days previously by a member of the Prison Officers' Association at a meeting of protest against the dangerously low ratio of staff to prisoners: "There is only one thing a man will slog his guts out for nowadays and that is money." The sermon was summarised by a number of weekly journals. The following extract is from the *Tablet* (3rd June, 1961):

"It would seem from the words of the prison officer that materialism is the great vice of our age," the Archbishop commented, but he went on—

"It is some comfort to remember that materialism was always said to be the great vice of every age. It corrupted and brought to ruin the civilisation of Greece and Rome. The ancient Hebrews worshipped the Golden Calf. Christ cast out those who traded in the Temple. Greed, lust for power, materialism—these are all names for the same evil—eventually destroys all whom it controls. But I am not convinced that our age is more materialistic than all others.

"We are told that England is now less Christian than ever before. But we may ask ourselves, was the nineteenth century really more Christian? It was not very enlightened in the year 1819. Then it was content to forbid the employment of children of eight years or less. Nineteenth-century law prohibited the employment of children of nine years for more than twelve hours a day. Even at the beginning of the present century, in 1901, Parliament forbade child labour before the age of twelve only *if* it prevented attendance at school . . ."

Dr. Heenan went on to say that those before whom he spoke, men devoting themselves to public service and public life, were themselves witnesses to the falsehood of the prison officer's remark that money is the only real incentive nowadays. He said that it was taken for granted that the new Lord Mayor, as a Catholic, would never seek the advancement of Catholic interests to the prejudice of the rights of non-Catholics:

"By God's grace you will be the servant of Protestants and Jews no less than those of your Faith. That we take for granted. But we

[275]

should also be able to take it for granted that all elected representatives regard themselves as pledged to the whole community. Yet increasingly those in local government are becoming partisans. Perhaps it was inevitable that parliament should have become the battleground of party politicians. But it is not necessary for councillors to view every measure with an eye to the party. Surely it would be better to return to the system in which the City Fathers debated the needs of citizens with the common good alone in view. Why should their minds be set and sealed before issues are publicly discussed? It is not progress to turn legislators into robots."

The importance of housing arises from the primacy of the family among human institutions. It was not only in Liverpool but in any city which provided a platform that I insisted on the Catholic teaching that the home and the family are more important than Church or State. I had already pointed out in an *ad clerum* letter that the growth of gambling could have a devastating effect on the family. Stories had reached me of mothers with bingo fever going out five or six nights in the week to hazard their housekeeping money while the family was left to look after itself. Some priests contended that the anti-bingo stories were spread by publicans suffering from the competition of the bingo halls and there may well have been some truth in this contention. It is true that many frequenting the bingo halls were former R.C.s (Regular Customers).

The county of Lancashire forms a large part of the Liverpool diocese (usually and inaccurately called the Liverpool archdiocese presumably because as a metropolitan see it has an archbishop). The diocese has undergone immense ethnological changes since the middle of the last century when Irish immigrants came in great numbers. During the present century most of the Irish arriving at the port of Liverpool have proceeded to London or the Midlands where greater opportunities await them. The docks provide the means of livelihood to the majority of workers but dockland is notoriously inhospitable to strangers. The Liverpool-Irish are mostly two or three generations removed from their land of origin. Like their similarly hyphenated cousins, the Irish-Americans, they are regarded as Irish but by outlook and education they are no less English than the Boston Kennedys are American. It is nevertheless true that inherited characteristics make the Liverpool Irish a different breed from the people of Lancashire.

Their demonstrative loyalty to the Church although not synonymous

[276]

with regular practice has become a legend. Less is heard of the Catholics of recusant stock. These are found in large numbers in Chorley, Ince Blundell, Wigan, Leigh, Crosby, Burscough and other small towns and villages. I remember being astonished at the familiar way in which the people of the tiny Benedictine parish of Brindle near Preston spoke of their local martyrs. It was as if they had known them personally. The children in school described the sixteenth-century martyrs as if they were recalling the exploits of beloved priests who had regrettably been recently transferred to another parish. The Lancashire people are not emotional but the depth of their faith is unique in my experience. I doubt if they were impressed by the Catholics who in the years after the Council turned against the Pope and bishops. Having seen what little account they made of the passage of time I imagine that they remained aloof from passing fashions.

There are few survivors of the old Catholic aristocracy still living in Lancashire but there was one old man whose simple devotion and prodigal generosity showed the quality of the faith his Catholic fore-fathers had bequeathed to him. What took place during our brief friendship is so astonishing that the account might come from one of the more imaginative lives of the saints. Perhaps he was a saint of the twentieth century. I give his story without embellishment.

One morning I received a letter asking me to see him to discuss a very personal matter. The writer, Geoffrey de Trafford, was very apologetic about asking for a lengthy interview but explained that his business was rather complicated. Furthermore it could be settled by nobody but me. If it had been possible to deal with his solicitor, he wrote, he would not have presumed to waste my time. I had not been in Lancashire very long at this time and had never heard of Geoffrey de Trafford. I thought it likely that the man had a matrimonial pro-blem which he was unwilling to discuss with his own priest. The address on the letter was Croston near Preston. I therefore asked Mr. de Trafford to come at midday on the following Thursday and promised to give him something to eat before he set off on his long journey home. The significance of the meal will soon appear. I had judged from his handwriting that he was an old man and I knew that Croston was one of the most distant parishes in the diocese. He had particularly asked to see me at Archbishop's House, Woolton, because the traffic in Liverpool confused him. Promptly at twelve o'clock my visitor arrived in an old but beautifully preserved motor car.

Captain Geoffrey Edmond de Trafford was the last of his line of de

Traffords. The family was one of the oldest in Lancashire with records going back to the twelfth century. It took its name from the village of Trafford near Manchester which is better known for test cricketers than confessors of the faith. Geoffrey belonged to the younger branch of de Traffords who moved to Croston towards the end of the sixteenth century. Croston Hall, the family seat, was a cold forbidding building with a chapel disproportionately large for the house. For reasons which he explained during his visit Geoffrey de Trafford now used only two rooms in the house—a large living-room which was also the bed-sitting-room of his crippled sister, Ermyntrude, and the room where he slept. The rooms upstairs were never used and the house was unheated. It must have been the most uncomfortable house in the village but the brother and sister who were utterly devoted to each other were quite content. The reason for their serenity in such austere surroundings came from an unemotional attachment to their religion. This was disclosed quite casually in the course of that first conversation with the Squire of Croston.

As soon as he was seated in my study Geoffrey de Trafford produced from his pocket a copy of his will. The purpose of his visit was to invite me to alter the wording in any way I saw fit. He intended to leave all his money and possessions, apart from legacies to retired servants, to the Church. The sole condition was that during her lifetime Ermyntrude was to have an annuity and the use of Croston Hall. Before agreeing to discuss the wording of the will I raised the question of his relatives. I pointed out that a large legacy could prove an embarrassment to the Church if the claims of family or dependants had not first been met. Geoffrey assured me that he had already made provision for the very few retired staff of Croston Hall who were still alive. "As for family," he said, "there are only Ermyntrude and I. We never married and we have no brothers or sisters." I reminded him that there were many de Traffords in other parts of England. Some of them might feel aggrieved if they were left out of the will. Geoffrey assured me that no problem could arise because those de Traffords who had remained faithful to their religion were all fairly rich. He was so positive about this that I did not question him further.

In the old will he showed me his estate was bequeathed to the Archbishop of Liverpool to be used to promote the Catholic interest in Croston. I suggested that this was too restrictive. The extent of the bequest after the sale of Croston Hall and its land might be more than two hundred thousand pounds—far too much to spend on Croston. I told him about the slum clearance in progress throughout Lancashire. Poor families were being removed from the squalor of the towns and rehoused in new estates. I asked him to re-word the will so that the archbishop of the day would have discretion to use the money for churches or schools wherever they might be most needed. He was quite happy to alter the will. He had been troubled in conscience at taking up so much of my time but now felt that his importunity had been justified. "I would never have thought of that," he said. "Obviously it would be absurd to spend the money on a handful of Catholics in Croston when poor people need churches and schools elsewhere." We agreed that the best phrase to cover the bequest was "for general ecclesiastical purposes". In case Croston itself were to become the site of future development we inserted its name with the proviso that the archbishop would not be bound to spend any of the money there. These expressions were later ratified by his lawyers who were satisfied that the archbishop of the day would have a completely free hand to use the legacy in any way he thought fit for the work of the Church in the diocese of Liverpool. I did not expect to be the archbishop concerned because Geoffrey de Trafford looked so spry and healthy that morning. Within two years he suffered a heart attack and died at the age of seventy-nine in 1960.

When we had finished our business discussion we had lunch. It is not my custom to scrutinise guests at my table but it was impossible not to notice the relish with which Geoffrey attacked the meal the nuns had prepared. His repeated expressions of appreciation for the plain food were clearly more than polite remarks. Under gentle cross-examination he revealed that this was the first cooked meal he had eaten for many months. Several years previously he had resolved to give all he possessed to the Church. Since that time he had avoided all unnecessary expense. A woman in the village prepared a hot meal each day for Ermyntrude. This was collected by Geoffrey who was content with bread, cheese and fruit. Croston Hall in his childhood had been full of servants. As they died or moved away they were not replaced. Those who lived in the village had rent-free cottages and an ample allowance. The old gardeners continued to cultivate the walled garden and the flowers and fruit in the greenhouses for their own commercial interests. Fair and generous to all tenants and former retainers Geoffrey de Trafford lavished all his care on his crippled sister. Ermyntrude, whom I visited later, was a witty, uncomplaining woman whose only grudge against life was her inability to attend daily Mass. In her childhood days there had been visiting priests to say Mass in the chapel.

Geoffrey de Trafford confessed during lunch to a weakness which he shared with Ermyntrude. Both liked to smoke cigarettes after the mid-day meal and occasionally Geoffrey smoked a cigar in the evening. He realised that this was a weakness but he doubted if he would ever overcome it. Smoking had such a hold on them both that the thought of Lent (when, of course, they gave up smoking with all other luxuries) cast a shadow over each new year. He was what is sometimes described as a garden-of-the-soul Catholic. His life was guided by the old maxims and devotions. The Mass and the rosary were his staple spiritual nourishment. Brother and sister spent as little as possible on themselves in order not to diminish the sum of money eventually to be used for charitable purposes. After Geoffrey's death Ermyntrude could not be persuaded to buy an up-to-date hearing aid to replace the clumsy instrument supplied by the National Health. She could not bear to spend money on herself. She was nevertheless delighted when I gave her a Christmas present of a neat hearing aid. In return she sent me an illustrated prayer book, velvet covered and complete with clasp, which had been in the family for generations. Ermyntrude did not long survive her brother. Nobody could possibly have provided the same loving care for this old lady who was entirely dependent on others. She also left all her money and possessions to the Church. The diocese of Liverpool had already inherited most of the estate. When Ermyntrude died the Hall was demolished.

CHAPTER

TWENTY

THE STORY OF THE BUILDING OF THE METROPOLITAN CATHEDRAL OF
Christ the King merits a whole book to itself. Little had been heard of
the proposed cathedral after 1939 when the war brought building to a
halt. Before the war Archbishop Downey had coined and popularised the
slogan 'a cathedral in our time'. His predecessor, Archbishop Keating,
translated from Northampton to the see of Liverpool in 1921, had
resolved with the enthusiastic approval of the Liverpool priests and
people to erect a cathedral under the title of the Good Shepherd in
memory of the much revered Archbishop Whiteside. At the time of his
death seven years later Archbishop Keating had collected one hundred
and twenty-two thousand pounds for this project. He had also begun
to negotiate the purchase of the old workhouse site on Brownlow Hill.
This was acquired a year later by his successor, Archbishop Downey,
at the price of one hundred thousand pounds. It was Dr. Downey who
appointed Sir Edwin Lutyens, the most famous architect of the day,
to design the new cathedral.

Opinions on art and architecture are always divided usually acrimon-
iously. The Lutyens design was no exception. Some regarded it as the
ecclesiastical masterpiece of the century. Others condemned it as the
monstrous creation of a pagan megalomaniac. It was pretentiously
large with a dome larger than that of St. Peter's, Rome. That aspect
of the Lutyens design rankled in Rome. Many years after the original
plans had been abandoned Pope John asked me why I wanted to build
the biggest cathedral in the world in Liverpool. There is no record of
the instructions Lutyens received from his client but it is unlikely that

[281]

he was told to dwarf St. Peter's. Dr. Downey was probably content to stipulate that the cathedral sited a few hundred yards from the beautiful Anglican cathedral should not be in gothic style. Dr. Downey had no wish to revive, still less perpetuate, religious competition on Merseyside.

When Lutyens submitted sketch plans he pointed out that he had carefully obeyed instructions to avoid anything gothic. He is alleged to have added: "My concept is renaissance spelt with a w—after Wren." This was a reference to his dome which was to have been no less than one hundred and seventy-two feet in diameter. An equally pleasant example of repartee is attributed to Sir Giles Gilbert Scott, the architect of the Anglican cathedral. He won the competition with a design submitted at the beginning of the century when he was scarcely out of his indentures. The building was well advanced when at the outbreak of the 1914–18 war young Scott enlisted. The story goes that serving in the Middle East he was busy erecting earthworks against a threatened Turkish offensive when fighting came to an end. The military aspect being no longer important he amused himself by making an architectural feature. A few days later a general making an inspection of the area was impressed by the imaginative design and sent for the officer responsible. "Young man," he said, "you have talent. I hope you will use it when you are demobbed. I shall give you a letter of introduction to an architect friend of mine in London. Have you ever tried your hand at this kind of thing before?" "Only Liverpool Cathedral, Sir," Scott replied.

Work on the crypt of the metropolitan cathedral began in the 1930s. Despite the estimated cost of three million pounds and although the cathedral would not be completed before the middle of the twenty-first century the clergy and people were not apathetic. Dr. Downey took the plans to Rome and Pope Pius XI gave them his approval. Such was the prevailing atmosphere that the Pope doubtless regarded the building of a vast cathedral in the industrial north as one more 'bulwark against communism'. He suggested that instead of Good Shepherd the dedication should be Christ the King to show the cathedral's significance. (The outlook of the public had changed so completely by the time the cathedral was opened that far from being regarded as a blow against communism the building of cathedrals or even of modest churches was likely to be condemned as playing into the hands of the communists.) Dr. Downey accepted the Pope's suggestion and told the people of Liverpool that the new cathedral would be "a noble edifice not merely in which but with which to worship Christ the King".

It was not to be. The second world war held up the building. Sir Edwin Lutyens died and his plans were set aside. The cost of the original building had now risen to an estimated twenty-seven million pounds but this was a vague and optimistic calculation. To replace Lutyens Dr. Downey chose Adrian Scott, the brother of Giles Scott, architect of the Anglican cathedral. He was designated not architect but continuator. In 1953 after Dr. Downey's death, Monsignor Godfrey was appointed to Liverpool and decided on grounds of cost to abandon the old design. Mr. Scott was instructed to draw plans for an entirely new building to be erected over the now half-completed crypt. Adrian Scott had an unenviable task. He had to tinker with a masterpiece. We do not know what instructions he was given but since he retained the vast Lutyens dome he must have been asked to preserve as much as possible of the original design. He prepared a sketch plan which invited unfavourable comparison because of the affinity with the Lutyens model. Mr. Scott undertook to have part of the building ready for occupation within ten years. He estimated that the cathedral could be completed soon after the close of the century. Architectural connoisseurs hoped that the Scott compromise (they used a cruder word) would never be built.

Archbishop Godfrey did not remain long in Liverpool. Three years after his enthronement he was translated to Westminster. William Godfrey was a man of prudence and—what is not at all the same thing—a man of great caution. Three years was not nearly long enough for him to put plans for the new cathedral into operation. He commissioned a series of drawings but never reached the stage of inviting contractors to submit tenders for the actual building. Work on the crypt continued in desultory fashion but little progress had been made since 1937 when Archbishop Downey had said the first Mass in an unpaved and roofless crypt. In view of the subsequent leap in building costs and the changed attitude to church building it was providential that Dr. Godfrey moved slowly. When he left Liverpool I was not encumbered with a scheme which had gone too far to be abandoned. In another three or four years the Metropolitan Cathedral of Liverpool would once again have been an unfinished symphony in stone. In December 1956 when Dr. Godfrey left Liverpool, the estimated cost of the project had risen to twenty million pounds. Even this was a low estimate. The Scott cathedral would never have been built.

In May 1957, as we have seen, I was translated from Leeds to Liverpool. It had been assumed that the biggest decision facing the new archbishop would be whether or not to proceed with the building of the metropolitan cathedral. I did not regard this as the chief of my problems. For me it was much more important to win the confidence of the priests and the people of my new diocese. Liverpool is only a short distance on the other side of the Pennines but to come from Yorkshire was not necessarily a passport to favour in Lancashire. I was also aware that clerical appointments made with apparently unwarranted speed in Leeds had not been forgotten. The clergy of Liverpool were bound to have misgivings and without the confidence of his priests a bishop cannot function. Unless he is accepted as the father by priests and people he is bound to fail. Paternalism is now a term of abuse but as St. Paul reminded the Ephesians, all paternity in heaven and earth is named from God.

I had expected to have to face many much greater issues than the cathedral but once in Liverpool I found that apart from the need for more grammar and secondary modern schools (this was before the advent of comprehensive schools) there were few problems. The welcome of priests and laity left me in no doubt that the Liverpool tradition of love and loyalty for their archbishop remained strong. I could not have been given a warmer welcome if, like most of my predecessors, I had been a Lancashire man. With so few difficulties to face I was able to give my attention to the cathedral much earlier than I had expected. My fellow bishops asked me as soon as my appointment had been announced whether I would 'scrap' the cathedral. It is worth recording that in Liverpool itself not a single person ever mentioned that possibility. The people of Liverpool had lived for generations with the idea of building a cathedral. The old were determined to make great personal sacrifices to achieve their goal. Those who picture the poor watching with angry resentment as a new church arises know nothing of Catholics. For them the church is their house and God's. Those who protest about new churches are so out of touch with Catholic life that they also put it about that Catholic parents don't really want Catholic schools for their children.

The curial offices to which I went each day were the only part of the old workhouse which had not been demolished. In these spacious offices all the administrative work of the diocese was done. The whole of the bottom floor was occupied by the office of Monsignor Turner who was the personification of the hope of 'a cathedral in our time'. He had devoted most of his priestly life to collecting funds for the metropolitan cathedral. He began his work in 1935 and did not retire until the cathedral was completed in 1967. Writing about his work Monsignor Turner gave a glimpse of the enthusiasm of his supporters. Apart from the many benefactors who could afford to subscribe one thousand pounds to become Founders there was an army of humble Catholics, mainly old age pensioners or school-children, who devoted their spare time to collecting waste paper, silver paper, milk-bottle tops and used postage stamps. Thousands of Catholics paid a pound to have their names inscribed in the Golden Book of the cathedral. Several chalices were made from jewellery and wedding rings presented in memory of relatives who had died without achieving their ambition of seeing the new cathedral.

Within a few days of taking possession of the see of Liverpool I resolved to concentrate all effort on completing the crypt and putting it into daily use as a temporary cathedral. At this time the crypt was still in much the same condition as it had been when the war put an end to building operations. Throughout the war one man had remained on duty. John Tiernan had been one of the small team which began work in the 1930s. He was still at his post (but now as clerk of works) when the new cathedral was solemnly opened nearly forty years later. Deliberately putting aside all consideration of the eventual shape of the building the cathedral committee was asked to concentrate all resources on the completion of the crypt. Mr. Scott was instructed to produce plans for the floor-paving. The organ well was converted into a sacristy and a wooden sanctuary was improvised. The archbishop's throne was brought from the old pro-cathedral.

The crypt was vast. Whether or not the Lutyens design would have produced a Christian building is a matter of opinion but there can be no dispute about the nobility of the crypt. It was not, of course, designed for the uses to which it was now to be put. The body of the temporary cathedral was designed as a processional way in which the clergy would form ranks before ascending to the cathedral proper. Here are some notes made by Adrian Scott to indicate the extent of the work required to convert the crypt into a temporary cathedral. Mr. Scott was a reluctant co-operator in these building operations. He was now an old man and must have regarded the new project as his architectural death warrant. Which indeed it was. Apart from the admitted poverty of his design for the new cathedral—for which we cannot fairly blame him without knowing his instructions relative to the original Lutyens plans— he did not give the impression of being in love with his foster child. Here are the notes which under pressure he prepared for the souvenir programme of the opening of the crypt. It gives some idea of the colossal proportions of the Lutyens cathedral. It must be remembered that this section, impressive and beautiful as it is, was no more than a crypt to be used as an ante-chamber to the cathedral and a burial place for the archbishops.

The carrying up of the existing complicated brick structure to a uniform level and the formation of an enormous paved and water-proof floor slab of some 32,000 sq. ft. complete with drainage and lighting systems. This involved the use of some 6¼ million bricks. The installation of a complete new floor heating system with the mains accommodated in the existing ducts below the Crypt floor, all leading to the new heating chamber. This involved the laying of about 7 miles of copper coils buried in a cement screed. The laying on this screed of 20,000 sq. ft. of marble paving to the two Chapels, processional way, and relic chapel. The patterned paving being in three shades of English purbeck freestone with a non-slip finish. The installation of a complete electric lighting system to the whole of the Crypt involving 8¼ miles of cable, together with special candelabra fittings to all the principal parts. The formation of a large new two-storied underground heating chamber which has been accommodated in a large existing quarry pit in the rock adjoining the Crypt. This is now nearing completion. The insertion of a new floor and roof to the original organ pit to form a new, large priests' sacristy with a strong room below and other sacristy accommodation adjoining. This involved the installation of a penum ventilation system for these underground rooms with no windows, with all the necessary ventilation ducts and plant and large structural inlet and outlet ducts leading to the outer walls. The installation of bronze metal windows and lead light glazing to all the windows. The provision of external and internal doors, the fixing of these being deferred till the existing structure has had time to dry out after many years of exposure to the elements. Meanwhile a lot of structural work was being done on the raising of the north west staircase to the same level as the existing north east staircase, prior to the completion of the large unfinished north sacristy which is being converted into an assembly hall.

The thought which led to the completion of the crypt was a simple one. In the diocese of Liverpool there had been constant talk of the metropolitan cathedral for two generations. It seemed obvious that there would still be no cathedral for many years. The astonishing building techniques which enabled the cathedral to be completed in less than ten years had not been envisaged. That is why I decided to let the priests and people enjoy the use of at least part of the cathedral for which they had made such great sacrifices for so long. Our forefathers built cathedrals for posterity. Modern Christians are less content to leave their children's grandchildren to enjoy the fruits of their self-sacrifice. In a pastoral letter read at the end of August 1958 in all the churches of the diocese I gave the dramatic news that the people of Liverpool were about to see some practical return for their money:

When I wrote to you last September I used these words: "Please God, you are soon going to see something really worthwhile." Now I can say: "Thank God, a crypt chapel will be open next month on the feast of Christ the King." That is the wonderful news I have for you today. Now let me tell you more about what has been happening. Last year I decided to concentrate on the crypt chapel. This does not mean that we are going to abandon hope of a great metropolitan cathedral. It means only that for the past year all work on the site has been directed to one objective. This objective was to provide without delay a spacious chapel, a permanent home for the Blessed Sacrament where Holy Mass will be offered day by day. As I told you last year, it is time that your generosity was rewarded and that you enjoyed the fruits of the sacrifices you have made. You will be astonished when you see the beauty of the crypt chapel. The workmen grew enthusiastic as the inspired dream of the architect took shape round them. Throughout the war years the crypt was waterlogged and desolate. Now it is alive with the cheerful sounds of busy labour.

An army of skilled men is at work. You will not see any mass-production in our cathedral. Every stone has come from the hands of craftsmen who respect the granite they fashion. But of the hardest work there is no evidence to be seen. Beneath the polished marble of the floor the rock foundation has been hewn for pipes and wires to be laid for the lighting and heating of the building. This vast operation is now finished. The feast of Christ the King will be the great day of the formal opening.

The opening of the crypt was made the occasion of a week of celebrations. It was important to give all the priests and people of Lancashire an opportunity of seeing what had been accomplished. This would stimulate continued interest in the plan to build the metropolitan cathedral. This scheme nearly defeated itself because everyone was so struck by the severe beauty of the improvised crypt/cathedral that some asked why we could not be satisfied with what we had now. This of course, was only a passing reaction to the first delighted sight of the finished crypt.

The following extracts from the souvenir programme give some idea of the excitement in the diocese when the opening of the completed crypt was announced. The first is from Monsignor Adamson, the Vicar General:

> The Clergy Day was undoubtedly one of the highlights of the 'Cathedral Crypt Week'. Some 400 priests from all parts of the archdiocese, together with 70 clerical students from Upholland College, gathered for the Pontifical High Mass sung by His Grace. There have been many great gatherings of the clergy at the pro-cathedral but on this occasion although the ceremony took place in the confined space of a crypt chapel, one sensed a spaciousness and a cathedral-like atmosphere which was something new and inspiring to the clergy of the diocese. It was singularly appropriate that on the occasion of this first clergy Mass in the crypt there should take place the solemn veneration of the sacred pallium recently received from Rome by the archbishop as metropolitan of the north. It was deeply impressive to witness the whole body of the clergy, led by the Chapter and dignitaries of the diocese, coming to the sanctuary at the end of the Mass to venerate the pallium as the sacred emblem of archiepiscopal authority in communion with the Holy See. The day was further made memorable by the election, a few hours previously, of the new Supreme Pontiff, John XXIII.

After the week of rejoicing the crypt was little used except for pontifical functions which hitherto had been held in the pro-cathedral. There was Mass at midday each day well attended by students and teachers from the university. Apart from this the crypt soon ceased to be a centre of interest or even a place of pilgrimage. A crypt however splendid is not a cathedral. I was pressed to make a fresh announcement about the cathedral with the least possible delay. I found out what is meant by the expression 'to think furiously'. I did a great deal of thinking and, to be sure, a great deal of praying. The Scott plans had now become as remote from reality as those of Lutyens. It would be folly to allow any more money to be spent on the present scheme. In the souvenir programme published after the opening of the crypt I flew a kite in a short article called "The Archbishop's Dreams":

In my dreams I see many buildings and they are not castles in the air. One day—and I have in mind a day in our own time—there will be a metropolitan cathedral either on the piazza above the crypt or near the site at present occupied by the open-air altar. There is no question of not building a cathedral. A considerable sum of money has already been subscribed. This is a sacred trust and cannot be diverted to any other purpose however worthy. The alternatives in my dream cathedral are either a building which will cost millions of pounds and be completed in the twenty-first century or a small but noble cathedral church which will cost less than £1,000,000 and be ready some time during the next decade. An impressive cathedral could be built at comparatively low cost on condition that future generations were left to embellish it. It seems clear that if we are to build quickly and economically we must begin anew.

In my dreams I see the metropolitan cathedral precincts as a centre of Catholic culture. In a matter of months the great cathedral hall by the side of the crypt will be completed. This will not be a social centre on the model of a parish hall. Forming part of the crypt chapel it could not be used for games and dances. It will be used for music, lectures and meetings. There is every reason to hope that it will become a source of spiritual and intellectual power for the city and the county. You know how those who dream sometimes stir uneasily in their sleep before settling down with a smile to enjoy an obviously satisfying vision. I see in my vision a convent of Sisters devoted to the service of the cathedral and to the cultural life to which it will give rise. Among their many activities will be the fostering of vocations and the care of an enquiry centre and library. This almost empty site will soon be alive with architecture in tune with the adjacent university. But we must not sleep and dream. Within the next few months our dreams will be changed into plans. When those plans are ready I shall publish something more useful and satisfying than the story of my dreams.

I suggested to the cathedral committee that it might be a good plan to pay Mr. Scott for his drawings and put the cathedral design out to public competition which I understood would not cost much more than ten thousand pounds. The committee had realised that the Scott plan must be abandoned but asked if the competition might not also produce a cathedral which could not be built for less than forty million pounds. To this I had a very definite answer. One of the conditions of the competition would be that the bulding and its fixed fittings must not cost more than one million pounds at 1959 prices.

I knew nothing about architectural competitions but once I had the support of the committee I began to make enquiries. I was not prepared to agree to the appointment of assessors who might be artistically sound but theologically incompetent. A cathedral, after all, is not a factory or a power house. (Two years later the competition was won by an architect who had never built church or chapel but had a world-wide reputation as a builder of power houses.) I wrote to the secretary of the R.I.B.A. (Royal Institute of British Architects) with a proposal to hold an open competition under R.I.B.A. rules with only three assessors of whom I would be one. Of the two architects one must be a Catholic and the other an active member of some Church. Within a few days the R.I.B.A. accepted my conditions and mentioned that their president, Sir Basil Spence, architect of Coventry cathedral, would be honoured to serve. David Stokes who had done a great deal of school and church building in the south was accepted as the Catholic architect.

With little delay the two architects came to Liverpool to discuss the competition with the cathedral committee (to be known henceforth as the promoters). Sir Basil Spence had long experience of competitions both as assessor and competitor. He was quite sure that with a Catholic architect on the panel no mistake would be made. I was amazed at our frequent meetings how confident both architects were that the best designs would commend themselves. They anticipated little likelihood of disagreement between us when the actual judging took place. They laughed at my nightmare in which I saw myself in a minority of one against the two architects. "You will see," Basil Spence said repeatedly, "that you have absolutely nothing to fear." He was right. My fear, like most fear, was fear of the unknown. Theoretically, of course, it was possible that the experts would over-ride the judgment of the amateur. But their role was not to insist on the selection being made according to their personal preferences but to protect their fellow architects against a judge incapable of recognising true merit. That is why the

R.I.B.A. will sanction a competition only if architects are in a majority on the panel of judges.

There were fifty items in the list of conditions and instructions issued to a candidate on payment of a deposit of two guineas (returnable after his design had been submitted). The brochure contained a series of photographs—including aerial views of the site—showing the surrounding buildings and the existing crypt in some detail. Apart from general conditions common to all architectural competitions e.g. "a design shall be excluded . . . if a competitor shall disclose his identity or attempt to influence the decision," there were specific requirements of which the following are samples:

(4) The award of the Assessors will be accepted by the Promoters, and within two months of the date thereof the following premiums shall be paid in accordance therewith, viz:

To the author of the design placed 1st by the Assessors . £5,000
To the author of the design placed 2nd by the Assessors . £3,000
To the author of the design placed 3rd by the Assessors . £2,000

(11) Each design and the report accompanying it must be sent in without name, motto or distinguishing mark of any kind and accompanied by a letter signed by the competitor or joint competitors and contained in the official envelope issued with these conditions, properly sealed, stating that the design is his or her or their own personal work, and that the drawings have been prepared in his or their own offices, and under his or their own supervision. A successful competitor must be prepared to satisfy the assessors that he is the bona fide author of the design submitted.

A number will be placed on each drawing and on the report and envelope contained in each package, and the envelopes will not be opened until after the award has been made.

(23) The new Cathedral may be placed by competitors anywhere within the building lines on the site plan. The crypt which is being completed to the designs of the late Sir Edwin Lutyens and which will be finished by 1961, occupies a part of the site as can be seen from the plans and photographs. It is mostly underground and is roofed with a paved terrace. This crypt formed part of the design for a vast cathedral which is not to be built owing to the enormous cost and this competition is being held for an alternative design to provide a cathedral to supply the needs of this generation and which can be completed within a decade.

It is desired to leave competitors as free as possible as to the style and materials to be used and also as to the siting of the new Cathedral and therefore it is left to competitors to decide the best relationship between the Cathedral and the Crypt and whether the Crypt be wholly or partly covered by the Cathedral or be entirely independent. The only condition in this connection is that there must be at least one internal access for the public from the Cathedral to the Crypt of good dimensions so that it can be used with dignity by processions (this in no way precludes steps) and it will be an advantage if access is such that the magnificent Crypt can be used easily by people from the Cathedral. None of the accommodation asked for is to be placed in the Crypt which will provide additional chapels to those asked for.

(26) The High Altar is the focal point of the Cathedral. It should be raised on three steps and covered with a canopy (suspended or on columns). It should be free standing and well away from any obstructions at the back. The Altar should be so designed that it will be possible for the Celebrant to offer Mass with his back to the people (the common practice) or facing the people (Roman Basilica style).

The brochure was prefaced by a letter from myself (*qua* archbishop not *qua* assessor). This was written at the suggestion of Sir Basil Spence. He said that although such a letter would not bind competitors it could infuse a spirit into the technical jargon in which the rest of the document had to be written. He said that he and his colleagues had found the letter written by the bishop most helpful when they entered the competition for Coventry cathedral (which, of course, Sir Basil won).

Letter from The Archbishop of Liverpool

My dear Architect,

The Metropolitan Cathedral of Christ the King will present a unique problem in design. The plans of Sir Edwin Lutyens were abandoned because the cost, after the second world war, had become prohibitively high. But his building, begun before the war, was resumed ten years later and the crypt is now almost completed. Not only by reason of its majestic beauty but because it has already cost over half-a-million pounds the crypt must not be abandoned. In some way it will have to be incorporated in the new cathedral.

That is your task. While free to design a building in any style, you must allow easy access between the crypt and the main building. If the crypt were virtually a half-built cathedral you might well be disheartened. But the crypt is mainly underground. It does not preclude an entirely new and distinctive design. Regard the crypt, therefore, not as an obstacle but as a challenge. The future use of the crypt need not pre-occupy you. The conditions make it clear that the siting of the high altar is for you to decide. The crypt, therefore, may be beneath it, as in existing cathedrals, or at the opposite end.

The high altar is the central feature of every Catholic church. It must be the focus of the new building. The trend of the liturgy is to associate the congregation ever more closely with the celebrant of the Mass. The ministers at the altar should not be remote figures. They must be in sight of the people with whom they offer the sacrifice.

Holy Mass is the great mystery of faith. The high altar is not an ornament to embellish the cathedral building. The cathedral, on the contrary, is built to enshrine the altar of sacrifice. The attention of all who enter should be arrested and held by the altar.

It may help you to know that the Holy Eucharist is not only a sacrifice but a sacrament. The bread consecrated at Holy Mass is given to the faithful in Holy Communion. But, in addition, the Blessed Sacrament is reserved both for the sick and for those wishing to receive Holy Communion when Mass is not being celebrated. During the day many come to visit Our Lord in the tabernacle. The Blessed Sacrament Chapel, therefore, should be the object of special thought and care. It is next in importance to the high altar itself.

The Assessors will not judge this competition in the light of any preconceived but undisclosed ideas. The conditions here set down will guide them as they must guide you. The figure of £1,000,000 obviously restricts the choice of materials. But this should not dismay you. New cathedrals need not be inferior to the old. You can use techniques which were not available to those who built the splendid cathedrals in the Middle Ages.

During the next twelve months the priests and people of Liverpool will beg God to enlighten you. Also you will have the powerful prayers of our children. It is for them and their children's children that you will build. May Christ the King inspire you to create a cathedral church worthy of His Holy Name.

†JOHN C. HEENAN,
Archbishop of Liverpool.
This letter does not form part of the conditions.

The number of applications for the brochure was amazingly high. I now realised why a charge of two guineas had been made. If the brochure had been free we would have received thousands instead of hundreds of demands for copies. After a pause of some weeks competitors began to send in questions and requests for clarification. Many were naturally repetitive but no less than 361 separate points were raised. The second brochure (which then had to be sent to everyone who had received the first) carried another preface—again at the suggestion of Basil Spence.

Letter from The Archbishop of Liverpool

My dear Architect,

In sending the answers to your questions I take the opportunity of thanking you for entering the competition for the building of the Metropolitan Cathedral of Christ the King. We have received 800 applications for the Conditions. The candidates represent no less than 25 countries. The largest group naturally is from the British Isles but considerable numbers are from other lands. These include Canada (67), South Africa (48), Australia (25), Rhodesia (22), Malaya (11) and Uganda (10).

It is most encouraging that this competition has aroused world wide interest. That many architects have already given deep thought to the project is clear from the questions which you will read. The Assessors have done their best to provide the information requested. If the answers are often terse you will understand that we were afraid lest our answers might create too many new conditions.

You have already noticed that the mandatory 'must' has been used sparingly in setting out the conditions. We are anxious that no architect should be excluded through neglect of some un-important feature of the building. We have left you as free as possible to use your imagination. After the winning design has been chosen it will still be possible for the architect to make any number of alterations and adjustments.

For your consolation you should know that the Assessors will look first for a splendid conception. You should not, therefore, worry unduly about the many details suggested in the 'should' clauses. We have been deliberately vague about the High Altar and Sanctuary which, as I have already told you, should be the focal point of your design. Liturgical practice is developing continually in the Catholic Church. That is why we have asked you to design the High Altar in such a way that Holy Mass may be celebrated from either side. This is the explanation of the apparent contradiction in the siting of the Archbishop's Throne and the Canons' Stalls. I hope that the answers to your questions will resolve any doubt you may have had.

I think I should tell you that the name of the Relics Chapel in the Crypt is misleading. It is, in fact, the burial place of two former Archbishops of Liverpool. That is why this chapel cannot be moved. But there is no reason why you should not allow for an entrance to this chapel from the main cathedral building.

We have asked only for block plans of the proposed convent and clergy house because we are not yet certain of the part they will play in the life of the Cathedral. I advise you not to concentrate unduly on the ancillary buildings but on the grand design of the Cathedral itself.

The prayers of our priests and people will be with you in the coming months as you perfect your plans. I have no doubt that you will receive rich inspiration in your work for the glory of God.

† JOHN C. HEENAN,

Archbishop of Liverpool.

This letter does not form part of the conditions.

Many of the questions put by competitors were purely technical and would be of interest only to architects. There are other questions which even the general reader is likely to find fascinating. Some questions (and answers) are unintentionally amusing. The questions give incidentally an indication of the complexity of the task facing competitors. It should be remembered that most of those asking questions were strangers to Liverpool. Some had never been to England. The following selection omits all the purely technical enquiries:

Q. 4.   Should more than one solution be entered, will it be necessary to forward to you a deposit of two guineas in respect of each?

A.   Yes.

Q. 9.   We would like to be informed if there is any objection to a British architect submitting a design in association with an architect of Italian nationality. If this were to be permitted the scheme or schemes would be prepared jointly by the two parties.

A.   Any person or persons of any nationality or calling may collaborate in submitting a design with a person or persons who are eligible to compete. *In this event* the design must be submitted in the name or names of those eligible and the letter submitted under Clause (11) signed by them. The letter should give the name(s) of the collaborator(s) under the signature(s), thus 'in collaboration with'. In the event of publication these names will also be published.

Q. 24.   Is the use of artificial shading media, such as Zippatone, allowed on plans, elevations or sections?

A.   Yes.

Q. 29.   May shade and shadow be used on the drawings to show the modelling of curved surfaces?

A.   Yes.

Q. 35.   It would be helpful if competitors could be furnished with a precis of those municipal bye-laws which could affect the design of the Buildings.

Climatic conditions:

(a) The incidence and severity of the rainfall.

(b) Is there much snow?

(c) Any other relevant information, such as prevailing winds, etc.

A.   Competitors must themselves obtain any general information they may require.

Q. 48.   What is the load bearing capacity of:

(a) Rock subsoil?

(b) Soil overburden?

A.   (a) Good.

(b) Nil.

Q. 95.   Levels please, in the vicinity of the existing boiler house?

A.   Can be deduced from information supplied.

Q. 123. Is limited modification to the Crypt allowed. For example, could the Relics Chapel be re-positioned in the Crypt?

A.   No. Only to provide access.

Q. 144. When the Mass begins is it most desirable that the Celebrant and attendant priests appear directly in front of the congregation and ascend directly up steps in front of the High Altar or can they ascend from the sides?

[296]

A. The High Altar should be accessible from the front, back and sides.

Q. 116. Would a layout of the Sanctuary similar to the layout as proposed in Sir Edwin Lutyens's scheme be acceptable, that is, the relative positions of the High Altar, Canons' Stalls and Choir?

A. The position of the High Altar was never finally decided in Lutyens's cathedral.

Q. 178. What headroom is necessary for cathedral procession?

A. 12 feet minimum.

Q. 192. Clause 44: Is sanitary accommodation for women required in the Sacristy?

A. No.

Q. 194. Sect. No. 27: What is the route that the priests will take when they move the Blessed Sacrament from its chapel to the High Altar?

A. The shortest.

Q. 196. Sect. No. 35: Where do the processions not originating in the Cathedral assemble?

A. Competitors need not concern themselves with this.

Q. 201. Can an approximate occupation programme be given, for typical week, for High Mass and the subsidiary chapels, by days and hours?

A. No.

Q. 230. When Mass is offered at the High Altar, does transubstantiation occur at the High Altar or at the Chapel of the Blessed Sacrament? If the latter is the case, should that part of the service be visible and audible from the main body of the nave?

A. At the High Altar.

Q. 235. Is public sanitary accommodation to be restricted to members of the congregation?

A. Yes.

Q. 243. If there are Holy Relics, at what distance must the High Altar be from them?

A. Not relevant to the competition.

Q. 249. Can the number of tourists visiting the completed cathedral be predicted and is any provision for their reception and circulation to be made?

A. No.

Q. 258. Would the Organisers please define what is meant by the requirement that the pulpit should be of reasonably large dimensions?

A.   No.

Q. 307. Does the site form part of a smokeless zone?

A.   Not yet, but probable.

Q. 354. Does the reference to Organ Pipes mean that an electric organ is to be precluded from the design, or is this a matter of choice for the competitors?

A.   Precluded.

CHAPTER

TWENTY-ONE

AT THE BEGINNING OF AUGUST 1960 ALL WAS READY FOR THE JUDGING
of the competition. The greatest problem had been to find premises in
which to display the drawings. Where could we find a building large
enough to put on display over three thousand exhibits on sheets of
double elephant size? This represented over two miles of drawings. In
addition there was the physical problem of mounting so many exhibits.
As so often since my days as a curate in Barking I took my problem to
the Ursuline nuns. The Prioress of the Ursuline Convent, Wimbledon,
took less than a minute to decide that her community could handle the
whole competition without any assistance. A Sister was appointed
secretary to supervise the whole operation. She planned the hanging of
the drawings in line after line on the walls of halls, classrooms and even
cloak-rooms of the convent school which had recently been considerably
enlarged. Energetic young Sisters joyfully undertook the enormous task
of arranging the display of drawings. By the end of the first week in
August all was in order. The plans were in place. The envelopes containing the names of the competitors corresponding with the numbers
on the exhibits were locked in a safe which would be opened only after
our decision had been made.

I accepted the hospitable invitation of the Ursulines to stay at the
convent while the judging was in progress. It meant that early and late
I could study the exhibits. After a few days of living with these plans
they became as familiar as family photographs. I have never served on
a jury but I imagine the experience must be similar to judging a competition. In both cases the public is not in a position to evaluate the
result. It is given the verdict but not told anything about the discussion

in the jury room. Without stretching the analogy to absurd lengths an assessor is a jury member with the difference that surprisingly little discussion takes place between the assessors. For the very first day or so we spent from nine in the morning until nine at night just moving singly from plan to plan. By the end of the first day I realised that what the architects had foretold was proving to be uncannily accurate. They had said that after a second or third brief inspection, that is by the end of the very first day, sheep and goats would have begun to identify themselves.

It is doubtless possible to produce attractive pictures which bear little resemblance to the plans they illustrate. This might deceive non-architects among assessors and for this reason perspective drawings are forbidden. The architects made no attempt to influence my judgment and scrupulously refrained from calling my attention to the merits of any particular design. Occasionally I asked one of them to sketch in perspective a building I could not visualise. It soon became obvious that certain designs were not worth further study while to others we found ourselves constantly returning. We rarely spoke except at meal-times when amazingly soon we began to refer to number 101 or 56 or 222 as old friends. I would not have believed it possible to become familiar with so many designs in so short a time. Those of great merit kept intruding themselves while others failed to cause a flicker of interest in any of us.

After a couple of days we were able to begin the process of elimination. We moved potential winners into the main hall so that we could give them closer inspection. As the layman I was enormously impressed by the demeanour of my colleagues. They completely justified the reassurance given by Sir Basil that I need have no fear that the professionals would 'gang up' against the amateur. It seems incredible that within forty-eight hours we were able to agree on the twenty or so designs worth detailed study. This first segregation did not, of course, represent a rigid or final choice. Each of us would go back to the other designs and occasionally bring one in to replace a design found wanting on further inspection. One or two splendid designs were obviously impossible to produce at the stipulated price. A quantity surveyor and a consultant engineer officially appointed to assist us were sent for when we had reduced the field to a round dozen. One plan which I found especially attractive was disqualified at a glance by the surveyor. Later he did his calculations and found that the building would have cost three times as much as the conditions permitted.

[300]

By the middle of the month we had chosen our three prize winners, six to be highly commended and a further twelve for mention. These commendations were not given lightly. Basil Spence and David Stokes said that it could mean much to an architect to receive special mention in an international competition. It was not a prize but it was compensation for the time and money spent on producing plans. When we had agreed on our choices—there was unanimity in deciding the winning number—we sent for the Sister with the envelopes containing the names. There was considerable tension while we awaited her disclosure. If we had chosen an architect with little experience or one living at the other end of the world there would be many problems. (The winner of the second prize was a young man from Kuala Lumpur.) It was no small relief to learn that the winner was an architect of vast experience with offices in London.

We managed to make contact the same evening with the winning competitor, Mr. Frederick Gibberd (on completion of the cathedral he was knighted). Genuinely surprised by his success, he told us how his design had been conceived. He was the head of the large firm of architects responsible for the planning of Harlow New Town in Essex. One of his Catholic partners Mr. Goalen (who had also entered the competition) designed the Catholic church in Harlow and Frederick Gibberd attended the solemn opening by the Bishop of Brentwood. Mass was a new experience for Gibberd, a Congregationalist. He found himself wondering about liturgy and ritual. Suddenly he remembered the competition for Liverpool cathedral for which he had entered but about which he had done nothing. During the Mass he became increasingly conscious of what was to him a new concept of liturgical space. After Mass he hurried home and told his wife that he intended to shut himself in his room until he had produced plans for Liverpool cathedral. He could scarcely believe that he was the winner. It was 15th August, feast of the Assumption of the Blessed Virgin.

The reception of the result of the competition was generous. There was general recognition that considerations of cost forced most architects to rely more on concrete than stone or brick. We delayed the press conference for four days to give the architect time to make a model of his cathedral. Since the chief idea he wished to express was spaciousness the production of a model was self-defeating. The human eye would never see the whole of the cathedral except from a great distance. The little model provoked mirth. "Just like a wigwam," said some. "More like a pagoda," said others. It was compared to a space ship and a rocket. One wag christened it the Mersey Funnel. Two loyal Catholics met Monsignor McKenna the future cathedral administrator after Mass the following day. "What do you think of the plan for the new cathedral?" he asked them. "The papers say the Archbishop thinks it's lovely," the man replied, "and he's no mug."

The report in the *Liverpool Post*, typical of the whole press, is given fairly fully for the sake of those who have never seen the new cathedral.

Liverpool's Roman Catholics will see their Metropolitan Cathedral of Christ the King completed in five years' time—and it will be a circular cathedral of startling modern design, swooping up in a conical shape to a height of 340 feet—only seven feet lower than the Anglican Cathedral and twenty feet lower than St. Paul's. The exciting shape was revealed yesterday when the first drawings were made avilable. Its soaring lines make it look like something ready to take off for the skies—a space-age cathedral.

Mr. Gibberd's concept of the new cathedral is a conical shape emphasising the vastness of the main shell of the building. Rising 340 feet above the Liverpool scene, the cathedral is topped by a huge crown of sixteen aluminium crosses. It has an underground car park and lifts for invalids from the entrance porch into the main body.

Mr. Gibberd, a Nonconformist, who has specialised in housing and civil design, told me of his plans for the new cathedral in London yesterday: "I think the design for the cathedral has very much to do with religion," he said. "I based the design on the idea that there should be a sanctuary in the centre with the high altar and that people should be grouped three-quarters of the way round and as close in contact as possible."

The result is a central altar round which 3,000 people can be accommodated, none of whom are more than seventy feet from the steps of the sanctuary.

"There are no pillars in the way and there is a tremendous intimate link between the holy places and the people themselves," said Mr. Gibberd. "It is not like a theatre. People are not going to watch a spectacle, they are taking part in it."

To increase the immediacy by giving a clear, uninterrupted view, the Derbyshire marble floor is dished down to the sanctuary, which is itself raised on steps. From outside, a series of sixteen slim, soaring, reinforced concrete ribs rise from the ground to above the main body in a vast conical shape which extends in the centre into the tower. This tower which rises above a copper roof, will be finished in coloured, one-inch thick glass and concrete so that a coloured shaft of scintillating light shines down on to the altar steps.

The difficulty of overcoming the lack of direction in a circular church has been overcome by erecting a huge triangular entrance porch, which also contains the bells. Electrically-operated bronze doors and a heated curtain of warm air give access suddenly from a 'tunnel' approach to the vast shell of the main body of the cathedral. Commenting on the winning design—which carries an award of £5,000 for the architect—the assessors said: "This was, in the view of the judges, clearly ahead of the field. The design is full of imagination and powerfully expresses the Kingship of Christ. The conception is itself a crown and the suggestion of the crowning of Christ is revealed in the details of the building with logic and restraint."

The Times gave a more guarded but still favourable report of the winning design after its architectural correspondent had visited the exhibition of the prize-winning and highly-recommended designs in the Building Centre, Bloomsbury, at the end of August. The conditions as originally published had promised that an exhibition of all designs would be held in Liverpool after the competition. On reflection it was seen that it would be enormously expensive to mount such an exhibition. It was therefore decided to hold the exhibition *in situ* at the Wimbledon convent at the conclusion of the competition. This involved no expense. It merely gave a great deal more work to the nuns, but as always, the Ursulines made light of the inconvenience when hundreds from all over England came to see the plans.

When the result of the competition was announced the priests and people of Liverpool were united in their sense of relief. They had been dismayed by the rumours of the rising cost of the original design which varied from the most modest estimate of twenty-seven million pounds to the more realistic figure of fifty million pounds. Not everyone was enthusiastic about the new design but all agreed that it was good to have put an end to speculation and be engaged on a scheme which could be realised in a few years and at reasonable cost. Nobody suggested that it would have been better to abandon the whole project of a metropolitan cathedral for the north. If there had been no cathedral project in existence in 1960 there would have been no overwhelming demand to provide one but there can be no doubt whatever that having grown up with the idea of 'a cathedral in our time' the Catholics of Liverpool were delighted that their hopes were about to be fulfilled.

I did not need to appeal to the people of Liverpool to hold to their resolution to build the cathedral. It was my more congenial task to persuade them that, although cheap by comparison with the old, the new design was not unworthy of a great diocese. Those who had seen the crypt in all its massive beauty recognised that concrete would lack the majesty of the Lutyens granite. There was nevertheless satisfaction that the Church was prepared to use a modern idiom in a cathedral which would dominate the university campus filled with glass and concrete buildings in the contemporary style. Two weeks after the result of the competition was announced the following letter was read from every pulpit in the diocese:

> The new Cathedral has been very much in the news during recent weeks. At last Archbishop Downey's slogan 'A cathedral in our time' seems likely to come true. After so many years of disappointment your generosity is about to be rewarded. In less than five years, please God, we shall have our cathedral. It was well worth while to hold a competition. During the past year you have prayed that the architects who entered the competition would be guided to produce a cathedral in honour of Christ the King of which Catholics might be proud. I believe that your prayers have been answered.
>
> When the people of the north see this great cathedral rising they will all—non-Catholic as well as Catholic—share our pride. I wish that I could find words to describe the beauty of the new building. Most of you will have seen the artist's impression which was rapidly sketched for the press. The drawing gives you very little idea of what the cathedral will really look like. In time for the Feast of Christ the King we shall have carefully drawn pictures and a new model. Then you will see why I say that your prayers have been answered.

At the end of the year I wrote a pastoral letter announcing the start of the building operations on the cathedral site:

> Picture an old age pensioner coming to the cathedral buildings with a hundred pound notes wrapped in newspaper. He hands it

[304]

to Monsignor Turner and says, "Here are my life's savings. Thank God for sparing me until I could collect a hundred pounds for our cathedral." This poor man is typical of very many old people who have dreamed of the new cathedral down the years. Daily they come with a few shillings, a bag of silver paper, a bundle of newspapers or a sack full of tin foil from milk bottles. Some of them can scarcely walk under the weight they carry. It needs little imagination to see Christ the King smiling on them as He did on the widow who brought her mite to the temple. I have great news for them and for you all. The building of the new cathedral is about to start. Work will not begin tomorrow because it is a Holy Day of Obligation. But on Tuesday the 2nd January the workmen will arrive. Many of you have seen the model kindly lent by Mr. Gibberd, the architect. Thousands of children from our schools have been to study it. They have the same spirit as the old people. They, too, have been collecting silver paper and tin foil. But in their enthusiasm they have also organised little bazaars in their schools, held concerts and made collections. They can now see what the new cathedral is going to look like. If you saw the model you know that the cathedral is not an ugly modern experiment. It is a lofty majestic cathedral which will translate the spirit of the builders of the old cathedrals of England into terms of today.

You know how I hate writing about money. But today I do so with enthusiasm. The Metropolitan Cathedral of Christ the King is at last about to become a reality. Barring a war or other disasters, the first Holy Mass will be offered there in the year 1966. But if your generosity were to fail, the whole project would have to be abandoned. I beg you, therefore, priests and people, to unite in this final effort to give the diocese and the north a worthy cathedral.

As soon as the diocese was committed to the new plan the cathedral committee was reorganised and enlarged. There was no shortage of liturgical scholars among the clergy and we were not without qualified laymen to give guidance in technical and financial matters. We were particularly fortunate in being able to call on Mr. Hall, the Principal of the Liverpool School of Building and Mr. Christopher Taylor, a lawyer of cultivated taste and wide business experience. The musical and acoustic problems were the special care of Dom Ronnie Wright, O.S.B., who had supervised the building of the organ at Ampleforth

Abbey. Regular weekly meetings, frequently attended by Mr. Gibberd and his experts, were held in the curial offices near the site. They were unlike any meetings I had hitherto attended. Nobody made speeches or bothered about details of procedure. At every meeting during the twelve months before building began practical decisions had to be taken. The texture and colour of material, the pattern of the paving, the positioning of drain pipes, the choice of artists for the coloured glass (there is more glass in this cathedral than in Chartres), the shape of lamp stands, the selection of craftsmen for iron work, details of heating, ventilation and seating—all these and a hundred other questions had to be decided by the committee.

It was instructive to watch the architect's tactics in dealing with this committee. Frederick Gibberd had never before been in such close contact with priests or Catholic laity. He nevertheless seemed immediately at home with them. He discovered that even the clerical members of the committee were surprisingly civilised. He felt reassured that the committee would not attempt to usurp his functions as architect. Each member of the committee stuck to his last. Monsignor Turner, the doyen, supplied the history of the building from its earliest days and in the smallest detail. On more than one occasion the information he provided saved us from repeating old mistakes. Monsignor Adamson and Monsignor McKenna were familiar with all that had gone on during the Downey and Godfrey years. It was useful to be told exactly what had been promised or agreed by earlier archbishops who had dealt personally with Lutyens or Scott. I was determined that there would be no private agreements between Mr. Gibberd and myself. This proved advantageous when I was appointed to Westminster with the building only half completed. Our meetings were never acrimonious. If the committee made no attempt to usurp the prerogatives of the architect he, in turn, was carefully reticent about matters which the clients alone had the right to decide. He would not insist on the employment of contractors or artists of his own preference but neither would he tolerate attempts by the committee to re-design his plans. We could comment, we could approve or we could reject. "But," Frederick Gibberd often used to say, "a committee is not an architect. It is a quite different kind of animal. A committee cannot draw plans."

One of the unique features of the Gibberd design was the colossal lantern to crown the cathedral, dominate the university and, at night, be a beacon visible from the sea beyond the harbour. For a long time many of us expected that the glass would be supplied by Buckfast

Abbey where the monks had a reputation for tasteful glass-making. Before any decision was made I paid a visit to Coventry Cathedral. This was partly to redeem a promise made to Sir Basil Spence and partly to study the Coventry glass. I was speechless when I saw the glowing beauty of the windows. I was especially impressed by the baptistry window. I was told that it had been designed by John Piper and made by Patrick Reyntiens. I resolved that if the committee were agreeable these talented artists would be commissioned to produce our lantern. A few days later the committee went on pilgrimage to Coventry and returned convinced that Piper and Reyntiens must be approached. Mr. Gibberd, himself a Coventry man, expressed great satisfaction at our choice. I was still in Liverpool while the main decisions, of which by far the most important was to appoint Taylor Woodrow the main contractors, were taken. From the window of my room in the curial offices I daily watched the swift rise of this exciting building. I was not destined to stay to see the end. I was translated to Westminster and had to leave Archbishop Beck, my successor, to find the money to pay the bills I had authorised. He bore me no grudge. When the solemn opening of the cathedral was due he requested the Holy Father to appoint me Papal Legate.

CHAPTER

TWENTY-TWO

DURING THE TWO YEARS FROM AUGUST 1961 UNTIL I LEFT LIVERPOOL
for Westminster my energy was directed, apart from routine pastoral
activity within the diocese, to Christian Unity and the Second Vatican
Council. Before the Council opened I had already begun to attend
meetings of the Secretariat for Unity in Rome. Now with the approval
of the bishops I set up a similar secretariat at home. This was desirable
not only to make our activities more effective but to give some public
sign that we were in earnest about our ecumenical declarations. Ten
years later nobody would have doubted our sincerity but before the
Council it was often assumed both at home and on the continent that
English Catholics were unfriendly to all their fellow Christians but
especially to Anglicans. To understand this it is necessary to recall the
anomalous preconciliar years when the relationship now taken for
granted among Christians was unthinkable.

It is not necessary to be deeply read in history to know that in the
sixteenth century religious faith was regarded as identical with loyalty
to the crown. *Cujus regio ejus religio* (a nation's religion is that of its
monarch) was like a family motto to the Tudors. For Protestants under
Mary and Catholics under Elizabeth life was precarious. It is easy to
forget in these tolerant days that hostility was handed down in families.
Sectarianism was dominant in Britain until citizens were drawn together
by wars for national survival. Modern religious rivalry had little to do
with the coming of the Irish workers. These immigrants came mainly
from the south of Ireland whose people are notably tolerant on religious

if not on political issues. Contrary to the conviction of continental Catholics bigotry among English Protestants was bitter until the present century. Thus opposition to the marriage of the young Queen Victoria to Prince Albert was due initially not to his German nationality but to the fact that so many of the Coburgs had Catholic relatives. Anxiety was increased because, although a good Protestant, King Leopold, the queen's uncle, had married a Catholic princess.

Apart from Cardinal Hinsley no Catholic archbishop had been on close terms with Anglicans since the restoration of the hierarchy in 1850. Manning, a convert parson, Vaughan, a Catholic aristocrat, and Bourne, the son of a convert, had all been tetchy in their dealings with the Protestant establishment. Cardinal Hinsley who came to Westminster at the age of seventy was like a Pope John born out of due time. During his early years in Westminster he was not known outside his own fold but his powerful broadcasts during the second world war made his name familiar throughout the country. He was passionately opposed to Hitlerism with which he sedulously refused to identify the German people. He was more than willing to lend his voice and influence to the effort to overthrow the Nazis. In this he was anxious to co-operate with other religious denominations to an unprecedented extent. As a result of his policy of friendship a letter was published in *The Times* signed jointly by the archbishops of Canterbury and York, the Moderator of the Free Church Federal Council and the Cardinal. It appeared on 21st December, 1940:

Sir,
The present evils in the world are due to the failure of nations and peoples to carry out the laws of God. No permanent peace is possible in Europe unless the principles of the Christian religion are made the foundations of national policy and of all social life. This involves regarding all nations as members of one family under the Fatherhood of God.

We accept the five points of Pope Pius XII as carrying out this principle:
(1) The assurance to all nations of their right to life and independence. The will of one nation to live must never mean the sentence of death passed upon another. When this equality of rights has been destroyed, attacked, or threatened order demands that reparation shall be made, and the measure and extent of that reparation is determined, not by the sword nor by the arbitrary

[309]

decision of self-interest, but by the rules of justice and reciprocal equity.

(2)   This requires that nations be delivered from the slavery imposed upon them by the race for armaments and from the danger that material force, instead of serving to protect the right, may become an overbearing and tyrannical master. The order thus established requires a mutually agreed organic progressive disarmament, spiritual as well as material, and security for the effective implementing of such an agreement.

(3)   Some judicial institution which shall guarantee the loyal and faithful fulfilment of conditions agreed upon and which shall in case of recognised need revise and correct them.

(4)   The real needs and just demands of nations and populations and racial minorities to be adjusted as occasion may require, even where no strictly legal right can be established, and a foundation of mutual confidence to be thus laid, whereby many incentives to violent action will be removed.

(5)   The development among peoples and their rulers of that sense of deep and keen responsibility which weighs human statutes according to the sacred and inviolable standards of the laws of God. They must hunger and thirst after justice and be guided by that universal love which is the compendium and most general expression of the Christian ideal.

With these basic principles for the ordering of international life we would associate five standards by which economic situations and proposals may be tested:

(1)   Extreme inequality in wealth and possession should be abolished;

(2)   Every child, regardless of race or class, should have equal opportunities of education, suitable for the development of his peculiar capabailities;

(3)   The family as a social unit must be safeguarded;

(4)   The sense of a Divine vocation must be restored to man's daily work;

(5)   The resources of the earth should be used as God's gifts to the whole human race, and used with due consideration for the needs of the present and future generations.

We are confident that the principles which we have enumerated would be accepted by rulers and statesmen throughout the British

Commonwealth of Nations and would be regarded as the true basis on which a lasting peace could be established.

COSMO CANTUAR,

Archbishop of Canterbury.

A. CARDINAL HINSLEY,

Archbishop of Westminster.

WALTER H. ARMSTRONG,

Moderator,

Free Church Federal Council.

WILLIAM EBOR,

Archbishop of York.

Today a joint letter from Church leaders would excite little interest or comment. This letter had a powerful effect on public opinion. It was the outcome of a new solidarity among believers which had begun with a movement founded by Cardinal Hinsley under the name of the Sword of the Spirit. In the summer of 1940 London was sheltering a number of exiled European governments and people. Among the French, Dutch, Belgians, Poles and Czechs there was a large proportion of Catholics. It was Cardinal Hinsley's plan to unite them and native British Catholics in an association for prayer, study and action. "Natural principles and the Christian way of life," he said, "are at stake in this war. We shall therefore fight for our cause till victory. After victory the reconstruction of Europe must be based upon these same natural and Christian principles." Christopher Dawson was appointed lay leader of the movement and Christians of every nationality and denomination were invited to co-operate. The Sword made a determined onslaught on such bigotry as still remained in wartime Britain. Looking back we can see that too much was expected too soon. Habits of generations cannot be discarded overnight. In May 1940 two vast meetings were held one of which was addressed by the Archbishop of Canterbury and the other by the Cardinal. This unprecedented co-operation between Anglicans and Catholics was expected to herald a new era. In fact it led to a temporary pause in joint Christian effort. The Catholics in the north—especially in Liverpool—were far from happy about the direction in which the Sword seemed to be pointing. Their more cautious approach was motivated by fear of religious indifferentism. They regarded it as dangerous for Catholics and Protestants to be members of the same religious organisation. When the constitutions were promulgated at the first annual general meeting in

[311]

1941 the Sword of the Spirit was an exclusively Catholic body. Full membership was open only to Catholics. The argument was that since the Sword was to uphold Catholic moral values it must be under the exclusive control of the hierarchy. Catholic bishops would have no right to give directions to those who did not acknowledge their authority. It was suggested that it would be safer to set up a parallel movement for non-Catholics under their own leaders.

This restrictive constitution was a painful rebuff to enthusiasts for Christian co-operation (later to be called ecumenists). They were saddened that the Catholic bishops feared a dilution of ethics if Protestant theologians were allowed a voice in laying down moral principles. The bishops' decision was not founded on prejudice. It arose from their conviction that there is no voice to speak with authority outside the Catholic Church. Before the coming of ecumenism Catholics were genuinely ignorant of the grave offence given to non-Catholics by this exclusiveness. On this occasion Catholics were not allowed to remain long unaware of the chagrin of their fellow Christians. The sensitively high Anglican *Church Times* published an indignant article under the title "Not Excalibur":

> The hopes engendered by the launching a year ago of the Sword of the Spirit Movement have not been fulfilled. The Movement was founded by Cardinal Hinsley, and adopted as its fundamental aim "the restoration in Europe of a Christian basis for both public and private life, by a return to the principles of international order and Christian freedom". What was unusual about the Movement, and excited unusual expectation, was that the organisers went out of their way to solicit the co-operation of Churchmen and Nonconformists. . . . The enthusiasm of those who were ready to co-operate with their Roman Catholic fellow Christians has had an unexpected cold douche.
>
> At the first annual meeting of the Movement, held in London last Saturday, it was made very plain that nothing which could be claimed to be a national Christian movement was to grow from the Sword of the Spirit. The secretary disclosed in public for the first time the details of the Constitution under which the Movement is in future to be operated. The rules allow non-Roman Catholic participants to march and cheer, but to have no real part in the Movement. At Saturday's meeting the secretary explained that its original purpose was to unite all men of good will in a crusade in

[312]

defence of the Christian tradition and natural law. It was a crusade under Roman Catholic leadership, with associated members from other communions. The secretary admitted that the term 'associated member' was not intended to imply difference of rights, but to distinguish Roman from other Christians. . . .

So far as Churchmen and Nonconformists are concerned, the Sword of the Spirit Movement, despite renewed allusions at the annual meeting to co-operation with 'the other Christian bodies', has now, alas! no more title to be considered in the light of a brave experiment in Christian collaboration than any other exclusively Roman Catholic organisation. The support of other Christians is accepted, almost as it were on sufferance, but neither corporately nor individually have they any *locus standi*, any say in the direction of policy. A great opportunity has been lost. In these days, above all, words must be supported by action, and fine sentiments butter no parsnips. The Sword of the Spirit Movement might have become a national Excalibur. Instead, those who have forged it and are wielding it have decided that it shall have no more significance or striking power than any other weapon of exclusively Roman Catholic piety and propaganda.

Such fighting words, however justified, might have made any further co-operation impossible. Fortunately Dr. Bell, Anglican Bishop of Chichester was more magnanimous than some of his friends. He wrote at once to the *Church Times*:

Sir,

I hope your readers will not rush to the conclusion that the hopes engendered a year ago are all in vain. Informal consultations have been and are proceeding as to possible ways and means for establishing a real co-operation, on equal terms, arising out of the Sword of the Spirit Movement, between Roman Catholics and non-Roman Catholics, with due regard for the dogmatic principles valued by each. Although difficulties exist, it would be a mistake to take it for granted that no way through can be found. Nor must the difficulties be assumed to be all on one side.

The Movement, as you point out, excited unusual expectations; given patience and a full understanding on all sides, there seems to me to be no reason why there should be any retreat.

In your leading article you speak of Excalibur. That sword had two mottoes, on one side of the blade, "Take me," on the other,

"Cast me away." When King Arthur took it, Merlin counselled him—

"Take thou and strike! the time to cast away is yet far off."

So, I trust, may the Sword of the Spirit be taken and used now as an instrument of real co-operation, on equal terms, between all Christians, by which to beat their foemen down.

These early misunderstandings sound trivial but to understand ecumenism in this country it is essential to know something of its English development. Mutual mistrust is a legacy inherited by the Protestants and Catholics of the British Isles. It would be misleading to suggest that those war-time Christians found it hard to co-operate because they were still brooding on the sufferings of their ancestors in the fires of Smithfield or on the Tyburn gallows. The record of violence is far less remote. The Gordon riots in which hundreds were killed and the Catholic churches and chapels in London destroyed took place towards the end of the eighteenth century. There is another pertinent consideration. Although Ireland no longer dominates English politics as it did until the early years of this century Irish affairs still disturb the peace of Parliament. The difference is that nowadays the religious issues no longer divide Christians in Britain. Almost without exception the press abstains from presenting Irish troubles in terms of religious faith. It prefers to stress the co-operation of responsible Protestants and Catholics. It is a remarkable tribute to the determination of Christians in England to pursue the path to unity that ecumenism suffered no set back at the time of the so-called sectarian murders in Northern Ireland.

The changes in outlook among Christian people are so far-reaching that the Irish are often the most active Catholics in the ecumenical field. It is not surprising that converts are not always to be found in the front line of fighters for ecumenism. Some, in fact, regard ecumenism as a sort of betrayal. Having changed their religious allegiance for the most part on grounds of lack of authority in their own Church they are not disposed to discuss theology on the equal terms demanded by the rules of ecumenical dialogue. Among Catholic ecumenists nevertheless are many former Anglican clergy who once sacrificed friends and security to embrace the Roman Catholic faith. Having left the Church of England as a matter of conscience they did not lose their admiration for the dignity of Anglican worship or their affection for their former colleagues. For them reunion has nostalgic as well as theological attraction.

Until the Secretariat for Christian Unity was set up under Cardinal

Bea in preparation for the Second Vatican Council there was little attempt in England at serious ecumenical action. There were, of course, some enthusiasts among Anglicans who never spoke of Christian Unity without Rome in mind. They did not think in terms of submission but of mutual recognition. They were under the double disability of being unwilling to deal with the leaders of the Church of Rome in England and of not being recognised as official emissaries by the Church of England when making contacts abroad. The Malines conversations between Lord Halifax and Cardinal Mercier are the best known example of negotiations about reunion between Anglo-Catholics and foreign Roman Catholics. They came to nothing partly because theologically each used a different language. The constant element in these conversations was the assumption that Anglicans are more likely to be understood by the French and Belgians than by their fellow countrymen. From the days of Abbé Portal continental Catholics have been able to believe that English Catholics are so ill-disposed towards their non-Catholic brethren that fruitful conversations can take place only abroad.

The growth of harmonious relations between Catholics and other Christians in England since the Council has rendered foreign intervention more than ever an obstacle to Christian Unity. Abbé Portal and other continental clergy in the last century were convinced that they understood religious conditions in England far better than the English clergy and laity. Lord Halifax and his friends gave French and Belgian Catholics the impression that they were typical Anglicans. Even today many foreign Catholics think that Anglicans are all Anglo-Catholics. Portal who first met Halifax in 1889 when both were wintering in Madeira for their health, formed a picture of the Church of England which would have astonished most Anglicans. He assumed that Anglicans go regularly to Mass and indeed to Confession. He was told of the many communities of Anglican monks and nuns scattered over England and of the fidelity of the *Ecclesia Anglicana* to the doctrines of St. Augustine. He pictured English Roman Catholics on fire with resentment because their cathedrals and parish churches had been taken away by the Protestants. Their hostility to the Church of England was so great that they refused to listen to the Anglican bishops who were all longing for reunion with Rome. They understood that the Roman Catholic hierarchy would become redundant once the Church of England made a pact with the Holy See. Furious and blinded by fear for its status and livelihood the hierarchy was virtually unapproachable.

[315]

More than a quarter of a century before Malines—the conversations took place after the first war—Abbé Portal and other French clergy had been trying to arrange a settlement between Rome and Canterbury. Unfortunately Canterbury was not officially aware of what was afoot. Archbishop Benson whose son, Hugh, had become a Catholic priest in the diocese of Westminster was no great admirer of the Anglo-Catholic party in the Church of England. According to his biographer he was "deeply annoyed and made no attempt to dissimulate his feelings" when the Abbé was "sprung upon him by Lord Halifax". The Archbishop of Canterbury was annoyed because he felt that Portal would mis-inform Pope Leo XIII about the true nature of the Church of England of which, he told the Bishop of Rochester, "M. Portal has seen nothing but with Halifax's eyes". The Abbé had in all innocence given Pope Leo a quite false picture of the Church of England whose clergy and people he had described as praying daily for union with Rome. The Venerable Leo—eighty-five years of age at the time (1893)—was urged to write personal letters to the Archbishops of Canterbury and York offering them the utmost concessions if they would bring back the Church of England to the centre of unity. "I would gladly say my *Nunc Dimittis*," the Pope declared, "if I could make the smallest beginning of such a reunion."

It was fortunate that in the end the Pope did not write the suggested letter. It was decided instead that Cardinal Rampolla, papal secretary of state, would write to the Archbishop of Canterbury. The letter was duly delivered to Archbishop Benson who was not impressed. He objected to the expression '*Mater et Magistra*' to describe the Church of Rome and denied that the Holy See could be called "the only centre of unity". The immediate result of Abbé Portal's Roman journey was the setting up of a commission to consider the validity of Anglican Orders. Before its negative findings were published in the Bull *Apostolicae Curae* (1896), Pope Leo wrote his celebrated *Epistola ad Anglos* (1895). This letter, not specifically addressed to the Archbishop of Canterbury or even to Anglicans, was a non-polemic appeal to the English to pray for reunion. It was remarkably well received by all except the most bigoted. Dr. Benson seems to have thought the letter quite good but thought it was spoiled by mention of prayers to the Virgin Mary. He thought "the Pope was trying his best to be honest and it might not be said that his letter had compromised doctrine or held out any hope of modification".

The anticlimactic end of the Malines conversations which lasted intermittently from 1921 to 1925 is well known. What is not so well known is that their chief result was to postpone the coming of ecumenism to England by causing much resentment among English Catholics. Whenever Anglicans are encouraged to deal with foreign Catholics instead of their own fellow countrymen the cause of Christian Unity suffers. Cardinal Bourne was grieved that his eminent brother in Brussels had arranged talks with Anglicans without consulting the English bishops or even notifying them. More incredibly, Cardinal Mercier had sent the Archbishop of Canterbury confidential reports of the talks while ignoring the Archbishop of Westminster. This eventually led to a spirited correspondence. Cardinal Bourne did not make any immediate or direct protest but Father Woodlock, the well-known Jesuit preacher, in the name of English Catholics voiced a protest at what he called the mystery of Malines. Father Woodlock had earlier written privately to Cardinal Mercier but his letter had not been acknowledged. He therefore wrote to the *Tablet* suggesting that the Belgian Cardinal was being falsely represented as sharing the fanciful views of Portal and Halifax. The Anglican peer on his return from Malines had declared that "reconciliation with Rome does not involve any denial of the historic claims of Canterbury" i.e. that the faith and orders of Anglican archbishops are precisely the same as those of St. Augustine the first Archbishop of Canterbury. Could it be assumed by the public that Mercier had agreed to the assertion that the Church of England is continuous with the pre-Reformation Catholic Church in England? Father Woodlock put the question rhetorically in a sermon at Farm Street. Commenting on this sermon the *Church Times* demanded an enquiry: "There is certainly enough in these utterances to justify an enquiry as to which of the two represents most nearly the prevailing Roman spirit. Is it the benevolent and venerable Cardinal at Malines or is it the Jesuit in our midst?"

The Jesuit in our midst was unperturbed. The letter which Cardinal Mercier forbore to acknowledge had been written at the instigation of Monsignor Carton de Wiart. This Belgian priest, Vicar General of the Westminster diocese, felt embarrassed by the intervention of the Cardinal of Brussels in English ecclesiastical affairs. He had urged Father Woodlock to write to Cardinal Mercier. Carton de Wiart knew from his own early experience how easy it is for a foreigner to imagine that he understands the Church of England. He thought that a letter from the distinguished Jesuit might put Cardinal Mercier on his guard against the extravagant ideas put about in all innocence by the pious

Lord Halifax. It was only when his personal letter was ignored that Woodlock wrote to the *Tablet*. He did not mention that Cardinal Mercier had ignored his letter but confined himself to asking if the teaching of the Catholic Church was really different in Brussels and Westminster. Cardinal Mercier at once wrote a letter which was so abusive of Father Woodlock that the editor of the *Tablet* refused to publish it on the grounds that it would disedify both his Catholic and non-Catholic readers. It is unlikely that a modern editor would withhold a letter from such a distinguished correspondent for fear of disedifying readers. Uncharitable correspondence is far more likely today to appear in religious than in secular newspapers.

The editor of the *Tablet*, Ernest Oldmeadow, realised that for a layman to refuse to publish a letter from a Prince of the Church might seem presumptuous. He therefore consulted Bourne who agreed that to publish Mercier's letter "would be productive of serious harm to religion". He promised to write to Brussels himself. The Cardinal undertook to write his letter as principal trustee of the *Tablet* (the journal is now completely under lay control). He explained to Mercier that apart from any other consideration it would be against English usage for a cardinal to reprehend a priest in the public press. For the editor to have published the letter would therefore have been injurious most of all to Cardinal Mercier himself. Cardinal Bourne then proceeded to give expression to the indignation of the hierarchy that Cardinal Mercier had presided over meetings of Anglicans without saying a word to English Catholics or inviting their co-operation:

> ... Your Eminence has kept honourably the silence imposed upon or accepted by you. But it is manifest that the same discretion is not being observed by Anglicans, and they openly declare that the views on the Holy See held at Malines are not the same as those taught by us in England. The Abbé Portal is allowed to speak in Belgium, and we are not allowed even to have an accurate account of what he actually said. The Anglicans are treated as friends—we, the Catholics of England, apparently as untrustworthy.
>
> I am powerless to intervene, for Your Eminence has thought well to leave me—who after all am the principal Catholic prelate in this country and your colleague in the Sacred College—absolutely in the dark. It would have surely been but right and seemly that Your Eminence should have stipulated from the outset that there should be no secrets from me. Yet, with the exception of

Your Eminence's communication at the end of 1923, I have been treated as if I did not exist. The Archbishop of Canterbury has been given the fullest information of the proceedings at Malines—I have been excluded from all such knowledge and thereby a grave wrong has been done both to me and to the Catholic Church in England. Out of respect and affection for Your Eminence I have been patient and have kept silence, with the result that I am quite unable either to correct or to control free-lances like Fr. Woodlock who has many sympathizers both here and in Rome.

Had I in a matter affecting Belgium acted towards Your Eminence and the Belgian Bishops as Belgium has now acted towards us in a matter most profoundly affecting the Catholic Church in England there would have been just cause for complaint. . . .

The main interest of the Malines Conversations is now only cautionary. Anglicanism extends beyond the British Commonwealth and in England it is also the Established Church. We may speculate whether the next Pope will be an Italian but it is quite certain that the next Archbishop of Canterbury will not be a Frenchman, German or Spaniard. It is possible but improbable that he will come from Africa or India. The chances are that the next Archbishop of Canterbury will be British. That is one reason why the cause of Christian Unity requires the closest possible co-operation between Anglicans and Roman Catholics in England itself. Foreign Catholics, no matter how ecumenically wholesome, make small appeal to English Protestants outside Anglo-Catholic circles. Perhaps as a result of inhabiting an island the English, without being actually xenophobic, treat foreigners with a certain reserve. After the failure of the Malines conversations the reactions of Hensley Henson, Bishop of Durham, were not untypical of those of more lowly Anglicans:

Always the dramatis personae of our insular drama are the same. The ardent Anglican yearning at any cost for Reunion; the convenient Roman cleric who acts as the bustling and unwearied go-between; the courteous but cautious Roman prelate: the benevolent intimations from the highest quarters; and then, in due time, when the whole proceeding has been fully exploited by the partisans on both sides, the inevitable *non possumus* of the Vatican, and a train of resultant recriminations. Age after age, they emerge, play their part and vacate the stage.

[319]

Cardinal Bea, a German Jesuit was, despite his great learning, a simple and approachable man. The Cardinal had been in close touch with most of the great scripture scholars in the world both Christian and Jewish. As is the way with serious scholars they estimated one another's worth not in terms of race or religion but of academic integrity. Augustin Bea, an acknowledged authority on the bible, was the ideal choice for first president of the Secretariat for Christian Unity. He had been provincial superior of the German Jesuits and had pastoral experience of Lutherans and Calvinists. The guilt all Germans feel for the treatment of Jews by Nazi Germany doubtless reinforced his per-tinacity in fighting for a generous pronouncement on the Jews by the Vatican Council. Although not familiar with the English scene he was, of course, acquainted with the works of English biblical writers. He was also a close friend of Pope John who had complete trust in his judgment on ecumenical matters. It is not without significance that Cardinal Bea had also been an intimate of Pope Pius XII who gave the first impetus to Catholic ecumenism.

There can be few countries in which ecumenism presented more problems than in England. It was not a question of hostility between Church leaders but of the almost total lack of contact between the various religious communities. "I've got nothing against them. We have some living down our street and they are quite nice people." These words were used by a broad-minded white speaking of blacks but could equally well have been said by an English Protestant of his Catholic neighbours. At least until recent years Catholics were inclined to keep to themselves. This was probably a relic of the days before the Catholic Emancipation Act (1829) when they were legal outcasts. There was little active hostility but Catholics had social contact with few non-Catholics outside their own family circles. Only funerals and weddings provided occasions for entering non-Catholic places of wor-ship. It is, therefore, not surprising that there was little enthusiasm for ecumenical enterprise among English Catholics before the Council. Traditional interference by continental Catholics made the bishops wary of the activities of Cardinal Bea. Few of the bishops were instinc-tive ecumenists. The more sturdy their English stock the harder it was to persuade them that ecumenism is not a betrayal of their Catholic forefathers. All priests of earlier generations have been sustained during the rigours of the long seminary course by the thought of the conversion of England (which would begin in earnest after their own ordination). It was theologically difficult and psychologically almost impossible to

The solemn opening of the Cathedral, May 1967: as the former Archbishop
of Liverpool I was nominated Papal Legate.

Last look at the Cathedral building before leaving Liverpool.

Last ceremony as Archbishop of Liverpool – Confirmation of the handicapped.

dersuade such men to approach Protestants without any intention of converting them. For Catholics the central problem of ecumenism is how to conduct honest discussions while insisting that the Catholic Church is the true Church of Christ. The contradiction involved in Catholic ecumenism is only apparent. The end and purpose of ecumenism is the eventual reunion of all Christians in one Catholic Church. This seems at first sight to involve submission to the Church of Rome but ecumenists rightly claim that this is only an assumption. By study and prayer true ecumenists try to find good in others and faults in themselves. What is true of individual Christians is true also of religious communities. Through honest self-criticism both Catholics and Protestants learn that their religion does not require them to uphold rigidly all its traditional attitudes. Not long ago, for example, Catholics regarded it as sinful to take part in a non-Catholic religious service. The Church itself has made that rule of faith redundant. Some say that it is not the Church but the times which have changed. They argue that the old rule was right because in the past joint prayer would have promoted indifferentism. Whatever its explanation the change is undeniable. The Church has a completely changed outlook on sharing worship with non-Catholics. Development of doctrine can, in fact, reverse earlier teaching. If such development were not possible there could be no place for ecumenism which is primarily an examination by Christians of each other's doctrine with the object of discovering to what extent religious differences are more a matter of expression than of substance. It is astonishing how often frank discussion reveals substantial identity of belief beneath apparently contradictory formulae.

Another example of the altered emphasis in Catholic teaching is to be found in the exercise of authority in the Church. The First Vatican Council in 1870 was brought to an abrupt halt by the outbreak of the Franco-Prussian war. At that time the Council was half-way through its agenda and had dealt only with the question of papal authority. Episcopal authority was still to be discussed. In the event, the infallibility and primacy of the Pope were promulgated without any complementary statement regarding bishops. When the Council was recalled nearly a hundred years later under the name of the Second Vatican Council ('Vatican Two' to the *cognoscenti*) the doctrine of episcopal collegiality was developed. This put the authority of the Bishop of Rome in the context of the episcopal college of which he is head. This evidently makes acceptance of the special position of the Pope as Chief Pastor of the Church and Patriarch of the West more easy of acceptance by Protestants. This does not make it likely that pictures of the Pope will displace those of King Billy in the Orange Lodges of Belfast but it serves to remind us that papal infallibility is one of the most easily misunderstood dogmas of the Church of Rome. Perhaps it would be more accurate to say that infallibility in practice is so different from the popular notion of papal infallibility that the objections of those outside the Catholic Church have become almost academic. Theoretically the Pope could, of course, define a doctrine in an encyclical, sermon or radio talk. In fact no Pope would attempt to define doctrine except after consultation with the bishops of the whole Church. The only example of a proclamation of dogma in modern times is the definition of the Assumption of the Blessed Virgin by Pope Pius XII. This was not done until after prolonged discussion throughout the Church. This particular definition was, in fact, superfluous. No section of the Catholic Church, East or West, has ever denied the Assumption. Since Anglo-Saxon times it has been one of the major feasts of the year. This one exercise of papal infallibility was not of dramatic significance. Today the Pope is likely to be a stumbling block less to Protestants than to the Orthodox.

It was my task to make the idea of ecumenism acceptable to the bishops, priests and laity of this country at a time when to most Catholics the word as well as the notion was new. This was early in 1962 before the opening of the Council. It is difficult if not impossible to judge the actions of men before they were enlightened. Our ancestors would not have burned witches if psychiatry had been available to them. Catholics would not have been so suspicious of ecumenism if they could have foreseen the decree on ecumenism to be promulgated by Pope Paul on 21st November, 1964. In letter and spirit it is totally different from the encyclical *Mortalium Animos* of Pope Pius XI in 1928 which contained a solemn warning against becoming too tolerant of heresy ". . . *agitur enim de vita et salute*" (for it is a question of life and salvation). The ecumenical outlook has developed with such amazing speed since the Council that today the language of the decree may already appear cold and grudging. Protestant sects are referred to as 'ecclesial communities' to avoid calling them Churches. The decree explicitly states that "it is through Christ's Catholic Church alone, which is the all-embracing means of salvation, that the fulness of the means of salvation can be obtained."

Before considering the first joint ecumenical efforts of the English bishops we may note that Pope John's idea of ecumenism was rudimentary. He has been given the reputation of a liberal if not radical prelate, a rollicking Nonconformist, an ecclesiastical Khrushchev. Historians who will be guided by his words and actions will present a very different picture of good Pope John. Ecumenism in his view meant being kind and loving to separated Christians thus facilitating their return to mother Church. He regarded the unity of the Church of Rome as self-evident (unity of faith was undermined in the name of theological pluralism only after Pope John's death). He took for granted that Protestants were yearning to return to unity with the See of Peter. In opening the Council Pope John turned towards the Observers who had come from many religious bodies as he said these words:

Unfortunately, the entire Christian family has not yet fully attained to this visible unity in truth.

The Catholic Church, therefore, considers it her duty to work actively so that there may be fulfilled the great mystery of that unity, which Jesus Christ invoked with fervent prayer from His Heavenly Father on the eve of His sacrifice. She rejoices in peace, knowing well that she is intimately associated with that prayer, and then exults greatly at seeing that invocation extend its efficacy with salutary fruit even among those who are outside her fold . . .

The Church, surrounded by divine light, spreads her rays over the entire earth. This light, however, is one and unique, and shines everywhere without causing any separation in the unity of the body. She extends her branches over the whole world by her fruitfulness; she sends ever farther afield her rivulets. Nevertheless, the head is always one, the origin one, for she is the one mother, abundantly fruitful. We are born of her, are nourished by her milk, we live of her spirit.

There was a great deal of adverse comment by the Observers after this speech of Pope John. They were especially worried by his contention that "those Christians separated from this Apostolic See aspire to be united with us." This was their first contact with Pope John. They had not appreciated that his views on Christian Unity would hardly be different from those of other bishops. Pope John for his part had not imagined that his words could give offence to the Observers. Two days later when Cardinal Bea brought the Observers to a special audience, the Pope without withdrawing his reference to a return to the Apostolic

See tactfully made it clear that he had not intended to score a point in his address on the 11th October:

> I confess to you that it was for me a day of great emotion. On that providential and historic occasion, I devoted all my attention to my immediate duty of preserving my recollection, of praying and giving thanks to God. But from time to time my eyes ranged over the multitude of sons and brothers and suddenly, as my glance rested upon your group, on each of you personally, I drew a special comfort from your presence.
>
> I will not say more about that at the moment, but will content myself with recording the fact. "Blessed day by day be the Lord." Yet, if you could read my heart, you would perhaps understand much more than words can say.

I have anticipated the opening of the Council (to which I shall return) in order to show that the English bishops were in good company. Cardinal Bea on more than one occasion had to coach Pope John gently on the mysterious ways of ecumenism. This was made less difficult because during the Council it became almost mandatory to call everything—even poverty—a mystery. Cardinal Godfrey, the Archbishop of Westminster, was frankly suspicious of the whole ecumenical movement but, passionately loyal to the Holy See, he was determined to follow Pope John's ecumenical lead. He was not sufficiently enthusiastic to open an office in Westminster to direct the work of Christian Unity but made no objection to my setting up ecumenical headquarters in Liverpool. I made it clear in a statement to the press that ecumenism which hitherto had attracted more criticism than support would henceforth be under the direction of the bishops:

> With the warm approval of the Holy Father and encouragement of Cardinal Bea, the hierarchy has appointed the following bishops to act in their name: The Bishop of Shrewsbury (Monsignor Murphy), the Bishop of Clifton (Monsignor Rudderham), Bishop Cashman and Bishop Holland. The committee will meet from time to time under my chairmanship to give guidance to the clergy and faithful. It is the earnest wish of the bishops that all Catholics will share in an apostolate so close to the heart of Pope John. Christians of all denominations will now have an organisation to supply in England what Cardinal Bea's secretariat provides in

Rome—'a place to go'. God grant that the work of our unity committee will deepen the faith of Catholics and show those outside the Church that the hierarchy is determined to reflect the Pope's fatherly zeal for Christian Unity.

One of the first actions of the new committee was to announce a national conference on ecumenism to which every bishop and major religious superior was asked to send a priest. Little as we then knew about ecumenism we realised that it would become a merely academic exercise if we did not train local priests in ecumenism. Joint demonstrations addressed by religious leaders were no longer a novelty. Work for unity must be done in the parishes if it was to achieve results. We decided to hold a conference at Heythrop College, the Jesuit house of studies at Oxford (Heythrop has now moved and forms part of the school of divinity of London University). I asked Cardinal Bea to be the chief speaker. I invited him as the greatest living authority on Catholic ecumenism but also because I wanted him to meet the bishops in a relaxed conference atmosphere. For reasons already given foreign cardinals are not highly regarded in English Catholic circles as authorities on the religious situation in this country. I hoped that personal acquaintance with Cardinal Bea would reassure the Archbishop of Westminster and my other brethren. This hope was only partially realised. Nobody could doubt the humility and learning of the German cardinal but not having lived in England he was obviously far from understanding the phenomenon of the Established Church. Like most foreigners he had a picture of the typical Anglican which applied only to high churchmen. He had yet to learn that the branches of the Church of England range from Anglo-Catholic Papalists to Evangelical Protestants.

This visit of Cardinal Bea to England did not dispel the suspicions of some English bishops that he was responsible for the slow progress of the cause of canonisation of the Elizabethan martyrs. Cardinal Bea was thought to have been persuaded by the Archbishop of Canterbury to obstruct the cause in the interests of ecumenism. Events are still too recent to be open to full investigation but it may be said that Cardinal Bea's insistence on visiting the Archbishop at Lambeth Palace before the Heythrop meetings did nothing to reassure the bishops. It was a matter of embarrassment to me that Cardinal Godfrey was unable to offer the visitor hospitality in Westminster. It is true that there was only one rather poky visitor's room in Archbishop's House. Cardinal Godfrey might, however, have done more to welcome his German brother but for the disfavour with which he regarded the Lambeth visit. Today nobody would question or misunderstand social exchanges between religious leaders but we have moved far ahead since 1962. I recall the earnestness with which soon after Dr. Ramsey's enthronement Cardinal Godfrey attempted to dissuade me from accepting an invitation to dine at Lambeth Palace.

The papers of the Heythrop ecumenical conference were printed in a paperback[1] of which the publishers said: "The picture it gives is all the more encouraging for being extremely balanced and sober. No-one imagines that the disastrous divisions of five hundred years can be papered over by a decade of mere friendliness but part of the excitement of this remarkable book lies precisely in the fact that it is a beginning." In the introductory chapter to this book (of which I was editor) I explained that in the caution with which the English bishops approached the ecumenical movement they were typical of the Catholic community. Nothing could be further from reality than the picture of eager priests and laity being held back from ecumenical endeavour by a bench of reactionary bishops.

I was given striking proof of this when a few days after the Heythrop conference had ended, I went to lay the foundation stone of a new Cistercian abbey at Portglenone, Northern Ireland. I was to preach at a Mass to be celebrated in the open air instead of in the temporary church in order that the friendly Protestant neighbours might attend. It would have been inconceivable for them to enter a Catholic place of worship. (It is important to remember that the year was 1962, long before the renewal of civil strife in the unhappy Province.) In the course of my sermon of which every word was meticulously chosen, I said that the friendship which had sprung up between the monks and the Protestant farmers did credit to them all: "You are all brothers in Christ," I said. "Remember that being a Christian is more important than being Catholic or Protestant." The congregation seemed delighted with the sentiments I had expressed. The Protestants came to shake my hand after Mass. "I never thought," one young farmer said, "that I would ever shake the hand of a Catholic bishop and feel proud to do so. My old father will be turning in his grave this day!"

The sermon was widely reported in the press and I was interviewed on Ulster Television. It did not occur to me that I had said anything startling yet I had scarcely reached home when letters of protest began

[1] *Christian Unity: a Catholic View* (Sheed and Ward, London, 1962).

to arrive from clergy and laity. Not one came from Ireland. All were from outraged English Catholics. Here are extracts from two letters typical of very many. The first letter shows that not all the laity were straining at the leash in their eagerness for contact with the separated brethren:

I have read today in *The Times* that you said "This new spirit has been created because Christians have come to realise that what matters most is not that they are Catholic or Protestant but that they are fellow Christians". My heart sank when I read this because if it is true then why have I, my husband and many converts who have sacrificed so much in order to become Catholics ever bothered to do so? How much easier for us all to have remained Christians, as it were, in the Church of England—where life in this present age is made so easy with divorce and birth control being allowed and no discipline being exercised—if that is what matters most. Your words may very well cause converts, especially among the young, to slip back into the Protestant church and give up their Faith. Our young family have had to fight hard for theirs and your remarks will not make it easier for them. Surely what we need now is more encouragement to hold the true Faith and more clear exposition of the reasons for the truth of the Catholic Church and the untruth of the Protestant churches.

Incidentally, I see today that in their New Testament they are intending to leave out the word 'Virgin' in Isaiah's prophecy which will lead, as it already has among modern churchmen, to a repudiation of the Virgin Birth. Are these the Christians with whom we are to cultivate a precious new friendship and that it is to matter more that we should be one with them than that we should be Catholics and belong to the one true Church? For what did our martyrs suffer torture and agonizing death if what mattered most was that they should be Christians whether Catholic or Protestant? But *The Times* does misquote and I hope that this may be the case on this occasion.

The next letter came from a priest:

May I bring to your notice the enclosed cutting from *The Times* of today, with deep respect and humility? The plain common-sense meaning to ordinary men and women can only be that to be a Christian is something over and above being 'Catholic' or 'Protestant', and it is time we put that something first . . . whatever *branch* of the Christian Church we belong to.

This is precisely what my Anglican neighbours in this very staunch and intelligently Anglican area want to be told, and I have no doubt I shall get this remark back from them in a short time. It is surely most confusing for the average good Catholic boy or girl, it makes for indifferentism, prevents conversions, and offers no reason why any little girl should belong to a branch of the Church of Christ which is so very old-fashioned and stiff about birth control for instance. I do realise that what one actually said is not what appears in the public press, but there has been a certain amount of this kind of reporting also in the Catholic Press of late, and one wonders if it is necessary to so devalue the word 'Catholic' as synonymous with 'Christian' in order to restore mutual friendship between Catholic and Protestant? Anyhow, the Fathers of the Church always did their best to avoid just that way of speaking.

The most trenchant of the letters came from a lawyer claiming to be my devoted admirer and therefore convinced that I had been misreported. A man of old Catholic stock, he objected vehemently to the suggestion that 'being a Christian' was in some way superior to 'being a Catholic'. My reported sermon was an attack on truth because a Christian who denied any part of Catholic doctrine was to that extent in error. He held daily Mass precious beyond anything on earth and was grateful to the martyrs who preserved it for him by suffering a barbarous death at the hands of 'fellow Christians'.

The priests who assembled at Heythrop for the conference were not all enthusiastic ecumenists. It was precisely to make sure that in every diocese and religious community there would be priests with some knowledge of ecumenism that they had been sent to Heythrop by their bishops or superiors. It was assumed that after a week in the company of Cardinal Bea they would learn Pope John's mind on Christian unity and be ready to follow it. At the opening session Cardinal Bea produced a letter addressed to me by Cardinal Cicognani, Secretary of State, in the name of Pope John. It gave the conference the initial impetus it needed. If Pope John were with us all would be well:

[328]

Secretariat of State
of His Holiness

Vatican City
July 26th 1962.

My Lord Archbishop,

The Holy Father has been informed of the Ecumenical Meeting of the secular and religious clergy of Great Britain which is shortly to be held at Heythrop College, and He has kindly directed me to convey His paternal greetings to Your Grace and to the assembly.

His Holiness bids me to say that He was greatly pleased to learn of this meeting which Your Grace's zeal has prompted you to organise on the approach of the Second Vatican Council, and He cherishes the prayerful hope that it may be productive of much spiritual fruit.

This meeting of the priests of Great Britain might well derive inspiration and guidance from the words of St. Paul, *'Veritatem facientes in caritate'* ('speaking the truth in love'). While clergy and laity must adhere absolutely to all the truths of their Catholic faith and show firmness and loyalty in propounding them, at the same time they must practise the maximum of charity, in accordance with the admonition of the Apostle. (Cf. 1 Cor. 13). Therefore, endowed with genuine humility, they should show respect and regard for their separated brethren, treat them with benevolence and render them assistance wherever possible.

The Pontiff fervently invokes the enlightenment of the Holy Spirit upon the deliberations and discussions of this meeting, and, as a pledge of the copious spiritual fruit which He ardently hopes will result therefrom, He cordially imparts to Your Grace and to the assembled clergy His paternal Apostolic Blessing.

Gladly do I renew to Your Grace the assurance of my high esteem, and, with cordial personal regards, I remain,

Yours sincerely in Christ,

A. G. CARD. CICOGNANI.

After the Heythrop conference ecumenism began to be taken more seriously. The conference was given good coverage by press, television and radio. In a broadcast during the course of the conference I introduced Cardinal Bea to viewers and interpreted his words which were spoken in English which was scarcely intelligible. He read English with little difficulty but had no practice in speaking the language. Two others who took part in the television programme were Father Bernard Leeming, S.J., and Father Henry St. John, O.P., the best informed of all Catholic ecumenists. As a young clergyman Father Henry had been present at the Edinburgh conference during which modern ecumenism was born. He had heard Protestant missionaries of many sects declare that if the Christian message was to reach the unconverted it must no longer be given in contradictory versions. During the conference Father St. John gave a brief history of the ecumenical movement and insisted that the fundamental obstacle to unity was what he called the unconscious war-psychology of Christians in dealing with their brethren of a different tradition.

Cardinal Bea impressed the assembled clergy less by what he said than by his sheer goodness. Holiness is sometimes almost palpable. Cardinal Bea resembled Pope John in the serenity of soul shining in his face. He was eighty-one years of age when he came to Heythrop but was full of the vigour which he retained throughout the Council. He died soon after the end of the Council. His work was done. At a Requiem Mass in Westminster Cathedral I tried to describe Cardinal Bea's character and achievement:

> Augustin Bea was a man of God. I am thinking not of his achievements but of his priestly character and life. What a man is matters more than what he does. He was a man of intense prayer and, therefore, of great peace of soul. I stayed with him often both before and during the Council and had every opportunity of observing his rule of life. It was a lesson to see him at his prie-dieu.
>
> . . . Ecumenism was largely unknown in the Church of Rome at the start of the Council. Cardinal Bea set out to teach his brother bishops. He did it so well that by the end he was generally recognised to be if not the most eloquent certainly the most practical and persuasive speaker in the Council.
>
> Cardinal Bea came here to preside at our first great ecumenical conference and was due in Westminster only last month. The very week he died he was to have come to Oxford to receive an honorary degree. Like Pope John he had not only love but genuine feeling for his fellow Christians. I doubt if he really appreciated the delicacy of the religious situation in England. I am quite sure that he never fully understood the outlook of the English Catholic community. Thus when the Archbishop of Canterbury was to

make his official visit to the Pope he wanted to lodge him and his fellow bishops in an hotel. He and his advisers on the Secretariat for Christian Unity could not see how important it was to English Catholics that their Anglican friends should be guests of the English College in Rome. The Cardinal did not realise that the warmth of personal relations between us and our friends is in no way diminished by the peculiar historical difficulties which only time can lead us to solve. In the end Pope Paul himself insisted that the Archbishop and his colleagues should be given the apartments of the hierarchy in the English College. This I mention only to show that as his Vice-President I did not regard the President of the Secretariat for Christian Unity with blind idolatry.

The influence of the Heythrop conference spread very slowly. The experience of the Council itself was needed to impart a sense of urgency into ecumenical effort. From unity headquarters (the ecumenical disguise for Archbishop's House, Liverpool) I issued various directions to promote interest but I was not conspicuously successful. I was given the strong impression that Catholics were notably less enthusiastic about ecumenism than their Anglican and Nonconformist brethren. Later I was to discover that the proportion of really keen ecumenists is roughly the same in every Christian community and in each there is a small number of ecumaniacs (people who jeopardise the whole movement by exasperating their own co-religionists with ecumenical excesses). In a pastoral letter published in March 1962 I gave certain rules for ecumenical conduct which caught the attention of press and radio. Intended only for the Catholics of my own diocese the message was found to be widely acceptable:

1. Never accuse non-Catholics of being in bad faith. God judges both them and us. Assume that members of other religions are at least as sincere as ourselves in their beliefs.
2. Always keep calm when the ignorant attack what they wrongly believe to be Catholic doctrine.
3. Be ready to answer questions about the Faith, but never argue if you are unable to keep your temper.
4. In discussions with non-Catholics never, in an effort to please, pretend that differences in doctrine do not matter. That would be insincere and untrue.
5. Don't deny that the Catholic Church claims to be the one true

Church. But don't allege that only Catholics can be real Christians. That is not only false but absurd.

6. Christian charity does not require us to take part in the worship of other religions, but we should not be more Catholic than the Pope. We may recite publicly the Lord's Prayer and the Apostles' Creed with other Christians. We may also pray with them in private. That is a different matter from taking part in public worship in which we do not believe.

7. Join with non-Catholics in working for the good of the whole community. In the social services, trade unions and political parties Catholics should give an example of public spirit.

8. While fostering Christian unity we must never forget our duty of bringing all men to a knowledge of the truth. Remember that the tragedy of England is not that many Christians are not Catholics but that so many citizens have no religion at all.

It is some indication of the speed of ecumenical progress that those rules are already out of date. The Catholic Church is now much less restrictive regarding joint religious activities. Permission is now sometimes given for the marriage to take place in the church of the non-Catholic partner of a mixed marriage. The question of inter-communion is constantly under review by the Holy See and the authorities of other Christian Churches. At one time it would have been unthinkable to allow non-Catholics to receive Holy Communion in our churches but today Orthodox Catholics and Roman Catholics are permitted to receive Holy Communion in each other's churches in the absence of a church of their own. Nobody knows the future shape of the ecumenical movement.

CHAPTER
TWENTY-THREE

DURING THE SPRING OF 1962 THE THOUGHTS OF CATHOLIC BISHOPS WERE on the coming Council. Many of us had already been called to Rome for meetings of commissions which were oddly styled pre-preparatory. The semantics were never explained. Despite their preoccupation with the Council bishops had to continue their normal pastoral activities. They were, in fact, busier than ever in anticipation of the many weeks they would have to spend in Rome during the Council. I usually made a visitation of two parishes each week but I now increased the number of visitations but made them shorter. This routine pastoral work aroused no interest in the press unless, as in Robsart Street, I ran into trouble.

There is no way of predicting which events will be given publicity. Solemn occasions in the cathedral or the Liverpool Philharmonic Hall usually passed without notice. An address prepared with fastidious care and distributed in advance would be ignored or dismissed in a small paragraph. A speech replete with delicate nuances or appeal was likely to inspire something like the following from the *Southport Bugle and Lancashire Trumpeter*: "Dr. Heenan who has Southport in his Lancashire diocese said that the public owed a debt of gratitude to landladies. He himself was no longer a keen athlete but he strongly believed that every man, woman and child was all the better for indulging in the sport of his (or her) choice." I shall not give examples of the doubtless splendid oratory which fell on the ears of the faithful without attracting the notice of the press. The only speech about that time which was reported at length was made to the nurses at a cottage hospital in Billinge, a suburb of Wigan. It was not an occasion on which I had expected to meet the country's ace reporters. The ensuing flood of publicity was due to the perspicacity of a young man from the *Wigan Observer* who realising that my words could affect a national issue telephoned the text to the Press Association. As reported in the *Daily Mirror* and *Daily Mail* the speech verged on the sensational but even in *The Times* and *The Daily Telegraph* it sounded dramatic.

In 1962 nurses had been making one of their periodic pleas for fair remuneration. I decided to use the Wigan prize-giving as a platform to gain support for their cause. To obtain a reliable briefing I gave tea at Archbishop's House to the matrons of some of the Liverpool teaching hospitals. These ladies produced figures which convinced me that the nurses, especially those below the rank of ward sister, were disgracefully underpaid. Shortly after the prize-giving a rally of nurses from all over the north was due to take place in Manchester. I hoped that the local papers would report my words and thus encourage the Lancashire nurses (of whom a large proportion were Catholics) to attend the rally. The strike is the weapon used by industrial workers in their fight for fair wages but in 1962 nurses and teachers, members of two notoriously underpaid professions, regarded it as unethical to strike. Nurses preferred to suffer themselves rather than inflict suffering on the sick by withholding their services. Their high-minded refusal to do anything likely to hurt their patients made it the duty of the rest of us to fight their battle for them. That was the burden of my speech at Billinge Hospital. Here are some of my words to the nurses:

> Money should not be the incentive for nurses any more than for priests and doctors but you must be given the money you need. You should not be at a disadvantage compared with those in other professions or in industry. If the pay were so high that it provided the main attraction to nursing it would be most undesirable. But this is not the position. The rate of pay is so low that only nurses without family obligations can manage to live on their wages.
>
> I have ascertained the facts from matrons of Liverpool hospitals who are facing a crisis because many have left the profession and many suitable candidates have turned away because the remuneration is so low. The post of theatre superintendent at the largest hospital in Liverpool has been advertised no less than eight times. In two other teaching hospitals posts for tutors have been vacant for years. Young doctors are already leaving this country in search

of well paid employment and it is possible that nurses will soon follow their example. If nurses were prepared to degrade their profession by going on strike the public—that is the patients—would suffer but the Government would have to give way to the pressure. The public—and many people are ex-patients—must exert that pressure on behalf of the nurses. Thousands of cured patients bid a tearful good-bye to their nurses. "I can never thank you enough," they say, "for what you have done for me." Here is a chance to say thank-you by writing to the Prime Minister to plead the nurses' cause. I hope that chivalrous consultants and members of hospital boards will also join the fight.

The nurses were delighted and grateful for the prominence given to their claims but such are the hazards of press publicity that within a few hours of making the speech I was under attack. "RC Archbishop in Row" the *Daily Mail* headlines proclaimed. "Says High Pay Could Degrade Nurses." The text beneath said "Nurses' union leaders replied angrily to a critical outburst by Dr. Heenan, Archbishop of Liverpool." The London editor of the *Daily Mail* must have been using different agency reports from those guiding the editor of the northern edition of the *Daily Mail* whose headlines read: "Battle Plan for Nurses in Pay War: Archbishop Aims to Win Them a Square Deal". The *Daily Mirror*'s Cassandra must also have been given a misleading extract on which to build his column. He wrote a rebuke under the title "The Dignity of Penury": "Dr. Heenan supports the cause of better pay for nurses," wrote Cassandra, "but says that high pay would be the worst thing that could happen to the nursing profession and that any profession is degraded when money becomes the incentive. This sort of stuff is unworthy of Dr. Heenan. Dedication is not enough. The dignity of penury is no substitute for self-respect and a proper standard of living."

Bishops no less than politicians need to develop some of the toughness of pachyderms. If they are too sensitive of criticism their addresses will be strictly anodyne. Soon after being made a bishop and becoming the quarry of newshounds I was told by an experienced journalist that there is only one way of avoiding sensational reporting. Before being released to the press, he said, a speech must be filleted. All memorable phrases must be excised because they alone are quoted in the press. This is obviously not a practical policy. It is easy to delete flashy epigrams but to omit every striking phrase is oratorical suicide. In these days when audiences hear only microphonised sound it is no longer possible to rely

[335]

on the magic of the human voice. Personal appearance and elocution help but even the eternal truths must be presented in an arresting way. I am glad to have been credited with views I have never expressed or held because the experience has made me cautious of accepting reports of what other men are alleged to have said. It is a recognised rule of law that what the soldier said is not evidence. What a listener says he heard is sometimes even less credible.

Before relating my experiences during the early days of the Council I must make brief mention of my last controversial utterance in Liverpool. A few years previously I had sponsored a diocesan weekly journal called the *Liverpool Catholic Pictorial*. The object of the paper was to give easily digestible news for those unable to read serious papers. Occasionally I used the *Pictorial* for a message which for some reason I did not wish to deliver in a sermon or pastoral letter. On my return from the first session of the Council in February 1963 I wrote an article in the *Pictorial* which was intended primarily for dockers and factory workers. Industrial unrest is never far from the surface on Merseyside. Liverpool's reputation is such that firms tendering for a contract add a percentage to cover loss from strikes. There is a large percentage of Catholics among the workmen but unfortunately few of the practising Catholics take an active interest in trade union affairs. Once a year the Catholic men of Liverpool attend a bank holiday Mass at the cathedral. Traditionally the archbishop preaches a sermon on the duties and opportunities of Catholics in industry. Year after year I used to exhort the men to attend union meetings and combine with other Christians and men of goodwill to elect sound men as officials to the unions. I warned them if militants captured all the influential posts Merseyside would never enjoy industrial peace. There was never any need to tell these men that their archbishop was not 'on the side of the bosses'. They knew that in Liverpool the archbishop had been recognised as the champion of the workers since the days of Archbishop Whiteside.

The cathedral was crowded for this bank holiday Mass but the thousands of workers of whom many were only nominal Catholics would not be at this or any other Mass. It was such as these that I hoped to reach through the short article in the *Pictorial* on the foolishness of allowing communist shop stewards to ruin their industry and thus rob them of their livelihood. It is well known that communists of all kinds (Trotskyists, Maoists and Stalinists as well as members of orthodox Soviet communism) contrive to have themselves elected shop stewards because hard-working unionists rarely bother to attend branch meetings. That is why a small band of militants can control thousands of workers and destroy the economy. To my astonishment—it was the first and last time such a thing happened—the *Pictorial* article was reported and reviewed by every paper in the country from *The Times* to the *Daily Worker*.

The substance of the article lay in two paragraphs in which I pointed out that being a shop steward is a dangerous job because it is often taken for granted that it will be held by a communist:

> Apart from overtime the best known sources of extra pay are dirt money and danger money. I am sometimes inclined to think that shop stewards ought to be given a bonus on both counts. Such is their reputation for making mischief that when a man becomes a shop steward his good name is endangered. Wherever there is industrial trouble the public blames the shop steward. The reason is that it is assumed he will be a communist. But not all the shop stewards are wreckers and communists.
>
> The good shop steward is in the job because he genuinely wants to safeguard the rights of his mates. The bad shop steward is there because he wants to use his fellow workers for his own purposes. It is this type of man who has given shop stewards a bad name. I want you to face the facts. They are quite plain and simple. A member of the Communist Party may be under orders to become a shop steward by hook or by crook. [The scandal of the electricians union—E.T.U.—with its communist-rigged elections was still a recent memory.] It is not usually necessary for Marxists to use crooked means to secure election because so few decent workers have the good sense to take an active part in union business or elections.
>
> Communists can walk into key positions almost at will once they set about the work of disruption. In the U.S.S.R., their spiritual home, they would be shot out of hand for starting strikes. The Soviet countries do not believe in the liberty of the worker to take industrial action. Take an interest in your unions. Elect shop stewards who have compassion for their fellow workers and will fight for their rights and save them from exploitation by the communists. It is sometimes right to strike but wild-cat strikes are rarely justified. You will nearly always find communists behind them. The official strike called by the union may well be brought about by the injustice or arrogance of the employers. Boards of

directors are blind not to see that if they declare annual profits and dividends running into millions of pounds the people who produce the wealth are going to demand an increase of pay.

The reaction of the press was predictable. Almost without exception they applauded what they called 'a timely warning'. The heart of the matter, a Birmingham paper said, was that mischief-makers not only disrupt relations between management and men but destroy the unions themselves. Most union leaders, it went on, are responsible and sensible men who are entitled to the loyalty and respect of those who elected them. The *Daily Mail* not surprisingly approved the 'blistering attack on communist shop stewards'. The religious press—including the *Baptist Times*—published approving editorials noting that I had not condemned all shop stewards but only the guilty minority. It was pointed out that many Christians had become shop stewards precisely to counteract communist intrigue. This was especially true in certain key areas of national security such as airports where militants were skilled and relentless. No journalist drew attention to the fact that the readership of the original article was mainly in dockland. If I had been writing for the country at large I would have made reference to the infinitely more dangerous infiltration of Marxism in the disguise of liberal materialism into artistic and academic circles.

The *Daily Worker* issued a remarkably mild editorial rebuke without, of course, making reference to my accusation of undue communist influence among shop stewards. It regarded my attack on communism as slanderous and suggested that it was an insult to the intelligence of the workers to say that they could be fooled into striking by scheming shop stewards. It accused me of trying to create divisions among the workers thus serving their class enemies in the Tory government. The editor commented darkly that De Gaulle and Adenauer were both members of Catholic political organisations and perhaps the Archbishop of Liverpool was trying to set up something similar in Britain.

The most original comment was in a letter to *Time and Tide* under the heading 'A Change of Jobs':

Sir,

After Archbishop Heenan's denunciation of Communist shop stewards—why not Heenan for Prime Minister? I certainly would not mind Mr. Macmillan as Archbishop—especially after his audience with the Pope.

S.W.1.   P.O.B.

CHAPTER
TWENTY-FOUR

LIKE ALL CATHOLIC BISHOPS I DEVOTED MY SPARE TIME IN 1962 TO study in preparation for the Council. We in England were theologically as well as geographically cut off from the Continent. We had no idea of the religious metamorphosis which had taken place in Europe. Although the war had ended more than a decade earlier and English bishops had frequently visited the Continent their journeys had been mainly to France and Italy. Germany and the Netherlands remained *terra incognita*. I had known Nazi Germany quite well but since the war I had been in Germany only twice—once to visit the English troops in the Rhineland and on another occasion to attend the centenary cele-brations in honour of St. Boniface, the apostle of Germany, who was an Englishman. I had not at that time ever visited Holland. We did not know what the Dutch were thinking and were quite unprepared for the later discovery that some Dutch Catholics had made almost a new religion of ecumenism. Impatient of all dogmatic differences they were ready to barter any doctrine in the cause of external unity. When the Secretariat for Christian Unity was first set up there were no less than four members from Holland. This did not seem significant at the time because the rest of the Church was unaware of the vast religious changes in Holland since the war.

Looking back it is clear that the English-speaking bishops were quite unprepared for the kind of Council the rest of the northern Europeans were planning. The Americans were even less prepared than the British. They made no contribution at all to the first session which was largely a probing battle between the old and new theological ideas. Most of the bishops as busy pastors (more than a third were missionaries) had not read the latest theological writing and were unfamiliar with the changed thinking in Europe since the Hitler era. Having been forced into a defensive alliance with Protestants against Nazi paganism Catholics in Germany and German-occupied Europe (chiefly France and the Netherlands) were bent on eliminating all trace of the counter-reformation in Catholic thinking. The contrast between East and West was evident to the bishops from countries—mostly English-speaking—which had not experienced enemy-occupation. Bishops from countries which had suffered Soviet occupation were more than ever tenacious of the authority of Rome. The bishops of Poland and Yugoslavia (no bishop from Czechoslovakia or Hungary was allowed to attend the first session) had a quite different theological outlook from that of their western brethren. Social and political conditions in Germany and German-occupied territories had led Christians to regard doctrinal differences as relatively unimportant but there were virtually no non-Catholic Christians in Russian-occupied Europe. Persecution therefore had different results in the two zones. In the one it threw Christians into each other's arms while in the other it made Catholics look more longingly than ever to Rome.

The differences between the northern bishops and the rest grew less as the Council proceeded but during the first session there was some-times emotional disagreement. This was dramatised by journalists who divided Council Fathers into progressives and conservatives. These labels unfortunately remained throughout the Council and for some time afterwards a bishop was liable to be called progressive if he con-tradicted the Pope and conservative if he defended any doctrine of the Church. After a few days of the first session the star journalists returned to their own countries and left reporting to their juniors. These were often Catholics and among them was a surprising number of ex-seminarists. These men were regarded (and came to regard themselves) as qualified theologians and were responsible for interpreting the teach-ing of the Council to the world. They received most of their information from priests who had been brought to Rome by their bishops. These were not official theologians to the Council (*periti*) but were usually so-regarded by the journalists to whom they gave regular press con-ferences. Hence the inaccurate and often alarmist reporting during the first session. The Council was more than half over before the Vatican was sufficiently wise to provide information in official press conferences. Then the journalists gave reliable reports but by that time the damage was done. Every bishop had to be type-cast as progressive or conservative.

Before the opening of the Council I asked priests to instruct their people on its meaning and importance. Everyone knew from Pope John's speeches that no definitions of doctrine were in prospect but few knew the purpose of the Council. This was largely due to Pope John's insistence that preparatory documents must be kept confidential. The secrecy of the proceedings of the pre-preparatory commissions was regarded as essential and inviolable. Even in the Secretariat for Unity we had to take an oath to observe secrecy about what we were discussing. For the first year the fiction of secrecy was maintained regarding speeches in the Council chamber (the aula) although the substance or, more often, the complete text was available to enterprising journalists. Because few understood the purpose of the forthcoming Council I wrote a pastoral letter to be read in four sections at Mass on the Sundays of September 1962. This was part of the spiritual preparation of the Liverpool diocese for the opening of the Council on 11th October. The first nine days of October were to be devoted to a novena of prayer.

The pastoral letter is of significance not for its intrinsic worth but for its evidential value. Some years later hostility to authority was to be fomented by those who felt frustrated by the Council. They could not bring themselves to see that Pope John wanted the Council to alter Catholic attitudes not the Catholic faith. The bishops always regarded it as Pope John's Council although he died before it was half over. They would have considered it disloyal to his memory to tamper with doctrine. The following extract from what proved to be my last pastoral pronouncement in Liverpool is given to show that even before the Council opened bishops were quite clear about its purpose. After the Council persistent efforts were made to persuade the faithful that the Council changed everything in the Church. It is because what was written before the Council cannot be prejudiced against its findings that this unremarkable piece of pastoral prose is worth quoting:

> . . . What will the Vatican Council decide? That we cannot say. We have been told some of the things which the Council will discuss. But nobody knows more than that. We can, of course, say what the Council will not do. It will not alter the Catholic Faith. If the Faith is going to be the same after the Council, what is the point of holding the Council at all? In the first place, the Council

can teach us a great deal more about the Faith. The Church is like any normal person. She learns by experience.

. . . Since it is nearly a hundred years since the last General Council there must be many things needing fresh examination. It is true that the Holy See is always in touch with every part of the Church. But that is a very different matter from gathering together the bishops of the whole world to discuss the needs of the Church in our time. Nobody can foretell what new strength and knowledge will come to us through the Vatican Council. Although, as we have said, the doctrine of the Church does not alter there may be many changes to make in the day-to-day life of the Church. So we are right to look for new benefits from the coming Council. The Pope has told us that he called the Council to renew the whole life of the Church. You have probably heard or read in the papers that Pope John has invited as observers to the Vatican Council theologians belonging to other Christian bodies. Some have already accepted the Pope's invitation. One of the first to accept and to nominate theologians was Dr. Ramsey, Archbishop of Canterbury. We have grown so used to the friendly and courteous actions of our fellow Christians that we have begun to take them for granted. It is well for us to thank God for this welcome change in relations between ourselves and members of other Christian bodies in this country.

We must not imagine, however, that Pope John has altered the nature of the Catholic Church. This striving for Christian unity is no new thing. Already in the time of Pope Pius XII, of happy memory, the Holy See had instructed the bishops of the whole Church to promote this work. The late Pope encouraged Catholics and Protestants to study together means of fostering closer relations. What Pope John has done is to quicken the pulse of the movement for Christian Unity. We may be sure that, with Pope John to guide them, the Fathers of the Council will not hurl anathemas at those who reject the Catholic religion. The intemperate language of more robust days will certainly not be used in the Vatican Council. It will avoid expressions which are known to give pain to non-Catholics. Only a few years ago the ceremony on Good Friday was altered so as not to give offence to the Jews. This does not mean that the Council will be afraid to proclaim the truth. It means only that in proclaiming the truth the Council will avoid hurting those not of the Household of the Faith.

Catholics do less than credit to non-Catholics by thinking that they expect us to be silent about the claims of the Church. Those of us on terms of the closest friendship with other Christians know that they never want us to disguise the Church's claims. They know where we take our stand. They respect an honest statement of the Catholic position and despise those who paint a false picture. We ought to thank God for the growing understanding that is drawing Christians together. The ultimate aim of all sincere Christians is to be united in one Faith.

The proceedings of the Council have been described so often that it is unnecessary to give any detailed account. Looking back it is easy to see how psychologically unprepared bishops were for what happened during the first session. Most of us arrived in Rome in October 1962 without any idea of the anti-Italian mood of many Europeans. This eventually crystallised into a specific hostility towards the curia, the Vatican bureaucracy. The political state of Europe may have been in some measure responsible. During their fascist phase there was a certain bombast about many Italians and Roman ecclesiastics were no exception. The cowardly attack by the Italians on the already defeated French and their subsequent defection from the Germans made them contemptible in the eyes of both. If the curia had not been manned mainly by Italians it would not have been the object of so much vituperation. It is nevertheless true that after the Council when curial posts were occupied by non-Italians the curia remained the chief target of peripatetic theologians. By that time the dog had acquired a bad name.

The conciliar fathers for the most part shared Pope John's illusion that the bishops of the world had come together as brothers in Christ for a short convivial meeting. Pope John and the fathers were quickly brought to a sense of reality. The first General Congregation (as meetings of the Council were called) had scarcely begun when the northern bishops went into action. I have described the scene at length in a book published shortly after the close of the Council.[1] Here I give only a very brief summary.

The bishops were handed books containing names of those who during the preceding two years had been members of the preparatory commissions. Cardinal Liénart, Bishop of Lille, rose to make a speech of protest. It would be absurd to vote immediately for members of

[1] *Council and Clergy* (Geoffrey Chapman, London).

commissions, he said, because as yet the fathers were unacquainted with each other. It would be much wiser and fairer to allow time for bishops to exchange information and discuss the merits of the proposed candidates. If votes were taken at once the bishops would be voting for men with whom they were unfamiliar even by name. The qualifications and worth of individual bishops are usually not known outside their own country of origin. The cardinal proposed that the various hierarchies should first consider what talent they could offer and then pass on to other hierarchies the names of their strongest candidates. As soon as the French cardinal sat down his German friend, Cardinal Frings, Archbishop of Cologne, rose to second the proposal. He claimed to be acting in the name of all German-speaking bishops. This drew a sustained burst of applause from the fathers who evidently thought that the Council had been saved from disaster. The reaction of the bishops was unmistakable and the Secretary General thought it superfluous to put Cardinal Liénart's motion to the vote. The first General Congregation of the Second Vatican Council was suspended after exactly fifteen minutes.

For the next three days national hierarchies met and sent each other lists of names regarded as most suitable for election to the commissions. There was a generous exchange of views through envoys who went round the national colleges where the various hierarchy meetings were being held. When all available information had been collected each hierarchy was able to produce a comprehensive list. A model international list was drawn up under the inspiration of Cardinal Montini by the Italian hierarchy.

Bishops were determined not to form national groups and as the Council proceeded it became clear that there was never the slightest danger of nationalism. Before the voting took place bishops had sufficient knowledge of candidates to vote intelligently. They knew, at least at second-hand, who were best qualified to serve on a commission. The bishops from the north acted in concert from the beginning and were in frequent touch with their English brethren.

All consultation had to take place between Saturday's abortive meeting and the following Tuesday when the Council was due to resume. The intervening days were perhaps the most strenuous of the whole Council. It was useless to put forward the name of a candidate without letting groups of bishops know something of his background and worth. Even using every spare moment it was impossible to learn enough about sixteen people for each of the commissions. It was, therefore, inevitable that the bishops gave votes for some candidates knowing little about them beyond their names. The important thing was that at least a nucleus of members would be recognised as competent in their subject. The voting duly took place and an army of seminarians was recruited to count the votes. This was no simple matter. After debates in the Council specially designed voting papers were counted by electric computers in a matter of minutes but you cannot put foolscap pages into computers.

Within two or three days the result of the voting was known and the list of successful candidates included most of the original names. The Holy See had chosen members of the preparatory commissions not because they were thought to be docile but because they were known to be competent. For making this choice—as, indeed, for many other actions—the curia has been judged harshly. It is true that some of the elected bishops had not been chosen for preparatory commissions but many more bishops were needed for the new commissions. Furthermore a bishop's abilities may be known to his colleagues but not to the Holy See. An obvious example was Dr. Grimshaw, Archbishop of Birmingham. Bishops in England were aware of his life-long interest in the liturgy but abroad his name was unknown. As soon as other bishops were informed of his domestic reputation they adopted him. His name was near the top of the list of successful candidates for the liturgical commission.

The diary I kept until the pace of the Council made it impossible reflects the excitement of October 1962.

9th October, 1962: Left Archbishop's House on a foggy day. The orphan children from Knolle Park were waiting for me in the front garden with the Sisters. They sang "Faith of Our Fathers" and "God Bless the Pope". We said a prayer and then I blessed them and drove off with Father Barry to the airport. Here hundreds of children were assembling. They came from all the neighbouring secondary schools. The aircraft was delayed over an hour to the immense satisfaction of the children. I went round the various groups and when the plane was ready to fly I was taken out to the apron by the airport commander. These children also sang "Faith of Our Fathers". Photographs were taken and the children shouted good-byes. After I had settled down in my seat the senior steward and Mr. Wilson, Director of Starways, asked me to go to the top of the steps to wave and give the crowds a blessing. Mr. Wilson also gave me a box of cigars which, he said, might prove useful at a conference if things were not going my way.

At London Airport I found the Bishops of Brentwood and Southwark. They were being seen off by various people including my old Barking friends, the Forans. Bishop Craven, Auxiliary of Westminster, was also on our plane. Uneventful and pleasant journey to Rome airport where we were met by Monsignor Clarke and Father Loftus. Most of the bishops had already arrived. Cardinal Godfrey called a meeting for six p.m. to discuss domestic details. Everything possible had been done for our comfort by Monsignor Jock Tickle, the rector. He and his students had worked like slaves each day until the early hours for the last few weeks to make ready this wing of the English College called the *piano nobile*. My own apartment is especially roomy because, the rector says, I shall have more visitors than the other bishops. He said I must expect members of the Secretariat for Christian Unity to call and perhaps some of the non-Catholic observers but the real reason for my splendid accommodation is that the rector happens to be my old friend Jock Tickle.

We were told what to do about correspondence, transport, Mass, money, meals and informed of the various people who would be at our service. It was clear that the atmosphere of home would be provided.

Went to St. Peter's for a glimpse of the Council Chamber (aula).

10th October: The vigil of the Council. All the bishops said a Red Mass of the Holy Ghost. Everyone wanted to know hundreds of details about arrangements for the Council. It was clear to all that the supremely important preliminary task was the selection of members for commissions.

A large palazzo in the Via della Conciliazione off the Piazza S. Pietro had been taken over as administrative offices. Most of the bishops had signed on there and received various documents. Among them was the *Ordo Concilii Oecumenici Vaticani II Celebrandi*. This gives all the procedural rules and details of the officials and their tasks. The second booklet is the list of all the Fathers of the Council under country, rite or religious congregation. The third booklet was called *Methodus Servanda*. This gave the *ordo missae* and the ceremony of the solemn opening of the Council together with the prayers to be recited daily before and after each Congregation (meeting).

This was a busy day because everyone felt that if voting for members of commissions was to take place on the second day of the Council it was a matter of urgency to learn whom other hierarchies intended to vote for. We are all expected to find out what we can and report back to a meeting to be held this evening. In the event I am better placed than most to make contacts because of my friendship with the bishops on the Secretariat for Christian Unity. In fact I had little to do because during the day the Bishop of Bruges (de Smedt) phoned and said he wanted to see me urgently on behalf of the Belgians, Dutch and Germans. He came round in the early evening. The Bishop of Bruges was rather reluctant to meet any other bishops as his communication was highly confidential but I persuaded him that G.P.D. was safe and that his knowledge of French would help.

Bruges' news was indeed startling. The Cardinals of Brussels, Vienna, Utrecht and Lille were of the opinion that the voting list would be put before us by the conciliar authorities under the guidance of Cardinal Ottaviani (Holy Office) and that little real choice would be given regarding candidates. Since most of the work will be done by the commissions it is important that the members should be really representative.

Bishops had another meeting in the evening to piece together rumours and impressions. The Cardinal is still suffering the effects of an operation last year and it is hard to put a point which he can grasp quickly or clearly. So far no vital decisions have had to be made.

11th October: Went to Vatican after Mass at five thirty a.m. The Archbishops were to vest (cope and white mitre) in the Hall of Inscriptions which is through the bronze doors and onwards and upwards (hard for old men) for a very long way. On the way up I passed groups of bishops (Scots, Irish, American, Australian, New Zealanders) whom I knew. I was with Archbishop Grimshaw of Birmingham and eventually we were in a group which included Archbishop Knox, Apostolic Delegate in India (once my host in Tokyo), Archbishops Krol (Philadelphia), McQuaid (Dublin) and the Archbishop of San Francisco.

The procession—our part at least—began to move just before nine a.m. By the time we reached the bronze doors the men were about to hoist the Pope on the *sedia gestatoria* to go to the piazza. The archbishops (about a hundred and fifty of us) were cut off and told to turn round and enter St. Peter's by the portico. This we obediently did. When we arrived at the seats in the basilica we found that most of them were already occupied. But Archbishop Grimshaw and I managed to find seats in an excellent position. We were very happy—but not for long. Within two minutes we were turned out of our seats and sent upstairs to the tribune reserved for *periti* (theologians attending the Council) where we most unpopularly took the seats of men who had been in them for two hours. However we were given no option. My resolution not to grumble about anything throughout the Council paid dividends. Instead of glowering and fretting about 'being pushed around' I was cheerful. I became even more cheerful when I realised that being displaced persons had given us a far better view than any other of the bishops.

The scene was one of the most beautiful and inspiring I had ever seen. The colourful blaze of the vestments of nearly three thousand bishops with different shades of purple, and contrasting flashes of more brilliant shades from the orientals, and the rich scarlet of the cardinals was really breath-taking. As a show it was magnificent and needed no impresario. Of course the ceremony was too long. All pontifical ceremonies are too long. The most boring features were the repetition of the Profession of Faith by the Pope and Archbishop Felici and the homage of the cardinals who each kissed the Pope's hand. Fortunately only one man was chosen to represent respectively archbishops, bishops, abbots and religious. The Pope's speech was remarkably to the point. On such an occasion platitudes are to be expected but Pope John's talk was concrete. He condemned pessimists and said the world was not going down to destruction. The Council would not spend its time condemning but showing compassion. The Church, he said, did not necessarily thrive when States tried to be friendly. The Chuch often did better when the State kept its distance. A good speech—it seemed long because the ceremony had already lasted too long. But it could hardly have been shorter. Came away from St. Peter's well satisfied.

12th October: Free day—continual coming and going by bishops re voting lists.

13th October: At St. Peter's by nine o'clock. The English bishops were in a group—no places have yet been allotted. Archbishop Felici announced that elections to the commissions would take place at once. The fathers had already received the booklet with the lists of all serving on the preparatory commissions. Scarcely had Felici spoken than Cardinal Liénart of Lille stood up and proposed that no voting should take place today and the session prorogued until next Tuesday by which time bishops would have had the chance of knowing men of other nations. Cardinal Frings of Cologne seconded this motion and there was a tense pause while the Presidency (a dozen cardinals) considered the proposition. Both speeches had been greeted with loud applause. Some obviously felt that this was a typical example of the Roman Curia in action—listed names of men conditioned by three years of prepararory work in Rome.

[348]

The rest of the day was spent lobbying. Bishop de Smedt of Bruges was on the phone and came round for the second time. His story was that when Liénart asked to speak the chairman, Cardinal Tisserant, Dean of the S. College and a fellow countryman, refused. Cardinal Liénart asked again after Mass. Once more leave to speak was refused. He therefore just took the microphone and spoke. His example was followed by Cardinal Frings. Collapse of some Italian cardinals (*"Scandalo!" "Che spettacolo divanti del mondo!"*)

On his first visit Bruges had discussed names with me. He had given some names that the Belgians, Dutch and Germans intended to back. We gave some of our names—Dwyer, Beck, Grimshaw—and those we knew from elsewhere. On this visit we discussed more names. He said that a final list was being drawn up at a meeting then in progress at the Anima College (German house of studies) under the presidency of Cardinal Frings. This list would be available by nine o'clock the next day. Meanwhile, many names had been given and it was hoped to make this list fairly international. It would attract the votes of missionaries—e.g. the Congo has many Belgian bishops.

Bruges was triumphant: He felt that his victory for freedom of the bishops augured well for the Council.

It was now time for another bishops' meeting of our own. Cardinal Godfrey said (wrongly I think) that we had to draw up a list only of our own people—one for each commission. I did not agree but I could not convince H.E. so we had to let it go. I also did not think it sensible to give a name for *every* commission. It would have been strange indeed if the small English hierarchy had that number of geniuses. We picked a list and gave it to Ireland, Scotland, Australia, New Zealand, India and, of course, to the Belgians, Germans, French and Dutch.

It has often been alleged that the cardinals in Rome were dismayed by Pope John's decision to hold a Council. If this be true it is not likely that the motive for their dismay was entirely discreditable. There is no reason for believing that they feared the loss of power which might result from a Council. Those who work in a curia are among the most devoted priests in the Church. Some, of course, are ambitious and self-centred but so are some bishops, curates, laymen and atheists. Few bishops join the chorus of detractors because they have constant and direct dealings with the curia. Only those on the fringes of ecclesiastical affairs challenge their integrity and zeal. The curia is the civil service of the Catholic Church. There is a certain similarity with the criticisms made of all civil servants. The unfeeling, tea-drinking bureaucrat is a favourite character of comedy but those who actually deal with civil servants in this country admire their courtesy, incorruptibility and sense of duty. Ecclesiastical civil servants may be less well trained for their professional duties but they are not less unselfish or honourable than servants of the crown in England.

End of extracts from my diary

TWENTY-FIVE

POPE JOHN INSPIRED SUCH ADMIRATION THAT, LIKE WINSTON CHURCHILL'S, his real greatness is still to some extent obscured by a mountain of myths. Angelo Joseph Roncalli was crowned Pope John XXIII on 4th November, 1958. From the first days of his pontificate he was completely at home in the Vatican Palace. There was no trace of the peasant born in Sotto il Monte, a village near Bergamo, on 25th November, 1881. Eighty-one years later to the day Pope John told the story of his birth to the English bishops when we went to the Vatican to offer him our birthday greetings. We did not realise that he would be dead before another year had passed. He told us that his mother and father, Marianna and Giovanni, were delighted that their third child (there were to be ten more) was a boy. Here is the story in Pope John's own words:

> Thank you, beloved brothers, for coming to greet me on this anniversary of my birthday. But you don't realise that it is also an infinitely more important anniversary—I was baptised on the day I was born. My mother was so delighted that her third child was a boy—the first two were girls—that she packed my father off to church with me at once. It was such a terribly cold and wet day, my father told me, that despite his big umbrella he was soaking wet when he arrived at the village church. The parish priest not at all pleased at being dragged out on such a night to baptise a perfectly healthy baby scolded my poor father unmercifully.

The Romans were amazed that a man of seventy-seven could so quickly be at home in his new position. Although in the homily at his coronation Mass he disclaimed any title to be 'a statesman, diplomat or scholar' he was all three and much more. He was a pastor who loved his flock. Furthermore he regarded all men as belonging to his flock. "We have at heart our task as shepherd of the entire flock. All the other human qualities—learning, diplomacy, tact and organising ability—can help but they are no substitute for being a shepherd." It was against protocol to grant interviews to the press but Pope John invited five hundred journalists to a special audience after his coronation. He gave them frank and homely advice. He told them never to manufacture news. He gave them the example of the press reports of what was alleged to have taken place at the conclave which elected him. He smiled broadly when he said "attempts were made to penetrate the secrecy of the conclave but I do not find a word of truth in any of your stories. Journalists have made formidable efforts but the secrecy of conclaves will in future be even more strongly preserved." Pope John then told the journalists the story of Joseph meeting the brothers who had sold him into slavery. He made the words of the patriarch his own: "I am your brother Joseph," he said. This was Pope John's striking way of pleading with journalists not to put words into his mouth. Pope John became their hero and—such is the power of press, radio and television—they soon made him the hero of the world.

Pope John could not possibly have foreseen the result of his decision to hold a Council. He had been pope only three months when on 25th January, 1959 during a ceremony at the basilica of St. Paul he disclosed his intention of calling an ecumenical council. Although he described himself as 'trembling with emotion' there was something almost casual about the announcement which came towards the end of his address. There are several reasons for thinking that the Pope did not fully appreciate the significance of the events he was setting in motion. In the first place the gathering at St. Paul's with only a handful of cardinals present was not an ideal occasion to make the announcement if he regarded it as truly momentous. The obvious moment would have been during the consistory six weeks earlier (15th December, 1958). At that time John had been pope for little over a month and had probably not even thought of a council. For the consistory the Pope had created twenty-three new cardinals raising the number of the Sacred College to the unprecedented figure of seventy-five.

When in the following month Pope John gave news of the Council he did not appear to regard it as the most important of the events he was announcing:

Leaving Liverpool.
Arriving for enthronement at Westminster Cathedral.

Westminster Cathedral: after the enthronement.

With Pope Paul.

We announce, venerable brothers and beloved sons, . . . a two-fold celebration: a diocesan synod for the city and an ecumenical council for the Universal Church. . . . They will lead happily to the desired and awaited bringing-up-to-date (*aggiornamento*) of the Code of Canon Law, which should accompany and crown these two tests of the practical application of the provisions of ecclesiastical discipline. . . . The forthcoming promulgation of the Code of Oriental Law will give a foretaste of these events.

The synod of Rome was duly held and the *aggiornamento* turned out to be a series of fresh restrictions on clerics living in Rome. The synod was such a failure that after a few days it was dismissed even as a topic of conversation. It is unlikely that any Roman cleric today could name a single canon the synod laid down. Its chief result seems to have been to kill all diocesan synods. Until Pope John's synod the canonical custom of holding a synod every ten years was generally observed. Today diocesan synods are unknown. Pope John—contrary to popular opinion—was a priest of intense self-discipline and a great believer in law. From both his studies and his travels he knew that law is the surest safeguard of human liberty. That is why he regarded the revision of Canon Law as the goal of his pontificate. The synod and council were to be crowned by the production of the new codex of canon law. The word 'juridical' was to be treated as obscene after his Council but to Pope John himself the notion of law was sacred. The 'spirit of Pope John' has become synonymous with *laissez-faire* and opposition to law and the rule of faith. This is unimaginably far removed from the true spirit of the Pope John I knew. We find out what Pope John was really like by reading his spiritual autobiography, *The Journal of a Soul*. There could be no more complete refutation of the caricature current after his death.

Pope John's Council, unlike his synod, became fruitful in the end but he did not live to see it recover from the chaos of its first session. As the Council progressed Pope John grew more and more depressed but, of course, the Council was not alone responsible for his sufferings. The cancer which was to kill him may have begun to destroy him emotionally as well as physically. He never complained to the bishops about his pains though he spoke to us very freely of his problems. One of his chief worries was that many bishops seemed in no hurry to finish the Council and go home to look after their flocks. This was especially true of bishops from Africa and Asia for whom the club-like atmosphere of

Rome and the company of their fellow bishops were delightful. Whenever he received a group of bishops in audience Pope John would ask them if they thought it necessary to hold a second session of the Council. He had imagined the Council as a glorified synod of Rome which would provide the bishops with the chance of a reunion in the home of their common father. Pope John saw the Council as an episcopal safari. During the grim November days when Pope John had to intervene to rescue the Council from the deadlocked debate on the sources of revelation he must have thought his Council less a safari than a siege.

The debate on revelation brought to light the extent of confusion regarding ecumenism. Although the debate was ostensibly and immediately about scripture and tradition the point of the underlying disagreement was ecumenical. Some of the fathers were evidently determined that Catholic doctrine must be stated only in terms which were acceptable to Protestants. They did not, of course, put it in this way even to themselves. They took their stand on the Reformers' contention that the Bible is the only authentic source of doctrine. (Scriptural texts are rightly quoted to support all Catholic dogmas but it is taking a liberty with language to say that the Immaculate Conception and the Assumption are biblical truths. Some over-enthusiastic ecumenists would jettison all Marian dogma in the quite mistaken belief that this would please Protestants.) It must be stressed that ecumenists of the Cardinal Bea school would tolerate no diminution of Catholic doctrine. Their view was contained in the Council's teaching that in the hierarchy of truths some are less important than others but not for that reason expendable.

Most of the eastern bishops were puzzled by the controversy among their western brethren. They are proud of the long tradition of devotion to the Mother of God in the East. They observed the feast of the Assumption of the Blessed Virgin, for example, long before it became popular in the West. The antiquity of their tradition rivals that of Anglo-Saxon times when the feast of the Assumption was by King Alfred's order made a public holiday. The Orientals hold that there is only one source of revelation—the tradition of the Church. They had understood this to be universal Christian teaching. So, in fact, it was but in the West Catholics had always spoken of a two-fold source of revelation—written (scripture) and unwritten (oral tradition).

If they could have looked into the future the Orientals might have been still more puzzled. After the Council an entirely novel version of revelation was introduced by catechists whose reading had been confined to post-conciliar popular theology. Revelation was described as 'ongoing'. It did not, as the Catholic Church has always taught, cease with the apostles but continues through the reflections of Christians on their own daily experience. It is obviously true that private revelations are possible but the Church insists that they can never be part of the faith. Catholics are free to accept or reject any private revelation. They must make up their own minds whether to accept or reject stories of apparitions and cures at Lourdes or Fatima. The new concept of revelation was not mentioned in the debate on the sources of revelation. This was fortunate because it could only have further darkened an already obscure discussion. Apart from dedicated ecumenists and those fathers who feared that ecumenism would lead to a dilution and eventual denial of truth, few of the fathers understood why revelation was causing such a furore. Now that ecumenism is better understood it is easier to see why so much time was spent on this discussion. The fact is that during the first session of the Council many bishops knew so little about ecumenism that they had to learn how to pronounce the word.

With the debate on the sources of revelation Pope John's hopes for his Council reached their nadir. A brief examination of what occurred will illustrate the shambling gait of the Council in its opening phases. Before a document was debated in detail—chapter by chapter and word by word—a general discussion took place to decide whether a schema was worth discussing at all. The fathers were impatient of these wide-ranging debates because they knew that the same ground would be covered all over again in the detailed discussion. In the whole course of the Council whenever the closure of a general debate of this kind was proposed it was invariably carried unanimously. This debate on revelation was the one exception. When the puzzled bishops felt the rising heat of dissension about what they had hitherto regarded as simple Catholic teaching—that revelation comes through the bible and tradition—they grew alarmed. Many were ready to scrap the whole document. Others wanted to end a discussion in which they saw no chance of agreement between what they erroneously thought of as ecumenists and anti-ecumenists. They wanted the general discussion to finish so that each side might be given the opportunity of debating the details of the decree. Then the Council could decide which was orthodox doctrine. Other bishops, bored by the question whether the bible or tradition came first, regarded it as the theological equivalent of the chicken and the egg. The upshot of this early disarray illustrates the problem of three thousand people attempting to pronounce on any issue. The fact that all were speaking Latin did not lead to ease in debate.

Archbishop Felici, the Secretary General of the Council, announced that the fathers must vote either to discontinue the general debate and begin the detailed discussion or to reject the decree absolutely. The fathers were instructed to vote *placet* (yes) if they wanted the debate to stop and *non-placet* (no) if they wanted it to continue. It requires no genius to see that this was a twisted way of presenting the vote. The normal and obvious method would have been to vote *placet* to continue and *non-placet* to stop the debate. Not many fathers at the end of the meeting on 20th November were really clear what had been decided. Some suspicious bishops set it about that the terms of the motion had been manipulated to prevent the document being rejected. This would have required a two-thirds majority. The Council re-assembled on 21st November in troubled mood. To their immense relief they learned that Pope John had intervened. He had decided to appoint a special commission to consider the draft decree and, if necessary, re-word it before bringing it back in the second session of the Council. The joint chairmen of this papal commission were Cardinal Ottaviani (President of the theological commission) and Cardinal Bea (President of the Secretariat for Christian Unity). The other members of the commission were those of us who belonged to one or other of these bodies. This device of a special sub-commission was Pope John's way of banging our heads together. He shrewdly judged that men who made flaming and intransigent speeches in the aula of St. Peter's might behave more reasonably in private.

I learned more of the psychology of the bishops from this small commission than from listening to the debates in the aula. Cardinal Ottaviani proved to be a genial chairman and Cardinal Bea was firm, gentle and humble. No disharmony was generated by the chair. In the Vatican apartment in which we met there was no echo of the rancour which had marred the debate in St. Peter's. The bishops were determined to find a peaceful solution. The only discord came from the advisers (*periti*) in attendance. A German theologian addressed us in a voice often rising to a scream. The chairmen wisely decided that if we were going to be subjected to a repetition by theologians of the kind of speech already made by bishops we would make no more progress in private than we had in public. It was therefore resolved to break up into small sub-committees, each working on one section of the new draft decree. There was need for speed because the mutual hostility shown by some of the fathers had disedified the whole assembly and given great pain to the ailing Pope John. Despite the need for speed, however, I proposed that there should be joint chairmen of each sub-committee. Cardinal Ottaviani felt this to be unnecessary but I insisted that if it was necessary to have joint chairmen for the whole committee it was essential to follow the same procedure for each part of it. Other-wise—since each cardinal was chosen on one side or other for his known views—the findings of a sub-committee with a powerful personality in the chair might be suspect.

"Are you suggesting," asked Cardinal Ottaviani with a smile, "that anyone would be afraid to disagree with me as chairman?" To which I replied amid some laughter: "Your Eminence, I would not be afraid to disagree with you at any time but some bishops might be unable to stand up to some cardinals." I could not give names but I had in mind men like Cardinal Ruffini, on one side, and the mercurial Cardinal Léger, on the other. Cardinal Bea agreed with me so the matter had to be put to the Pope personally after the meeting. Pope John also agreed that joint chairmanship of each sub-committee was desirable and to make this possible nominated two more cardinals to this special com-mission. We were then divided into small groups with equal numbers of sheep and goats. I found myself with three other bishops in a group under the joint chairmanship of Cardinal Liénart of Lille and Cardinal Ruffini of Palermo. This was the beginning of a warm friendship with Cardinal Liénart who after the Council came to stay with me in Westminster. These sub-committees went swiftly to work and within two or three days produced wording sufficiently ambiguous to satisfy rabid ecumenists and fanatical ultramontanes. When the revised decree on divine revelation was brought to the Council the following year it was briefly and uncontentiously debated and unanimously approved.

Despite his reputation as an ogre Cardinal Ottaviani showed himself to be a gentle person. I was destined to disagree with him on more than one occasion. A clash, which though not belonging to this period may conveniently be told here, took place soon after my appointment as Archbishop of Westminster. When the Council of Christians and Jews was formed the *ex officio* presidents were the Archbishop of Canterbury, the Chief Rabbi, the Moderators and the Archbishop of Westminster. This organisation to combat anti-semitism is strong in London where there is a large Jewish population. After the war Cardinal Griffin unexpectedly received orders from the Holy Office in Rome to resign his presidency. It is thought that the Holy Office (which rarely gives reasons for its ukases) was displeased by the speech of an English Jew at a Geneva conference in which he was alleged to have attacked Christian schools. Whatever the reason for such drastic action by the Holy See Cardinal Griffin, who at that time was in failing health, was obliged to comply. Cardinal Godfrey made an approach to the Holy Office after his succession to Westminster. To his request to be allowed to resume the presidency of the Council he received a blunt *non expedit*. By the time I was appointed to Westminster the religious atmosphere had totally changed. The Vatican Council had issued its Declaration on the Jews in the production of which I had played a modest part. The Holy Office itself had been under considerable fire for its autocracy. Such indeed was its unpopularity that after the Council the name Holy Office was expunged in favour of the clumsy and near tautologous title of Sacred Congregation for the doctrine of the faith.

Although, as I have said, this episode does not belong to my time in Liverpool it helps to explain the evolution of Catholic customs in recent years. As soon as I returned to Rome for the second session of the Council I called on Cardinal Ottaviani at the Holy Office. I explained why the Archbishop of Westminster ought to resume office as one of the Presidents of the Council of Christians and Jews. I took with me Bishop Holland, a colleague on the Secretariat for Christian Unity, to support my contention that the continued absence of the Catholic archbishop was harmful to our relations with the Jews. I was able to tell him that the Americans had now formed a national section and that the Spaniards had begun negotiations to found a branch of the Council of Christians and Jews in Madrid. The Cardinal was courteous but unconvinced that the time had come for a change of policy. Given the tradition of the Holy Office I did not expect Cardinal Ottaviani to withdraw the ban formally. It was sufficient for my purpose to have stated that it was pastorally desirable to resume the close connexion of English Catholics with the Council of Christians and Jews and that the start of a new episcopate in Westminster made the moment opportune. On my return to Westminster I wrote an official letter declaring that as a matter of conscience I intended to accept the invitation of the Archbishop of Canterbury and the Chief Rabbi to join them. Before doing so I promised to consider any reasonable objections the Cardinal might make. The answer was silence. I took it to be the benevolent silence which gives consent.

On 22nd January, 1963 Cardinal Godfrey, Archbishop of West-minster, died at the age of seventy-three. He was a gentle, prayerful

[358]

man who made no great impact on the non-Catholic public. He had spent much of his priestly life in seminaries. For many years he taught theology at Ushaw where I came to know him. Subsequently he replaced Monsignor Hinsley as rector of the English College in Rome. He took up duty during my last year in Rome when, although ordained, I was still a student. He had been kind to me in my schooldays at Ushaw although I was never actually his pupil. He always gave me his friendship which was a source of inspiration during most of my life as a priest. William Godfrey made little mark as a bishop largely because during his robust years he was in the diplomatic service of the Holy See as the first Apostolic Delegate to Great Britain. The good diplomat is anonymous and Dr. Godfrey never had the slightest difficulty in keeping silent. He was already sixty-three years of age when as Archbishop of Liverpool he was in a position to exercise overt leadership. It was too late for him to establish himself as a national figure but he was superlatively successful in the more important and much more difficult task of giving his priests and people an example of personal holiness. This was achieved not by what he said—he was a dull speaker—but by what he was.

As an old friend and disciple I was invited to preach the panegyric at his funeral in Westminster Cathedral. The following extract is an unrhetorical tribute to an archbishop whose chief attributes were his faith, strength of character and deep love of the Church:

He had a rare degree of self-control, and could not be betrayed into making angry or incautious statements. Probably he never needed to retract any words he had spoken. It is possible, of course, that sometimes his prudence led him to an excessive caution. He did not take easily or kindly to new ideas. He arrived at decisions so slowly that he found it hard to yield to argument or to alter judgments he had made. In this he appeared to some as stubborn and self-opinionated. But, in fact, it was not his practice to force his views on others. He was merely content to rest on the opinions he had formed because they were invariably the fruits of prayerful consideration.

On the death of Dr. Downey the Holy See appointed the Apostolic Delegate to the vacant see of Liverpool. By reason of his enthusiastic loyalty for the Holy See, it was an immense sacrifice for him to cease to be its representative. He became more reconciled to the change when he saw what joy his coming gave to the priests and people of the North. Here in Westminster when he succeeded Cardinal Griffin he just as quickly won the confidence of his priests and people. He regarded himself not only as the father but the servant of the youngest and weakest among them. Despite failing health he forced himself to make the last journey to Rome to take part in the opening session of the Council. He spoke frequently and always in faultless Latin at the daily meetings. None of his brother bishops then knew that he was suffering from a fatal disease. But he knew and had known for months. It is some measure of his heroic unselfishness that he refused to embarrass others by mentioning his own ill-health.

There is always widespread speculation when the see of Westminster falls vacant. The reason is that although the strength of the Catholic Church is greatest in the north of England it is to Westminster that Catholics and the general public look for an official Catholic voice. Inevitably the press canvassed names of possible successors to Cardinal Godfrey and published the guesses of anonymous clergy and laity. Canonically there is no primatial see in the Catholic Church in England but the diocese of Westminster is so regarded and therefore enquiries about candidates are more wide-ranging than for other vacant sees. The Apostolic Delegate consults not only the bishops of the Westminster province but all the bishops of England and Wales. He also tries to ascertain the views of clergy and laity. The voice of the laity is especially useful for suggesting the type of bishop needed in a diocese. It is of little value in determining whether a particular priest has the required qualities. The true priestly character is not easily discerned. Only priests and bishops are in a position to assess their brethren and even their judgment is fallible because a good priest is an extremely private person. To be a good pastor he has to be like Melchisedech "without father, without mother, without genealogy, having neither beginning of days nor end of life" (Heb. VII : 3). The effectiveness of his public life depends to a unique degree on his spiritual life. This can be known only to God and in some measure to a few people close to him. His personal attitude to his people, fellow priests and those set over him is the real test of a priest's holiness. The externals of a priest's ministry—praying, preaching, organising—are easily seen but they portray only a man's public face. A priest may spend hours in prayer and preach moving sermons on charity while not living at peace with clergy in the same house, with parishioners or with superiors who do not let him have his way. It is difficult to diagnose holiness in anyone but almost impossible to know if a priest (or bishop) is his own man or God's.

The present method of appointing bishops is not perfect but the alternative of a straight election would probably be much worse. Elections are satisfactory if the candidate is to hold office for a short period before being subject again to the judgment of his constituents. That is the basis of parliamentary democracy. A bishop is not part of a democratic machine nor does he receive power from his priests and people. He is appointed by the Pope acting in the name of the Church. This does not rule out elections but it makes episcopal elections essentially different from any other elections in the Church. When, for example, a religious superior is to be elected the community knows a great deal about the likely candidates. Many will have lived in the same house. The diocesan priest is well known to very few. For an election to be worthwhile personal information about each candidate would need to be circulated to all the' electors. It is easy to list a man's paper qualifications and public achievements but it is impossible to assess his priestly character without knowing his virtues and vices. That is why confidential enquiries are made about every priest whose name is proposed for a bishopric. It has become fashionable to question the propriety of any sort of confidential enquiry yet without such enquiry it is foolhardy to fill a post of responsibility. A dishonest man should not be entrusted with money and a sadist must not be put in charge of children. Lecherous or intemperate men are security risks. All this is recognised by the civil authorities in every land. No government would appoint anyone to high office without the most searching enquiries. The Church has a sacred duty to seek trustworthy priests for the episcopate. Bishops must admit that mistakes have been made—perhaps in their own case—but many more would be made if the Pope relied on opinion polls. It is true that the apostles cast lots to find a successor to Judas Iscariot but they put only two names into the hat and they were presumably well vetted.

The Holy See is aware that in the post-conciliar Church more consultation of priests and laity is desirable. As a first step bishops are now encouraged to discuss appointments with their senate of priests and pastoral council. One of the most important questions to be settled is whether a local priest or one from another diocese is more desirable. It is not uncommon for a diocese to need someone from outside to give it new life and direction. It is also true that some excellent candidates for the episcopate need new pastures if they are to be good shepherds. For many reasons it is best for the ultimate choice to be left to the Holy See. The Church will never again leave the choice to the state—concordats which leave the last word to heads of state are being anxiously re-negotiated. Although the Pope nominates every bishop it is obvious that he can know few candidates personally. He is advised by the Congregation of Bishops which meets in the Vatican six times a year to consider names proposed for the episcopate. There are differences of procedure in various countries but, apart from the very few dioceses in in which the chapter of canons has by tradition the right of election, bishops are chosen by the Pope on the recommendation of the Congregation of Bishops.

The names to be submitted to this Congregation are decided only after a thorough and lengthy process. When a see falls vacant in England the archbishop or, if the metropolitan see itself is vacant, the senior bishop of the province presides at a meeting of the cathedral chapter. At this meeting three names (the *terna*) are chosen by secret vote. These names are communicated to the bishops of the province who send them with their comments and, if they wish, with additional names to the Apostolic Delegate. It is his duty to obtain confidential views on each candidate from those in the best position to assess his qualifications and character. The most recent regulations from the Holy See instruct papal envoys to compile lists of suitable priests (*episcopabiles*) for use if the *terna* does not contain the name of a suitable candidate. The list of names together with biographical details and confidential assessments are then sent to the Congregation of Bishops in Rome. The Apostolic Delegate also sends to Rome a report on the state of the vacant diocese together with a summary of the opinions expressed by the local clergy and laity regarding the type of bishop the diocese needs.

The Congregation of Bishops has a staff of experienced bishops and priests with a cardinal at its head. These are the permanent officials experienced in assessing the kind of information required. The Apostolic Delegate is almost certain to be asked for further comment on some candidates and may be asked to supply more names. When sufficient material has been assembled the documents are printed for private circulation to members of the Congregation. These are cardinals and bishops from all parts of the world. Members who like myself live outside Rome are not expected to attend every meeting. We are not sent the highly confidential documents unless we propose to attend a meeting. The curia being now truly international there are bound to be some members at every meeting with first hand experience of the countries for whom bishops are to be appointed. After the experience of many meetings I still find the procedure most impressive. Members

[362]

are not summoned merely to give formal approval to decisions already arrived at by a national hierarchy, a papal delegate or the permanent officials. Each cardinal and bishop is required to express a personal opinion on each candidate. On some occasions I have seen the entire list of candidates rejected as unsatisfactory. A see is sometimes left vacant for more than a year but a long process is more satisfactory *sub specie aeternitatis* than a snap election in the home diocese. While the appointment of bishops remains life-long it is wise to proceed with caution. Some day bishops and parish priests may be appointed only for a term—as with abbots and most religious superiors.

During the weeks immediately following the death of Cardinal Godfrey the press occasionally published rumours of the imminent appointment of a successor. Although my name was frequently mentioned I did not think it likely that I would be asked to leave Liverpool. I did not share the view that the Holy See would be obliged to leave me in Liverpool until the building of the cathedral was completed. I regarded myself as an unlikely choice for a quite different reason. Although born and educated in England I have an Irish name. There have been other Archbishops of Westminster with Irish parents—Wiseman, for example, Bowne and Hinsley—but their names did not sound Irish. In the past it has been used as a slur on the Church that it is foreign ('the Italian Mission'). Apart from converts and traditionally Catholic families, mainly in the north, Catholics in this country are mostly Irish or of Irish origin. In the East End of London, for example, Irish and Catholic used to be interchangeable terms ("Yes, Father, I'm a Catholic. I turned Irish to marry her.") The Holy See is naturally not disposed to foster the myth that the Church in this country is a foreign institution. That is why I thought it likely that if possible a man with an English-sounding name would be appointed to the see of Westminster.

There was considerable delay in nominating a new archbishop. Evidently the Apostolic Delegate did not regard any candidate as an obvious choice. There was sufficient uncertainty to delay the appointment for several months. Pope John and Archbishop O'Hara, the Apostolic Delegate, were both dead before the see was filled.

The death of Pope John came after a painful illness whose course was followed by the public as if it were an international crisis. The interest shown by people of every creed in the Pope's struggle on his death bed was unprecedented. The illness of its chief citizen is bound to be newsworthy in his own country but Pope John's illness was the most important news all over the world. Not much more than ten per cent of the population of Britain is Catholic but press and radio kept the country as fully and frequently informed of the Pope's condition as if he had been one of our own royal family. The fact is that most people did regard him as one of their own. The achievement of Pope John was to win the love of millions to whom the papacy itself has hitherto been anathema. It will be for historians to examine all the reasons for his astonishing popularity but it is already possible to see how he was unique among the successors of St. Peter.

International figures employ Public Relations Officers but Pope John had the free services of thousands of journalists. They took him to their hearts from the time of his coronation and kept him there throughout his short reign. Pope John was so evidently genuine in his love of people for their own sake that journalists had to shout the good news to the whole world. Until recently Vatican protocol made what journalists call hard news almost impossible to obtain. By custom papal decrees are official and binding only after appearing in the official Vatican publication the *Acta Apostolicae Sedis*. Advance information may be given *sub secreto* to enable bishops to handle publicity in their own dioceses but the device of issung embargoed material to the press had not been found acceptable. Pope John humanised press relations by discouraging the hagiographic style of the Vatican newspaper and giving journalists what help he could.

Pope John's death agony lasted four whole days. He was occasionally comatose but more frequently lucid and sharply aware of his condition. Never losing his serenity he offered his sufferings for world peace and Christian Unity, two objectives of his pontificate. On the evening of Friday 31st May, 1963 to the gnawing pain of a stomach tumour was added the anguish of peritonitis. All Saturday and Sunday the agony continued but he was fortified by the prayers being offered throughout the world. In addition to members of his own flock, millions of people, Christians and non-Christians, in churches and chapels, synagogues and mosques, were interceding for a beloved father. He was shown a telegram from the men he had visited in the Roman gaol: "Holy Father we are close to you with immense love. Convicts of Regina Coeli prison." That message came on Whit Sunday as if to remind Pope John of the new Pentecost to which he had compared his Council. After reciting the litany of the saints one of the priests at his bedside asked him to bless the Council and the Church. By now Pope John was too weak to raise his hands but he smiled and nodded his head.

On Whit Monday the B.B.C. decided to include in their programme

Panorama a tribute to the dying Pontiff. The producer telephoned Liverpool to ask me to go to the B.B.C. studios in Manchester. I had to refuse because on a bank holiday the East Lancashire Road is almost solid with traffic. Half-an-hour later the B.B.C. rang again. They had managed to hire a private plane to fly me to Manchester. It must have cost the B.B.C. hundreds of pounds to transport me to their Manchester studios but no price was too high to give the public news of Pope John. The Heron aircraft brought me to Manchester in less than half-an-hour. Well before eight o'clock I was in the studio ready to talk about the dying pope. At two minutes to eight the studio telephone rang. Broadcasting House, London, was on the line to say that Pope John had died at ten minutes to eight. Panorama became a panegyric.

Catholics may not be the best judges of the esteem in which the Pope was held. They, after all, honour the Vicar of Christ irrespective of his personal qualities. The following short editorial gives a fair idea of the average non-Catholic Englishman's attitude to the dying Pope John. The article appeared in the *Sunday Express* on 2nd June 1963 under the title "A Man of God":

During the last few hours something has happened which is almost unique in history.

Virtually the whole of civilised mankind, including millions of militant Protestants and even many who do not call themselves Christians at all, have been united in grief for the Pope.

In grief for the Pope

Think what a change those words represent in men's hearts. For the messages of sympathy which have poured into Rome this week-end have not been merely the usual expression of polite, diplomatic regard for the head of a great religious community. . . . Pope John has for ever put hundreds of millions who accept Rome's leadership in the forefront of the fight for tolerance and world peace. Indeed, it may be that history will single out Pope John as the man who changed the world by his amazing decision to offer the hand of humanity and friendship to Moscow . . . He was an ordinary man who also had the inspiration and the greatness to apply the simple, decent God-given standards of ordinary men to world affairs. In doing so he wrought a miracle.

He hoped fervently to unite all Christians. But, far more effectively than by needless technical arrangements and concordats between Churches, he has already united us—in sorrow and hope.

It is too soon to assess the place John XXIII will hold in the history of the papacy. His greatest achievement was to have become universally loved without any conscious effort to court favour. He did nothing so spectacular as Pope Paul who was to fly to New York to address the United Nations, go on pilgrimage to the Holy Land and attend congresses in India, Latin America and the Far East. Pope John hardly moved out of the city of Rome, made few speeches and wrote only two encyclicals of any weight—*Mater et Magistra*—a modern version of the social encyclicals of Leo XIII and Pius XI—and *Pacem in Terris*, an appeal for a cessation of the arms race and a just and generous attitude of the rich towards the poor nations. Pope John's achievement is the more baffling because it happened in the second half of the twentieth century when the Church as an institution was being attacked and ecclesiastics were nowhere near the top of the popularity charts.

What will historians of the late twentieth and, if time has not run out, the twenty-first century say about John XXIII? Mary Pickford, the film star, used to be called the world's sweetheart. Pope John was her first serious rival for that title. The astonishing thing is that the contender was not an international television performer, an Olympic champion or the first man on the moon. He was a jovial, hard-working, prayerful man who would have made an excellent parish priest in a country town or a bishop in a small Italian diocese. Angelo Roncalli was not the first peasant to ascend the papal throne in this century. Giuseppe Sarto, a peasant from the north of Italy, became Pope in 1903 under the title of Pius X.

There was no great mystery about Pope John's election. He was chosen because he was a very old man. His chief duty would be to make Monsignor Montini, Archbishop of Milan, a cardinal so that he could be elected Pope at the next conclave. This was the policy of the cardinals and it was carried out precisely. That will present no problems to posterity. The problem will be to gauge his greatness from the raw material of his recorded words and deeds. Popularity is ephemeral. Nobody is more dead than yesterday's hero. The one significant fact that historians will be unable to blink is that by the time of his death Pope John had become the best-loved man in Christendom. Who else has a greater claim? St. Antony? St. Francis? Thomas More? Winston Churchill? John F. Kennedy? All may have been greater men but none was so beloved by so many.

His popularity will be no more than a footnote in the story of Pope

John. The overwhelmingly great event of his reign was the Vatican Council. We have seen something of the only session of the Council which took place during his lifetime. I have described its dramatic opening and the wrangling over the speculative question of the source or sources of revelation. I remained Archbishop of Liverpool throughout the first session and I must complete the picture. The bishops were still only becoming acquainted when the session came to an end. A few of the fathers had become well known through their interventions (speeches). Almost all were cardinals because they were given the floor each day before any of the bishops. Consequently the cardinals monopolised the first hour of nearly every congregation (meeting). The result was that they covered all the main issues and often rendered subsequent speeches pointless. The president constantly urged speakers not to be repetitious but a bishop who had come five thousand miles to say something usually insisted on saying it.

At the close of the first session little had been decided but many ideas had been ventilated. The subject most fully debated was liturgical reform. It might be more accurate to say that the bishops were under the impression that the liturgy had been fully discussed. In retrospect it is clear that they were given the opportunity of discussing only general principles. Subsequent changes were more radical than those intended by Pope John and the bishops who passed the decree on the liturgy. His sermon at the end of the first session shows that Pope John did not suspect what was being planned by the liturgical experts. The only development to which the Pope made specific reference concerned St. Joseph who "from today has his name shining in the canon of the Mass all over the world". It is ironic that after the Council it would be 'in the spirit of Pope John' that so many liturgical antics would be performed. There is a certain poetic justice in the humiliation of the Catholic Church at the hands of liturgical anarchists. Catholics used to laugh at Anglicans for being 'high' or 'low'. We said that they did not believe in their Church but only in the vicar who happened to cater for their liturgical fancy. Catholics no longer laugh at Anglicans. The old boast that the Mass is everywhere the same and that Catholics are happy whichever priest celebrates is no longer true. When on 7th December, 1962 the bishops voted overwhelmingly (1,922 against 11) in favour of the first chapter of the Constitution on the Liturgy they did not realise that they were initiating a process which after the Council would cause confusion and bitterness throughout the Church. Priests and people accustomed to a Mass unchanged for centuries sometimes became so angry that they were irrational in their opposition to reform.

There can nevertheless be little doubt that the liturgical decree was one of the great triumphs of the Council. The decree cannot justly be held accountable for priests who in defiance of the Pope devise their own liturgy and de-sacralise the Mass by dispensing with vestments and sacred vessels. Nor can the Council be blamed for the disappearance of Latin and the suppression of the beautiful chants and melodies bequeathed by the great composers. The uninspiring music used with the vernacular liturgy will have a short life. Musical appreciation is developing so rapidly in our schools that the next generation is not likely to tolerate third-rate music in church. Refusing to recognise the enormous spiritual benefits of the vernacular some Catholics set their faces against any reform of the liturgy. They were unfamiliar with the history of the liturgy and unaware that the shape of the Mass has varied at different times in many parts of the world. The liturgy of Salisbury ("the Sarum Use") was used extensively in England before the Reformation—it was the basis of the Prayer Book of Edward VI. It would have surprised our forefathers if they had been told that in the twentieth century some Catholics would make a fetish of one stage in the development of one rite (the Roman). Some Catholics were said to have given up the practice of their faith for lack of what they call 'the Tridentine Mass'. The Council is in no way responsible for extravagant reactions of this kind.

The chief arguments in the debate on the liturgy concerned the use of Latin in the Mass and the sacraments. This important debate, eminently practical and pastoral as well as theological, yielded a great deal of fresh knowledge. Men who had vehemently opposed the use of the vernacular in early speeches were completely won over by the arguments of learned liturgists and eventually supported it by their votes. Nobody living comfortably in the West could remain unaffected by the pleas of bishops behind the iron curtain. Archbishop Seper, Primate of Yugoslavia (who later succeeded Cardinal Ottaviani at the Holy Office) told the fathers how impossible it had become to teach the faith except through the liturgy. In communist states there are neither Catholic schools nor religious instruction for children. It was not enough to be able to preach homilies because these were liable to be overheard and misrepresented by agents of the secret police. The best way to teach the Catholic religion was through the Mass and the sacraments. This obviously required the use of the mother tongue. Bishop Kobayashi from Japan explained that the language and rules of the Roman rite were essentially western and alien to Orientals. Even the significance of colours is different. White, for example, is the colour not of joy but of mourning in the East. "Is our unity with the Holy See so tenuous that it has to be maintained by a rigid uniformity?" he asked.

The debate on the liturgy was splendid. It brought the fathers together in a way that other schemata had failed to do. Few bishops had been professional theologians before being given charge of their dioceses. They were far more at home with pastoral questions than with speculative theology. The debate taught them the complexity of liturgical problems and made them realise how harmful it would be to the Church to sustain their preconceived attitudes. They also learned how impossible it is to attempt to maintain complete uniformity in the modern Church. Most Catholics at some time have pointed with pride to the near miracle of a Mass identical in word and gesture throughout the world. It was not easy for bishops on their return from Rome to explain how its abandonment at home helped eastern Europe and the missionary lands. They had given a practically unanimous vote for the vernacular while fully appreciating the cost of losing uniformity in a world-wide Church. This they did the more readily because they were assured that the Latin Mass would remain the norm while the mother tongue would be employed only where pastorally desirable. The text of the vote they approved read in part: "The use of the Latin language except by particular dispensation is to be preserved in the Latin rites. But since the use of the mother tongue . . . may be useful to the people it may be extended . . . in the first place to the readings and directives and some of the prayers and chants . . ."

It is interesting to speculate whether the bishops would have approved the decree so overwhelmingly if they had realised that in practice it would mean the extinction of a common language in the Catholic Church. Today even in so-called Latin countries a Latin Mass is rarely heard.

One consequence of the Council will not be fully felt for at least two generations. The official documents of the Church are still in Latin. Bishops of different nations are thus spared the confusion arising from nuances of meaning in translations from multi-lingual announcements. If Latin were to be completely abandoned bishops would need to study the matrix document which almost certainly would be in Italian, French or German. The hazard of relying on translation is illustrated in *The Council Daybook*, the quasi-official account of the Council published by the United States hierarchy (N.C.W.C., Washington). In the very passage on the vernacular it quotes the words of the Vatican spokesman, Cipriano Vagaggini O.S.B. "Pope John . . . has strengthened the bishops to look unflinchingly at these horizons: '*Duc in altum* (lead upward)'". It happens that *altum* in Latin can mean high or low. In the context (Luke V : 4) '*Duc in altum*' means not 'lead upward' but 'launch into the deep'. If future bishops have to rely on translations of the documents of the Holy See the Church will be worse off. Poor as their conversational Latin may have been the bishops at the Council were at least using the same documents in a dead and therefore unchanging language. Some priests ordained since the Council have never said Mass in Latin or studied the Council decrees in the original. The advantage of a vernacular liturgy is beyond doubt but the good of the universal Church requires a rescue operation on behalf of ecclesiastical Latin before the belief of Catholics has become fragmented through differences of language. *Lex orandi lex credendi* (the rule of prayer is the rule of faith) has wider implications than those considered by the Vatican fathers.

There was no other positive result of the first session of the Council. It is true that there were three other debates—Communications, Unity, the Church—but to use a colloquialism then coming in vogue, all were non-events and as such can be dismissed in a few words. The schema on communications was as inept as any other amateur attempt to do the work of professionals. There are hundreds of Catholics in journalism, radio and television of whom some are very distinguished indeed. At this stage of the Council we had not thought of giving the laity an active part. It was not until after the first session that they were allotted even a passive role. They were then promoted to the same division as the non-Catholic Observers and given the title of *auditores* (listeners). It might have been possible to produce a useful document on the mass media if Catholic journalists had been employed but it was too late to make drastic alterations when the schema was presented. The debate began on Friday 23rd November and proved so uninspiring that by Monday 26th the fathers had heard enough. By a standing vote—not a standing ovation—the bishops ended the discussion with a recommendation that the whole schema be re-written.

The debate on Unity received (and deserved) a no better fate. The incompetence which marked the technical side of the first session of the Council though deplorable was in no way surprising. The last Council had taken place nearly a hundred years earlier (1869–70) and the one before that had been the Council of Trent (1545–63). There was nobody at the Second Vatical Council who had any recollection of the First. It is true that there was one bishop present who had been alive during Vatican One but as he was now a centenarian it was not thought practical to put him in charge of Vatican Two. We therefore had to learn as we went. Small wonder that the first session was full of mistakes and annoyances. The debate on Unity was an example of consummate mismanagement. One might have supposed that this important debate —important because there had been so much talk of unity and the Observers were awaiting this debate above all others—would have been conducted under the baton of Cardinal Bea, the greatest ecumenical authority in the Church. That was not at all how the authorities viewed the situation. Cardinal Bea was regarded as an authority on Protestants and in the long Vatican perspective a Protestant is a Johnny-come-lately.

The unity of Christendom was first broken in the fifth century when the Nestorians and Monophysites separated from the Church of Rome and Constantinople. The schism in the eleventh century which split the Orthodox from the Catholic Church was the second and greater source of disunity. The sixteenth century saw the greatest schism of all when wholesale apostasy from the Catholic Church led to the formation of several Protestant bodies. It seemed obvious to the Holy See that the first and most important step in building unity was to reconcile the Eastern Churches. That is why it was not Cardinal Bea but Cardinal Cicognani, President of the Oriental Churches commission, who was entrusted with the schema.

It is some measure of the confusion caused by hurried and inadequate preparation for the Council that no less than three schemata on unity had been made ready for the fathers. The first considered the Orthodox. The second, which was concerned with Protestants, had been drawn up by the theological commission. A third dealt with general principles of ecumenism and was prepared by the Secretariat for Unity. In the end Cardinal Bea's secretariat was left to deal with all ecumenical questions. This schema on unity vanished after a few days of debate, never to reappear. The discussion centred on the Orthodox Churches but some of the Catholic Orientals used the occasion to air grievances not against Constantinople but Rome. Catholic Orientals (Uniates) are in a somewhat embarrassing position. They are unacceptable to many Orthodox who regard them as ecclesiastical quislings. Towards their Roman Catholic brethren the sensitiveness of some Orientals borders on the pathological. Maximos IV, the Patriarch of Antioch, who refused to speak Latin at the Council could hardly ever resist attacking his western brethren. This may have been his way of making an ecumenical gesture towards his Orthodox brethren. The oriental patriarchs sat on a special bench above the western bishops exactly opposite the cardinals to whom they regarded themselves as superior both in antiquity and prestige.

The debate on unity produced no memorable speeches. The schema was inadequate as a basis for a thorough discussion on Christian Unity. It would have been more unceremoniously rejected had it not been presented by Cardinal Cicognani, the Pope's Secretary of State (a prelate much loved by the English and American bishops—he had been Apostolic Delegate in the U.S.A. for the record number of twenty-five years). The debate was allowed to continue for four days during which time homage was paid to the Orientals. The fact that their sacraments and orders are certainly valid was stressed. It was suggested that seen in the perspective of collegiality the Pope need not be an obstacle to reunion. The best point in the debate had nothing to do with the subject under discussion. A Mexican bishop protested about the way the schemata had been drawn up. He complained that although this Council was supposed to be primarily pastoral the texts were not. He criticised the rules of procedure which made debating impossible. There could be no give-and-take, no real argument. "Alas!" he said, "we are the victims of an interminable flood of monologues."

To this interminable flood I contributed as a member of the Secretariat for Unity. My contribution was pedestrian though it was subsequently reported[1] that "Archbishop Heenan of Liverpool put his finger on the crux of the matter when he spoke of the problem of authority as the real issue dividing the Churches, not doctrine as such. It would be a miracle if the Orthodox were to 'submit' to Rome but that there was no reason for discouragement. Hitler by persecution had united the Christians of central and western Europe. Perhaps the communist persecution would unite the Christians of eastern Europe. He deplored the absence of representatives of the Ecumenical Patriarch of Constantinople among the Observers." I also drew attention to the anomaly of a scheme on Christian Unity containing no mention of Protestants. I reminded the bishops that the Anglicans were always the first to respond to ecumenical initiatives. The following day the schema was smothered by over two thousand votes and passed to the Secretariat

[1] Xavier Rynne, *Letters from Vatican City* (Faber and Faber, London, 1963).

for Unity to extract any good points for incorporation in a new schema on ecumenism in the next session.

Pope John was in such a hurry to finish the Council that he had fixed 12th May, 1963 for the opening of the second and last session. Few bishops could face that prospect with any pleasure. It is true that other ecumenical councils had taken bishops away from their dioceses for months or even years but now that air travel enabled bishops to be back in their dioceses within twenty-four hours none was prepared to camp out in Rome between sessions. To return home for only a few weeks seemed futile. Bishops would barely have resumed their pastoral programme before it was time to return. Many of us therefore let the Pope know that we thought it unsatisfactory to return to our dioceses only for Christmas and Easter. Although it meant prolonging the Council he gave way and postponed the opening of the second session until 8th September, 1963. Presumably Pope John knew that he had little time left. He doubtless hoped to finish the Council himself but he was dead long before the second session began.

The final debate of the first session was on the schema *De Ecclesia* (the Church). This was the work of the theological commission under the presidency of Cardinal Ottaviani. It was given a generally hostile reception. Nobody alleged that it contained positive errors but it lacked all signs of the new outlook the Council had been called to provide. It was criticised for being too juridical, insufficiently ecumenical and not sufficiently rooted in the bible. These three complaints were repeated constantly during subsequent sessions in every conceivable context. (As with all clichés they eventually became worn out and useless.) There were some outstanding speeches in this debate but they were to prove of little practical use for the very good reason that Pope John had decided that all schemata must be re-written without delay. Two days before the close of the session (6th December) he made Cardinal Cicognani president of a new committee whose task was to co-ordinate the work of all conciliar commissions in preparation for the second and final session of the Council when a few brief schemata were to be proposed for discussion.

Since the schema *De Ecclesia* together with all the schemata was to be withdrawn for re-drafting the speeches had no impact on the subsequent voting. They were nevertheless among the most memorable of the Council. Chief among them was a philippic by the Bishop of Bruges in which he coined the oft to be repeated word 'triumphalism'. He said that it was time to drop attitudes out of tune with the social outlook of the twentieth century. He had especially in mind the pompous style of ecclesiastical pronouncements and the aggressive Catholic manner of claiming always to be right. He wanted less pride in the Church Militant and more humility in a Church which, like its Master, came into the world to serve. He accused the schema of containing clericalism of a most unattractive kind. It spoke as if the Church were a pyramid with the pope and clergy on top and the people at the base. It gave no hint of the whole Church being the People of God. The Church was made to appear formidable instead of being a sheepfold or, to change the metaphor, the mother of men. This was the best-known speech made at the Council if only because it gave currency to the new word 'triumphalism'. All new words are misunderstood and few have been more thoroughly misused than this one. It was widely employed to discredit ritual and liturgical solemnity of all kinds. Bishop de Smedt, however, is no puritan. Anyone who has seen the Procession of the Precious Blood held annually in Bruges will have admired the dignified splendour of the colourful costumes worn by enthusiastic young men, women and children. This is not triumphalism any more than were the silver trumpets sounded from the dome of St. Peter's at the elevation during the Pope's Mass. Latter day Cromwells would strip our churches of all splendour. English people with their love of ceremonial and sense of occasion are baffled by the wanton abandonment of glorious pageantry and music in the Church of Rome.

Cardinal Suenens of Brussels also made a notable speech. As was his custom he directed his words less to his colleagues in the aula than to the world outside. He said that the Church must provide the answers for which the world was looking. It must give a lead in all that concerns decency and the dignity of the human person. It must give thought to the population explosion, the third world, peace and war. It was stirring prose and gained almost as much applause as that of his colleague from Bruges. There was another speaker that day who was unable to coin phrases or produce oratorical fireworks. A quiet, thoughtful man, he had not spoken until this last week of the first session. Nor was he to speak again during the Council. He was Giovanni Battista Montini, Cardinal Archbishop of Milan. His intervention spoken in the now well-known flat voice contained no rhetoric. It would not have commanded attention but for the fact that Cardinal Montini was thought to have the ear of Pope John. He spoke against the schema and said that it must be re-written by the theological commission with the help of the unity secretariat. He said that the old approach was no longer fruitful.

It was pointless to talk of the rights of the Church in those parts of the world which regarded the Church with suspicion. The Church must not think of itself merely as a society founded by Christ but as the very body of Christ to be used as the instrument for the salvation of men.

The last meeting of the first session took place on 7th December. It was the happiest gathering of the session. This was partly because it was the last day of term and by this time even the oldest bishops were feeling like schoolboys. There was another reason for relief and rejoicing which was not voiced. There had been no signs of schism. Many had feared that the hostility of the north Europeans and the lack of imagination of some of the curial cardinals might have led to something more serious than verbal clashes. There were bishops who, recalling the history of the First Vatican Council, feared that there might be a Döllinger among the north Europeans. Some had feared the possibility of a National Church in the Netherlands. Now they felt that all was well. Despite fierce and sometimes bitter arguments and recriminations the bishops were united by their love of the Church and personal devotion to Pope John. An Ottaviani or a Ruffini on one side and a Suenens or a Léger on the other might give outsiders the impression of different creeds but beyond any shadow of doubt each of these cardinals would have laid down his life for the One, Holy, Catholic and Roman Church. Passionate disagreement in debate is compatible with essential unity of faith.

All the bishops were happy to be going home but not all were going home satisfied with the results of the first session. Some regarded the Council as a shameful waste of time and money. With so much talk about the third world's starvation they felt it was criminal to spend millions of pounds on a conference. A few bishops thought it not only a waste of time but a positive disaster. They were persuaded that in their very different ways Cardinals Bea, Suenens and Alfrink would destroy the unity of the Catholic Church. It is impossible to say how many fathers shared this gloomy view but the number was certainly not large. By the end of the session a very large majority had been won over and had become enthusiastic about the Council's potential for good. This would not have been true at the beginning or even half way through the session. By the end of those eight intensive weeks, however, almost everyone saw the value of the Council and was confident that with the lessons of the first session learned the second session would be rewarding. Most diocesan bishops agreed with Pope John that the second session must be the last. Some of the missionary bishops so

[375]

enjoyed the companionship of their colleagues that they would probably have been prepared to return to Rome every year.

The last meeting was presided over by Cardinal Liénart who expressed his gratitude to the fathers for their hard work and good spirit. He had been to the fore in some of the controversies but had never become impatient, emotional or in the slightest way uncharitable. He was the very model of a conciliar father. He began the meeting with the unexpected and joyful announcement that Pope John, who had been too ill to hold his customary audiences with groups of bishops during the previous week, was much better and later in the morning would make his first appearance in the aula since the solemn opening on 8th December. The rest of the morning was spent in rather desultory speech-making. One contribution of interest was that of Cardinal Koenig, Archbishop of Vienna, who challenged remarks which had been made by Bishop Griffiths, Auxiliary of New York, a few days earlier. The bishop, one of the few scholars among the English-speaking bishops, was a member of the theological commission. He had disagreed vehemently with some of the views pressed by German theologians and was convinced that they were bent on a course which might deliver the Church into the hands of the Lutherans. He also thought Karl Rahner so fanatically devoted to his own theological opinions as to be unteachable. That is the background to his publicly expressed complaint that the Council had been a waste of time. "Lord," he quoted, "we have laboured all night and have taken nothing."

Cardinal Koenig, one of the best brains in the Church, would have none of it. "Venerable Brethren," he said, "we have certainly not done everything but in the last two months we have accomplished great things. By our exchange of views within these walls we have come to a much greater appreciation of the Church as she really is. We have had our differences but we have maintained the charity of Christ. We have prepared ourselves to present the world with the truth and love of Christ in the next session." That was the authentic voice of the Council. One or two bishops spoke in similar terms. The words of the last speaker were drowned by the cheering of the fathers when, promptly at eleven o'clock, Pope John appeared in St. Peter's. That last speaker was Abbot Butler of Downside who later became Auxiliary Bishop of Westminster.

Pope John told us during his surprise visit that he had little to say. He would be addressing us formally at the Council on the following day during its solemn closure. He just wanted to say a warm personal word of thanks to the bishops for having 'spoken the truth in charity'.

He expressed his satisfaction at the sight of the whole Teaching Church united in study of what to express through the Council. He told us how moved he had been two days earlier when the bishops, hearing that he had recovered, had rushed out of St. Peter's to salute him as he gave his blessing to the crowds. The bishops in their purple and scarlet "stood out like a flame in St. Peter's Square. It was a thoughtful, festive encounter . . . The Father with his sons and all our brothers in the episcopate gathered together to pray and rejoice with us in a hymn of gratitude to Our Lord and His mother. We thank you with all our heart for this proof of your warm affection."

The following day Pope John presided at the ceremonial closing of the first session of the Second Vatican Council. The words he spoke are of particular interest because they were in a way his last will and testament to the fathers of the Council. He had failed to persuade the bishops to make their respite brief in order to re-open the Council in May. Almost certainly the Pope knew he would never see us again. The shadow of death was already beginning to fall on him. There was a sadness in his voice, a wistfulness perhaps for the Council of his dreams, i.e. a brief encounter with his brother bishops. As he spoke I felt I was listening to the valediction of a much loved Father in God. I was distracted as I thought of the words of Tennyson:

> The old order changeth, yielding place to new,
> And God fulfils Himself in many ways . . .
> I have lived my life, and that which I have done
> May He within Himself make pure. But thou,
> If thou shouldst never see my face again,
> Pray for my soul.

It was no more than a distraction but for me it made Pope John's words more memorable.

In fact there was nothing remarkable in the Pope's address. He started with a tribute to the Blessed Virgin on whose feast-day the Council both began (11th October, the Divine Motherhood of Mary) and was now ending (8th December, the Immaculate Conception). He said how fitting it was that the Council should take place "in the radiance of the grace of her who is God's Mother and our own". He recalled the opening of the Council in what can only be called triumphalistic terms. "The one, holy, catholic and apostolic Church was revealed to all humanity in the splendour of her perennial mission, in

[377]

the firmness of her organisation, in the persuasiveness and attractiveness of her teaching. We recall the delegations from the various nations at the solemn inauguration of the Council. The whole world has been an admiring witness of these events." It was strange that while acknowledging the presence of the diplomats he made no reference to the Observers who had faithfully attended every congregation. It was still more strange that Pope John made no reference to Christian Unity and did not mention either the Orthodox or the Protestants. He did have a word of reassurance for non-Christians but this was perhaps an echo of his years as papal nuncio among infidels ". . . countless children of ancient and glorious civilizations which the light of Christianity does not desire to destroy but in which she could develop the richest seeds of religious vigour and human progress. Our heart casts its glance in that direction."

The Pope declared that he had been in no way worried by the sharply divergent views expressed by the fathers. There was good reason for disagreement and it was quite consistent with charity. It is the way God's providence arranges for the triumph of truth. The disputes would demonstrate to the world that Catholics enjoy the liberty of the sons of God. He then asked the bishops to study the revised schemata which would be sent to them during the recess. He realised that they would be preoccupied with their pastoral duties after their long absence from their dioceses but when they came back in September he wanted them to show that they had learned the lessons of the first session. He wanted no more time wasted. The next session must proceed "more surely, more steadily and more quickly". He wanted the Council to be over by the following Christmas at the latest. He was sure that this was the hope of all Catholics: ". . . there is hope that the conclusion awaited by all our faithful children may be reached in the glory of the incarnate Son of God in the joy of Christmas in the centenary year of the Council of Trent". (The Council of Trent ended on 3rd December, 1563.)

Pope John said that the most important phase of the Council would be the last. It would see:

> Pastors united in the gigantic effort of preaching sound doctrine and applying the law . . . with diocesan and regular clergy, nuns and laity seconding the efforts of the bishops with a most joyous and faithful response. It will be a new Pentecost and the Church will extend her motherly care to every human activity . . . These, Venerable Brethren, are the feelings of our heart which issue in

hope and prayer. You are going back to your own countries and to the precious flocks committed to your care. Be our faithful messengers in telling your priests and people how great is our affection. I make my own the words used to the bishops by Pope Pius IX at the First Vatican Council: "See, Brethren, what a blessed and joyful thing it is to go forward in harmony in the house of God . . . As Our Lord Jesus Christ gave peace to His apostles so I, His unworthy vicar, give you peace in His name. Peace, as you know, casts out fear; peace shuts its ears to what is said without real knowledge. May this peace be yours all the days of your life." During the companionship of recent months I have felt the full flavour of those words of Pope Pius IX . . . the Supreme Shepherd will have loving care of you in your pastoral care of your own dioceses which will not be dissociated from your pre-occupation with the Council . . . A heavy responsibility therefore rests upon our shoulders but God Himself will sustain us on the way. May the Immaculate Virgin be with us always. . . .

The alleged sayings of Pope John were many and remarkable. It became tedious during the Council to be constantly confronted with opinions attributed to him. Pope John's reign was so short and his pronouncements so few that a mythology was inevitably created to explain the impact made on the world by an apparently simple old man. It is too early to seek explanations of Pope John's fame in myth-ology. If we confine our judgment to his actual words and actions the picture of the Church in the mind of Pope John is clear in outline. He did not regret having called the Council even though it had not turned out in the way he had hoped. Like most of his bishops Pope John had no premonition of the storms that would shake the post-conciliar Church. It is easy to forget what the Church was like at the time of Pope John's death. The most dutiful Catholics in the world were to be found in the English-speaking countries. They were devoted to the Pope and deferential to the authority of the Holy See. With the exception of the Dutch the Catholics most scrupulously observant of the minutiae of curial regulations were the Americans and the English. The picture changed rapidly. The Dutch and the American Church reacted violently against their erstwhile conformity.

It is essential to recall this in order to form a true picture of the Church at the close of the first session. Otherwise it would be quite impossible to understand how the joy of Pope John's Church so soon gave way to the misery of the early years of Pope Paul's. It was only after the first session of the Council that Catholics began to oppose the Pope and bishops. The spirit of revolt had been spreading through civic and scholastic institutions for some years and was certain eventually to affect the Church. The Council was the occasion rather than the cause. Although a spiritual organism the Church remains part of the material world. Whether a worker, student, soldier or astronaut the Catholic belongs both to the mystical body of Christ and to secular society. As violence spread in the world it spread in the Church. In St. Peter's during a later stage of the Council we celebrated a Requiem Mass for the assassinated President of Vietnam (his brother, a bishop, was present among the Council fathers). Shortly afterwards there was a Requiem Mass for President Kennedy who was also murdered. It was not surprising that violence, if only by refusal to submit to authority, overtook the Church. The once docile American Church produced both clerical and lay rebels—among whom the most militant were the former clerics. Chastity and obedience were derided, priests and nuns forsook their vows, doctrines opposed to the fundamental teaching of the Catholic religion were taught by theologians who nevertheless refused to leave the Church. They were guided by a self-made magisterium. Priests and laymen without qualifications set up as theologians. Everyone except the Pope became infallible.

All this happened soon after the death of Pope John and was a turbulent interlude in the life of the Church. People suffering emotionally and spiritually as a result of the changes in the Church blamed the Council for all these unattractive features of the post-conciliar scene. The fact is that the Council was not responsible for their misery—as they would have discovered if they had only read its decrees. Unfortunately few Catholics read the decrees of the Second Vatican Council. That is why they so easily accepted as due to the Council ('the spirit of good Pope John') the onslaught on Catholic doctrine and devotion by authors of whom not a few later renounced the priesthood, the religious life or the Catholic faith. There were no signs of this theological anarchy in December 1962. As we left Rome after the first session we were able to thank God with Pope John that despite differences of opinion, often expressed with vehemence, there was no sign of heresy.

The storms which were soon to batter the Catholic Church did not, as many Catholics believe, have their origin in the Council. They were the ecclesiastical counterpart of the world-wide onslaught on authority. The result was that for some years the liberating reforms of the Council were given no real chance to be tested. Catholic rebels used the reforms to undermine authority and discipline in the Church. This was disastrous in an organisation which describes itself as the Mystical Body of Christ. It was self-destructive to repudiate self-denial, obedience and the cross. The cult of softness was sedulously preached by theological journalists both lay and clerical. Inevitably the flow of converts (the most reliable sign of spiritual health in any religious body) slackened and virtually ceased. Vocations to the priesthood and the religious life failed to keep pace with the defections. Dismayed by the cynicism and apathy of their elders young people developed a disillusioned view of the Church. What had once been cherished as a loving mother was now disdained as a cold institution.

Pope John and his Council cannot fairly be blamed for the sickness which overcame the Church in the late 'sixties. It was a coincidence that the Council was held at the very time when restlessness was sweeping the world. Accepted moral standards were everywhere being discarded. The Church could not have escaped even if there had been no Council. Thus the decree on the renewal of the religious life came before the cloisters began to empty but it cannot be held accountable for the strange behaviour of monks and nuns which followed. The worldliness of some nuns caused confusion to the laity. At the very moment when the Church, with an eye to the third world, was preaching the 'mystery' of poverty men and women with solemn vows of poverty were buying new clothes to replace the religious habit and cultivating hair styles which made them figures of fun to the young. The laity who had always been proud of the Sisters were sometimes made to feel ashamed. By comparison with Canada and the U.S.A. religious in these islands were little affected by this itch for change but orders with branches abroad often caught the infection.

The barque of Peter was ill-equipped to face a tornado. An unchanging Church does not know what to do when change sets in. To gain a hearing reformers had to eschew the word 'change'. They had to talk of *aggiornamento* or 'renewal'. Only in this way could people be persuaded that the new proposal was made in the spirit of Pope John, that is, the spirit of religious liberty. It is astonishing how many crimes were committed in its name. Obedience was demoted and became not a virtue to be practised under vow but a weakness to be overcome· To hasten the process superiors were silenced or abolished. Schools were abandoned not because there were no religious but because there were fewer religious willing to teach. At the time of Pope John's death the

[381]

normal work of the Church had not been interrupted. No religious doubted that God's work was to be found in school or hospital. They accepted the self-sacrifice of community life and the frugality of communal living. The monks and friars also remained disciplined while Pope John was still alive. Everyone recognised that they had bound themselves by vow to follow a much stricter rule of life than diocesan priests. As missionaries they went to foreign lands to preach the Gospel and administer the sacraments. There came a sad change after the Council. It became fashionable to preach a gospel according to Marx not Mark. In dress, speech and behaviour the diocesan clergy were seen to be much more like priests than the religious and for that reason much more acceptable to the people. Catholic people are always ill at ease with priests masquerading as laymen.

It can be said without reservation that no document of the Vatican Council and no word of Pope John can justly be blamed for the woes of the post-conciliar Church. The *aggiornamento* of which Pope John spoke was entirely different from that of the post-conciliar pundits. Licence had no part in the plans of John, the lover of law. His name was nevertheless constantly invoked after his death by those whose 'insights' led them to defy the authority of his successor. The more charismatic theologians were talking of Vatican Three. The prophetic gifts of clergy and laity must no longer be hampered by pope and bishops. Authority was out. Community was all.

During this disastrous but brief period the Church in this country was saved by the good sense of the laity. Anti-papal theologians abounded but most of the laity regarded them with contempt. The publishers of their works soon went out of business. The people who accepted this modernist theology (not to be confused with the genuinely new theology of the Council) had usually read no theology until their interest had been aroused by the Council. For the most part they were students or teachers in schools and universities. Their little learning led to a great deal of bickering in the Church. Parents are apt to mistrust any teaching different from that which they received as children. This applies to arithmetic or language but, with Catholic parents, especially to religion. There was continual press controversy and widespread misgiving. Catholic parents feared that their children would be taught not the Catholic faith but some new religion created by unorthodox theologians. By God's mercy Pope John died long before his name was invoked by those who created such deep unhappiness in the Church he loved so passionately.

TWENTY-SIX

I RETURNED WITH JOY TO SPEND CHRISTMAS WITH THE PRIESTS AND people of Liverpool. Whatever effect absence had on their hearts it had certainly made my own grow fonder. The homecoming was spoiled by the death soon after Christmas of my old friend and master, Cardinal Godfrey. I have already described his Requiem and the sorrow his death brought to the Catholics who knew him well. There were few to whom his full spiritual stature was known. Very few indeed were allowed to know of the painful cancer from which he suffered during the last few months of his life. Most men would have regarded this as an adequate excuse for staying at home during the first session of the Council. Cardinal Godfrey not only went to Rome but was in his place in St. Peter's almost every day. It was only after his death that I learned of his daily agony during those weeks in Rome. The bishops were staying in the English College where we were constantly in each other's company. I sat next to the Cardinal at meals and was able to have long talks with him every day. Yet throughout the session he never once mentioned his health. Nor did he let any of the bishops know that he had to go to hospital three times a week to have his wound dressed. Refusal to seek human sympathy is less spectacular than facing physical danger without flinching but it is no less brave. Cardinal Godfrey was mourned deeply by the people of Liverpool who had recognised his holiness without knowing that it was in some ways heroic.

The next few months which proved to be my last in Liverpool were uneventful. There were one or two more television appearances. In the first I had to answer the questions of a group of mostly unbelieving young people. There was another and rather moving programme in which the children of St. Vincent's School for the Blind took part. Most people were touched by the way these children who would never themselves see television were intent on showing viewers how they felt about their faith. One of the twelve-year-old performers was an intelligent boy who later joined the Cardinal Allen grammar school and was soon top of his class. Six years later he won a scholarship to Cambridge where in his third year he became President of the Union. Had we known what the future held for him we could have made the T.V. programme more exciting still.

There had been no auxiliary bishop in Liverpool since the death of Bishop Halsall. There was no need to appoint a successor because Bishop René Boisguérin who had been expelled from China during the communist persecution was living in the city. Born in Falaise in the diocese of Bayeux Bishop Boisguérin had been appointed by the Holy See to look after Chinese exiles in Great Britain. His flock being small and sparse he was able to give me all the help I needed. When we returned from the first session of the Council we both undertook a busy programme of Confirmations so that as many parishes as possible would receive a visit before we had to leave for the second session of the Council. The next few months were the quietest I spent in Liverpool. The cathedral site was gradually taking shape. There was not yet much above ground but once the foundation work is completed a concrete building rises with unbelievable rapidity. During the spring of 1963 a purpose-built crane (said to be the biggest ever constructed) arrived from France to become a landmark and incidentally a reminder that after all the frustrations the metropolitan cathedral was at last becoming a reality.

The two greatest events between sessions were the death of Pope John and the election of Pope Paul. It was felt that, after Pope John, choosing a pope would matter to many besides Catholics. Earlier elections had been regarded as more or less domestic affairs but there had been a considerable shift in public opinion. Pope John had come to be regarded as a symbol of sheer goodness. Many non-Catholics and even non-Christians while not acknowledging his spiritual authority nevertheless regarded him as personifying hope for world peace. Nobody had been impervious to his influence. Even Khrushchev's son-in-law sought audience with him. Communists had been as impressed as Christians by his encyclical *Pacem in terris*. Sensitive and intelligent people knew that anger, ambition or despair among the super powers might lead to the destruction of the planet. Balance of nuclear armaments is an unstable guarantee of world peace. John XXIII showed that despite Stalin's reported sneer in Yalta about the number of armoured divisions deployed by the Vatican, the Pope could be a powerful instrument of peace.

Hence the unprecedented interest among non-Catholics in a papal election. Apart from issues of war and peace there was world-wide curiosity about who would take the place of the Pope whom everyone loved. There could be no question of finding another Pope John but the hope was that the next pope would continue the same broad policies. There was never any doubt about the result of the conclave and not surprisingly it took less than two days to find a successor to Pope John. There were few alternatives to Cardinal Montini. The situation had been very different following the death of Pope Pius XII when the cardinals had to find a successor for a Pope they regarded as irreplaceable. The most popular runner had been Cardinal Agagianian who, like Stalin, was born in Transcaucasian Russia. Many felt that the time had come to choose a non-Italian pope and Cardinal Agagianian might have been an admirable choice. An Oriental by rite (a former Patriarch in Beirut) he had command of several languages and was a priest of deep spirituality. The cardinals—on this occasion surely guided by the Holy Spirit—chose instead an old man of whom few had heard—Angelo Roncalli.

A glance at the press of June 1963 shows that journalists, both secular and religious, greeted the choice of the Archbishop of Milan as the Church's declaration of intent to follow the direction set by Pope John. Cardinal Montini was known to have been his intimate friend. Although he gave only one speech in St. Peter's during the first session of the Council he was consulted by many bishops to find out the mind of Pope John. He was a friend of Cardinal Bea and an enthusiastic supporter of ecumenical work. There was universal satisfaction within the Church when the result of the election was known. "The speed of the election," I said in a press release from Liverpool, "shows that the cardinals were not deaf to the voice of the people. If they wanted to find a pope to follow the policy of Pope John, Cardinal Montini was the obvious choice."

The *Irish Times* is, for some reason, a reliable mirror of Protestant opinion in the British Isles. The leading article from the issue of 22nd June, 1963 can be taken as an accurate reflection of what those outside the Church thought of the new Pope:

The election of Cardinal Giovanni Battista Montini of Milan as Pope took a comparatively short time to effect, and there is little doubt that he was the most popular as well as the most likely candidate. No Pope can ever have embarked on his career with more good will or with quite the same responsibility; for it is felt by most that this is not merely a succession to the See of Peter, but the inheritance of a special trust, a legacy from Pope John who died before his work was accomplished. . . . All the omens are favourable to Pope Paul . . . who was the first cardinal appointed by Pope John, and was close to him in his work preparing for the Council. . . . To speak of Cardinals as being of the Left or the Right is to push them into categories in which it may be assumed they have a distinct reluctance to fall. . . . But this terminology is loosely used to divide all men into sheep and goats. . . . The Archbishop of Liverpool, whose influence since the election of Pope John has extended beyond his diocese, and who has contributed not a little to the new mood so fatal to bigots of all persuasions, has declared that the new Pope has chosen as his patron St. Paul and, "like St. Paul, he will reach beyond his own flock to embrace all mankind." It needs no prophet to see that this humble man who refused a Cardinal's hat will continue to follow the pattern of humility and model himself on his much-loved predecessor. Scholar, diplomat and pastor of souls, his election has given heart to his own Catholic children and to all men of good will.

It is a pity that the journalists' habit of awarding progressive (liberal) or conservative (reactionary) labels to bishops has been accepted even in Church circles. The assumption is that change means progress. A change for the worse is accepted as impossible. A further implication is that bishops make every judgment along party lines. The truth is that bishops, like all responsible people, make up their minds on the merits of each case. Before God a bishop must do what he believes to be for the good of souls. By fidelity to prayer he becomes less vulnerable to his natural desire to win popular favour. With the years he discovers how untypical of the clergy and faithful are those who are always agitating. Knowing how easy it is to enlist supporters for any demonstration wise rulers are influenced not by agitation but only by reasoned argument. In 1963 when Pope John died the papacy was popular and the new Pope's appointment was especially welcomed by 'progressives'.

[386]

"John's Friend Takes Over" was a typical headline. Equally typical was the view expressed by the *Daily Sketch*:

There was never much doubt that the 'Archbishop of the Workers' would become the new Pope . . . The gaunt-eyed intellectual from Milan was always favourite. He is a progressive and is generally considered one of the Church's most dynamic leaders. Montini had powerful backing—he was the friend and nominee of the beloved Pope John. His triumph in the election is a crushing defeat for the Church's conservatives. When the new Pope appeared on the balcony for ten unbroken minutes cheering rose from the scorching heat of the sun-blazed piazza. There was jubilation among the Church's progressives because their leader had broken an ancient superstition that the man most popular before a conclave never sits in St. Peter's Chair.

His scholarship won from the Belfast *Northern Whig*, a tribute which would have astonished the new Pope if he had been a reader of that journal: "As an intellectual he is formidable. He is as likely in conversation to quote Thomas Mann or Spengler as Dante or Thomas Aquinas."

I must disappoint future historians looking for samples of Pope Paul's scintillating conversation and confess that in the many audiences I had with him during the following decade he never quoted Mann, Spengler, Dante or, I regret to say, the Angelic Doctor. In less fanciful rhetoric the report continued: "He is regarded as a 'Liberal', open to new ideas and concerned with modern social problems. To Italians he is known as 'the Archbishop of the Working Man' but he shuns publicity."

My own view of the new Pope is recorded in press statements and most clearly of all in a *Sunday Times* article for the Sunday following the election. Since this took place on the previous Friday my article must have been written within a few hours of the news reaching Liverpool. Here are the concluding paragraphs of the article which provide more reliable evidence than any later recollection of my reaction to the election of Cardinal Montini:

If, therefore, the Cardinals were dissatisfied with the pontificate of Pope John they would not have looked to Milan to find his successor. But it is incredible that the Catholic Church would deliberately undo the work of the last reign. It would scarcely dis-

[387]

sipate the rich treasury of goodwill which Pope John accumulated through a simplicity and goodness which conquered all hearts.

The swift decision to choose a declared admirer of Pope John's outlook will be reassuring to the whole world as well as to the faithful of the Church. Nobody need fear that the outstretched arms of the Vicar of Christ will now narrow the scope of their embrace.

No Pope is ever a mere replica of his predecessor. Pope Paul VI will emulate the wide charity of Pope John XXIII but will bring to his sacred office considerable qualities of his own . . .

. . . It is not surprising that the hopes of Catholics ride high. It is natural that they will look for even the smallest sign that the new Pope will match the achievements of Pope John . . . The Borghese Pope Paul V held office when Christendom was in ferment and part of Italy in schism. Pope Paul VI assumes the Fisherman's Ring as Christendom strives for unity and the whole world yearns for peace.

In view of the delight of 'progressives' at the result of the papal election an intriguing question for future historians will be—what went wrong? Was it Pope Paul or the progressives who changed? Was he really a crafty conservative pretending to share Pope John's ideas in order to achieve a personal ambition to occupy the chair of Peter? There is undeniable evidence that before his pontificate was very old Pope Paul had earned the angry contempt of his fellow progressives. He was a great disappointment to them. An interesting question which nobody has yet asked is—were his fellow progressives a disappointment to Pope Paul?

The answer may provide the solution to the infinitely complex problem of what exactly went wrong in the Church after the death of Pope John? The simplest explanation is lack of leadership. There is a happy and ubiquitous band of critics who explain every disaster in the world in terms of lack of leadership or failure of communication. Few realise that lack of leadership is usually good leadership. Fewer still appreciate that much of the world's misery is caused by communication. Most communication is hostile or, if friendly, is a substitute for action. This sounds cynical but it is a plain statement of fact. The proportion of time spent at local, national and international conferences has become scandalously high compared with the time given to work. Political, academic, religious and industrial discussion is becoming a substitute

[388]

for action. Resources are consumed on travel and hospitality which could be used for the relief of those in need. The Church's troubles in the 'sixties are attributable more to universal social trends than to the activities either of Pope Paul or of his critics.

Pope John was spared the agony of seeing the Catholic Church in decline. At the time of John's death there was no hint of impending disintegration. The neo-modernists and Catholic anarchists who changed his successor into a man of sorrows were yet to appear. Nothing ever disturbed Pope Paul's inward peace but he became a sad man when he had to keep warning priests and people against the enemies within the Church. Those who within a few months of Pope Paul's accession began the attack pointed out the contrast between him and good Pope John who had never condemned anyone or anything. Pope John, on the contrary, had rebuked prophets of doom at the opening of the Council and had promised that there would be no more anathemas. The critics now accused Pope Paul of being incapable of speaking except in jeremiads as he pointed out the disarray in the Church. They did not say that the disarray had not appeared in Pope John's day. There can be no doubt that Pope John would have condemned what Pope Paul condemned. The theological errors, the liturgical extravagances, the laxity of clerical and religious life were in direct contradiction to the spirit of Pope John's Council. Jesus wept over Jerusalem and John would have wept over Rome if he had foreseen what was to be done in the name of his Council. It was no wonder that Pope Paul wept.

What of the universally high hopes entertained in 1963 when Cardinal Montini was elected? Were they justified? Whether or not they were justified they were undoubtedly frustrated. This was due not to the papal leadership but to revolt against that leadership. The revolt began not as a personal attack on Pope Paul but in a rejection of prayer. The religious orders were the first to give up prayer. Inevitably the infection spread to the seminaries and last of all to the laity. Only the stalwarts continued to make any thanksgiving after Holy Communion and to keep hold of their prayer books and rosaries. The roots of revolt lay in a loss of faith in everything supernatural. The attack on the priesthood was subtle and sustained. Catholic priests had hitherto been outwardly distinguished from others by celibacy and clerical dress. It was now argued—as the sixteenth-century reformers had argued—that celibacy is unnatural. Clerical dress was attacked on the grounds that it separated the priest from his people. Similar arguments were used against the religious habit which was said to alienate the nun from the children, the sick and poor. This gave rise to many anti-nun stories which are now repeated with many a chuckle throughout the world. Here are two examples: an American bishop is remonstrating with a Sister for never wearing her religious habit. "This is not true, Bishop," she replies, "I always wear my habit in demos." The second story is of the nun in lay clothes who thought she was being followed by a man and rushed to a policeman for protection: "Help me, Officer, I'm a nun and I'm being followed." "How did you know I am a policeman, Sister?" the officer asked. It was not until after the Council that the mass exodus from the cloister and defection from the priesthood took place. Nobody has claimed that this was all part of the spirit either of the Council or of good Pope John. It was, in fact, the tribute paid by the Church to the world.

We are still too close to events to be sure of what went wrong. The way many Catholics both lay and clerical reacted to Pope Paul's decision to leave unchanged the teaching of his predecessors on con-traception was the greatest shock the Church has suffered since the Reformation. Yet it was only a symptom of a far more serious disorder in the Church. Theological revolutionaries, mainly in Europe but with eager disciples in North America, claimed that the Council was a failure because it had not really changed the Catholic religion. They contended that its only function had been to serve as a stepping-stone to real theological reform. Selective theology under the name of pluralism became the fashion. In worship a kind of liturgical geiger counter was applied to the Constitution on the Sacred Liturgy to detect anything not primitive. Neither the early Christians nor the Protestants wor-shipped Christ in the Holy Eucharist. St. Thomas Aquinas with his *Adoro Te devote* was regrettably medieval. This word had become pejorative and, like pristine, was rarely used correctly. Post-conciliar churches were built like Lutheran or Calvinistic chapels with no pro-vision for adoration of the Blessed Sacrament. Mysteries, miracles and devotion to Our Lady were discarded. This was the situation Pope Paul had to face. He had to implement the decrees of Pope John's Council in the face of self-appointed leaders of anti-Catholic renewal. In the golden days of Pope John Catholics had not talked about the 'institu-tional' Church nor had they been obsessed with 'structures'. Pope John had departed this life before structures became the rage in ecclesiastical, academic and even political circles. Many lay theologians left the Church while new-style priests and nuns began to practise the evangelical virtues unhampered by vows. Outraged by the lack of love in their own communities they sought Christ in each other's arms.

For the five years immediately following the Council Pope Paul was the target of abuse from all recognised progressives. He was a scourge sent to afflict the People of God. 'People of God' had meanwhile acquired a meaning quite different from that intended by Pope John. When he made use of this expression he meant the whole Church from himself to the most recently baptised baby. People of God now came to mean the laity and eventually the laity with special insights and charismata. The critics predicted that the Catholic Church would continue to decline ('to lack credibility', 'to be irrelevant') until a new Pope came to its rescue. The first acts of the new Pope would be to sanction contraception, divorce and abortion, abolish clerical celibacy and ordain wives as well as their husbands. The millennium would have arrived.

This part of my story ends with my departure from Liverpool for Westminster. I cannot therefore describe the odyssey which took Pope Paul from popularity to obloquy and back again. Eventually, when his most strident critics had left the Church or the priesthood, people took a second look at the Vicar of Christ. Even those outside the Church began to see that if Pope Paul had remained silent there would have been no voice to protest at the immorality, unalarmingly called permissive morality, which threatened Christian civilisation. A Pope who in old age visited every continent to plead the cause of justice and peace must, they realised, be less reactionary than his critics claimed. Some held that Pope Paul might turn out to have been a modern Gregory the Great, a twentieth-century champion of Christendom.

In England Catholics naturally connected Pope Paul's election with the vacant see of Westminster. The diocese had been without a bishop and the Catholic community without a spokesman since the beginning of the year. For much of that time Pope John had been ailing. That was accepted as sufficient explanation for the delay in making an appointment to Westminster. It would have been unthinkable to have no Archbishop of Westminster to lead the bishops at the second session of the Council. An appointment was therefore daily expected. Then, scarcely a month after the election of the new Pope, Archbishop O'Hara, Apostolic Delegate to Great Britain, fell sick and died. It is the task of a Delegate when a see is vacant to canvass local opinion and advise the Holy See. Gerald O'Hara was a most conscientious man and lost no time in preparing his report for Rome. It is probable that he had sent all the information requested by the Vatican before Pope John died—otherwise Pope Paul could hardly have made the nomination to Westminster with such speed. Since the confidentiality of this kind of information is inviolable in the Church only those bound by the oath of secrecy know which names were recommended.

I had taken for granted that no appointment would be made until we had a new Apostolic Delegate. I did not, as I have said, regard myself as the most likely choice but I would have been blind not to know that most of the papers had already sent me to Westminster. My own preference was for George Andrew Beck, Bishop of Salford. The architect of the modern system of Catholic schools he was highly respected by priests and people throughout the country and much admired by the teachers and education officials who had dealt with him over the years. Unfortunately he had to spend some months in hospital about this time and it is possible that this was thought to unfit him for the strain of Westminster. It is, perhaps, necessary to say that I have no more knowledge today than I had in 1963 of which names were submitted to the Pope or of how the final choice was made. The papers were full of rumours. Roman correspondents repeated the gossip of unofficial spokesmen. The following report in the *Sunday Times* of 14th July, 1963 was from James Stuart in Rome. He gave an account of the current gossip:

> Pope Paul VI is expected to announce soon a successor to Cardinal William Godfrey, Archbishop of Westminster, who died last January. Although 58-year-old Archbishop Heenan, of Liverpool, has been persistently mentioned as the most likely successor, some Vatican circles are inclining increasingly towards 59-year-old Bishop George Andrew Beck, of Salford. . . . Another candidate now widely mentioned is 61-year-old Archbishop Grimshaw, of Birmingham, who is seen as a possible 'compromise' choice for Westminster.

Towards the end of August I was informed by telephone of Pope Paul's decision to send me to Westminster. The frustrating interval between an episcopal appointment and its publication is usually about a week. It is frustrating because the bishop-elect is not free to inform even his own secretary whom he sees making appointments for him which will never be kept. For a reason never explained the announcement of my appointment was delayed for nearly two weeks. This was

[392]

particularly trying because September was already a week old. Thus within less than three weeks I had to settle my affairs in Liverpool, take possession of the see of Westminster and arrive for the second session of the Council.

These were the most rushed few days of my life. The permanent secretariat at Archbishop's House, Liverpool—Monsignor Tom Barry and Jean Jones—recruited the Sisters of Notre Dame and any man, woman or child, clerical or lay, who was breathing and capable of addressing an envelope. I had to be in London by 19th September. There were ten days in which to answer all the greetings and to write personal letters to all the civic, academic and religious officials who had given me their friendship during my years in Lancashire. Since I was to spend the rest of the year in Rome it was clear that any letter not written at once would not be written at all. With all the voluntary clerical help and loyal co-operation of the Franciscan Sisters who had remained with me since coming to me at the Mission House in London I disposed of a mountain of correspondence. Those rushed days were not without their drama. One Saturday afternoon a telegram sent in the name of the priests and people of the Isle of Man came from Monsignor Turner, the parish priest of Douglas. On Sunday afternoon another message informed me that he had died suddenly after Mass. Tom Turner had been on the Island for nearly thirty years and was much respected by all Manxmen. Inconvenient as it was I had to abandon my correspondence in Liverpool to fly to the Isle of Man to preach the panegyric and preside at Monsignor Turner's funeral. *Relinquendus Deus propter Deum* (You must leave God's work for God's sake) is as valid today as in the time of St. Augustine.

The massive operation was completed by Tom Barry, Jean and the nuns. Leave-taking, of course, I had to do in person. The most important places I had to visit were St. Vincent's Hospice for the dying, the orphanage at Knolle Park and St. Vincent's School for the Blind. Other institutions had to be satisfied with farewell notes but these old friends had to have personal visits. Saying good-bye to the blind children was hard—it is never easy to part from any kind of deprived child. They are affectionate beyond measure and feel the loss of anyone they love much more keenly than other children. One of the greatest blessings of my life as priest and bishop has been frequent contact with children. Leeds, my first diocese, has the only Catholic residential school for the deaf. In Liverpool we had the only Catholic school for the blind in the country. It was only coincidental that my last ceremony in Liverpool—arranged months earlier—was the Confirmation of eighty mentally handicapped children. Confirmation was at one time regarded as a sacrament for the adolescent but the Holy See had recently given directions for babies to be confirmed if in danger of death. (In the Eastern Churches Confirmation has always been given at Baptism.) If babies are fit subjects for the sacrament of Confirmation, the Church reasoned, these other innocents are equally entitled.

I had not expected that the press would salute my appointment with a stream of abuse but I was surprised that the appointment of an archbishop to Westminster was regarded as an event of national importance. I doubt if such an appointment would attract much attention today when religion no longer ranks as top news. It has to have what journalists call an unusual angle for a religious event to win space outside local journals. Church leaders are now accorded mention only when they contribute to current controversies. When fired with moral indignation people usually solicit the support of the Archbishops of Canterbury and Westminster. Churchmen are still expected to issue statements on domestic or international crises. They are urged to denounce every breach of the moral law and every act of violence.

Apart from receiving copies of correspondence sent to royalty and government ministers an archbishop receives frequent requests to be a joint signatory to protests and appeals. I have usually found such requests embarrassing. I feel no sympathy for those who unwilling to make protest alone seek safety in numbers. Nor do I like to sign a letter which is not my own. When I see an array of names of people 'in every walk of life' at the end of an open letter I am not in the least impressed by the number, variety or eminence of the walkers. I merely wonder who actually wrote the letter and why it was printed with names of people who could not possibly have had any hand in composing it. It is true that those who solicit signatures often express willingness to make alterations but these would obviously not be acceptable if they were substantial. One of the greatest trials of being at the head of a religious community is to be constantly urged to become a patron, sponsor or vice-president of praiseworthy causes. During an average month a bishop may be asked to support a law making chlorinisation illegal (or compulsory) abolishing censorship (or making it stricter) building more Catholic schools (or abolishing all such religious ghettoes).

There is also the difficulty of being asked to support (or condemn) every political or moral movement which happens to be in the public eye. It is a deplorable waste of time to have to explain to numerous correspondents why silence is not necessarily guilty. Anyone in public life who is continually pronouncing or denouncing soon becomes ineffective. This simple fact often escapes otherwise intelligent people who do not realise that to cry wolf too often is self-defeating or, as the politicians prefer to say, counter-productive. The same names appear regularly in support or condemnation of almost anything. A bishop has to learn not to dissipate his influence for good by talking too much and too often.

That the influence of bishops has diminished with the years is beyond doubt. In September 1963 the interest in the appointment to Westminster was by no means confined to the Catholic press or to what have come to be called the quality papers. I give examples from the popular press not only because they are agreeable but because they show how even so short a time ago routine ecclesiastical events were still regarded as newsworthy. A few years later papers would be less likely to report bishops' moves than priests' marriages. Here is how the *Daily Mirror* treated the news:

A Man with a Mission

Good news that Dr. Heenan has been chosen as the new Archbishop of Westminster and leader of Britain's 4,000,000 Catholics.

He is already widely known outside his own Church and widely respected.

Millions have seen him on television as Archbishop of Liverpool and warmed to this smiling, outspoken prelate with a winning personality.

Good news, too, that one of Dr. Heenan's first statements on his new appointment was in the cause of Christian Unity.

He pledged himself to "continue the co-operation, which is getting much greater, between non-Catholics and ourselves." He spoke of striving to promote the cause of unity in both the religious and social sense.

Friendship

People who know Dr. Heenan speak of his great gift for friendship throughout a life's work which began as a parish priest in London's East End.

Among his personal friends is the Archbishop of Canterbury, Dr. Ramsey. An important friendship at a time when the eyes of forward-looking Churchmen are fixed on bringing the churches closer together.

Dr. Heenan has always had this cause at heart.

[395]

In his six years as Archbishop of Liverpool he has made a notable impact.

When he moves to Westminster, Britain can expect to hear a lot more of this forthright Church leader.

The *Sunday Times* printed an interview from which the following is taken:

One of Dr. Heenan's first acts at Westminster will be to summon a meeting of his clergy to explain to them his policy. Foremost among this will be the advancement of Christian unity. His friendship with the Archbishop of Canterbury, Dr. Ramsey, will help co-operation in these matters.

Dr. Heenan, appointed to the Secretariat for Christian Unity by Pope John, referred to this: "What I have seen during my six years in Liverpool is a growing friendliness between the Catholics and the rest of the community. They have accepted me as one of their own. I have enjoyed especially close friendships with the Bishop of Liverpool and the Free Church leaders here."

The Archbishop of Canterbury said last night: "My old friend, Archbishop Heenan, will have the prayers of Anglicans throughout the country as he goes to Westminster. It is my great hope that our Churches may together bring home to the people the claim of God's love and righteousness."

The Yorkshire, Lancashire and Midland press also carried articles. No doubt remembering the famous debate in Bolton a dozen years earlier the *Bolton Evening News* carried a leader:

The appointment of Dr. John Heenan as Roman Catholic Archbishop of Westminster has delighted most people and surprised no one . . . the right man goes into the right job. Dr. Heenan has become well known to many people outside the Roman Catholic faith. This is in part due to television, but many priests have appeared on television without making so much impact. The qualities of Dr. Heenan's mind (he is formidable in argument) together with a certain warmth have brought him friendships beyond the usual range of the Catholic bishop. He is known to be strongly in support of Christian unity and his friendship with the Archbishop of Canterbury is not only proof that certain walls are down but a good augury for further developments . . .

The *Daily Worker* was less enchanted. It reported my appointment and listed as my sole achievement that I had remained alive for nearly sixty years:

New Archbishop of Westminster
    Dr. Heenan, Archbishop of Liverpool, has been appointed Archbishop of Westminster. He is 58.

Nothing remains to relate of my years in Liverpool but the finale. I have told of the tradition of love and loyalty which the Catholics of Liverpool have always given their archbishop. I was the second archbishop to be taken from them to be sent to Westminster. When Cardinal Godfrey left Liverpool for London he was given an emotional farewell. I was therefore not surprised that my own leave-taking was the occasion of a similar demonstration of love. I was amazed that so many people contrived to be at Lime Street station to see me off. Monsignor Barry had arranged for an open car to drive us to the station. ("They'll want to see the last of you, Your Grace.") Small groups were gathered outside schools, churches and hospitals as we passed but I was totally unprepared for the immense crowd which had gathered outside the station. It was touching that so many had taken time off work to be there to say good-bye. The occasion was too overwhelming for my recollection to be very clear. The only incident I recall distinctly was the urgent request of the station master that I would crouch into the corner of the compartment so as to remain out of sight. Among the thousands on the platforms were hundreds of children. There was a risk that if I went near the window they would rush forward and be pushed under the train. It was a very real danger and my last few minutes in Liverpool were filled with anguish lest an accident to a child were to turn drama into tragedy.

Here is an account of the leave-taking from the *Liverpool Daily Post*:

A waving, singing, cheering crowd gave Archbishop John Heenan a tumultous send-off yesterday afternoon, as he left Liverpool to take up his appointment as Archbishop of Westminster.

From the time the Archbishop, smiling but visibly moved by the warmth of his reception, entered the train, until it moved off fifteen minutes later, many thousands of people swamped Lime Street station. Platform Seven disappeared beneath a sea of humanity.

They cheered, clapped and alternated "For he's a jolly good fellow" with the Catholic hymn "Faith of our Fathers". . . . The massed crowds swarmed after the official car, coming in from Lime Street, until they completely blocked the platform.

Earlier the pavements in London Road and Lime Street were lined with patiently waiting crowds, come to say a last good-bye. By half-past one, when the procession was due to appear, they were two and three deep in London Road, and denser still in Lime Street.

They waited in near silence. Their mood was summed up by an elderly woman who remarked—"We can't afford to lose a good man like him from Liverpool". Children carried shakers in the Papal colours, yellow and white.

There was a striking contrast between the quiet of the waiting crowd and the wave upon wave of cheering that greeted the Archbishop when he appeared with an escort of two mounted police on greys, and followed by three limousines carrying senior priests of the archdiocese.

Then as the procession moved into Lime Street, the car was halted as thousands of people broke through the police cordon and surrounded the Archbishop. It had been intended that Archbishop Heenan should leave his car and give a blessing to the crowd from St. George's Plateau. The dense crowd made this quite impossible. After a few steps he had to return to his car.

Police struggled to clear a path so that the Archbishop's car could move into the station forecourt. . . . Many of the crowd who had been waiting in London Road ran to enter Lime Street station from the Nelson Street entrance and an estimated 10,000 people were finally gathered there to watch his departure. . . .

I shall not relate all that has happened in the years since that September afternoon when I left Liverpool. Owing to a bomb scare my train was delayed and arrived very late at Euston Station where the good priest of Somerstown had brought his people to greet me. From Euston I was taken with all possible speed to Westminster Cathedral where a large congregation was waiting patiently. They were determined to show that Liverpool had no monopoly of warm hearts. After we had prayed together we all walked round the corner to Archbishop's House. There I waved from the balcony and thanked them for their great welcome. It was a pleasant homecoming after twelve years' exile.

Clergy of every Church are loved and respected by their people but the love of English Catholics for their priests is unique. It seems to bear little relationship to piety. Even those who have stopped going to Mass usually retain their love for the priest. I have seen this in all parts of the country and London is no exception. The bishop also receives his due measure of affection. He is not so well known as his priests but he has a special place in the hearts of the flock.

As Archbishop of Westminster I have had abundant consolation but I have also tasted sorrow. Many a thorn was added to my crown during the stormy 'sixties. A shepherd suffers when his flock is scattered. He is desolate when a priest he ordained abandons his sacred calling. After the Council many were led astray by fellow Catholics claiming to speak with the voice of Pope John. A bitter attack on the Catholic Church was mounted by her own children.

At one time the vision of the Church as Mother was lost to sight. She became an institution. She was corrupt. The Vicar of Christ was vilified. Gradually the storm abated. The faithful revolted against the prophets of doom and looked to their bishops and priests for protection and guidance. Eventually the true spirit of Pope John prevailed. Faithful priests and people began by God's grace to rebuild the Church. It had been a fierce struggle with many casualties among the priests and nuns. The struggle had been long and it was only in 1973 that light began to break through.

> In front the sun climbs slow, how slowly
> But westward, look, the land is bright.

Index

Compiled by Robert Urwin

Adams, Alice (Allie), 162–3
Adamson, Monsignor, Vicar-General at Liverpool, 218, 222, 288, 306
Adenauer, Konrad, correspondence with J.C.H. on victims of Nazi regime, 250–1
Adrian IV, Pope (Nicholas Breakspear, the only English Pope), 256
Agaginian, Cardinal, 154, 256, 385
Ahmadiyya, Pakistan Moslem sect, 105
Alexander the Great film, 198
Allen, Cardinal, Grammar School, Liverpool, 247–8, 384
Ampleforth Abbey, 305–6
Anderson, Father Andrew, 196
Andrew, Father Agnellus, 80, 101
Andrews, Sir Linton, 74, 209
  article on J.C.H. broadcast controversy, 74–7
  letter to J.C.H., 77–8
Apostolicae Curae, Papal Bull, 316
Archbishop's House, Liverpool, 277, 393
Archer-Shee, Colonel, 107
Armstrong, William H. (Moderator, Free Church Federal Council), 311
Asquith, H.H. (later Earl of Oxford and Asquith), 42
Atlantic House, seamen's club, Liverpool, 243, 244
Attlee, Clement (later Lord Attlee), 46
Australia, J.C.H.'s visit to, 155–60
  attends Eucharistic Congress, 155–60
  speech on Communist menace, 155–6
  Canberra, impressions of, 156, 157
  meeting with Archbishop Mannix, 158–9
  Movement, the, pressure group, 101
  New Australians, impressions of, 156–7
  proportion of Catholics in, 103
Australian Redemptorist missioners, Singapore, 153

Baird, John Logie, 89
Baltic, S.S., 159, 160
Baptist Times, 338
Barbados, J.C.H.'s visit to, 197–8
Barcelona, *see also* Spain
  International Eucharistic Congress (1952), J.C.H. at. 41–53
  visits to: *barracas*, 51–2; lepers' home, 45, 54; prison, 45, 48–50
Barracas, the, *see under* Barcelona
Barry, Father, 185, 186, 194, 345
Barry, Monsignor Tom, 393, 397
Bea, Cardinal, 256, 259, 262, 314, 320, 323–5, 354, 356, 357, 371, 375, 385
  visit to England, 325–6, 328, 329
  Requiem Mass for and J.C.H.'s tribute to, 330–1
Beck, George Andrew, Archbishop (J.C.H.'s successor at Liverpool), 248, 307, 349, 392
Becket, Thomas (St. Thomas à Becket), 264
Beda College, Rome, 22

Belfast Telegraph, 227
Bell, Dr., Bishop of Chichester, 313
Benson, Edward, Archbishop of Canterbury, 316
Hugh (his son), 316
Bernard, Father, 194
Bevan, Aneuran, 32, 33
Bianchi, Bishop of Hong Kong, 124, 125
Binks, Rev. A., 259
Bishops, methods of selection and appointment of, 21–3, 361, 364–6
Bishop's House, Leeds, 172–3, 175, 209
Bittenfeld, Herwarth von, 250, 251
Blue Nuns (at St. Andrew's Hospital), 17
Bogert, Brigadier, 140
Boisguérin, René, Bishop, 384
Bolton, public debate on Communism at (1951), 11–14
Bolton Evening News, 12, 396
Bourke, Brigadier, 119
Bourne, Francis, Cardinal Archbishop of Westminister 42, 260, 309, 317, 318
reaction to Malines' Conversations, 318–9
Brannigan, Jim, 171
Breakspear, Nicholas, *see* Adrian IV, Pope
Brentwood, Bishop of, 301, 346
British Broadcasting Corporation, *see also under* Heenan, John Carmel
J.C.H.'s association with, 56–78, 361–2
first broadcast, 56
first High Mass televised, 79–80
differences with and controversy over reference to Northern Ireland, 57–8, 59, 60, 62–78
House, Francis, correspondence with, 69–74
British Council (in Singapore), 148
British Guiana (now Guyana), J.C.H.'s visit to, 191–4
Queen's College Hall, address to, 192–3
Scarboro Fathers, 193
Broadhurst, Father, S.J., 123
Brookeborough, Lord, 69, 74, 76
Browne, Bishop of Galway, 349
Buckfast Abbey, 306–7
Bullen, Alfred, 246
Butler, Abbot (later Anciliary Bishop of Westminister), 376
Butler, R.A. (now Lord Butler), 249

Cardinal Allen Grammar School, Liverpool, 247–8, 384
Carter, Father, S.J., 185
Carton de Wiart, Monsignor, Vicar-General of Westminster, 317
Cashman, Bishop, 324
Catechism, the, revision of, 171–2, 175
Revised Catechism of Christian Doctrine, publishing of, 172
Cathedral House, Leeds, 173, 209
Catholic Education Council, 249
Catholic Emancipation Act (1829), 320
Catholic Gazette, 15
Catholic Missionary Society, 11, 12, 15, 37, 48, 55, 162, 233
Catholic Officers' Association, Singapore, 152
Catholic Society of the University at Canberra, 156
Catholic Truth Society, 232
Catholic Women's League Refugee Committee, 250
Central Religious Advisory Council (C.R.A.C.), 71, 74, 205
Chadwell, Dr, Protestant "supply" Bishop in Korea, 132
Chancellor, Sir Christopher, 144
Cheshire, Group-Captain Leonard, 250
Chiang Kai-shek, 123
Christian Unity, *see* Ecumenism
Church Times, 317
reaction to Sword of the Spirit Movement, 312–4
Churchill, Sir Winston, 31, 44, 56, 60, 253
Cicognani, Cardinal 328, 371, 372
letter to J.C.H., 329
Clark, Barbara, 163
Clarke, Father Kevin, O.P., 195
Clarke, Monsignor, 346
Clegg, Sir Alec, 38
Coggan, Donald, Archbishop of York, 273
Cohen, Saul, 44
Columban Fathers, in Korea, 134
Comet aircraft, early disasters of, 104, 113–41, 116
Communist Party of Great Britain, 13
Constance, Sister, superior at Little Sisters of the Poor, Auckland, New Zealand, 160
Contraception, Church's attitude to, 11

Cornelia Marie, O.P., Sister, 176, 180, 181, 183, 184, 186
Cotton, Colonel, 125
Council Daybook, The, account of Second Vatican Council, 369–70
Council of Christians and Jews, relations with the Vatican, 357–8
Council of Trent, 371, 378
Courchaine, John and Helen, 135
Coventry Cathedral, 307
Cowgill, Joseph, Bishop of Leeds, 24, 25 81, 96, 158, 260
Cowley, Father John, 196
Cot, Sir Geoffrey, 100, 101
Craven, Bishop, 346
Cronell, Father, 12
Crosby, Bing, 165
Croston Hall, Croston, 278, 279
Cruzen, Admiral (and wife), U.S. Navy, 122–3
Cunningham, Bill, 144
Curates' strike, Leeds, 24–5
Cushing, Cardinal, 131

Dalton, Brigadier, 127, 130–1
Darlinghurst parish, Sydney, 156
Davey, Colonel (and wife), 116, 117, 118, 121, 153, 144, 148
Davies, Major, 130
Day, Robin, 101, 240
Delaney, Father Dick, 100
De La Salle Brothers, 120
De Smedt, Emile, Bishop of Bruges, 259, 260, 347, 349, 373, 374
Denson, Mrs. Winifred, 236
Denver, Colorado, J.C.H.'s visit to, 165–6
Loreto Heights College, 166
De Trafford, Captain Geoffrey (and his sister Ermyntrude) visit to J.C.H., 277–80
estates bequeathed to Church, 279–80
De Valera, Eamon, 159
Devas, Father Raymond, 196
Devas, Wing-Commander, 123
Devell, Father, O.P., 189
Dimayo, Father Paul, 196
Dinn, John, 23
Diocesan administration, and problems of, 25–40

Dowling, Father, 196
Downey, Richard, Archbishop of Liverpool, 19, 223, 235, 259, 281, 282, 283, 304, 306
Driver, Christopher, article on religious 'apartheid', 269–71, 272
Dwyer, Bishop of Leeds, 349

Ecumenism, and the move to Christian Unity, 200–4, 211, 227–8, 273, 308–32
J.C.H.'s work for, 308, 322–32
friendship with Archbishop Ramsey, 227, 269, 273–4, 395, 396
rules for ecumenical conduct, 331–2
background to Churches' mutual hostility and suspicion, 308–9, 311–22, 325
Congress on "The Four Gospels in 1957", 227–8
Pope John's work towards, 259–67 (see also under John, Pope)
Archbishop Fishers contribution to, 262–3, 267–8
mixed marriages problem and, 230, 231–4
Pope Paul's decree on (1964), 322
Secretariat for Promoting Christian Unity, 259, 308, 340, 346
Vatican Council, Second, 339–50 352, 362–3, 367–82
national theological differences and ecumenism, 339–41
Education Act, 1944, provisions for Catholic Schools, 204, 218, 246, 249, (see also Liverpool Education Act)
Education Conference, Harrogate, 1956, J.C.H.'s address at, 204, 205–6
Eglin, Mr, Your City articles, 271
Elwes, Val, 124
Emmigration problems, see under Heenan, John Carmel, and West Indies
English College, Douai, 247
English College, Rome, 23, 31, 331, 359
Etrangères de Paris Missions, 118
Eucharistic Congresses, International Barcelona (1952), J.C.H. at, 41–53
Bombay (1964), Pope Paul at, 41; J.C.H. at, 41

England (1908), 41–2
Sydney (1953), J.C.H. at, 54, 102, 154, 155–60
Express, Sunday tribute to Pope John, 362
Eyre, Marney and Wilfred, 165

Faber, Father (*All For Jesus*), 258
Fairlie, Henry, 100
Fava, Lieutenant-Colonel, 121, 150
Felici, Cardinal, 261, 262, 348, 356
Ferris, Paul, 266, 267
Field, Father, O.P. (later Bishop of Grenada), 194, 195, 196
Fisher, Geoffrey, Archbishop of Canterbury, 210–21
   background and personality, 262–3
   correspondence with J.C.H. 262–3
   retirement of and J.C.H.'s tribute to, 273
   visit to Rome and attitude to Christian Unity, 262, 263, 267–8
Fisher, John (Bishop of Rochester during Reformation), 264
Fitzgerald, Father, 190, 193
Foley, Bishop, 120
Foot, Sir Hugh (late Lord Caradon), 176, 177, 185
Foran family (of Barking), 346
Forest Lawn, Los Angeles, J.C.H.'s visit to, 163–5
Francis-Williams, Lord, 99
Franco, General, 47, 48, 50, 53
Franklin, Colonel, 121
Frings, Cardinal Archbishop of Cologne, 344, 348, 349
Frost, David, 101
Fulford, Roger, 189
Furstenberg, Monsignor, 132

Garbett, Cyril, Archbishop of York, 151, 227
Gardner, Father Joseph, 143
Garrone, Cardinal, 256
George VI, King, J.C.H.'s tribute to, 57–60
Gibberd, Frederick (later Sir Frederick), designer of final plan for Metropolitan Cathedral, Liverpool, 301, 302, 305, 306, 307

Gilroy, Cardinal Archbishop of Sydney, 54, 55, 102, 156
Glasspole, Mr., Minister of Labour, Jamaica, 183–4
Gloucester Valley battle, Korea, 139
Goalen, Mr. (partner of Frederick Gibberd), 301
Godfrey, William, Cardinal Archbishop of Westminster, 199, 206, 223, 283, 325–6, 346, 349, 358, 363, 397
   death of and J.C.H.'s tribute to, 358–60, 383
Goody, Bishop, 156
Gordon Riots, 314
Gordon, William, Bishop of Leeds, 24, 26, 260
Goss, Bishop, 222
Gracias, Cardinal, 154
Grayson, Colonel (and family), 150, 153, 154
Greeley-Rossi survey of Catholic education, 166
Greene, Graham, 178
Grenada, J.C.H.'s visit to, 194–6
Griffin, William Bernard, Cardinal Archbishop of Westminster, 84, 162, 357–8, 360
   death of, 194, 198
Griffiths, Bishop of New York, 376
Griffiths, James (vice-chairman of Parliamentary Labour Party, 1955–9), attitude to aid for church schools, 249
Grimshaw, Archbishop of Birmingham, 248, 345, 346, 349, 392
Guilly, Bishop, S.J. (of Georgetown), 191, 193
Gut, Cardinal, 256

Haegy, Henry, 184–5
Haig, Sir Douglas (1st Earl Haig), aphorism of, 27
Halifax, Lord, Malines Conversations with Cardinal Mercier, 315–6, 318
Hall, Mr. (Principal of Liverpool School of Building), 305
Halsall, Bishop, 218–9, 384
Hansard, extract from an J.C.H. broadcast, 65–8

Harding, Gilbert, 78, 79
Harkin, Jim (and family), J.C.H.'s Christmas TV programme with, 91–6
Harris, Kenneth, 268
Harrison, Father Bernard, 34–7
Hawkeswell, Monsignor, Vicar-Capitular and later Vicar-General at Leeds, 21, 23–5, 26, 27
Heenan, Father, O.P. (of Trinidad), 187, 190, 194
Heffernan, Father, 178, 180
Henry, Father Pat (senior RAF chaplain, Malaya), 122, 125, 145
Henson, Hensley, Bishop of Durham, 319
Heythrop College, Oxford, conference at 325–6, 328, 329, 331
Christian Unity: a Catholic View, paper on, 326
Hinsley, Arthur, Cardinal Archbishop of Westminster, 10, 20, 24, 31, 260
founder of Sword of the Spirit movement, 311
joint letter (with other Churches' leaders) to The Times, 309–11
Hiroshima, see under Japan
Heenan, John Carmel
death of brother, 9
appointed Bishop of Leeds (1951), 9
Consecration, 11–12, 16, 17, 19–22
Bishop's dependence on parish priesthood, 9–11
reflections on duties and spartan life of Bishop, 25–40
views on Communist menace 32–3 (see also Public relations)
exchange of letters with Harold Wilson, 33–4
attends Eucharistic Congress, Barcelona, 41, 42–3, 45–54 (see also under Barcelona and Spain)
B.B.C. broadcasts: Radio—56–78, 219–20, 329. Television—First TV Mass 79–83; 'fan mail', 83–91; Christmas programme, 91–6; Press Conference programme, 92, 99–101; other TV appearances, 225–6, 238–40, 268–9, 326, 361–2
controversy on reference to Northern Ireland in B.B.C. broadcast, 64–78
correspondence with Francis House,

69–74
sermon on death of King George VI, 58–60
criticism of B.B.C. in, 58–60
friendship with Gilbert Harding, 78
audiences with Pope Pius XII, 103, 207
tour of Far East, 102–54 (see also under various place names)
attends Sydney Eucharistic Congress, 155–60 (see also under Australia)
speech on Communist menace, 155–6
return from Australia via New Zealand, Honolulu and United States, 159–69
revision of Catechism, 171–2, 175
parochial work in Leeds, 173–4
West Indies, visit to, 176–98 (see also under various place names)
emigration problems, in, 177–8, 180, 182–4, 187, 188, 199
Leeds University, inaugural lecture at, 200–2
appointed Archbishop of Liverpool (1957), 207–12
visit to Rome, 207
press reactions to, 208–10
enthronement ceremony, 218–9, 221–3
settling in at Liverpool, 220–8
tribute to Monsignor Ronald Knox, 226–7
friendship with Archbishop Ramsey, 227, 269, 273–4, 395, 396
mixed marriage problems, and attitude to, 229–34
involved in Robert Street riot, 235–7
interest in youth clubs, 242–4
work for Catholic education 245–9
meeting with Harold Wilson, 248, 249
relations with and regard for the press, 249–51
appeal to Chancellor Adenauer on behalf of Nazi victims, 250–2
attends funeral of Pius XII, 254–6
audiences with Pope John, 257–8, 260, 261
appointed vice-president of Secretariat for Unity, 259, 270
interpretation of anti-clericalism, 261
relationship with Archbishop Fisher, 262–3
tribute to on his retirement from Canterbury, 273

letter to *Observer* in defence of Protestant clergy, 266–7
receives Geoffrey de Trafford, 277–80
story of design and building of Metropolitan Cathedral, 281–307
interpretation of Papal dogma, 322
work for Christian Unity, 308, 322–32 (*see also* Vatican Council *below*)
sermon at Cistercian Abbey, Portglenone, 326–7
rules for ecumenical conduct, 331–2
Billinge Hospital, speech in support of nurses, 334–5; press reactions to, 335–6
article on industrial relations, and Communist manipulation of, 336–8
Vatican Council, Rome (1962), 333, 336, 339–50 352–8, 367–82
pastoral pronouncement before attending, 341–3
death of Cardinal Godfrey and tribute to, 358–60
article on election of Pope Paul, 387–8
and dissertation on his papacy to date, 388–91
succeeds Cardinal Godfrey as Archbishop of Westminster, 391–3, 399
press reaction to, 395–7
farewell to Liverpool 393–4, 397–8
Writings: My Faith, 172; *My Lord and My God*, 172; *Our Faith*, 172; *The People's Priest*, 196; *They Made Me Sign*, 233; *Council and Clergy*, 343
Hitler, Adolf, 13
"influence" on path towards ecumenism, 260
Hobson, Captain R.N. and annexation of New Zealand, 160
Ho Choy (Colonial Secretary, Trinidad), 188
Holden, Christine (Sister Thomas More), 106
Holland, Father, 15
The Catholic Church and You article, 15–16
Holland, Thomas, Co-adjutor Bishop of Portsmouth, 261, 262, 324
Hollis, Christopher, 69
Hong Kong, J.C.H.'s visits to, 122, 123–6 142–4
Wah Yan Jesuit college, Kowloon, 123
Wah Yan College, New Territories, 125

Honolulu, J.C.H.'s visit to, 160–1
House, Rev. Francis, correspondence with J.C.H. on controversial broadcast, 69–74
Humphreys, Mr. (diplomat in Korea), 133

Industrial relations
Church's impact on (in Germany), 101
J.C.H.'s article on, 336–8
International Brigade (in Spain), 46
Irish Times, article on Pope Paul, 385–6
Island in the Sun film, 198
Issa brothers, of Jamaica, 186

Jamaica, J.C.H. in, 176–86
Jamaicans attitude to marriage, 179, 180, 181–2
Holy Name Homesteads, 180
living conditions in, 180, 181–2
Japan J.C.H.'s visits to, 127–32, 142–3
meeting with British ambassador, 143
morale and conditions of Allied troops in, 127–30, 144
V.D. problem, 128, 131
prostitution in, 127–8
visit to Hiroshima, 131–2
visits to troops and hospitals, 127–31
Jardine Matheson company, 125
John XXIII, Pope, 11, 281, 330, 384, 385, 389 390, 399
early life, 351–2
elected Pope, 256, 288, 351
efforts to achieve Christian Unity, 259–67, 271, 328, 349
address to Vatican Council, 322–4, 348; and activities therein, 352–6 363, 373–82
J.C.H.'s visit to, 257–8
Journey of a Soul diary, 258
Mater et Magistra and *Pacem in Terris* encyclicles, 363
popularity of, 207, 221
receives Archbishop Fisher, 263–4, 267–8
illness and death, 361–4, 366–7
John, Father, O.P., 195

John o' London's weekly, 268
Jones, Jean (of Archbishop's secretariat, Liverpool), 393
Judah, Douglas, 184, 186
Judah, Father Charles, S.J., 178

Karachi
J.C.H.'s visit to, 105–15
prison and hospital conditions in, 107–15
political situation in, 105
Keating, Archbishop, 223, 281
Keegan, Father Bernard, 174
Keightley, General Sir Charles, 121
Kennedy, President John F., 13, 380
Kerala, Catholics of, 115
Keswick, John (and family), 124, 125, 126
All I Know About China, 124
views on American-Chinese relations, 143–4
Khrushchev, Nikita, 13, 156
Kieran, Canon, 247
Knights of St. Columba, 80
Knolle Park orphanage, Liverpool, 393
Knox, Monsignor, secretary to the Internuncio, Tokyo, and later Archbishop of Melbourne, 142, 143, Apostolic Delegate in India, 347
Knox, Monsignor Ronald, 15
death of and J.C.H.'s tribute to, 226–7
Koenig, Cardinal Archbishop of Vienna, 376
Korea, J.C.H.'s visit to, 132–41, 142
visits to troops, hospitals, etc., 132–9, 140
Field Punishment camp conditions, 130, 133–4, 135, 140
Gloucester Valley, 139–40
Krol, Archbishop of Philadelphia, 347

Lang, Cosmo, Archbishop of Canterbury, 311
Leahy, Father, 191, 193
Leeds, Bishop of, *see under* Heenan, John Carmel

Leeds Diocesan Schools' Commission, 38
Leeming, Father Bernard, S.J., 330
Léger, Cardinal, 357, 375
Leo XIII, Pope, 257
efforts to achieve Church Unity, 316
Epistola ad Anglos, 316
Liénart, Cardinal Bishop of Lille, 343, 348, 349, 357, 376
Lindo, Roy and Pam, 184, 185, 186
Listener, The, 63
Liston, Archbishop, 160
Liverpool
Catholic Education in, 245–9, 271 (*see also* Liverpool Education Act)
Church's and Archbishop's influence in, 274–7
industrial unrest in, 336
J.C.H.'s appointment as Archbishop of, 207
large Catholic population, 221
Irish influx, 221–2, 276
Metropolitan Cathedral at, 217–8, 219
story of design and building of, 281–307, 384
religious intolerance in, 218, 222, 233–8, 245, 261, 269–71, 272
mixed marriages problem, 229–35
Robsart Street riot, 235–7
J.C.H.'s departure from, 393–4, 397–8
Liverpool Catholic Pictorial (diocesan weekly), J.C.H.'s article on industrial relations, 336–8
Liverpool Daily Post, 397
report on final plan for Metropolitan Cathedral, 302–3
Liverpool Education Act, 1939, extract from, 245–6, 271
'Living Your Life' TV programme, 239
Lloyd, Geoffrey (Education Minister), 248
Lloyd George, David, 159
Loftus, Father, 346
Logue, Cardinal, 42
Longbottom, Rev. H. D., 274
Lynch, Father Tommy, 191, 193
Lysenko, and controversy on biology, 200–1
Lutyens, Sir Edwin, designer of first plans for Metropolitan Cathedral, 281–3, 285–6, 289, 291, 292, 306

McCarthy, Dr., 131
McConnell, Brigadier, 137
McCormack, Bishop, 19
McDonald, Air Commodore Bill (and wife Diana), 121, 144, 145, 153
McEleney, John, Bishop of Kingston, Jamaica, 176, 177, 180, 183
McIntyre, Bishop (later Cardinal), 162
McKenna, Monsignor, administrator of Metropolitan Cathedral, 302, 306
McKernan, Peter, Lord Major of Liverpool, 274
MacMillan, Father, 119
McNamara, Canon, 190
McQuaid, Archbishop, of Dublin, 347
McShane, Canon, 174
Madden, Father, 124
Magnay, Harold, Director of Education, Liverpool, 245
  work towards building of Cardinal Allen school, 246–7
Mail, Daily, 101, 235
Malacca, Bishop of, 154
Malaya, *see* Singapore and Malaya
Malenkov, Georgi, 132
Malines Conversations (between Lord Halifax and Cardinal Mercier), 315–6, 318–9
Malta, J.C.H.'s visit to, 112
Manchester Guardian, 177, 227, 269
  Weekly Guardian, extract from article by Christopher Driver, 269–71
Manila, J.C.H.'s visit to, 122–3
Manley, Dr. Worman, 193
Manning, Cardinal, 260, 309
Mannix, Daniel, Archbishop of Melbourne, background of, career, and meeting with J.C.H., 158–60
Mariella, Sister, of Webster Groves, 167
Martin, Clifford, Anglican Bishop of Liverpool, 238, 270, 273
Martin, Sir Charles, Chief Constable of Liverpool, 241–2, 243, 244
Mary, Queen, 60
Masso, Rafael, 43–5, 48, 51
Mathew, Chief Justice, of Malaya, 145, 146
Mathieu, Cardinal, 42
Maximos IV, Patriarch of Antioch, 372
Mercier, Cardinal, 42, 317, 318
  Malines Conversations with Lord Halifax, 315–6

Metropolitan Cathedral (*see also under* Liverpool)
  details of competition for final design of, 290–302
Miltenberg, Monsignor, Archbishop of Karachi, 106, 107
Mirror, Daily, 234, 334, 335, 395
  Cassandra comment on J.C.H.'s speech on behalf of nurses, 335
Missionary Society of Paris, Malaya, 149
Mixed marriages, problems of, 229–35
  J.C.H.'s views on, 231–2
Molloy, Father, 143
Montini, Giovanni Battista, Archbishop of Milan (and later Pope Paul VI), 22, 256, 257, 344, 363, 374 (*see also* Paul VI)
Moorhouse family, 97
More, St. Thomas, 264
Morley, George, 88–9
Morris brothers (Bolton parishioners), 12, 13
Mountford, Sir James, 247
Mountjoy prison, Dublin, J.C.H.'s visit to, 111
Moverley, Father, later Auxiliary Bishop of Leeds, 39
Muggeridge, Malcolm, 101, 226, 239–40
  editor of *Punch*, 226
Murphy, John, Bishop of Shrewsbury, 273, 324

New York, J.C.H.'s visit to, 169
  Blauvelt convent, 169
New Zealand, J.C.H.'s visit to, 160
Newman, John Henry, Cardinal, 260
  Dream of Gerontius, 56
News Chronicle, 100
Nicholl, Sir John, 118
Norfolk, Duke of, 80, 84
Northern Ireland
  J.C.H.'s controversial broadcast reference to, 64–78
  J.C.H.'s sermon at Portglenone and reactions to, 326–8
  sectarian problems of, 314
Northern Whig, Belfast, 387
Notre Dame High School, Leeds, 22, 174

O'Brien, Father Terry, 191, 193
O'Brien-Twohig, Sister, 143
Observer, The, 226
J.C.H.'s letter to in defence of Anglican clergy, 266–7
O'Donnell, Meg, 171
O'Donnell, Mr. (Lord Mayor of Leeds), 19
O'Donoghue, Father, 180
O'Dwyer, Dr Michael, 188
O'Dwyer, Father (of Trinidad), 188
O'Dwyer, Father, S.J., (rector of Wah Yan college, Hong Kong), 125
O'Hara, Gerald, Archbishop, 366, 391
Olçomendy, Bishop, 118
Oldmeadow, Ernest, editor of *The Tablet,* 319
Oliphant, Rev. D., of Yateley, 121
O'Meara, Brigadier, 127, 143
O'Reilly, Bishop, 222
O'Sullivan, Canon, (of Huyton), 248
O'Sullivan, Father, (Jamaica), 184
Ottaviani, Cardinal, 347, 356, 357, 358, 373, 375
schema *De Ecclesia,* 373

Pakistani Sisters, Karachi, J.C.H.'s visit to, 113
Palmer, Canon (of Ilford), 230
Papen, Franz von, 124
Parish priests, Bishops' dependence of, 9–11
Paul V, Pope, 388
Paul VI, Pope
elected Pope, 384–6
tributes to, 384–8
criticisms of, 388–91
internationalising of the Curia by, 256
Pacem in terris encyclical, 384
receives Archbishop Ramsey, 263
supporter of ecumenism, 322, 385
travels of, 363
Pearson, Father, 197, 198
Pecci, Cardinal (later Pope Leo XIII), 257
Petit, Bishop, 19
Petry, Father Jim, 132
Pink, Rev. H., 259
Piper, John, 307
Pitt, Father, naval chaplain, 120

Pius IX, Pope, 379
Pius X, 17
canonisation of, 18
Pius XI, Pope, 11, 282
Mortalium Animus encyclical, 322
Pius XII, Pope, 11, 22, 222, 256, 309, 385
address to midwives' congress, 97–9, 100
and pro-Nazi allegations, 207
initiates move towards Christian Unity 342
J.C.H.'s audiences with, 102, 207
death of and J.C.H.'s tribute to, 253–5
Pole, Cardinal, last Catholic Archbishop of Canterbury, 41–2, 268
Portal, Abbé, 315, 316, 318
Poskitt, Henry John, Bishop (J.C.H.'s predecessor at Leeds), 11, 200, 209, 211
early career, 22, 25
Press, the, J.C.H.'s views on, 249–51
(*see also* Public relations)
'Press Conference' TV programme, 92, 99–101
Prison Officers' Association, 275
Protestant Alliance, 42
Public relations, and the Bishopric, 29–30, 31–4, 249–51
Punch magazine, 69, 226
Pyke, Father, 196

Quinlan, Father, S.J., 193
Quinn, Father, 198

Raffles Hotel, Singapore, 151
Rahner, Karl, 376
Rampolla, Cardinal, 316
Ramsey, Michael, Archbishop of Canterbury, 227–8, 326, 342
friendship with J.C.H. 227, 269, 273–4, 395, 396
shares TV programme with J.C.H., 268–9
visit to Pope Paul, 264
Redmond, Father Patsy, 100
Regina Coeli prison, Rome
Pope John's visit to, 258
prisoners' message to, 367
J.C.H.'s visit to, 103

Reid, Father, 127, 130
Renison, Sir Partick and Lady, 193
Reynolds, Brian, 16, 18, 192
Reynolds, Mary (sister of J.C.H.), 9, 16–18
Reynolds, Michael, 18
Reyntiens, Patrick, 307
Rhys-Williams, Lady, 99
Ribo, Xavier, 53
Richardson, Maurice, 226
Roberts, Dr., Methodist theologian, 204
Robsart Street riot, 235–7 270, 272, 333
Rochester, Bishop of, 316
Rodney youth club, Liverpool, 242–3, 244
Rolwing, Rosie, 43–4
'Roman Catholic Mind' TV programme, 240
Roncalli, Cardinal (later Pope John XXIII), 256
Rosen (film director), 198
Rossi, Cardinal, 256
Rothstein, Andrew, 13, 14
Rowntree, Winnie (Mother Xavier in Georgetown), 192
Rudderham, Bishop of Clifton, 324
Ruffini, Cardinal, 357, 375
Ryan, Archbishop, of Trinidad, 187, 188, 191, 193
Ryan, Father (in Korea), 127, 134, 142, 143
Ryder, Sue, 250
Rynne, Xavier, (*Letters from Vatican City*), 372

St. Andrew's Hospital, 17
St. Anne's Cathedral, first High Mass TV broadcast from, 79–83
St. Bede's Grammar School, Bradford, 24, 171, 211
St. John, Father Henry, 330
St. Louis, Missouri, J.C.H.'s visit to, 167–9
    St. Annes' town experiment, 167–8
    Webster Groves college, 167
    lecture at, 168–9
St. Malachy's Catholic School, Liverpool, 261, 270
St. Thomas Aquinas (*Adoro Te devote*), 390

St. Vincent's Hospice, Liverpool, 393
St. Vincent's School for the Blind, Liverpool, 384, 393
Sanderson, Air Marshal, 118
Sarto, Giuseppe (later Pope Pius X), 363
Scannell, Father Brian, 192
Scott, Adrian, part-designer of Metropolitan Cathedral, 283, 285–6, 289 290, 306
Scott, Monsignor George (and family), 163
Scott, Sir Giles Gilbert, designer of Liverpool Anglican Cathedral, 282, 283
Shann, Mr. and Mrs. (and family), 181
Shead, Michael, 130, 137
Sheffield Council for Catholic Action, 14–16
Sheffield University, J.C.H.'s talk to Union, 203
Sheridan, Father, S.J., 123
Shoosmith, General, 142
Singapore and Malaya, J.C.H. at, 116–21, 144–54
    Australian Redemptorist missioners, 153
    'Impressions of the Far East' talk, 151–2, 153
    Missionary Society of Paris, 149
    visits to troops, hospitals, missions etc., 117–21, 144–53
Sing-Sing penitentiary, New York, 49
Sinn Fein movement and I.R.A., 159
    the Black and Tans, 159
Sketch, Daily, tribute to Pope Paul, 387
Smith, Father (of Georgetown), 191
Smith, Father (padre of the Cameronians), 119, 146, 147
Southwark, Bishop of, 346
Spain, *see also* Barcelona
    Church—State relationship in, 50, 52
    civil war (1936–9), 42–3, 46, 52–3
    atrocities in, 43, 48, 53
    contrast between rich and poor in, 50–2
    English-Spanish relations, 46, 47
Spectator, The, 100
Spellman, Francis, Cardinal Archbishop of New York, 118, 162
Spence, Sir Basil, 290, 292, 294, 301, 307
Stalin, Josef, 13
    death of, 156

Stamm, Camille and Beatrice, 136
Star, The, 99
Stepinac, Archbishop, of Zagreb, 32, 33
Stevenson, Adlai, 144
Stirling, Brigadier, 125
Stockwell, General, 145, 146
Stokes, David, 290, 301
Stuart, James, 392
Suenens, Cardinal, 374, 375
Suez fiasco (1956), 97
Sullivan, Father Ray, 180
Sunday Times, 392, 396
   J.C.H.'s article on election of Pope
     Paul, 387–8
Swan, Mrs., President of English Catholic
     Women's League, 153
Sword of the Spirit movement, 311–4

Tablet, The, 100, 149, 317
   report on J.C.H.'s sermon on 'material-
     ism', 275–6
Taylor, A.J.P., 239
Taylor, Christopher, 305
Taylor, George, 38, 39
Taylor Woodrow, contractors for Metro-
     politan Cathedral, 307
Tedeschino, Cardinal, 50
Telegraph, Daily, 42, 217–8, 227, 334
Templer, General (later Field Marshal)
     145–6
Tennyson, Alfred Lord, 377
Thompson, Monsignor Henry, 38
Thompson, Monsignor, Vicar-General
     at Leeds, 212, 213
Tickle, Monsignor Jock, 346
Tiernan, John, 285
Time and Tide magazine, 338
   article on Archbishop Fisher's visit to
     Rome 265–6
Times, The, 227, 303, 327, 334
   joint letter from leaders of Catholic,
     Anglican and Free Churches, 309–11
Tisserant, Cardinal, 349
Tito, Marshal, 32, 133
Tobin, Father, senior chaplain at
     Singapore, 116, 117, 118, 122, 125,
     144, 145, 148, 150, 154
Tobin, Father Superior, Jamaica, 180
Tong Heng (Singapore tailor), 117

Trinidad, J.C.H.'s visit to, 187–91
   slum conditions in, 189–90
Trinitarian Congregation, 49, 53
Truman, President Harry, 11
Turner, Captain Mike, 132–3, 134
Turner, Monsignor, (chief of curial
     offices, Metropolitan Cathedral)
     284–5, 305, 306
Turner, Monsignor Tom (of Douglas,
     I.O.M.), 393

Ullathorne, Cardinal, 260
United Nations Relief Organisation, 251
United States, *see also under various*
     individual place-names
   J.C.H.'s visits to, 161–9
   comparisons of U.S. and British
     universities and colleges, 166–7
Ursuline Convent, Wimbledon,
   handling of competition for design of
     Metropolitan Cathedral, 299–301,
     303
Ursuline Sisters, Forest Gate, 56
Ushaw (St. Cuthbert's College), 39, 40,
     163, 359

Vagaggani, Cipriano, O.S.B., 370
'Van-Dooze', Canadian regiment in
     Korea, 141
Vannutelli, Cardinal, 41
'Vatican and Kremlin' debate, Bolton,
     11–14, 193
Vatican Council, First (1870), 321, 371,
     375
Vatican Council, Second (1962), 10, 233,
     234, 258, 333, 336, 339–50, 352, 358,
     363–4, 367–82, (*see also under*
     Ecumenism)
   differing national views on ecumenism,
     339–41
   Council Daybook, The, 369
   Ordo Concilii Oecumenici Vaticani II
     Celebrandi and *Methodus Servanda*
     (booklets on procedural rules, etc),
     346
Vaughan, Herbert, Cardinal Archbishop
     of Westminster, 39, 260, 309
Villot, Cardinal, 256

Wallace, Father Peter, 161, 162
Wallis, Monsignor (at Eucharistic Congress, Australia), 156
Waring, Father George, 243–4
Waugh, Alec (*Island in the Sun*), 198
Waugh, Evelyn, 163, 164,
  The Loved Ones, 163
Wells, Lieut.-Gen., (C-in-C. British Commonwealth Forces in Korea) 132, 134, 137, 140
West Indies, J.C.H.'s visit to, 176–98
  (*see also under various place names*)
  emigration problems, 177–8, 180, 182–4, 187, 188, 191, 199
Whitby Abbey, J.C.H.'s farewell sermon at, 209
Whiteside, Thomas, first Archbishop of Liverpool, 221, 222, 223, 230, 231, 281, 330
Wigan Observer, report on J.C.H.'s speech at Billinge Hospital, 334–5
Willebrands, Cardinal, 256, 259
Wilson, Harold
  exchange of letters with J.C.H., 33–4
  meeting with J.C.H. on aid for Catholic schools, 248, 249
Wilson, Field Marshal Sir Henry, murder of, 160

Wilson, John Leonard, Anglican Bishop of Birmingham, 20
  Japanese prisoner-of-war, 204–5
Wilson, Monsignor Gladstone, 185
Wilson, Mr. (Director of Starways), 345
Wiseman, Cardinal Archbishop of Westminster, 366
Woodlock, Father, 317, 318, 319
Woodruff, Douglas, editor of *The Tablet*, 149
Worker, Daily, 337, 338, 397
World Agricultural Association, 180–1
Wormauld, Mrs. (educationist), 247
Worsborough Bridge school, Yorks, 171
Wright, Cardinal, 256, 349
Wright, Dom Ronald, O.S.B., 305
Wyle, Father Gabriel, 196
Wyvern, H.M.S., 160

Yorkshire Post, 208, 227, 240, 269,
  article on J.C.H.'s broadcast, 74–7
Young, Bishop, 156

Zalfrullah Khan, Sir M., 105